T0318809

Innovation, Entrepreneurship, and the Economy in the US, China, and India

Dedication

To the memory of my parents for all the sacrifices they made
To my wife, Shrida, and to my sons, Rishi and Yash,
for their affection, love, and support;
To all my family and to all my close friends especially
those in the Dallas area who have been my extended family
and support system through the roughly
thirty-five years of my life in this area and,
To all my teachers and mentors, too numerous to list,
for all that they have taught me
Rajiv R. Shah

To my parents,
My husband, my brother, and my friends,
Who give me endless love, consideration, help, confidence,
and courage to face difficulties
Zhijie Gao

To my sons Prashant and Krishna for their undying
love and inspiration;
To my parents O.P. Seshadri and Menaka for their
constant encouragement, support, and affection; and
To my sister Anuradha for believing in me
always against all odds
Harini Mittal

Innovation, Entrepreneurship, and the Economy in the US, China, and India

Historical Perspectives and Future Trends

Rajiv Shah

Zhijie Gao

Harini Mittal

AMSTERDAM • BOSTON • HEIDELBERG • LONDON
NEW YORK • OXFORD • PARIS • SAN DIEGO
SAN FRANCISCO • SINGAPORE • SYDNEY • TOKYO

Academic Press is an imprint of Elsevier

Academic Press is an imprint of Elsevier
32 Jamestown Road, London NW1 7BY, UK
525 B Street, Suite 1800, San Diego, CA 92101-4495, USA
225 Wyman Street, Waltham, MA 02451, USA
The Boulevard, Langford Lane, Kidlington, Oxford OX5 1GB, UK

First published 2015

British Library Cataloguing-in-Publication Data
A catalogue record for this book is available from the British Library

Library of Congress Cataloging-in-Publication Data
A catalog record for this book is available from the Library of Congress

ISBN: 978-0-12-801890-3

For information on all Academic Press publications
visit our website at store.elsevier.com

Printed and bound in the United States

Working together
to grow libraries in
developing countries

www.elsevier.com • www.bookaid.org

Contents

Part I
Innovation

Part IV
Conclusions

Preface

This book is about innovation and entrepreneurship and the role it plays in the US, Chinese, and Indian economies. Innovation and entrepreneurship have transformed the Western world, and especially the United States, from agricultural economies of the past, through the Industrial Revolution into the information age of today. The impact on the US economy has been to transform the United States into the most dominant economic power of today with the world's largest GDP. However, the information revolution and globalization that we are experiencing today are also transforming the world. Fundamental economics, easy and rapid access to information, ease of global travel, and opening up of societies, although in some cases to a limited extent, that were previously completely closed to the West are sowing seeds of change that have the potential of creating a future somewhat different from what we have been used to in the recent past.

The most significant among these changes is the rapid growth in the economies in other parts of the world—most notably China and perhaps to some extent India—while the growth in the United States has been sputtering. Besides, both China and India are increasingly becoming engines of global economic growth and are today the world's biggest emerging economies with high GDP growth rates. Although both China and India have followed different paths to global prominence, because of their peculiar interdependence, they are also sometimes referred to as "Asia's nonidentical twins" or "Chindia."

While these countries have received the most mention in the recent past, especially during the recent economic downturn in the United States and the resultant job losses, there is also significant growth in other BRICS countries and in the Asia-Pacific region, in general. However, in order to keep the scope of the book manageable, and given the expertise and experience of the co-authors, *in this book, we confine our attention to looking at the United States, China, and India.* Also, the case of China is especially compelling, given that by most accounts, its economy is expected to surpass that of the United States in the not too distant future.

While innovation and entrepreneurship have driven the United States to its present status as the most dominant economic power of today, can the United States continue on that path? China and India used to be dominant economic powers several centuries ago, when the United States was not even on the map or was not very heavily populated. With the rise of the West and due to a number of social and political reasons, these two nations lost their economic clout, and their economies were dwarfed by Western economies. While both these countries have shown significant growth in recent decades, can that growth be sustained? If we believe in the premise that innovation and entrepreneurship are indeed vital for long-term growth of a country, can these two nations exhibit that? *That brings one to the question, what are the factors that are important for innovation and entrepreneurship to thrive? The book looks at how these factors compare between the United States, China, and India, looks at the evolution of these factors in the past, and assesses the pointers they give us about the future and hence about the likelihood for continued growth in these economies.* A lot is known and has been written about in the context of innovation and entrepreneurship in the West, and the United States in particular. But the same is not true about China and India—not a lot is known in the West either about their distant past or about the recent evolution and the present state of affairs with regard to the fundamentals that drive innovation and entrepreneurship. What has been written about innovation and entrepreneurship in these two countries very recently, given the recent growth in their economies, is either very anecdotal or very prescriptive. So, the approach we take in this book is to delve far more thoroughly into the fundamentals of these issues as they relate to China and India and, for comparison, discuss their state in the United States.

The importance of innovation and entrepreneurship to any economy has been recognized since the pioneering work of Joseph Schumpeter. A number of books have been written on the subject of "innovation and entrepreneurship" since the landmark book by Peter Drucker on this subject. The importance of innovation has been studied and written about especially radical, transformative, or disruptive innovation by a number of authors in recent years, most notably, Clayton Christensen. However, while the impact and the results of innovation and entrepreneurship on the economy are generally easy to see, the task of mathematically relating them is extremely challenging. This is further complicated by the fact that macroeconomic theory for the best part of the twentieth century has been divided into two opposing philosophical and mathematical camps, which have not shown a sign of coming together until recently and has been discussed by Mankiw. While we recognize that a large number of other factors—monetary and fiscal policies, budget and trade deficits, inflation, unemployment, exchange rates, and a host of others—affect the economy in the near term, the long-term vector, an area of macroeconomics that is now known as economic growth, is driven by innovation and entrepreneurship.

Since the early and pioneering work of Solow, the impact of innovation and other factors on economic growth has been mathematically modeled by a number of economists and, in recent years, most notably, by Acemoglu, Aghion and Howitt, and Barro. A number of authors, especially Acs; Audretsch; Parker; Alfaro; Ghani, O'Connell, and Kerr; and others, have attempted to model the impact of entrepreneurship. These authors and a number of organizations, such as the World Bank and the OECD, have collected data on entrepreneurship and published entrepreneurial indices. Given the qualitative nature of the factors responsible for innovation and entrepreneurship and discussed in the earlier sections of the book, the task of modeling the impact on the economy is next to impossible, also leading to an area of research referred to today as "economic development" as opposed to "economic growth". *However, with this recognition, in the third section of the book, we attempt to relate innovation and entrepreneurship to the economy. As a backdrop, we provide a brief overview of the present state of macroeconomic theory and economic growth theory and an overview of the approaches to model the impact of innovation and entrepreneurship on the economy along with relevant previous data and propose an approach to be considered for detailed modeling in the future that could be used to tie to data.*

We conclude in the fourth and last section of the book with our thoughts and qualitative assessments about the future of innovation and entrepreneurship and its impact on economic growth and the economies of the United States, China, and India.

Introduction

The book is divided into four parts. *Part I, Chapters 1 through 9*, focuses on innovation; *Part II, Chapters 10 through 17*, on entrepreneurship; and *Part III, Chapters 18 through 21*, on the impact on the economy, and in *Part IV*, the fourth and last part, *Chapter 22*, we close with conclusions and our thoughts about the future of innovation and entrepreneurship and the resultant economic growth in these parts of the world.

We begin *Part I* with *Chapter 1* discussing what *innovation* is, since this is a term that has come to mean a lot of different things to a lot of different people. Since the entire first section of the book is devoted to innovation and the role of innovation, we define how we use the word innovation in our book. We also then discuss why innovation is important in any economy, and finally, we list the factors that we believe are important contributors for innovation to thrive. We further lay the groundwork for the first part of the book in this chapter by briefly comparing and contrasting general innovation trends in the United States, China, and India over the last few years using innovation indices and subindices of the United States, China, and India computed by INSEAD and WIPO.

In *Chapter 2*, we discuss the role that *history* plays in innovation. We look at historical GDP in China, India, and the United States and how the roles have reversed in the last couple of centuries. We believe that having had a history of innovation does provide a perspective on the intrinsic nature of a culture and its people and a potential proclivity towards reverting to that behavior under the "right circumstances." We, therefore, trace the role of technology and innovation in the phenomenal rise of China and India in the distant past and examine the factors that obstructed innovation in later years, which resulted in the subsequent decline of these economies. We then briefly compare that to the history of innovation in the United States. While a lot has been written about the latter and is fairly well known, not much has been written about or known in the West about the history of innovation in China and India. So, we first examine that history.

Among the "right circumstances" that encourage innovative behavior, one of the most important factors is the *economy*. The three key measures of economy that impact technological innovation are R&D expenditures, foreign direct investment and its impact on the flow of knowledge and technology, and the quantity and quality of intellectual property. In *Chapter 3*, we discuss these topics for China and India and trace their evolution and effect through time and compare these to the United States.

Even if a country has a history of innovation in the past and an economy that is growing rapidly, it may not have the *social and cultural factors* that encourage the spirit of innovation. This is an area that particularly may bring out the contrast between Western societies, such as the United States, and China and India. In *Chapter 4*, we delve into this topic and explore whether there are winds of change in Eastern cultures that might foretell a different future from that of the past.

In *Chapter 5*, we explore the role of government and other institutions and the infrastructure of *laws and regulations* and their impact on creativity and innovation. We discuss how these may have evolved over the years in China and India and how they compare with those in the United States and the impact these are having on innovation today and potentially in the future. In any developing or emerging economy, especially India and China, the presence of corruption and a significant size "parallel economy" is well known. What impact does that have on innovation?

It is commonly known that creativity and innovation are at their highest levels in a person's life during youth, and so is productivity. It is, therefore, important to understand how *demographics*, in general, and its quality in terms of level of education are evolving and changing in all these three regions of the world. The onset of an aging population and the resultant influx of immigrants in the West, and the United States in particular, are well known. China, on the other hand, is also beginning to face the problem of an aging population although, to a smaller extent, partly caused by its restrictive population growth policies, whereas India is forecast to have one of the youngest populations in the years to come. Chinese and Indian immigrants in the United States who were once considered a brain drain from these countries are now playing a significant role in driving innovation in China and India. In *Chapter 6*, we explore these issues and the impact this may have on the future of innovation in these countries.

In this advanced information economy, innovation requires a population that is technologically sophisticated. Hence, the *role of schools* and *universities and the education* they provide are very important. In *Chapter 7*, we explore how that is changing in China and India and contrast that to what is happening in the United States.

We then examine the role of *industry and market structures, as well as regional clusters* that seem to play an important role in innovation. In the United States, regional clusters in the Silicon Valley in the Bay Area and Boston's Route 128 are of legendary prominence. From an industry and market cluster perspective, we have seen the shift in the United States from innovation in traditional industries to the more technology- and software-oriented industries, as well as biotechnology, nanotechnology, pharmaceuticals, and energy. We discuss in *Chapter 8* these factors in China and India and compare them with those in the United States.

While innovation is most prevalent in the United States in recent years, in the sectors discussed in the previous chapter, innovation in China and India may be driven more by local factors and conditions relevant to those economies and societies. This thinking has recently spawned the notions of "innovation at the bottom of the pyramid," as well as "reverse innovation." The latter concept talks to innovating in developing and emerging markets to meet their cost and price points, and then, for comparison, we also discuss the areas that have a need for innovation in the United States. We deliberate on these issues in *Chapter 9*.

We begin *Part II* of the book and switch to the concept of *entrepreneurship* in *Chapter 10*. We begin by again defining what we mean by entrepreneurship, given the plethora of definitions since the early work of Joseph Schumpeter, and discuss how that is different from innovation. We discuss briefly the entrepreneurial process that results in the creation of new ventures and then talk about the factors that drive entrepreneurship.

In *Chapter 11*, we discuss the general business environment in the three countries and the *personal characteristics* that are necessary for entrepreneurial behavior. Personality traits such as the ability to spot opportunities and innovate, propensity for risk taking, achievement orientation, and an internal locus of control, among others, are conducive to entrepreneurship. We examine the personality traits of the people in the United States, China, and India and assess what role they play in the dynamics of entrepreneurship in these countries.

We then revisit *social and cultural factors* in *Chapter 12*, however, this time in the context of entrepreneurship. Here, again, there is a strong contrast between the US and the Eastern cultures of China and India. We discuss what impact this has on entrepreneurship. However, with a global economy, ease of travel, exposure to Western ways of thinking and working in this information age, and a growing middle class once again suggest things may be starting to change.

We address the role of *education*, in general, and *entrepreneurial education*, in particular, in contributing to the success of entrepreneurial endeavors in *Chapter 13*. Most entrepreneurs and academics in the field of innovation and entrepreneurship know that a good idea alone does not make a new venture. It takes a lot more than that. Entrepreneurship, as discussed earlier, is a process. Some people have the natural instincts to learn this along the way, very often the hard way through experience. For the vast majority, education in entrepreneurship can facilitate the process of launching new ventures. We look at the availability of this education in China and India and compare it to that of the United States.

In *Chapter 14*, we discuss some of the other key ingredients conducive to entrepreneurial activities. We group them under *"external environment"* and include within that factors such as legal, political, and institutional environments. Besides, the state of labor markets has a close link with the type of entrepreneurship prevailing in a country—the types of entrepreneurship in terms of whether it is necessity-driven or opportunity-driven. We look at these factors in China, India, and the United States.

Growth of a new venture into a thriving business depends not only on the legal, political, social, and institutional factors discussed in the previous chapter but also on the *physical infrastructure*—communication, energy, power, transportation, utilities, etc.—of the country. In the United States, this infrastructure is clearly very well built out and well established, but some of these may be aging, creating concerns about the future. In China, these are rapidly improving with a lot of new construction of airports, seaports, railways, roadways, and other sectors. In India, in spite of recent growth in some of these areas, lack of reliable infrastructure has been known to be a problem constraining growth. We discuss these factors in *Chapter 15*.

Capital is the "lifeblood" of a new venture. In the United States, various sources of capital—angel investors, venture capital for start-ups and early-stage companies, and private equity and, of course, debt and equity capital through major Wall Street banks, for the more "mature," late-stage new ventures—are well known. Government involvement and funding in new ventures are very limited in the United States. The question that we try to address in *Chapter 16* is whether similar channels for private capital exist in China and India and what role do they play in relation to public or government funding.

Entrepreneurship in well-established, middle-size to large companies, which has been termed *intrapreneurship*, is just as important, if not more important than entrepreneurship in new ventures. In fact, Joseph Schumpeter even went to the extent of saying that innovation and entrepreneurship are best carried out by large companies due to their access to financial, market, technological, and manufacturing resources. In the United States, this was in fact true until the mid-1980s and the emergence of the VC community and their willingness to take the risk of funding new ventures. Corporate innovation in the United States is, however, starting to see a revival out of the sheer necessity for growth through disruptive innovation. In *Chapter 17*, we look at intrapreneurship in the United States, China, and India.

We begin *Part III*, *Impact on the Economy*, with *Chapter 18*. Having discussed innovation and entrepreneurship at great length in the previous chapters, we now turn our attention to the impact on the economy, more specifically on economic growth. We provide a brief review of a previous work that models the impact of technology and innovation on economic growth, starting with the pioneering work of Solow and bringing it to the present state of the art in accounting for innovation in economic growth models. Entrepreneurship, of course, is a very challenging topic to model.

Innovation and entrepreneurship, while extremely important for long-term economic growth, are certainly not the only factors that affect the economy of a nation. A large number of other factors—monetary and fiscal policies, budget and trade deficits, inflation, unemployment, exchange rates, and a host of others—affect the economy in the near term. We, therefore, provide an overview of a *general macroeconomic framework*, in *Chapter 19*. In order to understand changes in the economy in the short run, one must consider a broader macroeconomic framework. This is especially important since, as the field of macroeconomics began after the Great Depression of the 1930s, it quickly evolved along two different schools of thought. These two schools of thought have been reconciled only in the late 1990s.

In *Chapter 20*, we draw from the previous two chapters and discuss ways to address not only innovation but also potentially entrepreneurship, in *an economic model*, drawing from techniques used in the fields of finance, physics, and engineering. While we invoke these phenomenological techniques to explain the survival and success of some of these ventures and their impact on economic growth, in either a start-up or a corporate environment, we draw upon analogies to other natural phenomena to attempt to provide a plausible explanation for these spurts in the economy.

In *Chapter 21*, we provide an overview of work done to date by others to measure and quantify entrepreneurship. We review these *innovation and entrepreneurship indices*, as well as *relevant macroeconomic data*. The ultimate goal, which we will defer to future work, is, of course, to be able to use a model such as the one discussed in Chapter 20 and relate that to a time series of entrepreneurship data and key macroeconomic factors.

We conclude with *Part IV*, and *Chapter 22*, and discuss our *conclusions from this work and our thoughts and qualitative assessments about the future of innovation and entrepreneurship and its impact on economic growth and the economies of the United States, China, and India*. We compare our views with the starkly contrasting, almost diametrically opposing, views of Josef Joffe, of Stanford University, in *The Myth of America's Decline: Politics, Economics, and a Half Century of False Prophecies*, on the one hand, versus those of Robert D. Atkinson, of the National Innovation and Competitiveness Strategy Advisory Board, and Stephen J. Ezell, in *Innovation Economics: The Race for Global Advantage*; Thomas Friedman and Michael Mandelbaum, in *That Used to be Us: How America Fell Behind in the World It Invented and How We Can Come Back*; and Steven C. Currall et al., in *Organized Innovation: A Blueprint for Renewing America's Prosperity* (Atkinson and Ezell, 2012; Curral et al., 2014; Friedman and Mandelbaum, 2011; Joffe, 2014), on the other, and with those of a number of others who have written on the subject of future potential of China and India, for example, Gupta and Wang (2009), Sharma (2009), Eichengreen et al. (2010), Bardhan (2010), Khanna (2011), Li (2013), and McKinsey & Company (2013).

REFERENCES

Atkinson, R.D., Ezell, S.J., 2012. Innovation Economics—The Race for Global Advantage. Yale University Press.

Bardhan, P., 2010. Awakening Giants, Feet of Clay—Assessing the Economic Rise of China and India. Princeton University Press.

Curral, S.C., et al., 2014. Organized Innovation—A Blueprint for Renewing America's Prosperity. Oxford University Press, New York.

Eichengreen, B., Gupta, P., Kumar, R., 2010. Emerging Giants—China and India in the World Economy. Oxford University Press.

Friedman, T., Mandelbaum, M., 2011. That Used to be US—How America Fell Behind in the World It Invented and How We Can Come Back. Farrar, Straus and Giroux.

Gupta, A.K., Wang, H., 2009. Getting China and India Right—Strategies for Leveraging The World's Fastest-Growing Economies for Global Advantage. Jossey-Bass/Wiley.

Joffe, J., 2014. The Myth of America's Decline—Politics, Economics, and a Half Century of False Prophecies. Liveright Publishing.

Khanna, T., 2011. Billions of Entrepreneurs—How China and India are Reshaping Their Futures and Yours. Harvard Review Press.

Li, P.P., 2013. Disruptive Innovation in Chinese and Indian Businesses—The Strategic Implications for Local Entrepreneurs and Global Incumbents. Routledge/Taylor and Francis.

McKinsey & Company, 2013. Reimagining India—Unlocking the Potential of Asia's Next Superpower. Simon & Schuster.

Sharma, D.S., 2009. China and India in the Age of Globalization. Cambridge University Press.

About the Authors

Dr. Rajiv R. Shah is a clinical professor in the Naveen Jindal School of Management at UT Dallas since 2008 and is also the founder and program director for the Systems Engineering and Management (SEM) program. At UT Dallas, he teaches innovation and entrepreneurship, corporate entrepreneurship and venturing, technology and new product development, and quantitative and numerical methods in finance and macroeconomics.

He specialized in solid state and laser physics, and quantum electronics and nonlinear optics, and prior to joining UT Dallas, he spent close to 30 years in industry working in areas that spanned lasers, semiconductors, computers, and wireless, optical, and Internet communications. He cofounded and is a managing partner at Timmaron Capital Advisors, a firm that provides advisory services to CEOs, BoDs, and PE firms. He also founded the indusLotus Group and provided high-level consulting to private equity firms and others on Wall Street. He worked on a $50 B telecom deal in 2007. He has been an adviser to Cerberus Capital Management LP, Pioneer Natural Resources, Ericsson Inc., CommScope Inc., Goldman Sachs Vantage Marketplace LLC, Nomura Securities' Private Equity arm, a council member on the Gerson Lehrman Group (GLG), a number of other private equity and hedge funds, and three separate engagements with McKinsey & Company. He has also worked as an evaluator and mentor with the Texas Emerging Technology Fund and STARTech, reviewing business plans and mentoring founders and CEOs.

Dr. Shah has served as CTO of Alcatel North America and was VP of Research & Innovation and Network Strategy at Alcatel for 4 years. Prior to that, he held senior management positions at MCI Worldcom over a 5-year period and was involved in half-a-dozen corporate-level M&A due diligence activities. Before that, he worked for Texas Instruments for seventeen years in various capacities, including R&D, manufacturing, business start-up, business strategy, and business development.

He served for 2 years on the faculty of the California Institute of Technology (Caltech) as Dr. Chaim Weizmann postdoctoral research fellow. He has an MS and a PhD in electrical engineering from Rice University, specializing in applied physics; an executive MBA from Southern Methodist University; and a BS in physics, mathematics, and statistics from Fergusson College, University of Pune, India, where he was the recipient of the National Science Talent Search Fellowship from the Government of India. Early in his career, he published over 50 papers in peer-reviewed journals, such as those of the American Physical Society (APS) and the Institute of Electrical and Electronic Engineers (IEEE), and had over twenty-five US and international patents issued to him.

Dr. Zhijie Gao is an associate professor with the College of Economics and Management, Northeast Agricultural University, Harbin, P.R. China, and was a visiting scholar at the University of Texas at Dallas from 2012 to 2013.

Her research areas mainly focus on analysis of entrepreneurial environment, cultivation of innovation ability, and development of agriculture-related industries. She participated in more than 10 research projects, such as "Research on Technological Innovation Capability of Small and Medium-sized Enterprises in Heilongjiang Province," "Research on Technological Innovation Strategy of Small and Medium-sized Enterprises in Heilongjiang Province," and "On Biomass Energy Industrialization in Heilongjiang Province," and published over twenty articles and one monograph—on potential and countermeasures about the development of biomass energy industry in Heilongjiang Province based on low-carbon economy.

She received her PhD in general management from the College of Economy Management, Northeast Agriculture University, Harbin, P.R. China; her MS in Macroeconomics from the College of Economy, Jilin University, Changchun, P.R. China; and her BS degree in Business Administration from the Business School of Beihua University, Jilin, P.R. China.

Dr. Harini Mittal is currently an assistant professor in the areas of Finance and Organizations, Strategy and International Management at Naveen Jindal School of Management, University of Texas at Dallas.

She has been actively involved in various activities, initiatives, teaching, and research in the field of innovation and entrepreneurship specifically in the Indian context. She also has a proven track record in strategic planning, execution, and formation of alliances and partnerships. She has published a number of peer-reviewed papers in Indian journals, made conference presentations at international conferences, written case studies and technical notes, and supervised PhD and MBA theses at CEPT University, Ahmedabad, Gujarat, India, where she was an associate professor and head of the department, Faculty of Technology Management, for 5 years, prior to coming to UT Dallas.

She received her PhD in management, from the Institute of Management, Nirma University, Ahmedabad, for which she worked on the impact of mergers and acquisitions on the performance of a firm. She received an MBA in finance from the B.K. School of Business Management, Gujarat University, and a BA in corporate secretaryship from the University of Madras, India.

Acknowledgment

We would like to acknowledge the UT Dallas Jindal School of Management and express our special appreciation to Dean Dr Hasan Pirkul of the Jindal School for enabling this undertaking in the first place and for his continued support of this work.

We would also like to thank Dr J. Scott Bentley, Melissa Murray, McKenna Bailey, Lisa Jones, and others on the editorial staff at Elsevier. We would also like to thank the reviewers of our manuscript for their comments and feedback.

One of us (RS) would like to acknowledge a number of folks: in the Jindal School administration, Drs. Varghese Jacob, Monica Powell, Diane McNulty, David Ritchey, Shawn Alborz and Jerry Hoag; all my colleagues in the Jindal School, especially, Drs. Greg Dess, Joseph Picken, Mike Peng, Habte Woldu, Robert Kieschnick, Alain Bensoussan, and Suresh Sethi; my colleagues at the Institute for Innovation and Entrepreneurship – Jackie Kimzey, Madison Pedigo, Dan Bochsler, Jonathan Shapiro and Bob Wright; also in the Jindal School, John Reeser, Sharon Pianka, Karah Hosek, Van Dam, Canan Mutlu, Craig Macaulay, Azar Ghahari and Amir Zemoodeh; my colleagues with the Jonsson School of Engineering and Computer Science – Dean Dr. Mark Spong, and Drs. Stephen Yurkovich, Mathukumalli Vidyasagar, Lakshman Tamil, Duncan MacFarlane, Bob Helms, Andy Blanchard, Cy Cantrell, Ed Esposito, Gopal Gupta and Ron Bose; in the UT Dallas administration – President Dr. David Daniel, Drs. Bruce Gnade and Don Hicks; at Timmaron Capital Advisors and the indusLotus Group, my colleagues and friends, especially – Dr. Jim Carlisle, Jack Mueller and Jack Wimmer, and Drs. Henry Sinnreich and Ljubisa Tancevski; Dr. Pradeep Shah and my early mentors in the US in the 1970's – Professors Dae Mann Kim, Thomas Rabson, and Frank Tittel at Rice, and Professor Ahmed Zewail at Caltech; I would also like to acknowledge the following people at various stages in my career – Phil Coup, Tom Engibous and Dr. Pallab Chatterjee at Texas Instruments; Tom Guthrie, Robert Ferguson, Robert Cronk, Eugene Smar, Jack Wimmer, Leo Cyr, Bob Finch, Fred Briggs and Dr. Vint Cerf at MCI Worldcom; Drs. Niel Ransom, Krish Prabhu, Christian Gregoire, and Ms. Joelle Gauthier at Alcatel; Peter Ewens at McKinsey and Co; Eddie Edwards at Commscope; Mikael Stromquist, Mikael Backstrom, Sten Andersson, Arun Bhikshesvaran, and Hal Thomas at Ericsson; John Masters at Nomura Securities; Wayne Huyard at Cerberus; Paul Klocek at Raytheon; and, ShaChelle Manning and Chris Cheatwood at Pioneer Natural Resources.

One of us (ZG) would like to acknowledge all those who helped and supported her to finish this work. She would like to thank the China Scholarship Council and the Northeast Agricultural University for giving her the opportunity and for sponsoring her for this project. Next, she would like to express her gratitude to her foreign partners and to her Chinese colleagues for their acceptance, team spirit, and understanding. Last, but not least, she would also like to express her deepest gratitude to her parents, her husband, her brother, and her friends, who give her endless love, consideration, and help and gave her confidence and courage to face difficulties.

One of us (HM) would like to express her deepest gratitude to Dr R.N. Vakil, ex-president, CEPT University, for inspiring her to explore the vicissitudes of the Indian innovation and entrepreneurship system. It would not have been possible for her to visit UT Dallas and work on the book had it not been for him. She would also like to thank Mr Harkesh Kumar Mittal, adviser and member secretary, National Science & Technology Entrepreneurship Development Board (NSTEDB), Department of Science & Technology, the Government of India. His enthusiastic response to the book project helped her gain access to several reports and resources pertaining to government initiatives and institutional frameworks in India.

Rajiv R. Shah
Zhijie Gao
Harini Mittal

Part I

Innovation

Chapter 1

Innovation

Chapter Contents

WHAT IS INNOVATION?

A lot has been written on the subject of innovation. More than 250 books were published with the word "innovation" in their title in just the first 3 months of 2012, and the term appeared more than 33,000 times in 2011 alone, in the annual and quarterly reports filed with the US Securities and Exchange Commission (SEC), a 64% increase from 2006 (Kwoh, 2012).

The word "innovation" has come to mean a lot of different things to a lot of different people, and as is typically the case with words in vogue at different periods in time, this word has been used and abused to the point where the word may have begun to lose its meaning. While the word is derived from the Latin noun *innovatus* and appears in print as early as the fifteenth century, the more modern interpretation and expounding of it go back to the famous economist Joseph Schumpeter and his writings in the 1930s (Schumpeter, 1934).

In 1934, Schumpeter added a definition of "innovation," or "development," as "new combinations" of new or existing knowledge, resources, equipment, and other factors. He pointed out that innovation needs to be distinguished from invention. The reason why Schumpeter stressed this difference is that he saw innovation as a specific social activity, or "function," carried out within the economic sphere and with a commercial purpose, while inventions in principle can be carried out everywhere and without any intent of commercialization. Thus, for Schumpeter, innovations are novel combinations of knowledge, resources, etc. subject to attempts at commercialization—it is essentially the process through which new ideas are generated and put into commercial practice. This "combinatory" activity he labeled "the entrepreneurial function" and the social agents fulfilling this function "entrepreneurs." For Schumpeter, these are keys to innovation and long-run economic change (Fagerberg, 2008).

After this early discussion of innovation and entrepreneurship, the next author- itative work on this subject was due to the famous management guru Peter Drucker in the 1980s (Drucker, 1985). Peter Drucker defines "*innovation*" in his 1985 book "Innovation and Entrepreneurship" as: "Innovation is the specific tool of entrepre- neurs, the means by which they exploit change as an opportunity for a different business or a different service. It is capable of being presented as a discipline, capa- ble of being learned, capable of being practiced. Entrepreneurs need to search pur- posefully for the sources of innovation, the changes and their symptoms that indicate opportunities for successful innovation, and they need to know and apply the principles of successful innovation." It is clear from this definition that (1) inno- vation is not just about inventions or about new technology, but about *new business opportunities* created through new technologies, products, services, processes, business models, etc.; (2) innovation is not something that just happens by itself, but is a *structured or systematic process that requires discipline* and that can be learned and practiced; and (3) in order to succeed at innovation, *you need to be proactive and search* for the sources of innovation and exploit them. Innovation is a process for creating and introducing something new, novel, or advanced with the intention of creating value or benefit (Hisrich and Kearney, 2014). Innovation is a process that begins with a new idea and concludes with market introduction.

In the 1990s and beyond, Clayton Christensen of the Harvard Business School wrote extensively on the subject (Christensen, 1997; Christensen and Raynor, 2003, Christensen et al., 2004; Dyer et al. 2011). In more recent years, there have been a plethora of writings on the subject of innovation and various interpreta- tions of the term. The intent of this work is not to debate the subject or to delve into the various interpretations, definitions, types, or applications of the term. Instead, we will first look at why innovation is important and what are the various factors that contribute to it and explore how these factors differ across some of the regions of the world, more specifically across the United States, China, and India. In order to facilitate that, we will use the definition of innovation as used by Schumpeter or by Peter Drucker, viz., innovation results from the application of knowledge and results in new business opportunities, regardless of whether these are the result of innovations in technology through innovations in process, product, or service or innovations in business models and business processes.

WHY IS INNOVATION IMPORTANT?

Innovation is important because it results in new business creation, which in turn drives economic growth. This is true whether these new businesses are new start-ups or whether they are new businesses within existing enterprises, and the latter has been described more recently as intrapreneurship. While these start-ups or existing enterprises benefit from these innovations in the form of increased revenues and increased profits, the net effect in the aggregate is a growth of the national and global economy.

Economic growth is measured as the annual rate of increase in a country's gross domestic product (GDP) and is a measure of the general well-being of the people in that economy. Economists, such as Schumpeter (1934), Solow (1956), and, most recently, Acemoglu (2009), Aghion and Howitt (2009), Barro and Sala-i-martin (2004), and others, who have studied factors contributing to economic growth, have shown that economic growth cannot be explained only by the increasing application of factors of production, viz., capital and labor. Specifically, per capita GDP cannot grow in the long run unless one assumes productivity also grows, which Solow refers to as "technical progress." What are needed in addition to capital and labor, to explain economic growth, are additional factors. Several innovation-based models have been used to explain economic growth. In one model, innovation causes productivity growth by creating new, but not necessarily improved, varieties of products (Romer, 1986a,b). Another model is based on "quality improving innovations that render old products obsolete" and hence involves the force that Schumpeter called creative destruction (Aghion and Howitt (1992) in Aghion and Howitt, 2009). We will discuss these theories and others in Part III of the book.

FACTORS CONTRIBUTING TO INNOVATION

The next question we address is what factors affect innovation in a given society. The Global Innovation Index (GII), prepared by the World Intellectual Property Organization and INSEAD for the year 2013, gives an overall score and ranking of innovativeness for 142 countries. These indices have been constructed using five input and two output subindices (Fig. 1.1).

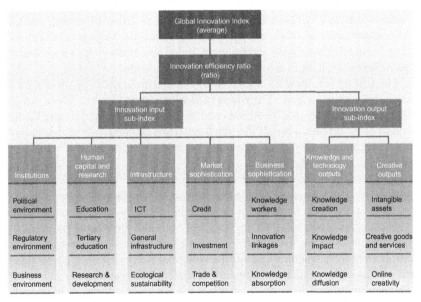

FIGURE 1.1   Framework for the Global Innovation Index (GII).

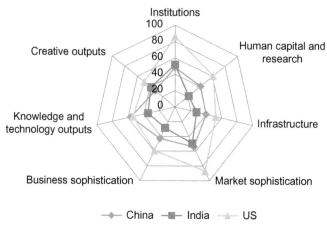

FIGURE 1.2   Global Innovation Index 2013. *(Source: Global Innovation Index 2013: The Local Dynamics of Innovation by WIPO and INSEAD.)*

The radar diagram (Fig. 1.2) shows the scores of the three countries for each of the seven subindices. From the diagram, it is evident that the United States provides good institution and market sophistication inputs, although in terms of human capital and research, infrastructure, and business sophistication, there is a lot of scope for improvement. In terms of output, the United States seems to produce more knowledge and technology outputs than creative outputs. China produces almost similar levels of knowledge and technology outputs as the United States and is better equipped than India in terms of human capital and research, infrastructure, and business sophistication. India produces more creative outputs than China and provides better institutional input and almost similar levels of input in terms of market sophistication.

The United States ranks 5th out of 142 countries in the GII, while China ranks 35th and India 66th. The overall GII score for the United States out of 100 is 60.3, while it is 44.7 for China and 36.3 for India. Both India and China need to catch up in almost all the input indicators as compared to the United States. Technologically, India seems to be lagging far behind the other two larger economies of the world.

This book goes into further detail and examines more factors that impact innovation specific to each of these three countries. The factors range from historical perspective (as an indicator of potential proclivity towards innovation), cultural factors, economic factors, laws and rules and the role of government and other institutions specifically geared towards promoting innovation (as indicators of infrastructural and institutional frameworks and overall business and market sophistication), demographics and education system (as indicators of human capital and research), to industry and market structures, including any industry or regional innovation clusters (as an indicator of level of sophistication of innovation across various industries of each of the economies).

Based on the analyses of the above factors, the section on innovation concludes by identifying the gaps in innovation in each of the economies taking into consideration the relevant local factors and conditions.

REFERENCES

Acemoglu, D., 2009. An Introduction to Modern Economic Growth. Princeton University Press.
Aghion, P., Howitt, P., 2009. The Economics of Growth. MIT Press.
Barro, R.J., Sala-i-martin, X., 2004. Economic Growth. MIT Press.
Christensen, C.M., 1997. The Innovator's Dilemma. Harvard Business School Press.
Christensen, C.M., Raynor, M.E., 2003. The Innovator's Solution. Harvard Business School Press.
Christensen, C.M., Anthony, S.D., Roth, E.A., 2004. Seeing What's Next. Harvard Business School Press.
Drucker, P., 1985. Innovation and Entrepreneurship. Harper.
Dyer, J., Gregersen, H.B., Christensen, C.M., 2011. The Innovator's DNA. Harvard Business School Press.
Fagerberg, J., 2008. A Guide to Schumpeter. Center for Advanced Study, pp. 20–22. (http://www.cas.uio.no/Publications/Seminar/Confluence_Fagerberg.pdf).
Global Innovation Index (GII), 2013.
Hisrich, R.D., Kearney, C., 2014. Managing Innovation and Entrepreneurship. SAGE Publications.
Kwoh, L., 2012, May 23. You call that innovation? The Wall Street Journal.
Romer, P., 1986a. Increasing returns and long-run growth. J. Polit. Econ. 94 (5), 1002–1037.
Romer, P., 1986b. Growth based on increasing returns due to specialization. Am. Econ. Rev. 77 (2), 56–62.
Schumpeter, J., 1934. The Theory of Economic Development. Harvard University Press, Cambridge, MA.
Solow, R.M., 1956. A contribution to the theory of economic growth. Q. J. Econ. 70 (1), 65–94.

Chapter 2

History

Chapter Contents

The reason history is an important factor in contributing to innovation is because the history of innovation in a country, both in the distant past and especially in the immediate past, or its recent "track record" sets societal or collective expectations in the psyche of a nation for innovations in the near future. Effectively, the expectation of innovation in the near future is an extrapolation of the history of innovation and hence is a factor contributing to innovation. In a sense, the "history of innovation" is the *net effect* of all other "hard factors," factors that can perhaps be measured and quantified, and "soft factors" that have contributed to innovation in the past and the outcome of that is captured by history. The "hard factors" might include the amount of capital invested, availability of a qualified and affordable work force, and level of infrastructure and industrialization of the country. In the near future, therefore, all of these contributing factors are expected to stay the same and hence history affects future innovation. Moreover, history also serves as a reflection of some of the "soft factors" that support innovation. These might include the country's political system, rules and regulations, value system, social opinions, and customs, which were gradually and unconsciously formed over a long period of time and which in turn affect expectations about innovation. Hence, we explore the impact of history on innovation.

THE UNITED STATES

The history of the United States as a nation is fairly recent, a little over 200 years, and yet the United States became a major force in innovation, especially starting around the late nineteenth century, after it emerged from the Civil War in 1865, to roughly the mid-twentieth century. The history of innovation in the United States and the growth of American economic power have been very well chronicled by a number of authors, most notably by Hughes (1989) of the University of Pennsylvania, Gordon (2004), and Morris (2012), and others. We, therefore, provide only a very brief synopsis here and refer interested readers to the very detailed, entertaining, and fascinating accounts by these technological and business historians.

We provide this very brief synopsis by quoting Heather Whipps, of LiveScience, from "A Brief History of US Innovation," "... however, the US did not begin its history as an innovation powerhouse. Despite encouraging inventions, those first few decades of its existence were spent relatively poor, both economically and in technological infrastructure. While other countries had their own very influential eras, America's distinction as a natural leader in technology came about in part from the fact that the U.S. peaked at a very opportune time. It was Britain and Germany that dominated science into the nineteenth century and also the early part of the twentieth century. While British engineers built the foundation for the Industrial Revolution, helped largely by the invention of the steam engine, German scientists developed key principles in the world of physics."

According to Thomas Hughes, with the framework laid in Europe, it was easier for the United States to excel when it finally emerged from the Civil War in 1865. No other nation has displayed such inventive power and produced such brilliant innovators as the United States during the half-century that began around 1870, wrote Hughes, who noted that the number of new patents issued annually in the country more than doubled between 1866 and 1896.

Further quoting Heather Whipps, "Americans were naturals at applied science, improving many ideas that were already in existence and bringing them to fruition with resources newly available during the Industrial Revolution: Samuel Morse did it in creating the telegraph; Thomas Edison did not invent the light bulb, but he made it practical and got his name in lights for the work; many men attempted to fly before the Wright brothers finally succeeded—under power and more or less controlled—at Kitty Hawk in 1903. During this time of 'independent' invention, it was often the last link in the chain that got credit. And that final link was often American."

The United States also became home to the brain power from around the world, due to the influx of people from other parts of the globe. During the nineteenth and early twentieth centuries, this influx of people was mainly from Europe—people escaping harsh economic or political realities at home— who were able to make huge contributions through their knowledge, creativity, and diligence to their new homeland. These contributions ranged from US atomic and space programs to US business economy and the military-industry complex. This influx of brain power has since continued into the late twentieth and early twenty-first centuries with people from other parts of the world. Significant contributions have come from these new immigrants to the Silicon Valley and to other parts of the United States in creating value for the US economy through innovation and entrepreneurship.

With the ease of communications and global travel, rise of the multinational corporations, and proactive involvement of foreign governments in supporting research and development, innovation and entrepreneurship have become more of a global affair. However, although science has become global, and while some technologies and innovations and, in some cases, entire industries moved to other countries, and skeptics wondered if there would ever be another era where US innovation would dominate as it did in the past, a new era of innovations dawned in the United States with the Internet (Whipps, 2009).

The spirit of innovation and entrepreneurship that spawned entirely new industries and built economic wealth in the United States from the mid-nineteenth to the mid-twentieth century that Hughes, Gordon, and Morris talked about in their books appears to be alive and well through the early part of the twenty-first century. While older industries matured and migrated to other parts of the world with lower cost structures, innovation in the United States gave birth to new industries such as computers, semiconductors, lasers, and wireless and optical communications. As these also matured and moved, at least partially, to the Far East, the United States saw the emergence of new innovation and value creation through companies such as Apple, Google, Amazon, eBay, Facebook, Twitter, and a host of other new innovative entrants in the software and Internet arena. The United States has also continued to be a leader in innovations in other sectors, such as pharmaceuticals, biotechnology, biomedical instrumentation, nanotechnology, and alternative energy, among others.

CHINA

Chinese history can be separated into three periods: (1) the feudal period, (2) the Republic of China period, and (3) the People's Republic of China period. We will discuss innovation in these three periods.

The Feudal Period (221 BC–AD 1911)

There are disputes among historians about the evolution of China during the feudal period. Chinese feudal society began in 221 BC with the Qin dynasty and lasted 2132 years through the Qing dynasty. By contrast, the United States became an independent nation in 1776 and evolved as a free market economy from the very beginning.

With regard to technology and innovation, this period can be further divided in two phases: in the first phase (221 BC–AD 1279), Chinese technology made significant progress, while in the next phase (AD 1279–AD 1911), the rate of technology, innovation, and resultant prosperity declined in China compared with that of the Western nations.

During this period, China was very advanced in many fields in relation to the rest of the world. China's agricultural technology was especially advanced. In order to take advantage of weather conditions to promote agriculture production, the Chinese created the lunar calendar and 24 solar terms in the lunar year (Wang, 1999). Some solar terms mean specific agricultural activities. For example, Grain in Ear (9th of the 24 solar terms, which is around 5th of June) means that the "bearded" summer-maturing crops, such as wheat and barley, are ripe and the "bearded" summer-seeding crops, such as grain and millet, should be sown. Other solar terms mean changes of weather, such as Rain Water, White Dew, and First Frost, which are important to agriculture. In addition to technologies in the areas of soil improvement, irrigation, fertilization, seed cultivation, hybridization, and grafting developed very well so that Chinese agriculture was extremely productive. Besides agriculture, Chinese silk, tea, jade articles, porcelain, and pottery were well known at that time, and the related technologies were the best in the world.

The four great inventions of ancient China—the compass, papermaking technology, gunpowder, and movable-type printing—made enormous contributions to the development of the world.

As far back as the period of the Warring States (475 BC–221 BC), people mastered the technology to indicate the north–south direction by using magnets. In the earlier Song dynasty (AD 960–AD 1127), another device was invented with a magnetic iron needle that pointed to the magnetic north, which was later used in navigation.

In the early western Han dynasty (206 BC–AD 24), paper was made from linen, which was the world's earliest kind of paper made from plant fibers. In the eastern Han dynasty (AD 25–AD 220), many kinds of new materials such as linen craps, rags, and used fish nets were used to make paper. After that, China had an advanced papermaking technology.

Lithographic printing was invented in the Sui dynasty (AD 581–AD 618) and was very common in the Tang dynasty (AD 618–AD 907). Also in earlier Song dynasty, movable-type printing was invented and baked clay typesetting started to be used.

Gunpowder was invented in the Tang dynasty and was used militarily on a large scale in the Song dynasty (AD 960–AD 1279). In AD 906, the last year before the demise of the Tang dynasty, "gunpowder made by machine" was used in the war of Hangzhou City, which is the earliest record of the use of gunpowder. In the Yuan dynasty, handguns, artillery, and other weapons began to appear (Wang, 1997).

So we see that China had some very advanced technologies before the thirteenth century, but most of these were not used commercially to develop the economy or to improve peoples' lives. In the thirteenth century and later, the art of invention in China declined and it gradually lost its technological advantage with respect to the rest of the world. Especially after entering the nineteenth century, because of the lack of a strong military capability, China was invaded several times and growth in China lagged behind the growth in Western countries, and this is indicated in Table 2.1 and Fig. 2.1. In AD 1000, China's share of world GDP was 22.7%, second only to India's with 28.9%, and over thirty times that of the United States. This share reached its highest level in 1820 at 32.9%. In the First Opium War of 1840, which was aimed at banning the

TABLE 2.1 China and India: A Look Back (Percentage of World GDP)

	The US and Other Western Offshoots	Europe	China	India
1000	0.7%	13.4%	22.7%	28.9%
1500	0.5%	23.9%	25.0%	24.5%
1700	0.2%	29.7%	22.3%	24.4%
1820	1.9%	32.3%	32.9%	16.0%
1913	21.7%	46.6%	8.9%	7.6%
1950	30.6%	39.3%	4.5%	4.2%

Source: Maddison (2003)

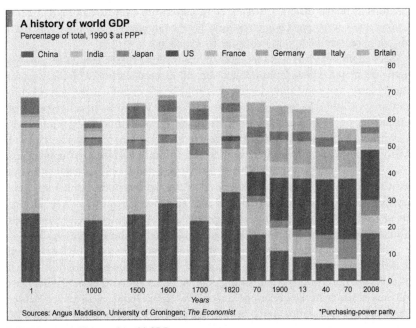

FIGURE 2.1   A history of world GDP.

addictive drug, China lost to Britain. After that, China was invaded by many countries and kept plunging into continual wars. During the same period, Western countries started to industrialize, and the West made significant advances in innovation and technology, resulting in greatly improving Western economies. By 1913, China's world GDP share was down to 8.9%, while that of Europe was at 46.6% and the United States was at 12.7%.

It was under these circumstances that China chose to learn technology from the West. Westernization Movement was the first time in Chinese history that technology was introduced on a large scale. During this movement, more than 30 schools were started in order to provide science education, and more than 200 students were sent to foreign countries to study electronics, medical science, mining, metallurgy, civil engineering, shipbuilding, building railroads, etc. (Chinese Modern History Collections: Westernization Movement [Z] Shanghai: Shanghai People's Publishing House, 1961).

With regard to innovation, the reasons why China moved from a period of great innovation and resulting prosperity to a period where it had lost its innovation advantage and a resultant weak economy can be understood as follows.

First, since 221 BC, China evolved as a highly centralized feudal system, which was the fundamental pattern of Chinese society. Under this system, all kinds of officials were appointed by the emperor and wealth distribution was also controlled by the emperor. As a result, people did not attach much importance to technology, innovation, commercialization, and the resultant wealth creation. They sought power and personal riches by aspiring to be and seeking positions as feudal officials. So, although there were a few technological innovations, they were not commercialized. For example, the compass was used only in geometry and gunpowder for firecrackers.

Second, in order to meet the political needs of the rulers, Confucianism was highly promoted. Other philosophies were all disused starting with the western Han dynasty, and neo-Confucianism was popular after the Yuan dynasty. Confucianism took ethics as the core and aimed to construct harmonious interpersonal relationships. It evaluated people only from the view of virtue, talent, and family background but ignored other key characteristics such as risk-taking, creative ability, and commercial awareness. Neo-Confucianism advocated "uphold justice, eliminate human desires," which greatly manacled people's thoughts. Under neo-Confucianism, women were deprived of the right to study, while men were required to just read The Four Books and The Five Classics for their official career (Sun, 2006). As a result, most people almost completely lost their spirit of innovation and any interest in doing scientific or technical research.

Third, the imperial examination system, which began in AD 605 and ended in 1905, had a negative influence on society. The imperial examination, which in itself was quite good, provided the poor an opportunity to change their lives and was better than the contemporaneous Western feudal lord system. Before the imperial examination system was established, China selected officials by the way of the "nine-grade system" (Zhang, 1999)—officials were separated by nine grades. Appointees to these nine grades were selected on the basis of their "virtue" and through an evaluation of their family backgrounds. In this system, a person with a "good family background," regardless of any other issues, could become an official, whereas a person without a good family background could not join these ranks no matter how talented the person is. The imperial examination system changed the way of selecting officials by defining selection criteria organized by subject areas and evaluating people along these criteria. So, compared with the "nine-grade system," the imperial examination system became the preferred system since one's family background was not a consideration. The imperial examination system played a very positive role in selecting qualified officials. But after entering the Qing dynasty, an eight-part essay (or stereotyped writing) became the main content of the imperial examination (Xiang, 1999). This often took the form of a written exam with a fixed format covering the Five Classics: the Book of Songs, the Book of History, the Book of Changes, the Book of Rites, and the Spring and Autumn Annals. As long as applicants were good at writing an eight-part essay, they could be appointed as officials. As a result, most Chinese did not really care about history and the reality of the times and certainly were not interested in natural sciences and technology. Their ideas and thinking were confined to the Five Classics and they lost their creative abilities. Intellectuals did not participate in social and economic practice and indulged in empty political talk.

Lastly, emperors of the Qing dynasty cut off communications with other countries. In the eighteenth century, uprisings against Qing governments occurred more frequently, and the emperor worried about Han Chinese colluding with Westerners through doing more international business with the West. The Qing emperors, therefore, adopted a closed-door policy, and embracing Western culture and influence was prohibited, and, of course, advanced Western technologies were also not allowed into China.

The Republic of China (1912–1949)

In this period, China went through great social upheaval. The period saw a Cultural Revolution, an antiaggression war, and a civil war. As a result, not only technology and innovation but also the economy and society developed very slowly. There are no data to directly relate to innovation during this period. However, since innovation results in economic development and is strongly related to education, education and economic developments are used as proxies to assess innovation during this period.

From the standpoint of economic activity, from 1912 to 1919, only 472 factories were set up, and the total capital deployed for production was about 95 M yuan. In 1947, there were about 12,000 factories. These factories were in the food industry (28%), textile industry (20%), chemical industry (19%), and the machine tool industry (13%). During this period, the average annual economic growth rate was 5.6%. From 1937 to 1949, economic growth reversed course because of wars, and the GDP was mainly from agriculture. For example, in 1933, agricultural products accounted for 65% of total output, and industrial products and commerce accounted for 10.5% and 9.4%. Although the economy and industry made some progress, inflation was rampant and was reflected in the national retail price index, which was 103 in 1937 and increased to 10,593,400 at the end of 1947. Especially in 1947, the national retail price index jumped from 846,333 in January to 10,593,400 in December—11.5 times in just 1 year. This is also evident from the data in Table 2.1, which shows that China's share of world GDP was only 4.5% in 1950, only about half of that in 1913 (The Statistics Year Book of the Republic of China).

In the Republic of China, higher education made some progress, especially after the New Culture Movement. The Imperial examination system was abolished, women's right to education was established, and Mandarin was used in teaching instead of the ancient Chinese language. In 1912, there were 115 colleges and universities, and only 4 of them were universities or independent colleges. Between 1913 and 1936, although the number of colleges and universities fluctuated with its lowest at 74 in 1928, universities and independent colleges grew during this entire period. After 1939, the number of schools of higher education, research institutes, numbers of teachers, and numbers of students all increased (Table 2.2). In 1946, there were about 130,000 students in schools of higher education. Law schools were the most popular, followed by engineering, and then business, humanities, and teacher training (Fig. 2.2). In 1929, about 1657 students studied abroad and that number declined to 450 in 1931. From 1931 to 1935, the number of students studying abroad increased every year with about 1038 in 1935. A sharp decline followed, with this number declining to 57 and 8 in 1941 and 1945, respectively. At the end of 1946, the number of Chinese students studying overseas increased but was still less than that in 1930 (Fig. 2.3). These data suggest that China had very little academic communication with other countries and avenues for obtaining new technology from abroad were very limited.

The People's Republic of China (After 1949)

After the establishment of new China, the People's Republic of China (PRC), the year 1978 was a big turning point for Chinese technology. So we separate this period into two phases: from 1949 to 1978 and then 1978 or later.

In the first phase, technological innovation was centrally planned and was targeted to meet the goals set by the central government. Innovation and the budget for innovation were allocated by the government. As a result, the innovator did not take any risks and hence did not benefit from the innovation either. At the same time, innovation was also heavily influenced by the economic and social development of the country, as well as by politics and relevant policy.

After years of war, the economy in 1949 was fragile, and the output of major industrial product fluctuated from 15% to 80% of peak levels. For example, cast iron production and steel production were 13.9% and 17.1% of their historical

TABLE 2.2 General State of Higher Education from 1936 to 1946

Year	Number of Colleges and Universities	Number of Research Institutes	Number of Undergraduates	Number of Teachers	Number of Graduates
1936	108	22	41,922	9154	7560
1937	91	18	31,188	5137	5657
1938	97	23	36,180	5025	6079
1939	101	30	44,422	5622	6514
1940	113	30	52,376	7710	7598
1941	129	36	59,457	8035	8666
1942	132	45	64,097	9056	9421
1943	133	42	73,669	10,514	10,536
1944	145	49	78,909	12,078	11,201
1945	141	49	83,498	14,463	11,183
1946	185	51	129,336	20,185	16,317

Source: The Statistics Year Book of the Republic of China

Distribution of majors among students

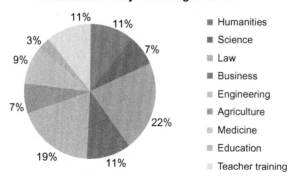

FIGURE 2.2 Distribution of majors in 1946. *(Source: The Statistics Year Book of the Republic of China.)*

peak annual outputs. Besides, agricultural output fell more than 20% and the output of all major agricultural products also greatly declined. As shown in Fig. 2.4, before 1970, except for the period from 1958 to 1961, primary industrial output exceeded secondary industrial output. This situation changed after 1970. The reason why the secondary industry developed fast from 1958 to 1961

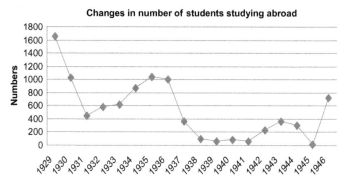

FIGURE 2.3   Changes in the number of students studying abroad. *(Source: The Statistics Year Book of the Republic of China.)*

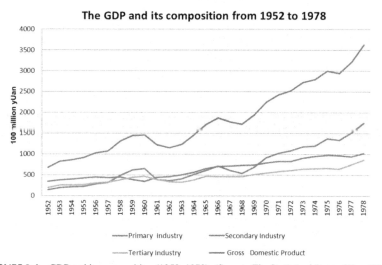

FIGURE 2.4   GDP and its composition (1952–1978). *(Source: The Statistical Data of New China Sixty Years.)*

was not because of technical progress but because of "The Great Leap Forward," which made an unrealistically ambitious plan for the Chinese economy and which eventually caused significant loss in output.

In addition, from 1959 to 1961, China suffered from very serious natural disasters. The total area covered by flood or drought in those years was about 172 M ha. "The Great Leap Forward" and the 3 years of natural disasters made for a very difficult period in China. This indicated that in the early years of the People's Republic of China, the industrial base was very weak and the industrial infrastructure was severely incomplete. China's industry made some progress with the help of the Soviet Union. However, due to political instabilities and system inefficiencies, China's industrial output was lower than its primary (agricultural) output. In this environment, vast manpower resources were tied to its primary industry and had no opportunity to learn about technology. This in turn hindered technological progress and innovation. The net result of all of this was that very little investment could be made in technological research and development.

In order to correct this situation and to accelerate industrial development, in the 1960s, a great deal of investment was made in industrial construction and the ratio of industrial investment to total investment was over 60%. Import of new technology from other countries was key to the completion of a large number of industrial projects. In the 1950s, China got technological assistance from the Soviet Union, and 156 projects, accounting for about half of the total industrial investment, were finished in the 1st 5-year plan and more than 24,000 sets of scientific and technical information documents were freely introduced in about 10 years (Yi et al., 2007). These technological documents contributed to the building of the Chinese industrial system.

Many big manufacturing factories were set up during this period. This, in turn, played an important role in the economic development of China. In the 1960s, the relationship between China and the Soviet Union changed significantly and China lost technological support from the Soviet Union, resulting in financial losses in many uncompleted projects. The influx of technology into China from the Soviet Union and Eastern Europe rapidly declined. From 1963 to 1966, China signed more than 80 technological contracts with Japan, the United Kingdom, France, Italy, the former Federal Republic of Germany, and other countries, and these were worth $280 M. In the 1970s, China imported a lot of technology from the Western countries, and by 1977, the actual external transactions reached $3.96B of which equipment cost was about $3.15B (Yi et al., 2007).

The state of education in this period also greatly influenced China's later technological innovation. Indicated in Table 2.3 are changes in the numbers of students at different levels. The Cultural Revolution began in 1966 and ended in 1976. This was a political movement intended to prevent the birth of capitalism. In this movement, many intellectuals were not only criticized at public meetings but also forced to work in the countryside in order to change their views. Students were also denied education and were required to settle and work in the countryside. Many people in this period did not even finish secondary school, and colleges were prohibited from enrolling new students.

As shown in the data in Table 2.3, during this period, graduate students were not permitted to enroll for about 12 years, studying abroad was forbidden for about 6 years, and there were no enrolled undergraduates from 1966 to 1969. According to some estimates, about 100 M undergraduates and 100,000 postgraduates lost potential educational opportunities. The Cultural Revolution had a disastrous influence on China's technological development. On the one hand, China lost huge amounts of valuable manpower because higher education was

TABLE 2.3 The State of High-Level Education in China (1949—1978)

Year	Number of Postgraduates (persons) Student Enrollment	New Student Enrollment	Number of Overseas Students (persons) Studying Abroad	Returned after Studying	Number of Undergraduates (in Units of 10,000) Student Enrollment	New Student Enrollment	Number of Students in Specialized Secondary Schools (in Units of 10,000) Student Enrollment	New Student Enrollment
1949	629	242			11.7	3.1	22.9	9.7
1950	1261	874	35		13.7	5.8	25.7	12.8
1951	2168	1273	380		15.3	5.2	38.3	23.0
1952	2763	1785	231		19.1	7.9	63.6	35.1
1953	4249	2887	675	16	21.2	8.1	66.8	19.4
1954	4753	1155	1518	22	25.3	9.2	60.8	15.0
1955	4822	1751	2093	104	28.8	9.8	53.7	19.0
1956	4841	2235	2401	258	40.3	18.5	81.2	46.2
1957	3178	334	529	347	44.1	10.6	77.8	12.3
1958	1635	275	415	670	66.0	26.5	147.0	89.5
1959	2171	1345	576	1380	81.2	27.4	149.5	70.0
1960	3635	2275	441	2217	96.2	32.3	221.6	106.6
1961	6009	2198	124	1403	94.7	16.9	120.3	16.7

Year								
1962	6130	1287	114	980	83.0	10.7	53.5	3.9
1963	4938	781	32	426	75.0	13.3	45.1	15.5
1964	4881	1240	650	191	68.5	14.7	53.1	24.9
1965	4546	1456	454	199	67.4	16.4	54.7	20.8
1966	3409				53.4		47.0	4.6
1967	2557				40.9		30.8	0.8
1968	1317				25.9		12.8	1.8
1969					10.9		3.8	1.3
1970					4.8	4.2	6.4	5.4
1971					8.3	4.2	21.8	21.3
1972			36		19.4	13.4	34.2	26.8
1973			259		31.4	15.0	48.2	29.4
1974			180	70	43.0	16.5	63.4	32.7
1975			245	186	50.1	19.1	70.7	34.4
1976			277	189	56.5	21.7	69.0	34.8
1977	226		220	270	62.5	27.3	68.9	36.6
1978	10,934	10,708	860	248	85.6	40.2	88.9	44.7

Blanks indicate that the data are not available.
Source: The Statistical Data of New China Sixty Years

prohibited during a crucial period when China's economy began to recover. On the other hand, it changed peoples' attitudes towards learning and seeking knowledge because intellectuals had a lower social status than the common workers and also because many intellectuals gave up their research due to persecution.

In 1978, the policy of reform and opening up was put forward, which emphasized science and technology far more than ever before, and scientific and technological progress was seen as one of the most important factors to promote socioeconomic growth. Although before 1989, technological innovation was not clearly evident, research in the areas of technological progress and technical and economic effectiveness was very active.

After 1978, industrial structure changed, and the proportion of secondary and tertiary industries significantly improved. This brought about rapid economic and technological development. Increasing labor demand from secondary and tertiary industries liberated labor from their attachment to land and resulted in many opportunities for them to learn new technologies. This improved the skill level of the workforce and contributed to technological progress. At the same time, with the development of secondary and tertiary industries, peoples' basic and survival needs were being met, and a significant amount of capital could be invested to promote innovation. For example, R&D investments gradually increased and reached about 0.7% of GDP long before 2000, while in 2002, it exceeded 1% for the first time and continued to grow beyond that (China Statistics Year Book, 1999–2003).

The number of scientific and technical personnel grew quickly in the 1990s, growing from 257.6 M in 1994 to 348.1 M in 2004. Higher education enrollment increased year by year after 1978. For example, as recently as 2000, China produced 949,000 undergraduates and 59,000 graduates. In addition, enterprises played more of a role in technological innovation, and more than 500 technological business incubators were set up in 2004 (Zhang, 2007).

INDIA

Technology, innovations, and entrepreneurship in Indian history can be viewed in four distinct parts—Ancient Indian period, medieval period, period of British rule, and postindependence–prereform period.

Ancient Indian Period (4000 BC–185 BC)

The history of India begins with the evidence of human activity of *Homo sapiens* as long as 75,000 years ago or with earlier hominids including *Homo erectus* from about 500,000 years ago (Bongard-Levin, 1979). However, the first well-known major civilization in India was the Indus Valley Civilization, although the prior existence of a Dravidian civilization in southern India has also been reported.[1]

---

1. Source: Michael Wood's BBC TV Series "India—An Epic Journey Across the Subcontinent."

Indus Valley Civilization or the Bronze Age (4000 BC–1900 BC)

Technological progress in India can be traced back to Indus Valley (Harappa) Civilization, also called the Bronze Age. This civilization spanned most of the northern Indian subcontinent that included much of modern Sindh, Gujarat, Rajasthan, Haryana, Punjab, and western UP. It was renowned for its superior architectural and urban planning skills and techniques characterized by well-constructed public and multistoried private dwellings made of fired bricks with separate toilets and kitchens, public granaries, warehouses for trade, public baths and public buildings used for common purposes, well-planned roads, and sanitation facilities that included underground drainage systems connected to every individual dwelling. These urban centers were planned near riverine or seaports to facilitate trade. Trade across these centers and with Babylon, the Persian Gulf, Egypt, and the Mediterranean region flourished during this period.

The civilization was also well known for its

a. expertise in the manufacture of copper and bronze products supported by advanced technology and instruments for the purpose and
b. proficiency in pottery and irrigation systems with appropriate fire- and flood-proof measures in place.

The civilization disappeared due to population pressures leading to social decay and disintegration. The disintegration manifested itself in the form of haphazard growth of urban dwellings and decline in the maintenance of irrigation systems, ultimately making it susceptible to natural disasters such as floods, droughts, fires, and earthquakes and eventually resulting in the extinction of this once vibrant civilization.[2]

Vedic Period (1700 BC–500 BC)[3]

Following the Indus Valley Civilization was the Vedic period and the written evidence of knowledge of sciences in India can be traced back to the Vedic times. The Vedas describe knowledge in pairs such as "groups of: logic (*Nyaya*) and physics (*Vaisheshika*), cosmology (*Sankhya*) and psychology (*Yoga*), and language (*Mimamsa*) and reality (*Vedanta*)."

Indian geometry also had its origin in the Vedic period. The "Pythagoras" theorem was described in Sulbasutra authored by Baudhayana and others. Binary numbers were known at the time of Pingala's *Chhandahshastra* in around the fifth century BC.

Indian astronomy is also said to have had its origin in the Vedic period. Cosmology as described in the Vedas believed that the universe goes through cycles

---

2. This section is based on the article "Technological Discoveries and Applications in India" from http://india_resource.tripod.com/technology.htm.
3. http://www.ece.lsu.edu/kak/grolier.pdf.

of creation and destruction with a period of 8.64 B years. The speed of light was estimated at 186,000 miles/s in those days.

Panini's grammar had 4000 rules for Sanskrit language in the fifth century BC.

Ayurveda, the Indian medicine system, is a holistic approach to health that builds upon the tripartite Vedic approach to the world. Much of the knowledge of Indian medicine was standardized and available in the classical textbooks of Charaka and Sushruta. Cesarean section, bone setting of high skill, and plastic surgery were the highlights of Indian surgery at that time. Sushruta Samhita has chapters on surgery that indicate many inventions of medical instruments and surgical operations.

Following the Vedic period, there were several other rulers including the Mahajanapadas, Persian, and Greek rulers and the Mauryan Empire.

Mauryan Empire (321 BC–185 BC)

This empire was one of the largest empires in the history of India extending in the west to what is now Afghanistan and some of the finest architectural structures were built during this period. The wood-based dwellings including grand palaces and public buildings built during the Mauryan civilization were destroyed due to extensive civil wars. This led to developments in construction technology bringing about durable, long-lasting buildings and dwellings. The Mauryans therefore developed skill and know-how in stone-based construction and sculpting and thereby marked the beginning of the use of hard-based construction materials in India.

The stone and other hard-based construction materials required hard metal-based tools and instruments. The discovery of iron played a role not only in monumental architecture but also in the mastery of metallurgical skills. Kautilya's *Arthashastra* (fourth century BC) had a section on metal extraction and alloying.[4]

Medieval Period (100 BC–AD 1600)[5]

This period was marked by several kingdoms, the most significant of them being the Gupta dynasty spanning the northern, central, and major parts of eastern and western India; the Pallavas and the Cholas from the south; and Islamic and Delhi sultanates followed by the Mughal Empire. India produced very prominent astronomer-mathematicians and made rapid strides in technological advancements in several fields in the medieval period.

The era of the Gupta dynasty (AD 320–AD 600) has been described as the golden period of Indian history marked by extensive inventions in science,

---

4. Source: http://india_resource.tripod.com/technology.htm.
5. This section is based on the article "Technological Discoveries and Applications In India" from http://india_resource.tripod.com/technology.htm and http://www.iisc.ernet.in/prasthu/pages/PP_data/105.pdf.

technology, engineering, art, dialectic, literature, logic mathematics, astronomy, religion, and philosophy. Aryabhatta in his book *Aryabhatiyam*, which dates back to the Gupta period, describes cosmic, planetary, and mathematical theories including the theory that the Earth spins on its own axis, theories of the lunar eclipse, reflection of sunlight by the moon and planets, and the theory of relativity of motion.

Technological advancements in the field of metallurgy continued in this period. The 23-feet high iron pillar built in the fifth century in Delhi has withstood more than 1500 monsoons without a trace of rust. Progress in the field of metallurgy led to the production of artilleries including a variety of weapons. In fact, the heaviest guns in the world were being cast in India.

The prevalent social and climatic conditions also played a major role in steering technological developments in the medieval period. The long dry months experienced in most regions of India caused innovations in water management such as the advent of a variety of water-harvesting techniques, construction of irrigation canals, wells of different types, storage tanks, and artificial lakes.

The needs of accurate prediction of monsoon led to advancements in astronomy. Post-Gupta dynasty, several astronomer-mathematicians continued to make significant contributions to the field. Brahmagupta who had contrary views to Aryabhatta wrote Brāhmasphuṭasiddhānta in AD 628, which was later translated to Arabic and became very popular in the Arabic world. He contributed to number theory and provided a solution of a certain second-order indeterminate equation. Bhāskara, a brilliant mathematician and astronomer from the twelfth century, was the author of the book Siddhanta Shiromani that was in four parts: (i) Lilavati on arithmetic, (ii) Bijaganita on algebra, (iii) Ganitadhyaya, and (iv) Goladhyaya on astronomy. Madhava from the fourteenth century was able to give accurate estimates of lunar positions (every 36 min) and planetary positions. He gave power series expansions for trigonometric functions and correct to eleven decimal places for pi. The contributions of Nilakantha Somayaji relating to the heliocentric model of the solar system and many other mathematicians from his time and region are considered to be far superior to those by the European mathematicians of the day.[6]

Climatic conditions also spurred the need to preserve and prevent spoilage of food, which gave birth to techniques for preserving fruits, vegetables, fish, and meat.

In addition to the above technologies, Indian medicine in its evolved stage was in place in the first century. An upshot of Indian medicine was the growth in the field of chemical technologies, which saw not only the production of medicinal substances but also the manufacture of glass.

Beyond the above innovations in the physical world, the psychological aspects of a human mind were also given importance. The role of color in

---

6. http://www.ece.lsu.edu/kak/grolier.pdf.

uplifting of mood was recognized, as a result of which newer ways of using colors for art, architecture, textiles in the form of dyes, and decoration of public and private spaces came into existence.

The Indian textile industry commanded a huge market share worldwide and the early British and German textile machines were modeled after the Indian machines. The thriving export market gave rise to an equally booming shipping and packaging industry.

One of the reasons for the flourishing of science, technology, and innovations in ancient and medieval India was the availability of state support in various forms from most rulers alike, be it the Guptas or the Rajputs or the Deccan kings or the Mughal rulers.[7] In fact, during the Mughal rule of India, science and technology developed mainly due to the interests of Emperors and Sultans, particularly in astronomy, agriculture, engineering, architecture, and medicine. A number of encyclopedias and dictionaries were also written.

Initially, dictionaries were needed as new ideas were being developed as a result of interaction between Sanskrit and other languages. During the later period of Mughal rule, new ideas were accepted from European science and technology inscriptions.

Limitations of Indian Science, Technology, Innovation, and Entrepreneurship[8]

Although India made rapid strides in science, technology, innovations, trade, and commerce, it had certain limitations that created an environment conducive for European conquests of India. Major impediments in the path of Indian science and technology in the medieval and ancient periods were superstitions, religious beliefs, reliance on astrology, numerology, or the advice of "seers," palmists, and fortune-tellers. Unfortunately, many a time, some of the scientific and rational principles were mixed with religious beliefs.

The second limitation was related to Indian manufacturing. Though it was of exceptional quality, it was highly labor-intensive. The Indian artisan was specialized and had trained hands. Labor-saving instruments and techniques were not found in these periods perhaps because the need for major expansion was not felt since production was sufficient to meet local demand. Due to the absence of well-developed transportation and communication systems, the village-level self-sufficiency economy existed, whose requirements were easily met by the production system that existed then.

---

7. A detailed list of ancient scientific discoveries and technological inventions has been compiled by the Indian Institute of Scientific Heritage (Ramaswamy, 2012).
8. This section is based on the article "Technological Discoveries and Applications in India" from http://india_resource.tripod.com/technology.htm.

The third limitation pertained to the occupational immobility due to the caste system till the onset of the nineteenth century. Commercial activities were a monopoly of the Vaishya caste and manufacturing activity was performed by artisans. There was a clear distinction between commercial activities and manufacturing.

The fourth limitation was the lack of political unity in India that hindered commercial activities on a larger scale and mobility, in general. Political and economic factors such as the absence of effective communication systems, primitive modes of transport that prevented secure movement of goods and people especially during the Mughal period, a network of customs barriers, and the existence of innumerable systems of currency (about 1000 in circulation) led to the development of regional markets or the so-called village self-sufficient economy.

The overall environment in this period was that of prosperity and, therefore, complacency. Harry Verelst (Senior Officer of the East India Company of Britain) described Bengal before Plassey quite succinctly: "The farmer was easy, the artisan encouraged, the merchant enriched and the prince satisfied." Europe was going through a totally contradictory phase with harsh climates, poor peasantry and working class, and a high requirement for technological breakthroughs and, therefore, huge capital requirement. The demand for Indian goods in Europe was great in the sixteenth and seventeenth centuries and the exploits of the East India Company further augmented the demand. Balance of trade was always in favor of India and Europeans had to import treasuries into India to finance their operations in spite of the restrictions imposed by their governments. One of the answers for the problems of Europe was the colonization of prosperous regions like the Indian subcontinent. The following section gives a description of science, technology, innovation, and enterprise in India during the period of European especially British dominance.

1750–1947: The Period of European Dominance[9]

Descriptions of science, technology, and innovation in India in English during the major parts of the eighteenth and the nineteenth centuries are mostly found in British archives. These archives are accounts of authors who visited India in the capacities of military, civilian, and medical servants of European governments or travelers or Jesuits from Europe. Dharampal (2000) studied in detail the works of various such authors and provided an analysis of the state of science, technology, and society during this period, which was a period characterized by European dominance.

According to him, these accounts were an outcome of the Europeans' quest for knowledge in the fields of science and technology in the non-European

---

9. This section is based on Dharampal (2000).

world. Dharampal (2000) found that some of the initial accounts did not present a comprehensive understanding of science and technological advancements in India as it was, due to the "lack of requisite comprehension amongst the learned of Europe of the prevailing non-European practices and technologies. Such lack of understanding was even more evident amongst the learned of Britain who, till about 1800, seem to have lagged behind some of the other parts of Europe in many scientific and technological fields by about 50 years." This statement is profound since it implies that the Indian science and technology in the eighteenth century was so advanced that it was beyond the comprehension of Europeans at that time (Dharampal, 2000).

Later as European needs started multiplying, the quest for knowledge became wider and more sophisticated, and the travelers became more interested in Indian science and technology.

The knowledge and expertise of Indians in astronomy and mathematics even in the eighteenth century intrigued the explorers. John Playfair, a professor of mathematics at the University of Edinburgh in his review of European knowledge of Indian astronomy written in the year 1790, observed that Indian astronomical observations were as old as 3012 BC and they could have been a product of observations made at the time rather than the result of complex calculations. He also found that the highly sophisticated astronomical observations and findings that the eighteenth-century Indian astronomer perused were products of the ancient Indian astronomers, which were passed on to the Brahmins of the eighteenth century. In his opinion, "the eighteenth century Indian astronomer had little knowledge of the principles on which his rules are founded and no anxiety to be better informed."

However, in 1769, M. Le Gentil visited India and took instructions and data from the very same Indian astronomers, as a result of which he was able to publish tables and rules in the Academy of Science in 1772.

The observatory at Varanasi, which was constructed in the eighteenth century, though some historians believe it was constructed in sixteenth century, housed some of the most sophisticated astronomical instruments used to track planetary movements and make accurate observations regarding the solar system, including its planets and their satellites. Similarly, observations were made by various other European scholars and authors who visited India who concluded that the Indians must have possessed a variety of telescopic instruments to have such detailed knowledge on the subject of various planets and satellites.

The astronomical calculations also revealed the Indian mastery of mathematics. Authors such as Reuben Burrows and H.T. Colebrooke presented an exhaustive review of Indian arithmetic and algebra. Burrows had pointed out that the binomial theorem originated in India and Colebrooke had speculated that Indian algebra may have had its roots in Greek algebra, but "by the ingenuity of Indian scholars," the algebra in its Indian form was far more advanced and developed.

Indian technology as it was recorded in the eighteenth century evinced considerable interest among the Europeans, be it in the field of medicine or construction or agriculture or metallurgy.

As far as medicine is concerned, the surgical operations performed by Indians were successful in removing ulcers and cutaneous eruptions of the worst kind with the process of inducing inflammation. Plastic surgery was also prevalent in western India. The practice of inoculation against smallpox was widespread in both the northern and southern parts of India in their own indigenous way. European authors had presented extensive reports on this practice in an effort to learn and improvise the practice for European use.

The mortar used for construction purposes as it was made in Madras using several natural ingredients was recorded by Isaac Pyke, the then-governor of St. Helena in 1732, so that the process could be replicated in the European world. The unique process for making ice was observed by Sir Robert Baker in 1775 in Allahabad, Mootegil, and especially in Calcutta where natural ice was never to be seen since the temperature was never below freezing point. Similarly, the process of making paper with various parts of *sunn* (*Crotalaria juncea*) and a few other ingredients was recorded by Lt. Col. Ironside in 1774.

The system of agriculture in India as observed in 1820 was based on a set of well-formulated code of rules for both cultivation and animal husbandry. Indian farmers then cultivated more kinds of grain than in any other part of the world using different types of tools, instruments, implements, and techniques that were appropriate for different types of soil. The drill plow, a very efficient and effective tool, which was used in India from time immemorial, was introduced in Europe only in 1662. Indian soil was fertile in general and the farmer was knowledgeable about every detail of his profession.

The *wootz* steel manufactured in India was on a par with the best steel available in Britain in the 1790s due to two reasons—the availability of superior-quality ore and the use of a superior technique that enabled the Indian steel to be made within 2½ h, while it required at least 4 hours or more to produce the same steel in Sheffield. In the field of shipping, the British adapted several improvements from India to their shipping.

Several other innovative, indigenous technologies and techniques such as the art of dyeing, the process of using lime in buildings, and the methods of making soap, gunpowder, indigo, ink, cinnabar, vitriol, and iron and alum, the substance *dammer*, which was used for covering the bottoms of ships or for paving the seams of parts above copper, were found to be in use in the eighteenth and nineteenth centuries.

Post-1780s and more after 1820, knowledge of the non-European world did not have much utility for the European world, and Indian science and technology met the same fate as its sovereignty and political systems. Post-1820s, most of the non-European world was described as backward and barbaric in European theory.

The superiority of India in science, technology, and industrial development disappeared because under the British rule, India was to be treated as a consumer of British goods, and therefore, manufacturing of finished goods was discouraged through hostile state policy. The economic breakdown of India under British rule and harsh fiscal policy eliminated indigenous sciences and technologies from both society and the Indian memory.

It was not as if India had not been conquered by foreign invaders earlier. While the early invaders "Indianized" themselves, the interests of the British were rooted in their home country. A new tradition unknown to Indians was introduced by them—foreign rulers and Indian subjects.

Some exploitative trade practices of the British were (i) forcing Indian planters to cultivate indigo at unreasonable prices so that it could be exported by them at fabulous margins, (ii) exploiting Indian artisans to deliver cotton and silk fabrics at below market prices, and (iii) either banning or imposing high duty on export of superior Indian goods while three-fourths of India's imports consisted of British goods and the remaining one-fourth was of a kind that the British did not produce.

Also as a backdrop, the Indian business community belonging to the Vaishya caste was confined only to trading and money lending and did not have any inclination to venture into manufacturing.

On the other hand, the British merchants set up agency houses in Presidency cities of Calcutta, Bombay, and Madras to facilitate remittances through trade and commerce. They also entered into banking and steam shipping businesses to facilitate financing and trade for the British.

At the same time, English secular education was spreading its wings. Some of the most important Indian scientists were also making an international mark such as Jagadish Bose (1858–1937) in electromagnetic theory and plant life, Srinivasa Ramanujan (1887–1920) in mathematics, Chandrasekhar Venkata Raman (1888–1970) in physics, Meghnad Saha (1893–1956) in astrophysics, and Satyendra Bose (1894–1974) in quantum theory. In addition to that, the birth of the "Protestant ethic" Brahmo-samaj also facilitated loosening the tight grip of religious and traditional ideas, superstitions, and dogmas.

Between 1837 and 1847, prompted by the changes in the cultural environment and inspired by the success of enterprises set up by the British agencies, Hindus from other castes also started entering the business domain in partnership with the British. These partnerships disappeared due to mismanagement. However, certain developments introduced by the British to enable their trade and commerce—such as the emergence of unified currency, abolition of irksome custom barriers, advent of liberal reformist movements, establishment of post and telegraph systems, and construction of roads and railways—helped in expanding markets and the horizons of business during the latter half of the nineteenth century. As a result, several enterprising Parsees and non-Vaishya Gujaratis entered the domain of entrepreneurship.

After the First World War, imports of essential commodities stopped. Indian industries were offered discriminatory protection albeit only in those industries in which India had to compete with some other country but Britain. Currency became more stable. At the same time, freedom movement to break free from the British rule promoted the "Swadeshi" (indigenous) concept, which gave a new upsurge to the demand for Indian goods. With these changes in the environment, the Indian Vaishya community across the country entered other industries, sugar, cement, textiles, construction, chemicals, newspaper, and publishing and a host of other fields with their enormous capital (Dharampal, 2000).

Postindependence and Prereform Period: 1947–1990

India became independent from British rule on August 15, 1947. At the time of independence, India inherited a distorted colonial economy. Food grain consumption had dropped; 70% of industrial employment was located in the Presidency cities and port-towns concentrated in a few sectors like agro-based industries, repair activities, steel factories, textile industries, and rudimentary cement and sugar industries; the transport network was linked only with metropolitan towns. A high proportion of agricultural workers in the labor force, female illiteracy, low levels of power availability and consumption, industrialization, literacy, and high density of population pointed to structured backwardness at the time of independence in 1947. The task of correcting the imbalances was set in the backdrop of the ideology of self-reliance, the seeds of which were sown in the freedom movement in the colonial era. This translated into a need for indigenous science and technology to avoid economic dependency and to have a significant presence at the global level. The rhetoric defined the formulation and implementation of goals and policies for science, technology, and innovations in the postindependence (post-1947) era.

The rhetoric resulted in both favorable and unfavorable outcomes. Foremost among the achievements was the establishment of a science and technology infrastructure that was far superior to that in most of the developing countries (Jayaraman, 2009). By the 1980s, India had

> *i) a nuclear energy sector with independent capabilities, ii) a space sector that rapidly moved from semi-experimental status to establishing strengths in communications infrastructure, and remote sensing capabilities, iii) a chain of industrial research laboratories that covered a wide range of fields ranging from leather technology to modern biotechnology, and iv) a network of defense research laboratories. In agriculture, India developed a national agricultural research system and an agricultural extension system alongside the Green Revolution that significantly increased agricultural productivity and helped increase the diversity of India's agriculture. In the field of health it established, though more slowly, a system of institutions of medical teaching and research that developed considerable capabilities in several areas of medicine.*

(Jayaraman, 2009)

Higher education in science and technology also grew in this period. Initially, during the colonial period, five engineering colleges, namely, the Guindy College of Engineering (1858) in Madras, Thomson College of Civil Engineering (1847) in Roorkee, Poona Engineering College (1856) in Poona, Calcutta Civil Engineering College (1856) in Calcutta, and Victoria Jubilee Technical Institute (1887) in Bombay, were established to cater to the needs of the British. These colleges focused on creating a pool of technical human personnel to fulfill the human resource needs for subordinate grades of engineering services of the then-British colony (Saha, 2011).

In order to impart arts and science education that could address the Indian needs, three nationalistic models were developed in the early nineteenth century. They were (i) the National Council of Education, Bengal, in 1906 by the nationalists, which became the Jadavpur University; (ii) the Banaras Hindu University in 1916 by Pandit Madan Mohan Malaviya; and (iii) the Indian Institute of Science, Bangalore (1909), by the industrialist Jamshedji Tata, as a research institute.

However, to address the need to produce scientists and engineers to support the economic and social development of India postindependence, the Indian Institutes of Technology (IITs) were set up starting from 1951. Parallel to the establishment of the IITs, a network of other engineering colleges of both a general and a specialized nature was also set up. Industrial training institutes and polytechnics were also established to provide skilled manpower. Basic science capabilities were also built across a wide spectrum of disciplines.

As shown in Figs. 2.5 and 2.6, the number of universities grew 6.3 times from 30 to 190 from 1950 to 1990 while the number of colleges grew 10.57 times from 695 to 7346.[10] The student enrollment also increased from 397,000 to 4,925,000, about 12.4 times (Fig. 2.7). The teaching staff increased 11.17 times during the

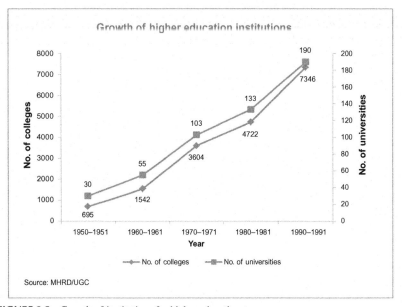

FIGURE 2.5 Growth of institutions for higher education.

10. All graphs pertaining to the growth of higher education in India in this section have been adapted from UGC (2012).

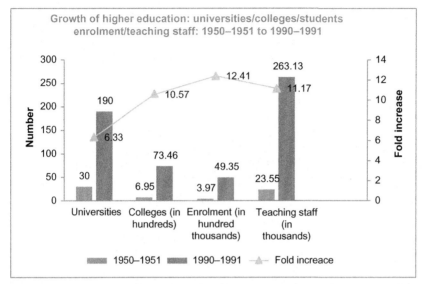

FIGURE 2.6   Growth of higher education: universities, colleges, student enrollments, and teaching staff (1950–1951 to 1990–1991).

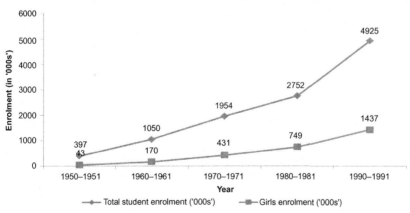

Source: MHRD for 1950-1951 and 1960-1961 and UGC for 1970-1971 onwards

Coverage: figures of students enrolment and teaching staff (1970–1971 onwards) pertain to regular courses in universities and colleges (excluding polytechnics, other diploma awarding institutions and non-formal system of higher education)

FIGURE 2.7   Growth of student enrollments (in 000s) in higher education.

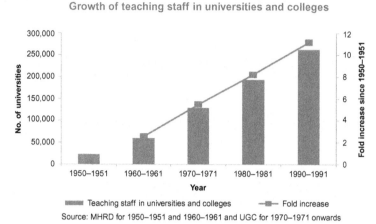

FIGURE 2.8 Growth of teaching staff in universities and colleges.

period, from 23,549 to 263,125 (Fig. 2.8). Educational expenditure as a proportion of both public expenditure and GDP was steadily increasing (Fig. 2.9).

However, colleges imparting professional education in the fields of engineering, technical, architecture, medical, education, and other such areas increased only 4.26 times compared with an increase of 13.17 times in the colleges imparting general education (Table 2.4). While India was trying to build its higher education base across various fields including science and technology, there was a widespread and disturbing trend of significant migration of highly educated scientifically and technologically trained manpower to other countries, especially to the United States.

Besides higher education, the Council of Scientific and Industrial Research (CSIR) with its 38 research laboratories was also set up to create an R&D infrastructure in the country. However, the above measures did not translate into radical technological and innovative developments in the country. The proportion of CSIR activities leading to industrial production was small except in certain sectors like leather and small-scale industries. One of the reasons was the ineffectiveness of the scientific knowledge to be translated into technology and thereby innovations for use by industry. In most instances when technology was required by the industry, it was imported and adapted to Indian requirements. The linkage between science and technology with industry was missing. Secondly, whenever the question of introduction of new technology came up, it was left to the public sector to produce and adapt the indigenous technology. As a result, the private sector did not develop the requisite innovative capabilities. In the background was the Industrial Policy Resolution intended to demarcate the roles between the public and private sectors through licenses and controls. Although there was new confidence generated after independence and the facilities provided for indigenous ventures, private enterprise, and business groups

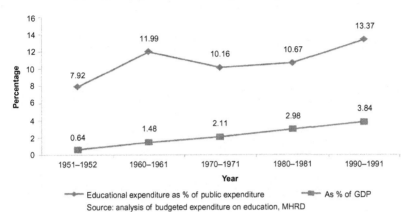

Educational expenditure as % of public expenditure and GDP

Source: analysis of budgeted expenditure on education, MHRD

FIGURE 2.9 Educational expenditure as a percentage of public expenditure and GDP.

TABLE 2.4 Growth of Recognized Educational institutions from 1950–1951 to 1990–1991

Statement 1: Growth of Recognized Educational Institutions from 1950–1951 to 1990–1991

Year	Colleges for General Education	Colleges for Professional Education	Universities/ Deemed Universities/ Institutes of National Importance	Total Institutions of Higher Education (2+3+4)
1	2	3	4	5
1950–1951	370	208	27	605
1955–1956	466	218	31	715
1960–1961	967	852	45	1984
1965–1966	1536	770	64	2370
1970–1971	2285	992	82	3359
1975–1976	3667	3276[a]	101	7044
1980–1981	3421	3542[a]	110	7073
1985–1986	4067	1533[a]	126	5726
1990–1991	4862	886	184	5932

[a]Includes Institutions for Post Metric Courses.
Note: Professional Education includes Engineering, Technical, Architecture, Medical, Education, and other colleges.

to diversify and enter into foreign collaborations, the public sector was still sad-dled with the responsibility of building those industries in which the private sec-tor investment either was not forthcoming or was a failure. While the planning process relied on the public sector as "national champions," the sector had its own problems of bureaucracy and lack of incentive for continuous improve-ment. Technological progress, as a result, varied across sectors and the growth in GDP was fluctuating (Table 2.5).

The economy grew steadily till 1965 at an average rate of 4.2%, followed by a decline of 2.7% up to 1975. From 1975 to 1989, the GDP growth rate

TABLE 2.5 Growth Performance of Indian Economy in the Planning Era, 1950–1989

		1950–1951 to 1964–1965	1965–1966 to 1974–1975	1975–1976 to 1988–1989	1980–1981 to 1988–1989
1	Growth of GNP at factor cost	4.2	2.7	5.0	5.6
2	Growth of per capita NNP	1.9	0.2	2.8	3.4
3	a. Rate of gross capital formation (refers to 3-year average of base year in each column)	10.0	16.8 (15.3)	18.9	22.5
	b. Average annual increase (Rs crores at 1970–1971 prices) in public investment		(−87)	356	
4	Growth of industrial production	6.6	3.3	5.6	7.7
5	Growth of food-grain production	2.9	2.1	2.6	2.5

Note: Figures refer to 1980–1981 prices unless otherwise stated. Rs 1 Crore = Rs 10 M
Source: Alagh (1992).

increased to 5%, and in the 1980s, it hovered around 5.6%. Per capita income and industrial production also followed the same trend (Alagh, 1992).

With the success of the green revolution, agriculture has been a sector of Indian sciences that has delivered the most. However, this revolution was not accompanied by the requisite institutional transformation including land reforms and, therefore, did not translate into successful poverty eradication measures (Jayaraman, 2009).

It was evident that the efforts in terms of schooling, health indicators, and employment outcomes were not commensurate with population pressures. Resource constraints were mounting and India was in the thick of a severe balance of payments crisis by 1989–1990. Hence, a series of economic reforms were introduced to liberalize and globalize the economy in 1991. India eliminated the main restrictions to domestic and foreign competition. The industrial license regime was revoked, in such a way that it continued to apply only to a few activities like services related to public health and security. Financial markets were also liberalized. The reform process has had its impact on technology, innovation, and entrepreneurship in India, the details of which have been explained in the following chapters.

In summary, in this chapter, in order to assess the role history plays in innovation, we looked at the historical GDP of China, India, and the United States and how the roles have reversed in the last couple of centuries. We believe having had a history of innovation does provide a perspective on the intrinsic nature of a culture and its people and a potential proclivity towards reverting to that behavior under the "right circumstances." We, therefore, traced the role of technology and innovation in the phenomenal rise of China and India in the distant past and examined the factors that obstructed innovation in later years, which resulted in the subsequent decline of these economies. We briefly compared that to the history of innovation in the United States over the last 200 years. We discussed the history of innovation in the United States only briefly, since a lot has already been written about it and is fairly well known, and spent most of the effort discussing the history of innovation in China and India, since not much about it is known nor has been written about in the West.

China started off as an economy with significant inventive capabilities but subsequently witnessed a decline due to the then-prevalent political, ideological, and social conditions. The opening up of the economy in 1978 gave a boost to science, technology, and innovation in the country and set the stage for ensuing growth and progress in China. India, on the other hand, had a rich science, technology, and innovation base to start with. The period of European dominance, particularly the British rule, adversely impacted the economy and its superiority in science, technology, and industrial development. After India's independence from the British, it went about building a strong science and technology infrastructure. While some of its efforts were fruitful, it did not result in building significant innovative capabilities in the industrial sector. The link between science and technology with industry was missing and the resultant economic performance was unstable. In spite of its very brief history, about

200 years, the United States has been phenomenally successful in contrast to China and India, in advancing and commercializing science and technology. The history of these countries brings to light the bearing that the political environment and ideology that a country espouses and develops over a period of time has on its innovative capabilities.

REFERENCES

Alagh, Y., 1992. Growth performance of Indian economy 1950–89, problems of employment and poverty. Dev. Econ. XXX (2), 97–116.

Bongard-Levin, G., 1979. A History of India. Progress Publishers, Moscow.

China Statistical Yearbook, 1999–2003, http://www.stats.gov.cn/tjsj/ndsj/2012/indexeh.htm.

Dharampal, 2000. Indian Science and Technology in the Eighteenth Century. Other India Press, Goa, India.

Gordon, J.S., 2004. An Empire of Wealth—The Epic History of American Economic Power. Harper Perennial.

Hughes, T.P., 1989/2004. American Genesis—A Century of Invention and Technological Enthusiasm, 1870–1970. The University of Chicago Press.

Jayaraman, T., 2009. Science, technology and innovation policy in India under economic reform: a survey. http://www.networkideas.org/ideasact/jan09/pdf/jayaraman.pdf (accessed 24/9/12).

Maddison, A., 2003. The World Economy: Historical Statistics. OECD, Paris.

Morris, C.R., 2012. The Dawn of Innovation. Public Affairs, Perseus Book Group.

Ramaswamy, 2012. Sage—scientists of India—the universe was their laboratory. Bhavan's J. 29–39.

Saha, 2011. Technical Education in India. Historical Lessons & Roadmap. National Institute of Science, Technology and Development Studies (NISTADS), CSIR, New Delhi.

Shanghai People's Publishing House, 1961. Chinese Modern History Collections: Westernization Movement [Z]. Shanghai People's Publishing House, Shanghai.

Sun, J., 2006. On confucianism character of ancient science and technology in China. J. Henan Univ. (Nat. Sci.). 36(4).

University Grants Commission, 2012. Higher Education in India at a Glance. University Grants Commission, New Delhi.

Wang, Z., 1997. Chinese ancient four great inventions and their effect to the world. J. Cent. Inst. Social. 2.

Wang, J., 1999. Discuss about the development of 24 solar-terms and its use. J. Suihua Teach. Coll. 5.

Whipps, H., August 4, 2009. A Brief History of US Innovation, LiveScience.

Xiang, Y., 1999. About Chinese imperial examination system. J. Qinghai National. Inst. March.

Yi, D., Li, H., Zhao, X., 2007. New China's technology introduction and its effect. Sci. Technol. Manage. Res. 4.

Zhang, X., 1999. Discussion about the disadvantage of nine grades system and its effect. J. Zhengzhou Univ. 32.

Zhang, J., 2007. On China's national innovation system historical evolution. China Youth Sci. Technol. 11.

Chapter 3

Economy

Chapter Contents

ECONOMIC GROWTH

In 2010, the United States ranked first, China ranked second, and India ranked ninth in terms of gross domestic product (GDP) in current prices, while they ranked first, second, and third on a purchasing power parity (PPP) basis in 2012 (Figs. 3.1 and 3.2).

While China and India are among the fastest growing economies in terms of GDP growth rates, the absolute GDP and per capita GDP of the United States have been much higher than that of the rest of the world (Figs. 3.3 and 3.4).

A number of factors affect the economy and economic growth. We discuss these factors quantitatively in Part III of the book. In this chapter, we confine our attention to the qualitative aspects of the impact of innovation, more specifically technological innovation, on the economy.

Technological innovation is an important driving force to grow the economy, and, in fact, its nature should be that. On the other hand, there is also no doubt that a strong economy and supportive economic conditions are necessary to enable technological innovation. There are at least three measures of the economy that can be considered in relation to innovation. First, R&D expenditure is an important factor that influences the level of innovation. Second, foreign direct investment (FDI) results in the flow of knowledge and technology through the capital between different countries. Third, the number and quality of patents issued are also indicative of the level of innovation in a given economy and, in turn, influence future innovation. We, therefore, chose to study the relationship between the economy and innovation by analyzing the above three measures.

As mentioned above, an important determinant of innovation performance is industrial research, as measured by the level of R&D spending (Chengqi and

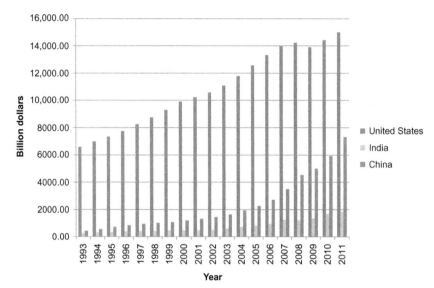

FIGURE 3.1 GDP in current prices. *(Source: World Bank (www.worldbank.org).)*

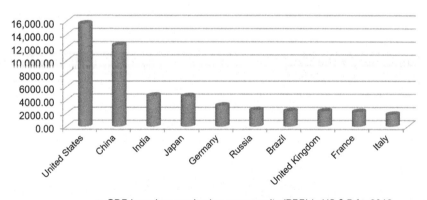

■ GDP based on purchasing-power-parity (PPP) in US $ B for 2012

FIGURE 3.2 GDP based on PPP in US $ B for 2012. *(Source: International Monetary Fund, World Economic Outlook Database, April 2013.)*

Kafouros, 2009). It is commonly thought that investments in R&D enable organizations to create an internal stock of scientific knowledge (Feinberg and Majumdar, 2001; Griliches, 1979; Hall and Mairesse, 1995) that may further lead to global knowledge diffusion (Buckley and Ghauri, 2004). This stock, in turn, assists firms in developing and introducing new products to the market, reducing production costs, pricing their products more competitively, and, consequently, improving corporate revenues and performance (Kafouros, 2008a,b).

FDI is viewed in both theoretical and empirical literature as a main channel for the dissemination of technological advances (De Bondt, 1996). With capital

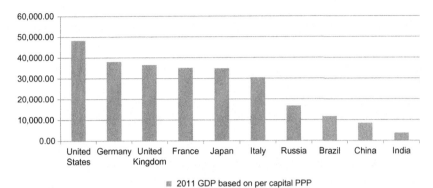

FIGURE 3.3   2011 GDP per capita based on PPP. *(Source: International Monetary Fund, World Economic Outlook Database, April 2013.)*

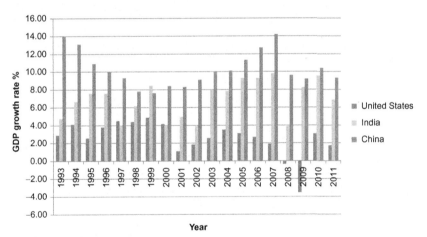

FIGURE 3.4   GDP growth rates—the United States, India, and China. *(Source: World Bank (www. worldbank.org).)*

investment, technology learners and absorbers seek technologies in which they are weak in their home countries but strong in host countries, to offset their home country technological weakness (Bas and Sierra, 2002). Conversely, technology creators and contributors accumulate strong technological capabilities and participate in new knowledge-generation activities in host countries, thus complementing the existing stock of knowledge in multinational corporations (MNCs) (Almeida, 1996; Bas and Sierra, 2002; Kuemmerle, 1999).

Patents have long been recognized as an important and fruitful source of data for the study of innovation and technological change (see Griliches 1990 for a survey of the use of patent statistics). The reason patents affect the rate of innovation is that the ability to file patents influences a firm's willingness to engage in R&D activities and the potential for profiting from the investment.

R&D EXPENDITURES

China and India have now become hosts for the R&D laboratories of many large MNCs such as GE, Intel, IBM, Microsoft, and Texas Instruments. China is one of the most research-intensive countries in the world. In 1995, the total R&D expenditure was only about $4.15 B in China, while it increased to $104.3 B in 2010, about 25 times that of 1995, and the average increment was over 20% per year. The ratio of R&D expenditures to GDP also increased to 1.76% in 2010 from 0.57% in 1995. By contrast, R&D expenditures in the United States were $397.6 B in 2008, about twice what they were in 1995 (China Statistics Year Book, 2011; United States Statistical Abstract, 2012). However, there was no big change in the ratio of R&D expenditures to GDP, from 2.5% in 1995 to 2.77% in 2008. In the case of India, R&D expenditure grew 6.77 times from $2.24 B (Rs. 74.84 B) in 1995–1996 to $15.16 B (Rs. 726.20 B) in 2011–2012, while the ratio of R&D expenditure to GDP increased from 0.67% to 0.88% (NSTMIS, 2011-2012).[1] Comparing China and India with the United States, although both China and India had high growth rates in the years mentioned, both the amount of R&D investment expenditures and the ratio of R&D expenditures to GDP were far behind that of the United States, far more in the case of India than China.

With regard to the R&D investment structure, R&D expenditure is composed of basic research, applied research, and experimental development. In China, from 1995 to 2010, basic research investment was almost at the level of 5% of total R&D and was the smallest of the three components. Experimental development not only had the biggest share but also continued to increase, reaching 83% in 2008, and this happened at the expense of decreasing investment in applied research. The United States has had a different trend with regard to investment in basic research, applied research, and development. In the 1960s, basic research was about 10%, applied research was about 22%, and development was about 68% of the total R&D budget, whereas in 2008, these same percentages were 23%, 30%, and 47%, respectively, indicating an increase in basic research and applied research and a significant decline in development (China Statistics Year Book, 2011; United States Statistical Abstract, 2012). The data suggest that even as late as 2010, much like the situation in the United States in the 1960s, China invested very little in basic research, which in turn adversely impacted applied research and development activities. As a result, it has been difficult to maintain sustainable innovation in China. In the United States, on the other hand, while a significant portion of

1. The figures were converted from rupees to US $ using the exchange rates for the respective years from the Economic Survey of India 2012–2013: Statistical Appendix.

R&D expenditures go towards development, there is not a very large difference in the relative investments in the three categories.

In the case of India, this breakup is available only for R&D in the government sector. In the year 1996–1997, about 17.3% of the total R&D expenditure of the government sector was spent on basic research, 39.8% on applied research, 32.9% on experimental development, and the remaining 10% on supporting activities, while in the year 2009–2010, 23.89% of the total expenditure was spent on basic research, 33.37% on applied research, 35.11% on experimental development, and the remaining 7.64% on supporting activities (NSTMIS, 2011–2012). The pattern in India is similar to that in the United States in the sense that there is not a significant difference in the relative investments in the three categories and India also has ramped up its investment in basic research over a period of time. Since 67% of R&D was carried out by the government sector in India in 2009–2010, the above trend is indicative of a major portion of R&D activities in India (NSTMIS, 2011–2012). Governmental R&D in India, however, is not very significant in the area of commercial applications. In recent times though, conscious efforts have been made by the government and these are slowly beginning to produce results, especially in the area of astronautics research (Mani, 2010).

In China, R&D was carried out mainly by enterprises, R&D institutions, and institutions for higher education. Expenditures on R&D by these various entities were 73.4%, 16.8%, and 8.5%. In the United States, 72.7% of R&D was carried out by corporations and about 12.9% by universities and colleges, while the remaining 3.9% was carried out by other nonprofit institutions. In India, in 2011–2012, 65.69% of R&D expenditure was incurred by the government sector, while 30.22% was spent by the private sector and only 4.06% was spent by institutions of higher education (China Statistics Year Book, 2011; United States Statistical Abstract, 2012). In both the United States and China, the biggest contributions to R&D came from industry as opposed to India, where the biggest contributor is the government. Increasing the share of R&D by business enterprises is a desirable trend as business enterprises generally implement and commercialize the results of their research rather quickly compared to the government. Although Indian industry has shown an improving trend in R&D spending, it still has a long way to go in terms of taking the lead like its counterparts in the United States and China. Industry R&D spending as a percent of sales revenues in 2009–2010 was a mere 0.82% in India with the public sector industry spending 0.27% and the private sector industry spending 0.66% (NSTMIS, 2011–2012).

Although China shows an increasing trend of R&D expenditures by the business sector, many of the public research institutes in China, according to the OECD (2008), were mechanically converted to business entities without creating the conditions for them to become innovation-oriented. Hence, it can be inferred that a part of the R&D expenditures from the business sector in China is contributed by these research institutes. Also, in China, many R&D institutions and institutions for higher education got R&D project funding from the government and not from the private sector. R&D from these efforts was thus

directed towards meeting the needs of the Chinese government and did not necessarily meet market needs. So, to some extent, some of these R&D expenditures were wasted.

There is also a big difference between China and the United States with
regard to how these funds were deployed. In China, industry spent 97.5% of
their R&D funds on experimental development, while less than 1% was
invested in basic research with the exception of the high-tech industry where
about 18.7% was invested in basic research. In higher education, 13.5% of
R&D funding was deployed in applied research and 30.1% in basic research.
As was the case with the enterprises, the largest component of R&D spending
(56.4%) went towards experimental development. However, in contrast to the
enterprise sector, R&D institutions spent 32.7% of their R&D budget on applied
research. By contrast, in the United States, industry spent 74.6% of their R&D
funding on development, 21.3% on applied research, and 4.1% on basic
research. In US universities and colleges, the percentages of basic research,
applied research, and development, respectively, were 75.9%, 20.6%, and
3.5%, whereas with other nonprofit institutions, basic research expenditure
got 52.7% of the share of R&D funding, followed by applied research
31.9%, and then development 15.3% (China Statistics Year Book, 2011; United
States Statistical Abstract, 2012).

Based on the above, it is clear that in China, enterprises invested almost all
R&D funds in experimental development. The net result of this was that Chinese firms were not able to develop a deeper understanding of the problems at
hand. Although the American industry also devoted most of their R&D funds to
development, applied research was not neglected. In terms of basic research,
although Chinese universities invested a greater percentage in this area compared with enterprises and R&D institutions, their investment levels were significantly lower than those by American universities.

It is also important to consider the various vertical sectors where these R&D
funds were being invested.

In China, the top five sectors with the highest R&D investments were (1)
telecommunications, computer, and other electronic equipment (17.1%); (2)
transportation (14.5%); (3) electrical machinery and equipment (10.6%); (4)
manufacturing and processing of ferrous metals (10%); and (5) manufacturing
of chemical raw material and chemical products (6.2%) (China Statistics Year
Book, 2011).

In the United States, on the other hand, the top five sectors that spent the
most on R&D were (1) computers and electronic products (20.8%); (2) chemicals and allied products (20%); (3) information technology (13.1%); (4) professional, scientific, and technical services (12.9%); and (5) aerospace parts and
products (12.7%). These patterns are very similar between the United States
and China, except for a couple of categories: processing of ferrous metals in
China and professional, scientific, and technical services in the United States.

In the case of India, the trends differ for both government and private sectors. The top five sectors with the highest R&D investments, which accounted

for more than three-fourths of the total R&D expenditure by the government in the year 2009–2010, were public administration and defense (25.97%); service sector (25.04%); agriculture, hunting, and related services (18.94%); electricity, gas, steam, and water supply (10.48%); and drugs and pharmaceuticals (3.69%). The top five sectors for industrial R&D expenditure in the year 2009–2010 were drugs and pharmaceuticals (29.08%); manufacture of motor vehicles (13.47%); computer and related activities (12.54%); manufacture of machinery or equipment (7.68%); and public administration and defense (5.48%) (NSTMIS, 2011–2012). As can be seen from the above figures, the government sector and business sector have different R&D spending patterns (Table 3.1). As mentioned earlier, governmental R&D in India has been focused more on public administration, defense, and service sectors and much less on commercial applications, while Indian industry has been consistently building its capability in pharmaceutical research.

If we look at the share of foreign companies in business sector R&D, it has been consistently increasing in the case of India from $59.1 M in 2002–2003 to $1.163 B in 2010–2011. According to the latest estimates available, the share of FDI in business sector R&D had increased to around 20% in the year 2007–2008 from a figure of 7% to 8% in the previous years. The figures also show a quantum leap in FDI in R&D in the recent years. The most prominent sector

TABLE 3.1 R&D Expenditure by FDI Companies in India

	R&D by FDI Companies		Total R&D by Private Sector Companies	Percentage Share of FDI Companies in Private Sector R&D
Year	(Rs. in Millions)	(US $ in Millions)	(Rs. in Millions)	
2002–2003	2860	59.10	34,983	8.18
2003–2004	3100	67.46	44,713	6.93
2004–2005	3570	79.45	60,390	5.91
2005–2006	5290	119.49	74,442	7.10
2006–2007	6680	158.11	91,281	7.32
2007–2008	22,230	552.15	111,929	19.86
2008–2009	40,566	882.00	NA	NA
2009–2010	45,000	949.03	NA	NA
2010–2011	53,017	1163.24	NA	NA

Source: Reserve Bank of India (Various Issues) and Department of Science and Technology, Government of India (2009)

that attracts the highest FDI in R&D in India is the ICT sector and a major part of the FDI in R&D comes from the United States. The availability of high-caliber scientific and engineering manpower at considerably lower compensation levels seems to be the reason for the increasing FDI in R&D. However, the investment so far is more focused on meeting market demands of the parent companies of the MNCs located outside than on the local Indian market. The linkages with domestic companies are limited only to the IT sector and only to a certain extent. In other sectors, these linkages are missing (Basant and Mani, 2012). This implies that the spillover effects to the local firms and R&D with the intent to augment the knowledge of local economy are limited.

FDI INFLOWS

FDI inflow has a significant impact on the level of innovation. First of all, FDI inflows bring new product, new technology, and advanced management experience into the recipient countries. Companies in recipient countries can learn from technologically advanced foreign corporations that bring in advanced technology as part of technology sharing, along with investment into their countries. Through this technology sharing, the level of innovation in the recipient countries can be improved, thus helping reduce the technology gap between the host and guest countries. Secondly, due to increased competition from foreign companies, domestic companies in the host country are forced to make significant investments in R&D so they can compete with foreign companies and survive. Thirdly, FDI is instrumental in improving the quality of the workforce due to professional training and education provided by foreign companies. These trained people in turn make significant contributions to domestic innovation. Finally, other domestic companies, such as service companies, processing and manufacturing firms, and design firms, that do business with foreign firms in their country are also forced to improve their technological capabilities and business processes.

With regard to the level of FDI inflow, after Deng Xiaoping's visit to China's southern coastal areas and special economic zones (SEZs) in 1992, China had a high growth rate of FDI inflows. China has become the second largest FDI recipient in the world, after the United States. For example, from 1995 to 2000, the average FDI inflow into China was only $41.8 B and it increased to $106 B in 2010, with a trend of gradual growth every year except 2009 (Fig. 3.5). The average FDI inflow into the United States from 1995 to 2000 was $169.7 B, more than four times as much as that into China over the same time period, and was also higher than that into China in 2010. The highest inflow of FDI into the United States was in 2008 at about $316 B, with a big dip during the Wall Street crisis of 2009. In 2010, FDI inflow into the United States grew about 49% comparing to that in 2009, which was $228 B. Although China was second after the United States in FDI inflows, there was still a big gap between China and the United States, with 8.5% and 18% of the global FDI

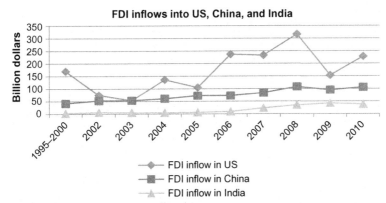

FIGURE 3.5   FDI inflows into China, India, and the United States. *(Sources: China Statistics Year Book, 2011; United States Statistical Abstract, 2012, Handbook of Statistics on Indian Economy 2011–2012, www.rbi.gov.in.)*

inflows. FDI inflows into India have been on the rise after the introduction of economic reforms in 1991. The average FDI inflow from 1995 to 2000 was a mere $2.19 B, and it increased to $41.8 B in 2009. FDI inflows saw a slight downward slide in 2010 when it decreased to $37.74 B. However, in the global FDI landscape, India's ranking as an FDI recipient is very low. FDI inflows into India in 2010 were three times lower than those into China and six times lower than those into the United States.

Where did the FDI inflows go? In China, manufacturing got most of the FDI inflow. For example, in 2010, 47% of inflows went towards manufacturing, followed by real estate at about 23%. The two sectors that received very little FDI inflows were (1) scientific research, technical service, and geologic prospecting (2.4%) and (2) information transmission, computer services, and software (1.9%). During the 2004–2008 period, the maximum FDI inflows into the United States were also in the manufacturing sector with a low of 15.5% in 2004 and a high of 48.9% in 2008. Also, FDI inflows into other sectors grew significantly as well. This ratio grew to 24.8% in 2008 from 10.4% in 2000. Similarly, the specialty and technological service sector and the information technology sector attracted only a small part of the FDI inflow, with average percentages from 2000 to 2008 of about 4.6% and 10% (except in 2005, where these were negative). It can be seen from these data that both in China and in the United States, the manufacturing sector attracted the most foreign investment. In China, some high-technology industries such as computers and telecommunications did not attract foreign funds and so that they could not take advantage of technology advancements brought about by FDI inflows.

As far as India is concerned, during the financial year 2012–2013, the service sector received the highest FDI of $4.8 B, which amounts to 21.55% of the total FDI. The service sector includes the financial sector, outsourcing, R&D,

and technical analysis and testing. The next sector to receive the second highest level of FDI is hotel and tourism at 14.5% followed by the construction development sector that received 5.9% of FDI.[2] If we consider the cumulative figures, the service sector received the maximum FDI from the year 2000 to July 2013 (19.10%) followed by construction development (11.20%). The telecommunications sector received the third highest FDI (6.42%). Computer software and hardware received the fourth highest level (5.94%) and drugs and pharmaceuticals the fifth (5.65%).[3] India has been a preferred recipient of outsourcing contracts, which is reflected by a consistently high level of FDI inflow into the service sector. The other sectors that have been receiving FDI in the last 13 years have been predominantly the various areas of the infrastructure sector, viz., construction, telecommunications, and power. There is a large demand–supply gap in the Indian infrastructure sector with demand far exceeding supply, which explains the relatively high levels of FDI inflows into the sector. The IT sector, which is considered to be India's forte, has also been one of the highest recipients of FDI. Of late, the hotel and tourism sector has been emerging as one of the top recipients of FDI.

FDI OUTFLOWS

FDI outflows help to improve a country's export of technology in a number of ways. First, R&D facilities can be set up in foreign countries. In these facilities, especially those set up in developed countries, advanced technologies can be developed because of the availability of well-trained resources, including excellent researchers, and access to advanced technology. Second, transborder corporate M&A activities are a common way to fill technology gaps and gain overall improvement in a company's technological capabilities. Some companies' primary motive for buying foreign companies is to acquire new technologies. Although motivations for other cross border M&A activities could be to increase market share or gain other specialized resources, they can also benefit from a technology perspective through communication between native and foreign staff or from technology bridging between backward and forward industries in the value chain. Finally, cross-border strategic alliances, especially technological alliances, can also result in the creation of new technologies through cross-border cooperation.

In the aggregate, FDI outflows from the United States (Fig. 3.6) were $125.9 B on an average from 1995 to 2000 reaching a high of $330 B between 2008 and 2010, with its lowest level of $15.4 B in 2005. While China had small FDI outflow, although with an increasing trend, it was only $2.5 B in 2002 and increased to $68 B in 2010. This was only one-fifth that of the United States during the same period. Indian FDI outflow, although miniscule as compared

2. http://dipp.nic.in/English/Publications/SIA_Newsletter/2013/apr2013/index.htm.
3. http://dipp.nic.in/English/Publications/FDI_Statistics/2013/india_FDI_July2013.pdf.

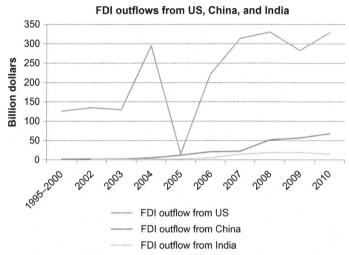

FIGURE 3.6 FDI outflows from China, the United Sates, and India. *(Sources: China Statistics Year Book, 2011; United States Statistical Abstract, 2012, Handbook of Statistics on Indian Economy 2011–2012, www.rbi.gov.in.)*

with those of both the United States and China, is also witnessing an upward trend from a mere $1.391 B in 2002 to $15.143 B in 2010.

With regard to the distribution of FDI outflows across various sectors, China invested most of their funds into leasing and business services (44%), financial intermediation (12.5%), and wholesale and retail trade (9.8%). Scientific research, technical service, and geologic prospecting sector (1.5%) and the information transmission, computer services, and software sector (0.7%) had very small shares of FDI outflow, and as a result, China got very little advanced technology through FDI outflows.

PATENTS

In 2010, China's total patent applications including domestic applications and applications abroad ranked third in the world, only after Japan and the United Sates, but domestic applications ranked first. During the same time period, the ratio of US applications to total global applications was 22.2%, while that ratio for China was about 17%. The number of Chinese patent applications filed globally was 306,793, and 95.5% of them were submitted to the Chinese patent office, with only the remaining 4.5% filed in a foreign patent office (China Statistics Year Book, 2011). The number of applications filed globally in the United States was 401,386. Of these, 60% were filed with the US patent office with the remaining 40% filed in a foreign patent office, and only 9.8% of those were filed in China (United States Statistical Abstract, 2012).

In India, the total number of patents granted during 2010–2011 was 7509, out of which only 1273 (17%) were granted to Indian applicants. The number of patents in force was 39,594 as of 31 March 2011, out of which only 7301 (18%) patents belonged to the Indians. Foreign companies and individuals who were granted patents in India were predominantly from the United States, followed by Japan and Germany. The number of patents granted to American companies and individuals (9034) exceeded that of Japan (3112) and Germany (2991) by a huge margin (Office of the Controller General of Patents, 2011–2012). According to Basant and Mani (2012), there could be two reasons for a higher share of foreign inventors in Indian patents. One could be due to TRIPS compliance of the Indian patent regime since January 2005, which has created a need for Indian patenting by MNCs so that Indian companies, and especially the pharmaceutical ones, may find it difficult to do incremental innovations. The second reason hypothesized by them is the possible increase in patenting in India by foreign R&D centers in India.

With regard to the different fields in which patent applications were filed, the top two categories in which the applications in China were filed were (1) chemistry and (2) electrical engineering. These two together composed about 73.9% of the total patent applications from 2005 to 2009. In the United States, as was the case with China, more patents were filed in chemistry and electrical engineering than in other industries, with the two fields together accounting for about 52.9% of the patents filed. Comparing China and the United States, in these two fields, in chemistry, China had half the number of patents as did the United States, and in electrical engineering, that ratio was 67.5%. As compared with China and the United States, the sectors that dominated the patent scenario in India were different. Out of the total granted patents in India, the top three categories were mechanical (22.34%), chemicals (19.67%), and computer and electronics (10.63%), totaling 52.66% of the patents granted over the years 2006–2011 (Office of the Controller General of Patents, 2011–2012).

The records of India and China in US patenting have improved since the introduction of economic reforms (Table 3.2). China has more US patents than

TABLE 3.2 Total Number of Patents Granted by USPTO to US, Chinese, and Indian Inventors

	Total Utility Patents Granted During the Period 1963–2011	Total Design Patents Granted During the Period 1977–2011
Total world	4,992,192	407,802
United States	2,837,050	252,607
China	12,647	4011
India	7091	233

Source: USPTO www.uspto.gov

India in both utility and design patent categories. However, the United States is far ahead of both China and India by leaps and bounds as far as US patenting is concerned. An analysis of the patent portfolio composition reveals that India has more utility patents than design patents in its US patent portfolio while one-third of China's US patent portfolio consists of design patents. Utility patents represent new inventions, while design patents represent ornamental appearance. It is possible that many design patents may be on the same inventions for which product patents have been filed (Basant and Mani, 2012). A surge in Indian patents in the United States has been due to the growing number of foreign R&D centers in India. Basant and Mani (2012) found that most of the foreign R&D centers in India active in US patenting are from the ICT sector. Although many international pharmaceutical companies are outsourcing portions of large R&D projects to Indian entities, especially in the area of clinical trials, patent-yielding foreign R&D projects are very few.

In China, patent examiners are paid more if they approve more patents, and Chinese academics, companies, and individuals are provided incentives to come up with patentable ideas. Quantity not quality, it appears, is what matters. Professors are given tenure, workers and students are given residence permits, corporate income tax is reduced, and companies are provided with generous government contracts, in return for obtaining patents. These benefits, to both patent examiners and potential patent filers, have led to perverse incentives and ideas of "dubious originality" and a lot of patents for "worthless ideas" or "junk." So, some patents in China's portfolio may not be worth very much in terms of their role in economic development. An indication of this can be seen from Table 3.3, which shows that in the top 50 ranking of patent assignees in 2011, there were 17 in the United States and 19 in Japan but none in mainland China or India. Comparing the number of patents granted, the United States had a total of 22,669 with a 36.1% share, while Japan had 24,777 with a share of 39.5%. It is evident that Chinese and Indian companies are far behind Japan and the United States with regard to the level of innovation.

In summary, there are at least three measures of the economy that can be considered in relation to technological innovation—R&D expenditures, FDI, and patenting. With regard to these three indicators, China and India have greatly improved in recent years but still lagged behind the United States. In R&D expenditure, while China and India spent far more than before, China's R&D expenditure is not structured to encourage sustainable innovative ability. Besides, some of the R&D work carried out by universities and institutions appears to be low on efficiency, since they appear to be disconnected from market demand. In India, the government has the most prominent share of R&D spending and most of its efforts are not directed towards commercial activities. Business sector R&D and patenting have shown improvements, and the incremental effects are more pronounced in certain sectors, such as ICT and pharmaceuticals, although investments made in these sectors are far less than those in the United States and in China. The recent influx of FDI into R&D spending and

TABLE 3.3 IFI CLAIMS® 2011 Top 50 US Patent Assignees

Rank	Grants	Company Name	Country
1	6180	International Business Machines Corp.	United States
2	4894	Samsung Electronics Co. Ltd.	Korea
3	2821	Canon KK	Japan
4	2559	Panasonic Corp.	Japan
5	2483	Toshiba Corp.	Japan
6	2311	Microsoft Corp.	United States
7	2286	Sony Corp.	Japan
8	1533	Seiko Epson Corp.	Japan
9	1514	Hon Hai Precision Industry Co., Ltd.	Taiwan
10	1465	Hitachi, Ltd.	Japan
11	1448	General Electric Co.	United States
12	1411	LG Electronics Inc.	Korea
13	1391	Fujitsu Ltd.	Japan
14	1308	Hewlett-Packard Development Co., L. P.	United States
15	1248	Ricoh Co., Ltd.	Japan
16	1244	Intel Corp.	United States
17	1164	Broadcom Corp.	United States
18	1095	GM Global Technology Operations LLC	United States
19	1005	Renesas Electronics Corp.	Japan
20	997	Honda Motor Co., Ltd.	Japan
21	994	Toyota Jidosha KK	Japan
22	980	Cisco Technology Inc.	United States
23	971	Fujifilm Corp.	Japan
24	947	Micron Technology Inc.	United States
25	935	Hynix Semiconductor Inc.	Korea
26	923	Qualcomm Technologies Inc.	United States
27	888	Brother Kogyo KK	Japan
28	880	Xerox Corp.	United States

Continued

TABLE 3.3 IFI CLAIMS® 2011 Top 50 US Patent Assignees—Cont'd

Rank	Grants	Company Name	Country
29	872	Sharp KK	Japan
30	851	Siemens AG	Germany
31	812	Silverbrook Research Pty Ltd.	Australia
32	794	Texas Instruments Inc.	United States
33	780	Honeywell International Inc.	United States
34	761	Semiconductor Energy Laboratory Co., Ltd.	Japan
35	721	AT&T Intellectual Property I, L.P.	United States
36	700	Koninklijke Philips Electronics NV	Netherlands
37	695	The Boeing Co.	United States
38	689	Denso Corp.	Japan
39	676	Apple Inc.	United States
40	663	Research In Motion Ltd.	Canada
41	643	LG Display Co., Ltd.	Korea
42	622	Bosch, Robert GmbH	Germany
43	622	NEC Corp.	Japan
44	617	Infineon Technologies AG	Germany
45	605	Mitsubishi Denki KK	Japan
46	587	Fuji Xerox Co., Ltd.	Japan
47	585	NokiaABOy	Finland
48	534	Electronics and Telecommunications Research Institute	Korea
49	529	Telefonaktiebolaget LM Ericsson	Sweden
50	523	El DuPont de Nemours and Company	United States

Sources: http://www.ificlaims.com/index.php?page=misc_Top_50_2011

the resultant growth in foreign R&D centers have contributed to an increase in patenting activities in China and India. However, while the number of patents applied for and granted has grown fast in China and India, these are still outnumbered by the number of US patents, and also the quality of these patents is far inferior to those filed in the United States.

REFERENCES

Almeida, P., 1996. Knowledge sourcing by foreign multinationals: patent citation analysis in the US semiconductor industry. Strategic Manage. J. 17, 155–165.

Bas, C.L., Sierra, C., 2002. Location versus home country advantages in R&D activities: some further results on multinationals locational strategies. Res. Policy 31 (4), 589–609.

Basant, R., Mani, S., 2012. Foreign R&D centres in India: an analysis of their size, structure and implications. Indian Institute of Management, Ahmedabad, Working paper No. 2012-01-06. http://www.iimahd.ernet.in/assets/snippets/workingpaperpdf/8040799502012-01-06.pdf (accessed 26/7/13).

Buckley, P.J., Ghauri, P.N., 2004. Globalization, economic geography and the strategy of multinational enterprises. J. Int. Bus. Stud. 35, 81–98.

Chengqi, W., Kafouros, M.I., 2009. What factors determine innovation performance in emerging economies—evidence from China. Int. Bus. Rev. 18.

De Bondt, R., 1996. Spillovers and innovative activities. Int. J. Ind. Organiz. 15 (1), 1–28.

Feinberg, E.S., Majumdar, K.S., 2001. Technology spillovers from foreign direct investment in the Indian pharmaceutical industry. J. Int. Bus. Stud. 32 (3), 421–437.

Griliches, Z., 1979. Issues in assessing the contribution of research and development to productivity growth. Bell J. Econ. 10, 92–116.

Griliches, Z., 1990. Patent statistics as economic indicators: a survey. J. Econ. Lit. 28 (4), 1661–1707.

Hall, H.B., Mairesse, J., 1995. Exploring the relationship between R&D and productivity in French manufacturing firms. NBER Working Papers 3956, National Bureau of Economic Research, Inc.

Kafouros, M.I., 2008a. Industrial Innovation and Firm Performance: The Impact of Scientific Knowledge on Multinational Corporations. Edward Elgar, Cheltenham.

Kafouros, M.I., 2008b. Economic returns to industrial research. J. Bus. Res. 61 (8), 868–876.

Kuemmerle, W., 1999. The drivers of foreign direct investment into research and development: an empirical investigation. J. Int. Bus. Stud. 30, 1–24.

Mani, S., 2010. The flight from defence to civilian space: evolution of the sectoral system of innovation of India's Aerospace Industry. Working Paper Series, No: 428, Centre for Development Studies, Trivandrum.

NSTMIS, 2011-2012. Science and Technology Indicator Tables. Department of Science and Technology, New Delhi http://www.nstmis-dst.org/SnT-Indicators2011-12.aspx (accessed 19/1/14).

Office of the Controller General of Patents, 2011–2012. Annual report of the office of the controller general of patents, designs, trademarks and geographical indicators. Ministry of Commerce and Industry, Government of India, New Delhi.

Chapter 4

Culture

Chapter Contents

Herbig and Dunphy (1998) defined culture as follows: "culture is the sum total of a way of life: it is the values, traits, or behaviors shared by the people within a region. The function of culture is to establish modes of conduct, standards of performance, and ways of dealing with interpersonal and environmental relations that will reduce uncertainty, increase predictability, and thereby promote survival and growth among the members of any society." This definition hints at the fact that culture is not stable but evolves to meet the needs of society. That culture is not fixed once and for all is underlined by studies mapping value change (Von Rosenstiel and Koch, 2001). Research conducted by Hofstede (1984) shows that those societies that score high on individualism and low on the power dimension have a higher economic growth and a greater tendency to innovate.

High individualism combined with low power distance and weak ambiguity avoidance can encourage pro-innovative culture and entrepreneurship (Hofstede, 1991). The essence of innovation is the originality in the science and the thought process, that is, to discover new problems and resolve them. With regard to culture, innovation needs an atmosphere of democracy, stability and equality, tolerance and respect for individual creativity, and encouragement of risk taking and change.

POWER DISTANCE AND BUREAUCRACY

Power distance is the perceived degree of inequality among people. In high-power-distance society, the "superiors," or those in power, perceive themselves, and are also perceived by others, to be at a higher level and, hence, have a great degree of control over others. While, in low-power-distance society, the difference between superiors and subordinates is not perceived to be very significant, and they are considered to be at the same level. China is a society with high power distance. There is a strong difference among various members of society and organizations because of hierarchy. As a result, people have to be very careful and cautious in their interactions with officials, elders, and authorities (Wang, 2009). They have to be careful not to question, criticize, or disagree with those supported by the people at "higher" levels.

Compared with China, the United States is a low-power-distance society. The Declaration of Independence states that "all men are created equal, and that they are endowed by their Creator with certain unalienable Rights, that among these are Life, Liberty and the pursuit of Happiness." The Bill of Rights protects the natural rights of liberty and property, including freedom of religion, freedom of speech, a free press, and rights to free assembly and free association, as well as the right to keep and bear arms. The lack of power difference is not only evident from the intent of these documents but also borne out by the conduct of social and business interactions in American society, to a large extent.

Indian organizations, especially from the small business sector, are high on power distance that commands loyalty and possibly accountability (Afza, 2005). The need for control in such small organizations is so strong that Indian entrepreneurs prefer to stay small than to lose control. The power distance can also be seen in the way large companies treat their suppliers. Suppliers are seen as "vendors" rather than partners, and superior power is used by large companies to manage these relationships.

Since Indian society and organizations continue to be hierarchical, employees in India yearn to transition to managerial positions very early in their careers (Sharma et al., 2012). Premature movement of the best technical minds into managerial roles weakens organizations' ability to innovate in domains where cumulative technical expertise matters (Krishnan, 2010).

Bureaucracy comes from "valuing official titles," which takes official rank as a social standard to measure a person's social status and individual achievement. A person with a higher official position has a higher social level and is regarded as having been more successful. Currently, in China, relative to other occupations, government officials earn higher income, have higher social status, and are more widely known. This attracts people to government jobs, so they can "learn for becoming an official." This "brain drain" to "officialdom" takes place at the expense of other fields of human endeavor, such as the creation of new businesses and industries. More seriously, the concept of "power being truth" makes administrative authority equivalent to academic authority and professional authority. Because "official" means the truth, others can only obey and believe that they have no right to say "no."

Chinese universities and research institutions are run by a highly centralized system, which results in a great deal of administrative constraint and control of scientific study, and there is no clear boundary between administration and research. There is a great deal of administrative intervention, very little scientific autonomy, rigid norms, very little human consideration, complex multiple-level pressures, and very little academic freedom. The net result is that scientific activities lose their vitality. Also, the government has considerable power to decide the agenda for educational and scientific work performed at universities. For example, the universities' grades, assessment, and approval of research projects carried out by principal investigators, overview and approval of research projects, and evaluation of scientific output are to a large extent controlled by the government. The government sets up universities and research institutions in administrative levels where the managers are appointed by higher government authorities. Hence, most research units focus their attention on the attitudes of their superiors and ignore the advancement of their own education and research needs.

By contrast, in the United States, education institutions and private corporations are fairly autonomous and independent of government intervention.

As far as Indian organizations are concerned, although the emphasis is on valuing relationships and loyalty, both Western and traditional management systems coexist. The traditional system with its absolute loyalty to the family at the expense of all else, cronyism, political patronage, absolute obedience of authority, centralization of power, and other similar considerations, coexists alongside Western management practices such as autonomy and participative style of management. Hence, while bureaucracy may be observed in some organizations, autonomy and people-oriented management are also found in many Indian organizations (Sinha and Kanungo, 1997).

COLLECTIVISM OR INDIVIDUALISM

Characteristics of individualism in the context of the social fabric are those in which the individual takes care of himself or herself in contrast to collectivism in which groups take care of the individual (Li and Zhai, 2010). China is a nation with a collectivist approach to human behavior. Collectivism takes collectivity as the center, and the collective interests are always above individual interests. So, in order to protect collective interests, individual interests may be sacrificed. In a collectivist environment, individuals are attached to groups and are especially dependent on the family. A person's "value" depends on his or her belonging to a group. Since an individual's rights are superseded by group rights, private property rights have not been protected well in the past, which, to some extent, decreased a person's motivation to innovate.

The United States is a nation that cherishes and celebrates individualism. Individualism takes the individual as the center and encourages everyone to be who they are and accepts differences among people and different ideas. The United States is a highly individualistic society. In every field, diverse ideologies and different theories coexist, which is conducive to academic prosperity and creativity in research and development.

Indian organizations exhibit medium collectivist orientation influenced primarily by the extended family, caste, and religious and linguistic affiliations, with the resultant in-group and out-of-group relationship orientations. The emerging Indian capitalist system that is associated with a high degree of competition is, however, slowly leading to an individualistic survival philosophy (Sahay and Welsham, 1997). This individualistic survival philosophy combined with Brahminic idealism makes Indians bad team players. Consequently, they have difficulty in engaging in mutually coordinated action to achieve shared goals. Their failure to accept criticism also inhibits their ability to work together on problem solving.

UNCERTAINTY AVOIDANCE

Uncertainty avoidance is the extent to which a society feels threatened by uncertain situations and avoids these situations by providing stable systems with formal rules.

Geographically, China is a closed country, with a trackless desert to the north, impassable mountains to the west and southwest, and a vast sea to the east and southeast. With this closed geography, China gradually developed a self-sufficient agricultural economy, and that formed the physical basis of Chinese culture. Agricultural production caused people to be attached to their land and live in unchanging ways and gradually formed the habit of seeking stability (Dong, 2009). Chinese culture advocated eternity, and anything breaking the stillness and stability would make the Chinese feel uneasy.

Unlike the Chinese, Americans like adventure, and their ancestors came from all over the world to make a new life in the United States, which in itself was an adventure. This adventurous spirit was handed down from generation to generation. US history is full of examples of adventurous activities, such as the Dunbar expedition, the Fremont expedition, the Columbia River expedition, and the polar exploration. The venture capital and private equity culture today is a display of the American spirit of adventure, and it greatly promotes innovation. In the United States, venture capital came into vogue just before World War II and began to flourish in the second-half of the twentieth century. As a complement to the mature capital markets on Wall Street, venture capital and private equity provided important financial support for technological development and innovation.

Indians, on the other hand, exhibit low uncertainty avoidance tendencies at work commensurate with the Hindu belief in karma, which promotes a sense of fatalistic acceptance of current uncertainty rather than proactive efforts to reduce it (Hofstede and Bond, 1988). Since their environment is characterized by uncertainty, a sense of insecurity, a general helplessness, named as "poverty syndrome" by Sinha and Kanungo (1997), exists. This syndrome prompts them to avoid futuristic thinking and risk-taking behavior. As a result, attitudes towards innovation and entrepreneurship and public acceptance of entrepreneurs are not well developed.

The "poverty syndrome" also displays itself in a general lack of confidence in Indian firms in their innovation capabilities. Indian firms have therefore traditionally believed that expertise, particularly technical expertise, is best found outside rather than inside. When they do innovate, it has been observed that a strong need for external validation exists. For example, well-funded groups like the Tatas chose to obtain government financial support for the "Indica" car and "Biosuite," a bioinformatics tool, not for want of funds but more for the need of external endorsement of their innovation activity. Similarly, it was found that relatively large firms sought support from the Small Business Innovation Research Initiative (SBIRI) of Government of India's Department of Biotechnology (Krishnan, 2010).

Another dimension of acceptance of current uncertainty also stems from the Hindu belief in several births or reincarnations. This belief of several births culturally manifests itself in a lack of sense of urgency or lack of a strong time orientation (Sinha and Kanungo, 1997). As a result, Indian organizations find it difficult to plan, compartmentalize, schedule, and have the sense of urgency that is needed for effective strategy implementation. Multinational organizations (e.g., Toyota) operating in India have had difficulties in implementing continuous improvement systems in India since deadlines are not viewed with high importance (Krishnan, 2010).

CULTURAL OPENNESS

Cultural openness means the communication, exchange, and acceptance of thoughts and ideas between different cultural groups and nations and the mutual influence, absorption, and integration of different cultures. China has a long history and a rich culture. It was, therefore, thought of as a "Celestial Empire" and looked up to by surrounding countries in the feudal period. China was very proud of its cultural heritage and, to some extent, looked down condescendingly upon the cultures of others. In the Qing dynasty, before the Opium War, the policy of "locking the door against the world" cut off Chinese people from the outside world, and new technologies and ideas could not be introduced into China (Chang, 2001). As a result, the Chinese gradually became very conservative and were reluctant to accept new ideas. After 1978, because of the policy of "opening up," China developed a more open culture, but the old and negative conservative thoughts have not been completely uprooted.

Compared with China, the United States has a very open culture. First of all, the United States is a country of immigrants and was thus destined to be a blend of different cultures. Second, the United States has through most of its history not been an "isolationist" country and has had significant contact with other countries, throughout its short history. On the one hand, there have been frequent exchanges among members of various occupations, such as teachers, researchers, medical workers, journalists, government officials, and social organizations with their counterparts in other countries. On the other hand, beginning in the second half of the twentieth century, more and more students from all over the world came to the United States to study, and they brought different cultures with them.

India, roughly the same size as Western Europe, also is culturally diverse with hundreds of indigenous languages and various ways of life. Some of its diversity is due to an influx of influences that have poured in from outside all through its history. Interestingly, these influences were engulfed into Indian culture bringing in complexity and heterogeneity without getting integrated into a melting pot. This led to the preserving of uniqueness of Indian culture, while at the same time, seemingly contradictory and inconsistent actions are integrated and balanced. These contradictory actions and beliefs in India are activated based on the three contextual components, viz., kal (time), patra (person), and desh (place), and the two dimensions of Indian culture, viz., context sensitivity and balancing. As a result, differing behaviors can be seen by the same person in three different contextual components. In other words, the solution for the same problem may be so vastly different depending upon the time and the place at which the decision is taken. Sometimes, such decisions may vary from person to person in the same organization.

This is in contrast to the United States, where people with different backgrounds and heritage seem, to a large extent, to get integrated, assimilated, and naturally "homogenized" into the American way, the quintessential American "melting pot," due to a uniform overlay of American institutions across the 50 states, while still allowing for subtle geographically local variations, and the retention of vestiges of original culture and heritage.

An example of contradictions in Indian culture is the differing preference of Indian firms for collaboration for research with different organizations. For example, Indian firms prefer to collaborate with research institutions than with each other. This comes in the way of joint working with other organizations and therefore has negative implications for innovation (Krishnan, 2010).

Another example of inconsistency can be found in the implementation of quality management practices. While Indian firms are keen to improve their operational processes and efficiencies, they do not make the requisite changes in information flows, delegation of responsibility, authority, genuine team-based functioning, and performance-based management and incentive systems that are needed to make the practices sustainable (Krishnan, 2010).

ACCEPTANCE OF CHANGE

Acceptance of new ideas and, hence, of change is the fundamental requirement of science and is also the essential characteristic of an innovative cultural environment. The level of readiness to accept change is an important factor that affects innovation. To change also means to be different, and to be different implies a degree of "separateness" from existing others. Chinese culture, on the other hand, emphasizes "sameness" and integration. The "book of changes" (Chinese name YI Jing) was the earliest philosophical literature that greatly influenced Chinese thinking. The philosophy put forth here promoted the idea that all separation is for the sake of integration, and integration is the basis of Chinese culture. After the Han dynasty, all philosophical ideologies were prohibited except Confucianism, which guided the ideology of the entire feudal period. Confucianism was used in every field, including politics, economy, education, imperial exams, and daily life. So, the whole society was very uniformly homogeneous. If someone was a little different, they would be condemned, and people were afraid of being different and standing out or leading new ideas.

US culture derives primarily from European culture, which has its roots in the ancient Greek culture, which is characterized by a pursuit of "truth," and emphasizes the scientific method and the search for the laws of nature. Furthermore, individualism made the United States a country with "difference and separation." In any field, to be different and to be willing to accept change were encouraged. To Americans, change means constantly breaking the "old mold," and this reflects the spirit of innovation. With this spirit, Americans will never be satisfied with their achievements and will refuse to settle for "status quo" and will strive for better and accept change that goes with it.

Indians have also been found to possess tendencies towards context sensitivity and balancing in organizational behavior as mentioned earlier. As a result, they tend to have a balanced behavioral disposition and therefore adapt themselves to changes in environment without taking extreme positions (Sinha and Kanungo, 1997). Since extreme positions are not taken, there is limited room for a high degree of experimentation.

OPINION ABOUT ACHIEVEMENT

In the Chinese traditional culture, the pursuit of a saint's personality was held in high esteem, and this meant that the Chinese placed moral conduct above all else. So, a person's greatest achievement was to act as the saint did. Because of the importance of Confucianism, the archetypical figure of the saint was Confucius, and his ideas and actions greatly influenced people. "Valuing loyalty and disregarding material interests" was one of Confucius' important teachings (Zheng, 2006). In other words, pursuit of material interests was shameful and was only done by villains and not by gentlemen. Under the influence of this opinion, it is not surprising that people did not care about practical and commercial technologies. However, after "opening up," a great deal of attention was devoted to developing the economy, and money has taken on more and more importance. At the same time, assessment of scientific research was closely tied to the numbers of articles published, projects completed, and government awards received. Facing huge career advancement pressures, scientific research was the only way to get money, and so, scientific study remained at a very superficial level.

In Western culture, by contrast, individual achievement in any form—in innovation, entrepreneurship, business, academics, research, sports, arts, literature, music, etc.—is cherished, celebrated, and promoted. Achievement is promoted not only at an individual level but also in group activities and in organizations of various sorts.

Indian culture encourages admiration of ascetic contemplators over practical doers. Indians are motivated by duty (dharma) to their life roles and family welfare rather than to the intrinsic value of occupational accomplishment, so an ambivalent attitude towards material success and a sense of sociomoral obligation, rather than to organizational commitment, persists (Amba-Rao et al., 2000). However, in recent times, India has been experiencing a social shift with Indians becoming more competitive with a drive to excel (Herstatt et al., 2008) and a taste for material success and material comforts. But the drive to excel seems to be limited to certain technology-based service fields (particularly software) than in manufacturing where logical and mathematical skills are more important. This is because, traditionally, Indian society has valued brainwork more than physical activity (Krishnan, 2010).

MASCULINITY OR FEMININITY

According to the Chinese, masculinity–femininity reflects on whether the dominant values are associated with the collection of money and things (masculinity) as compared with values associated with caring for others and quality of life (femininity) (Tu et al., 2011).

In China, the culture has the character of femininity. First, Chinese people show sympathy towards the weak in society; intuitive thinking is more prevalent than logical reasoning; emotional response is more common than rational action. Second, Chinese people take nature, society, and individuals as a whole, and they would like to be submissive. As a result of this psychology, there is lack of competition. Lastly, Chinese people tend to be nostalgic, always looking back to the bygone days. This, of course, provides them an escape from the present difficult times and takes the burden off of having to take risks in the present.

In American culture, human beings and nature are not necessarily "in harmony" in the Chinese way, and, historically, have often been in conflict, as people had to conquer nature to survive. This resulted in Americans being more independent and competitive or in other words a more "masculine" psyche as defined above. Also, Americans like to look forward, which makes them have less of a burden of history. On January 21, 1985, President Reagan said in his second Inaugural Address: "contemporary Americans did not indulge in retrospect. In this happy land, there is always a better tomorrow." This further provides support for the above opinion. So, Americans, in general, do not reminisce, "live in the present," and go forward without any particular concern for being "in harmony with nature."

India on the other hand can be described as a country with medium masculinity reflected in moderate levels of assertiveness and interest in acquiring money and things, relative to affiliation and social relationships (Amba-Rao et al., 2000).

CHALLENGES FOR THE UNITED STATES: RECENT CULTURAL EVOLUTION OF THE UNITED STATES

The characteristics we have described thus far have stood the United States in good stead over its 200-year history. However, US culture, as that of any other country, is not entirely static. US culture has been changing, and there are several broad thrusts to these changes.

First, a culture that emphasized education, especially in math and sciences, innovation, and risk taking may have been gradually changing since the 1980s. Like in a lot of previous civilizations, where developments in science and technology and in engineering and innovation led to economic progress and much affluence, the tendency is to forget what got the society there in the first place and for complacency and a feeling of satiety to set in. To quote Vint Cerf (Peterson et al., 2011), the "father of the Internet," and now the Chief Internet Evangelist at Google, "America simply is not producing enough of our own innovators, and the cause is twofold. . . . . a national culture that does not emphasize the importance of education and the value of engineering and science."

Second, without a cause to rally around, as they did in the past—such as World War II or the mission to "send man to the moon"—the national preoccupation has shifted from an emphasis on education and advancement of science and technology to an emphasis on entertainment, sports, and other pursuits and from producing to consuming. While entertainment and sports have always been key pillars of the US culture, social fabric, and national pastime, as they should be, their emphasis at the apparent exclusion of emphasis on education appears to be a recent phenomenon, getting more and more acute since the 1980s. This is further exacerbated by a cultural shift towards "instant gratification," rather than making sacrifices for longer-term gains. This is also evident in the business world from the emphasis on Wall Street, in the 1990s and beyond, on short-term—every quarter or every 6 months—corporate performance rather than investment with longer-term strategic objectives. There are, however, exceptions. There are a few companies in the United States that do take a longer-term view of their innovative pursuits, and they have done well. But these companies are an exception rather than the rule—more on this has been elaborated in the intrapreneurship chapter later in the book.

Third, starting in the 1960s, the US culture has been gyrating between wild liberalism, on the one hand, and extreme social conservatism, on the other hand, to the point where today, the country appears to be polarized between these two extremes.

While this did not adversely affect innovation from the 1960s through the 1990s, while the US economy was still vibrant and global challenges to its dominance were temporary, today, this could be an area of concern. Extreme social conservatism in large swaths of the United States, away from the major metropolitan areas and away from the two coasts, and their preoccupation with turning back the clock by, among other things, distancing themselves from the theory of evolution in favor of creationism and their disavowing the notion of global warming do not bode well for the future of innovative thinking in the United States.

Fourth, a culture that was based on science, engineering, and technology and the resultant economy driven by a substantial manufacturing base have now transitioned to a primarily service-based economy. The cultural mind-set, by and large, is that of people who are primarily consumers of products and services and providers of services rather than makers and builders of products. A reversal of this type of cultural mind-set will be difficult to pull off. The solution to this innovation gap proposed by some is to "in source" innovation by selectively allowing an influx of technically trained immigrants to create these innovative solutions, rather than adequately train those born and brought up in the United States.

All of the above present some significant mainstream cultural challenges to the United States as it looks forward to competing in the future in the global arena.

In conclusion, compared with Chinese and Indian cultures, the traditional American culture is very conducive to innovation. However, winds of mainstream cultural change in the United States that have affected its ability to innovate in recent years may be a reason for future concern.

The Chinese culture has the characteristics of relatively higher power distance and bureaucracy, more collectivism and uncertainty avoidance, high reluctance to openness and acceptance of change, ambiguous opinions about achievement, and higher levels of femininity—all of which have greatly hindered, in recent years, the nurturing of an innovative spirit. The barriers to innovation in Indian culture range from high power distance exhibiting itself in a strong need for control, individualism demonstrated by poor teamwork, high uncertainty avoidance leading to weak strategic outlook, achievement culture driven more by philosophical and intellectual pursuits rather than an action-orientation and physical work, to moderate levels of masculinity affecting degree of experimentation. Since 95% of Indian organizations are family-owned, their ability to innovate and adapt to new technologies is also a major challenge by virtue of their ownership structure and management style.

REFERENCES

Afza, M., 2005. Superior-subordinate relationships. VIKALPA 11–19.
Amba-Rao, S.C., et al., 2000. Comparative performance appraisal and management values among domestic and foreign firms in India. Int. J. Hum. Resour. Manage. 11 (1), 60–89.

Chang, Z., 2001. About the seclusion policy of Qing dynasty and its lesson. J. Guizhou Univ. (Social Sci.). 5.

Dong, B., 2009. A comparative study of Chinese and American culture and national character. Shi Ji Qiao. 12.

Herbig, P., Dunphy, S., 1998. Culture and innovation. Cross Cultural Manage. Int. J. 5 (4), 13–21.

Herstatt, C., et al., 2008. India's National Innovation System: Key Elements and Corporate Perspectives. Institute of Technology and Innovation Management, TUHH, Hamburg, Germany and East West Center, Hawaii.

Hofstede, G., 1984. Culture's Consequences: International Differences in Work-Related Values. Sage Publications, Beverly Hill, CA.

Hofstede, G., 1991. Cultures and Organizations. Harper Collins Publishers, London.

Hofstede, G., Bond, M.H., 1988. The Confucius connection: from cultural roots to economic growth. Organ. Dyn. 16 (4), 4–21.

Krishnan, R., 2010. From Jugaad to Systematic Innovation—The Challenge for India. The Utpreraka Foundation, Bangalore.

Li, H., Zhai, S., 2010. Chinese and American thinking patterns from perspective of collectivism and individualism. J. China Univ. Min. Technol. (Social Sci.) 2010 (4), 119–124.

Peterson, P.E., Woessmann, L., Hanushek, E.A., Lastra-Anadon, C.X., Fall 2011. Are U.S. students ready to compete? Educ. Next 11 (4), 50–59.

Sahay, S., Welsham, G., 1997. Social structure and managerial agency in India. Organiz. Stud. 18, 414–444.

Sharma, P., et al., 2012. India's national and regional innovation systems: challenges, opportunities and recommendations for policy makers. J. Ind. Innovat. 19 (6), 517–537.

Sinha, J.B.P., Kanungo, R., 1997. Context sensitivity and balancing in Indian organizational behavior. Int. J. Psychol. 32, 93–107.

Tu, Y.-T., Lin, S.-Y., Chang, Y.-Y., 2011. A cross-cultural comparison by individualism/collectivism among Brazil, Russia, India and China. Int. Bus. Res. 4 (2), 175.

Von Rosenstiel, L., Koch, S., 2001. Changes in socioeconomic values as a trigger of organizational learning. In: Dierkes, M. (Ed.), Handbook of Organizational Learning and Knowledge. Oxford University Press, New York.

Wang, X., 2009. Cultural analysis of differences in power distance between Chinese and American cultures. J. Heilongjiang Coll. Educ. 29(2).

Zheng, W., 2006. Discuss on the relationship between Confucianism and Chinese ancient technology. Popular Tribune. 3.

Chapter 5

Laws, Rules, and Role of Government Institutions

Chapter Contents

Laws and rules, as part of the regulatory infrastructure created by the government, provide the necessary assurance that enterprises need in order for them to invest in innovation. The protection provided by intellectual property rights (IPR), especially patent right protection, is a very important factor that contributes to promoting innovation globally. Nordhaus (1969) and later studies of innovation have emphasized the role of patent laws in determining the incentives to invent. Nordhaus pointed out that the incentives to invent increase with the strength of monopoly rights that are granted to successful innovators. Klemperer (1990) and Gilbert and Shapiro (1990) added the breadth of patent grants as a further policy instrument, thus capturing the range of technologies that are covered by each patent.

In addition, governments can use tax incentives, government procurement, and governmental financial support of projects to increase the motivation to innovate. Conservative economists and policy makers prefer to give businesses tax incentives based on the belief that tax policy is market neutral, in contrast to direct funding of projects that targets particular technologies or phases of the

R&D cycle (Tassey, 2007a,b). This philosophy has dominated economic growth policy in the United States for decades, in spite of an occasional argument to the contrary (Bozeman and Link, 1984, 1985; Surrey, 1969; Tassey, 1996, 2007a,b).

To the extent that tax preferences for R&D affect the user cost of risk capital, they can influence decisions by companies with respect to location of R&D facilities and operations. Billings (2003) estimated the effect of tax incentives by relating the average rate of growth in R&D spending in eleven countries relative to the comparable rate of growth in the United States for seven industries over a 10-year period (1991–2000). Industry years with tax-based incentives had an average annual increase in industry R&D spending of 9.61% compared to 2.24% average annual R&D spending growth for years without tax-based incentives. Thus, the average growth rate for industry years with a tax incentive is more than four times that of the average growth rate for industry years without such an incentive.

In the 1970s, a number of empirical studies explored the relevance of procurement to innovation (for an overview, see Mowery and Rosenberg, 1979; Rothwell, 1984; Rothwell and Zegveld, 1981). Rothwell and Zegveld (1981) compared R&D subsidies and state procurement contracts without direct R&D procurement. They concluded that, over longer time periods, state procurement triggered greater innovation initiatives in more areas than did R&D subsidies (see also Rothwell, 1984). Geroski (1990) also analyzed the quantitative and qualitative meaning of state demand for innovation and concluded that procurement policy "is a far more efficient instrument to use in stimulating innovation than any of a wide range of frequently used R&D subsidies" (Edler and Georghiou, 2007).

Also, institutional environment has a great impact on innovation. Hall and Jones (1999) and Acemoglu et al. (2001) found that differences in institutional social capability can account for a large share of the observed differences in income per capita across countries. North and Thomas (1973), in their classic, "The Rise of the Western World," argued that the institutions that evolved in late medieval Europe were key to Europe's later rise to world economic dominance. Following a somewhat similar line of reasoning, Rosenberg and Birdzell (1986) emphasized the importance of flexibility and innovation, in both the political and the economic spheres, to the emergence of sustained growth in the West (Chaudhary and Garner, 2007). Poor institutional rules infrastructure can result in significant rent-seeking and block innovation.

INTELLECTUAL PROPERTY RIGHTS

United States

The history of IPR in the United States can be traced back to its colonial days and its roots in Europe. Protection of intellectual property (IP) has been a critical function of the US government since the founding of the United States. Indeed, Article I, Section 8, Clause 8 of the US Constitution grants to Congress the power to "promote the Progress of Science and useful Arts by securing for limited Times to Authors and Inventors the exclusive Right to their respective Writings and Discoveries" (The US Department of Commerce, 2012). It has been refined over the years since then, with significant changes taking place since the early 1980s and more recently during the Obama administration (Administration's White Paper on Intellectual Property Enforcement Legislative Recommendations, March 2011, www.whitehouse.gov/sites/default/files/ip_white_paper.pdf).

The existence of this legal framework has afforded an opportunity for innovators and entrepreneurs to protect and hence benefit from the fruits of their creativity and labor and has been a major driving factor in the industrialization of the United States. Changes that have taken place in the US patent laws since the 1980s have enabled the patenting of software and business models and also living entities—an era marked by the general relaxation of patentability criteria. "They have resulted in major changes in the US system of innovation—more specifically in the increasing privatization of knowledge domains and activities that were previously public. The changes result from the combined effects of a response to US perceptions of increased foreign competition, of the emergence of major new technological opportunities in biotechnology and in information and communication technologies, and of a series of regulatory changes that have paved the way for the financial sector's increased involvement, via direct investments in firms whose main activity is comprised of R&D" (Coriat and Orsi, 2002).

A key driver for some of these changes was the debate raging among industrialists and academicians in the 1970s resulting from the loss of US competitiveness, especially in the semiconductor industry, which was at least partially attributed to, one, an overemphasis on basic research at the expense of applied research, especially at universities, and, two, the ease with which corporations could appropriate the results of research carried out using the US government funding. This resulted in the first major change in US patent law, the Bayh-Dole Act, or the Patent and Trademark Law Amendments Act of 1980, which allowed public research institutions and small businesses to patent their inventions although they were made using federal funding (Coriat and Orsi, 2002; Sampat, 2006).

On June 22, 2010, the US Intellectual Property Enforcement Coordinator (IPEC) issued the administration's first Joint Strategic Plan on Intellectual Property Enforcement (Strategy), which was developed in coordination with many federal agencies, including the Departments of Commerce, Health and Human Services, Homeland Security, Justice (DOJ), and State and the Office of the US Trade Representative. As part of the strategy, the Obama administration undertook to review existing laws to ensure that they were effective and to identify deficiencies that could hinder enforcement. Based on that review, this White Paper identified specific recommended legislative changes, designed to increase the effectiveness of US enforcement efforts (Administration's White Paper on Intellectual Property Enforcement Legislative Recommendations, March 2011). A number of these and other recommendations went into effect as changes to the patent law in 2013 and can be found at the website of the US patent office.

The objective of this segment is not to provide a comprehensive review of patent law in the United States or its history, for which extensive literature already exists, but more to point out its long-standing history in the United States in contrast to its recent vintage in China and India and to briefly allude to the more recent changes.

China

After the establishment of new China (1949), in August 1950, the Chinese government enacted the Provisional Regulations on the Protection of the Invention Right and the Patent Right and published a document, "Provisional Regulations on Invention and Patent Right Protection." This ordinance protected intellectual rights through invention and patent certificates and also rewarded the recipients of the certificates. In November 1963, this document was repealed, and Invention Award Regulations came into force replacing the invention protection system with an invention reward system. The patent system did not change for the following 20 years.

In 1980, China formally submitted the application for membership to the World Intellectual Property Organization (WIPO) and established the patent office (Zheng, 1986). Since then, China announced and implemented the Patent Law of the People's Republic of China, the Trademark Law of the People's Republic of China, the Copyright Law of the People's Republic of China, the Computer Software Protection Regulations, the Integrated Circuit Layout Design Protection Ordinance, the Copyright Collective Management Regulations, the Audio and Video Products Management Regulations, the New Varieties of Plants Protection Regulations, the Intellectual Property Customs Protection Regulations, the Distinctive Emblems Management Regulations, the Olympic Symbols Protection Regulations, and a series of related rules. From 1992–1993 to 2000–2001, legislations pertaining to IP were amended significantly and they were more consistent with international laws and regulations.

Although there has been progress in China with regard to IPR protection, there are still several problems. First, researchers and individual contributors in most Chinese companies do not appreciate the importance of protecting IP or its market value and hence do not take the necessary steps to protect it. Hence, when a scientific research project is complete, the emphasis is on publishing results and seeking ensuing recognition and financial rewards, rather than applying for patent protection, thus making core results of the research known to competitors.

Second, businesses do not pay attention to IP portfolio management. In China, 99% of small and medium enterprises do not have a department to manage IP. In fact, very few large companies have an IPR department, and patents are administered by the technology department, trademarks are managed by the legal department, and copyrights are handled by the publicity department. As a result, it is very difficult to ensure uniformity in the application of IP policies and procedures across the organization. This can be ascribed to the fact that a large number of scientific and technological achievements are lost to the patent filing process every year due to publication in the open literature, documentation of scientific output for the government, and public usage of the results of research. By some accounts, from 1990 to 2005, about thirty thousand Chinese innovations have been lost to the patent process. For example, in the field of Chinese traditional herbal medicine, up to May 2004, it is estimated that roughly 900 patents were filed by the Chinese but issued to foreigners (China Youth Daily, May 5, 2004).

Third, most advanced technology innovations are owned by foreign companies, and China needs a great deal of indigenous innovation. Data indicate that in the high-tech fields of information and communication, computers, aerospace, and biopharmaceuticals, foreign companies owned 60–90% of the patents applied for in China. For example, from 1994 to 1998, foreign patent applications in the field of information technology accounted for 90% of the applications, 70% in computers, 61% in pharmaceuticals, 87% in biology, 92% in communications, and 90% in semiconductors (Research Team of Institute of Finance and Trade Economics, 2002).

Fourth, the degree of commercialization of patented technologies is very low. According to World Bank estimates, the average conversion rate of Chinese scientific and technological achievements into commercial products is only 15–20%, the conversion rate for patents into commercial products is 25%, and the patent general usage rate ranges between 10% and 15%. In some developed countries, like Japan, the rate for scientific and technological achievements into commercial products is as high as 70–80% (Feng and Huang, 2009).

Fifth, marks of origin are not well protected. In international trade, it is common practice to indicate the place of origin of imported or exported items, especially the place of manufacture. This geographic identification is important especially as an indication of the quality and authenticity of the product. In the Trade-Related Aspects of Intellectual Property Rights (TRIPS) Agreement of the WTO, the geographic place of origin of the IP is especially important. In China, there is such little respect for the place of origin of the IP that there are a very large number of IP-related disputes.

Lastly, in China, there is a great deal of confusion about the rightful ownership of IP. This is true in at least a few different situations. Firstly, this is the case in job-related versus non-job-related innovation or invention. Secondly, this is an even bigger issue in collaborative projects between companies, universities, and research institutions, due to the lack of contractual clarity with regard to IP ownership, before these collaborations begin, resulting in a high rate of commercialization failures. Thirdly, this lack of respect for IP has become an issue in dealing with foreign companies, for example, the dispute between Cisco and Huawei over IP relating to Internet protocol-based routers.

India

The following legislation on IPR is in force in India:

- The Indian Copyright Act of 1957 governs the copyright laws in the country. India is also a signatory to international treaties pertaining to copyrights.
- The Patents Act of 1970 as amended by the Patents Act of 2005 along with the Patents Rules as amended by Patents (amendment) Rules 2006 and 2012.
- The Trade Marks Act, 1999, along with the Trade Marks Rules, 2002.
- The Designs Act, 2000, along with the Designs Rules, 2001.
- The Geographical Indications of Goods (registration and protection) Act 1999 and the Geographical Indications of Goods (registration and protection) Rules, 2002.
- The Protection of Plant Varieties and Farmers' Rights Act, 2001.

Other than enactment and enforcement of various laws in the country after joining the WTO and TRIPS, India has also acceded to various international treaties like the Paris Convention, Patent Cooperation Treaty (PCT), Budapest Treaty, Universal Copyright Convention, Phonogram Convention, and Madrid Protocol.

The evolution of India's IPR laws, more specifically its current patent regime, is a reflection of its journey from colonization to independence to globalization. Accordingly, Indian patent laws can be viewed in three time periods, viz., the colonial period, the postindependence period, and the globalization period (Mueller, 2006).

The colonial period of IP in India is characterized by the introduction of patents for the first time in India by the British. Their laws were enacted with the objective of enabling British patent holders to acquire control over Indian markets. The British implemented the first patent statute in India in 1856, based on the British Patent Law of 1852. Subsequently, a series of patent laws were introduced by the British with several amendments, the last in the series being the Indian Patents and Designs Act, 1911, which was viewed as being very "draconian" by the indigenous Indian drug manufacturers.

When India attained its independence from the British, the Indian government wasted no time in "reviewing the patent laws in India with a view to ensure that the patent system was more conducive to national interests." It set up two committees and based on their recommendations the Indian Patents Act of 1970 was enacted. The act repealed patentability of pharmaceutical products. It prohibited patents on "substances intended for use, or capable of being used, as food or as medicine or drug, or . . . relating to substances prepared or produced by chemical processes (including alloys, optical glass, semiconductors and inter-metallic compounds)." However, it provided for patenting of processes for making these products. The intellectual protection period for process patents was 7 years from the date of grant or 5 years from the date of sealing the patent, while all other types of patents had a term of 14 years. India quite bluntly set forth justifications for its broad limitations on patent exclusivity in the 1970 act with the statement of "general principles," viz., "That patents are granted to encourage inventions and to secure that the inventions are worked in India on a commercial scale and ... that they are not granted merely to enable patentees to enjoy a monopoly for the importation of the patented article. ..." "The law, conceived in postcolonial days when India still suffered from famines and the average Indian could expect to live only about 40 years, was intended to Ramasubramanian, 2009 encourage the founding of local industries and to break the choke hold of foreign chemical companies."

The 1970 act resulted in the ousting of several multinational pharmaceutical companies and a simultaneous dramatic turnaround of the indigenous pharmaceutical industry that was almost nonexistent at the time of independence. The indigenous firms were free to copy pharmaceutical products patented outside India as long as the process of production did not infringe on an existing Indian process patent. As a result, the production of generic drugs witnessed a phenomenal upswing driving down drug prices considerably, leading to major growth in domestic and export markets. Ever since then, India has emerged as a major supplier of affordable generic HIV and AIDS drugs and other critical pharmaceuticals around the world. The fallout of this trend was a lack of innovation capabilities in certain industries such as pharmaceuticals, agrochemicals, and agricultural products. This manifested itself in terms of lack of R&D and professional expertise to pursue new molecules or products and personnel with exposure to advanced technological tools and techniques.

In 1990, when India started its journey of liberalization and globalization in the wake of the acute economic crisis of the 1980s, it had no choice but to bring its patent laws into conformity with the WTO's IP rules as set forth in TRIPS, in order to gain the economic and political benefits of participation in the WTO's trading system. Also in the background was the need for transforming its patent laws so as to stimulate domestic innovation. However, India was also faced with a multitude of issues, such as a vast population, widespread poverty, lack of a health insurance system, deeply ingrained wariness towards foreign influences, a fragile coalition government that had opposing views on TRIPS compliance, and a vocal citizenry, affected by the relevant patent issues, aware of developments in patent laws. In addition to the above factors is the fact that traditionally, people in India did not believe in asserting rights over intellectual properties (Ramasubramanian, 2009). In fact, intellectuals were associated more with poverty than with property or prosperity, and people took pride in proclaiming that the Goddess of Wealth (Lakshmi) and Goddess of Learning (Saraswati) never coexisted. As a result, in spite of being faced with the task of complying with TRIPS requiring introduction of product patents and extending the term of patents to 20 years, India went about introducing changes in the patent laws gradually in three stages, viz., Patents (Amendment) Acts of 1999, 2002, and 2005, followed by amendments in certain rules in 2006 and 2012 and by taking advantage of the flexibility in the TRIPS system.

Furthermore, since it became obligatory for India to provide protection to new plant variety through either a patent or an effective "sui generis" system or a combination of these two systems, India opted for "sui generis" (a Latin phrase meaning "of their own kind") system and implemented the Protection of Plant Varieties and Farmers' Rights Act of 2001. This act has been enacted in such a way that adequate safeguards are provided to farmers by giving their rights while providing for an effective system of protection for plant breeders' rights and at the same time encouraging development of new varieties of plants. Farmer's rights include their traditional rights to save, use, share, or sell their farm produce of a variety protected under this act, provided the sale is not for the purpose of reproduction under a commercial marketing arrangement. The act also seeks to safeguard researchers' rights and the larger public interest.

The introduction of stronger IPR laws in India has given rise to an increasing trend of MNCs coming to India through various routes such as FDI, contract research and manufacturing, outsourced manufacturing, joint ventures, and setting up of green field ventures. The Indian Patent Office has been witnessing a dramatic increase in the number of foreign and domestic patent applications. Large and innovative companies have benefitted from the new IPR laws. However, small- and medium-sized companies, especially in the pharmaceutical industry, are facing difficulties. As mentioned in the earlier chapter on economy, while India is witnessing an increase in R&D spending by MNCs and foreign firms, the spillover effect on domestic firms is yet to be seen. The prices of patented pharmaceutical products in some instances are very high.

Some of the problems that warrant attention in the IPR system are as follows (Chaudhuri et al., 2010):

- Complex and lengthy legal recourse: although India has an independent judiciary, legal recourse in India in general is lengthy and complex due to the significant backlog of cases in the courts. To make the legal recourse with respect to IPR-related cases easier, the Intellectual Property Appellate Board (IPAB) has been created to resolve disputes prior to going to court. However, as far as IPR infringement is concerned, the industry still perceives the penal action on infringement as weak, lengthy, and complex. This is one reason often cited for lack of incentive for R&D by industry.
- All information regarding IPR is not available online: although the Indian Patent Office has made available a considerable amount of information online, there is a need for making all information pertaining to IPR available online and searchable, including published applications, granted patents, complete specifications, examination reports, patent office decisions,

details of oppositions filed, and correspondence between the applicant and the patent office. This will lead to increased transparency in the process for granting of patents.

- Inconsistency in the process for granting patents: in some cases, despite lack of relevant data, patents were granted, and in some cases, patents were granted to products that were not eligible for patents. In these cases, certain patent applications have circumvented the provisions that specifically exclude granting of patents, by applying on other grounds by careful rephrasing the patent application. For example, in the case of software patents, computer programs can be patented only when they are a component of a larger system, which is patentable when taken as whole. However, in spite of this constraint, patents have been granted to software that is not part of a larger system. Similarly, in the case of pharmaceutical products, "new use" or "methods of treatments" are not patentable. However, several "composition" claims that in fact appeared to be essentially "new use" or "method of treatment" claims have been granted patents as these applications were reformulated as "compositions."
- It has been found that in certain cases, patents although rejected by the US Patent and Trademark Office (USPTO) or by the European Patent Office (EPO) were granted by Indian Patent Office. This is despite the fact that the information pertaining to prosecution history of US applications is available online and the USPTO and the EPO have more liberal patentability criteria, when it comes to defining novelty and what is innovative.
- The Indian Patent Office has seen a manifold increase in the number of patent applications ever since India started the process of compliance with TRIPS. However, the infrastructure and human resources required for processing the volume of these applications are inadequate. Adequate training of all personnel is required to expedite granting of patents in a consistent manner.
- Many of the industry players are still not IP-aware. There is a need for the training of industry personnel on IP-related issues. This is especially true in the case of small and medium enterprises.

TAX POLICIES FOR PROMOTION OF INNOVATION AND ENTREPRENEURSHIP

United States

Federal government funding of corporate R&D has for a long time played a significant role in making the United States a world leader in innovation. Since the 1960s, the tax policy of the US government towards R&D spending by private corporations was designed to subsidize these expenditures at varying rates over time (Hall, 1993). The Research and Experimentation (R&E) Tax Credit, first introduced in 1981 as part of the Economic Recovery Tax Act, in particular has played a key role in encouraging firms to commit funds to innovation-focused activities. This act was recognition by the federal government that businesses tend to underinvest in R&D because they cannot fully capture returns on such investments due to spillover effects. The credit provided them an incentive to invest in R&D (Lee and Muro, 2012, The Brookings Institution). The R&E Tax Credit significantly increased corporate research by lowering the effective cost of research and helped increase innovation and job growth in the United States.

However, the R&E Tax Credit policy after being first introduced in 1981 was in effect for only about five years and had to be renewed every few years. This lack of permanence along with the associated uncertainty, in relation to similar more permanent policies introduced by a number of other nations, as well as the vagueness and complicated nature of some of the calculations needed, resulted in a gradual loss of the positive impact of these policies on R&D and innovation. The United States, therefore, no longer leads the world in innovation-based competitiveness.

The Obama administration, as well as a number of others, has proposed changes to improve US competitiveness (The President's Framework for Business Tax Reform, a Joint Report by The White House and the Department of the Treasury, February 2012). One of the key components of this framework includes a proposal to expand, simplify, and make permanent the R&E Tax Credit. The proposal also recommends simplifying the presently complex calculations with tax credits varying between 14% and 20%, to a simpler rate of 17%. It has been estimated that an expansion of this size would bolster the US economy by producing a $66 B increase in annual GDP, at least 162,000 new jobs, and an additional 3850 patents issued to American inventors (Lee and Muro, 2012, The Brookings Institution).

A proposal such as this would reduce uncertainty and encourage companies to invest in long-term planning and take on R&D projects with longer-term horizons, would bolster the impact of regional innovation systems, and would work to enhance the standing of the United States in the global economy both now and in the decades ahead.

China

Since China began to transform its science and technology system in 1985, a series of tax incentives were provided to promote technological innovation. In recent years, the influence of tax preference and its supporting policies on innovation has received much attention. The following provide a brief overview of the highlights of current preferential tax policies (Lu and Sheng, 2002; Niu, 2004; Zeng 2001):

1. *High-tech enterprises.* High tech primarily includes the following sectors: microelectronics and electronic information technology; materials science and new materials technologies; optoelectronics and opto-electromechanical integration technologies; life sciences and biotechnology; energy, new energy

sources, and energy efficiency technologies; ecology and environmental protection technology; earth science and marine engineering technologies; basic materials science and radiation technology; medical science and biomedical engineering; and other applications in traditional industries based on new processes and technologies. The principal preferential tax policies applicable to high-tech enterprises are tax exemption or reduction of income tax rates.

2. *Technology transfer and development.* The tax incentive here is to exempt sales tax, which is applicable to individuals and businesses (including foreign nationals and foreign enterprises) engaged in technology development, technology transfer and related technical consulting, and other technological services.

3. *Technology development appliances and accessories.* Import value-added tax (VAT), consumption tax, and imported duties may be waived or reduced on imported instruments and equipment, chemical reagents, and technical information used by research institutes and technology centers, if these items cannot be indigenously produced, or produced in adequate quantities, or if the items produced in China do not meet requirements.

4. *Nonprofit research institutions and university science and technology parks.* In nonprofit research institutions, sales revenues from technology development, technology transfer and related technical consulting, and other technological services are exempt from sales tax and income tax.

5. *Rewards to individuals for job-related technological achievement.* In research institutions and universities, employees who were given shares of stock or options as a reward for job-related technological achievement can be exempted from income tax. When reward recipients put their technological award or bonus for education, interest income from it is also exempt from individual income tax. Those who win scholarships given by provincial governments or ministries and commissions by State Council or international organizations are also exempt from individual income tax.

6. *Accelerated depreciation of fixed assets.* Fixed assets that were subject to rapid technology-related obsolescence can be depreciated over shorter periods or the depreciation allowance can be increased.

7. *Software companies.* Since January 1, 2007, the VAT rate of audio and video products and electronic publications decreased from 17% to 13%. VAT can be levied on publications like scientific and technical periodicals, books, and science and technology audiovisual products during the publication process but refunded later after a review by the tax authorities.[1]

8. *Environmentally friendly and energy- and water-efficient enterprises.* These types of enterprises can also have their taxes waived or pay a reduced tax rate.

---

1. http://www.cnnsr.com.cn/jtym/swk/20070119/2007011911274832756.shtml.

9. *Development of new products, technologies, and processes.* Expenses for developing new products, new technologies, and new processes, such as new product design fees, process planning fees, equipment adjustment costs, technical books and materials fee, costs of intermediate testing included in the national plan, the wages of staff in research institutes, depreciation of research equipment, and new product trial costs, may be included in administrative expenses and can be treated as tax-deductible.

Also, China enacted a new enterprise income tax law in January 1, 2008. Under this law, corporate tax rate is 25%, the same for foreign and domestic enterprises (Ding and Gao, 2009). Before this law was enacted, the tax rate was 33% for domestic enterprises, and it was only 15% for many foreign enterprises. The change of tax rate meant that since foreign companies no longer enjoyed a tax-preferred status, they are now incented to promote in their Chinese subsidiaries.[2]

The present Chinese tax system has some deficiencies that hinder innovation (Li and Zhou, 2003; Liu, 2002). First, although there are many preferential tax policies, the one used most often is tax rate reduction, regardless of whether it is income tax or revenue tax. This kind of tax preference treatment is very simple, but it is based on revenues and is less in support of innovation. If an enterprise fails in scientific and technological research and development, they cannot get tax preference. Tax base reduction, like accelerated depreciation and tax-deductible expenses, is not often used, and there are very strict restrictions on its use. Given these policies, many enterprises place emphasis on technology introduction but not on indigenous innovation.

Second, tax preferences are mainly targeted at high-tech enterprises, enterprises registered in certain places, and enterprises belonging to certain industries. For example, enterprises in special economic zones and high-tech development parks, software enterprises, foreign enterprises, and enterprises aided by the State to develop new products, technologies, and processes can all obtain some tax preferences. Most self-employed and small- and medium-sized enterprises are excluded from preferential policies, although they need far more help than other enterprises.

Third, the current preferential tax policies cannot promote human capital development. Personal expenditures on education are not excluded from individual income taxes. So, there is very little incentive to improve personal capabilities. Present rules for individual income taxes have not provided tax incentives to enterprises for giving awards to employees for innovation or invention or science and technology progress. There is little incentive for companies to encourage their employees to innovate. Finally, there is very little support for commercialization of science and technology and for scientific and technological venture capital. For example, in the current policies, there is

---

2. http://www.chinaacc.com/new/63/67/88/2007/3/wa060911316191370021122-0.htm.

no policy for tax preference for venture capital invested in scientific and technological enterprises.

India

In order to promote R&D and innovation in Indian industries, the Government of India provides a number of fiscal incentives and support measures to industries (Saha, 2006). Some of these incentives are (Saha, 2006) as follows:

1. Excise duty waiver for 3 years on Indian products patented in any two countries from the EU and/or in the United States or in Japan.
2. Publicly funded R&D institutions registered by the Department of Scientific and Industrial Research (DSIR) are eligible for taking advantage of the central excise duty waiver on the purchase of indigenously manufactured items.
3. In-house R&D units recognized by the DSIR in the area of pharmaceutical and biotechnology sector are eligible for duty-free import of specified goods.
4. Publicly funded R&D institutions registered by the DSIR are also eligible for benefiting from custom duty exemption on import of equipment, spare parts, accessories, and consumables.
5. Exemption from the Drug Price Control Order for a period of 5–10 years for bulk drugs produced based on indigenous R&D for drug price control.
6. Weighted tax deduction on R&D expenditures at 150% is available to companies engaged in the business of biotechnology or in the business of manufacture or production of drugs, pharmaceuticals, electronic equipment, computers, telecommunications equipment, chemicals, and manufacture of aircraft and helicopters.
7. Accelerated depreciation allowance is available for plant and machinery installed for manufacturing goods based on indigenous technology developed in recognized in-house R&D units, government R&D institutions, national laboratories, and Scientific and Industrial Research Organization (SIRO).
8. Commercial R&D companies approved by the DSIR before April 1, 2004 are also eligible for a 10-year tax holiday.
9. Income tax relief on both revenue and capital expenditures pertaining to R&D.
10. Weighted tax deduction of 125% for expenses on sponsoring research programs at national laboratories functioning under Indian Council of Agricultural Research, Council for Scientific and Industrial Research, Indian Council of Medical Research, Defense Research and Development Organization, Department of Biotechnology (DBT), Department of Atomic Energy, Department of Electronics, Indian Institutes of Technology, and universities.

The impact of the above tax incentives in promoting R&D has been analyzed by Mani (2008). He found that the tax incentive scheme has been targeted well and it has been somewhat successful in increasing R&D expenditures in targeted industries. The pharmaceutical industry has been able to garner maximum tax incentives as it has been a target of most of these financial incentives. The nine other industries targeted are biotechnology, chemicals other than pharmaceuticals, electronic equipment, computers, telecoms equipment, automobiles, auto parts, seeds, and agricultural equipment. However, there is not much accountability of these incentives and their outcomes, and there is still much opportunity for industry to use these incentives. High transaction costs in deriving these benefits and low importance that R&D has in corporate planning and strategy are cited as some of the reasons for the lukewarm effect of the tax incentives (Dahlman et al., 2007).

GOVERNMENT PROCUREMENT TO PROMOTE INNOVATION AND ENTREPRENEURSHIP

United States

In the United States, procurement legislation and supporting laws reflect the role of government procurement in promoting scientific and technological innovation. In 1933, Congress passed the Buy American Act, which required the government to preferentially buy United States-made products in its purchases (Xiong et al., 2011). When the federal government constructed public facilities, materials and services were required to be provided by domestic suppliers. Multinational companies set up in the United States were eligible to participate in government procurement tenders, only when at least half of the components and parts that went into their products were produced in the United States. The act was revised in 1954, 1962, and 1998. For example, it allowed US government procurement to pay 6% higher for domestic goods compared to the same goods if imported and 12% higher if buying from small-sized businesses or during a recession.

In the Federal Procurement Law, there is some content concerning purchase of innovative products. In the manufacturing sector, the share of government procurement at one time reached 40%, and these items were purchased at a price above fair market price. In the Buy American Act, government took effective measures to reduce the market entry risk of domestic technological products. If these products could not be produced in the United States, foreign companies were required to transfer technology if their products were bought by the US government. In 1989, when George H.W. Bush became president, federal procurement rules were revised in order to enhance government's role in promoting local technological innovation through government purchase of locally manufactured goods. In 1992, President Clinton explicitly proposed that elimination of government obstacles for innovation should be extended from the commercial arena to the military arena and the defense procurement system was greatly reformed (Zhang et al., 2009).

US government procurement did a number of good things to help promote innovation. First, US government procurement placed an emphasis on the support of high-tech cutting-edge industries. In the fields of aviation, computers, semiconductors, and other high-tech industries, government procurement played a more significant role than government-sponsored R&D investment that influenced the direction of innovation. For example, airplanes were made larger or faster, or computers were made bigger or smaller determined by capital flows from government procurement. In 1955, the federal government bought 40% of semiconductor products and that reached 50% in 1960, which greatly promoted the early development of the semiconductor industry (Zhang et al., 2009).

Second, R&D contracts were an important aspect of government procurement, because it meant that the government signed contracts with research units to commission necessary research projects driven by requirements of design, quantity, and quality. These contracts provided significant research funds and the necessary market for these products when complete, thus benefitting cooperation between research and production and ensuring that the research programs finished on time.

Finally, US government agencies actively promoted indigenous innovation even when they purchased items for daily necessities. For example, when government departments bought commodities like typewriters, computers, automobiles, and other nongovernment special products, they also tried to steer the direction of technical development. This kind of government procurement played a key role in the following ways: identifying areas where the specific design and technology made development costs too high and defining when government funds should go to R&D to support procurement versus when they should be given to basic research or general research. An alignment of interests between the government and private corporations in these areas strengthened the innovation capabilities of the enterprise.

China

Government procurement was first implemented as a trial in Shanghai and Shenzhen in 1996. In 1998, the Chinese State Council officially gave the Ministry of Finance the right for government procurement. This was implemented in far more places, in addition to Shanghai and Shenzhen. In January 1, 2003, the Government Procurement Law was formally implemented, which clearly defined the goals of government procurement, its operational mechanisms, etc. In the late 1990s, suggestions were put forward for using government procurement to promote development of high-tech enterprises. So the goals of government procurement were expanded from ordinary products to high-technology products. In 1999, the document stating "To strengthen technical innovation, to develop high technology and to achieve industrialization" was decreed by the Central Committee and the State Council of the Communist Party of China.

This document put forward a policy that directed and encouraged government departments, enterprises, and public institutions to purchase domestic high-technology products and related equipment through the use of government procurement policy. This document was an important policy basis for using government procurement to support innovation by businesses. In February 27, 2006, related policies about implementing "the national long-term science and technology development plan (2006–2020)" was issued by the State Council. This policy clarified how to effectively use government procurement to support indigenous innovation. In recent years, the software industry, the integrated circuit industry, and some important strategic technologies were supported through the use of the government procurement policy. In 2000, a document issued by the State Council required that the software purchased by government agencies and the software involving national sovereignty and economic security should use government procurement. Industries that were the primary consumers of software were the finance, telecommunications, and government sectors. For example, in 2001, the total outlay for government procurement was ¥65.32 B, of which about 14.1% or ¥4 B was attributable to software (Treasury Secretary of Ministry of Finance, 2002).

Although government procurement in China played a significant role in promoting innovation in enterprises, there are some shortcomings with this policy. First, the level of government procurement is lower than that in developed countries. For example, government procurement amounted to only ¥1 B in 1996 and increased to ¥213.6 B in 2004. Although the rate of increase was very high, the highest ratio of government procurement to GDP was under 3%, while this was over 10% in developed countries (Zhang, 2007). Second, the method of purchase was very simple. Although five methods of procurement were permitted by the government—public bidding, invited bidding, competitive bidding, price inquiry, and single-source procurement—only public bidding was often used in reality. Third, the related laws and rules were not complete. Government Procurement Law only ensured priority purchasing of domestic products under the same conditions. There is no supporting measure to promote development of new industries and industries important for national interests so that government procurement often lost its relevance for directing indigenous innovation. At the same time, during the bidding process, there were no clear guidelines for evaluating various businesses due to a lack of well-defined evaluation criteria. Finally, government objectives in the procurement process were somewhat misplaced, because the most important goal of local governments was to save money and the goal of supporting innovation in the enterprise took a backseat.

India

In India, public procurement has not yet been used to its fullest extent or potential (e.g., defense and food sectors, public health, and vaccine development). Almost all ministries and departments (e.g., telecoms, transportation, rural development, defense, and space) are responsible for the implementation of demand-side policy measures, in general. There are some cross-border schemes and programs in the areas of public health, environment, and climate change. In public health, Indian institutions have entered into a very large joint public procurement effort with the Bill and Melinda Gates Foundation. The Department of Health Research under the Ministry of Health and Family Welfare has created the following schemes for creating demand for health research and procurement:

- Promotion of clinical research units in stem cells and virus-related units.
- Spread of health-related information through various media among poor and rural populations.
- Combating spread of epidemics and health-related factors in emergency periods, such as floods and earthquakes.
- Nationwide immunization programs.

The government, through the Department of Science and Technology (DST) and Ministry of Health and Family Welfare, has entered into various collaborations for the development and production of vaccines. Research on the development of a malaria vaccine is under way with US collaboration. A government-led Hep B project in collaboration with the Global Alliance for Vaccines and Immunization and the WHO is being implemented with phase I complete and phase II in progress.

In the field of climate change, there are a few government projects in renewable energy and data sharing and management.

These demand-side policies face several barriers. First, demand-side measures do not completely align with and complement supply-side measures. Although public procurement in the defense, space, and other civilian sectors, such as urban development, has created a good deal of demand for innovation, enterprises suffer from underdeveloped technological capabilities. For instance, standardization in electrical appliances is not practiced widely, and wherever standardization exists, regulatory measures are not implemented or enforced. A similar situation exists with food and restaurant hygiene and food safety measures. Second, the level of funds allocated to demand-side measures is well short of requirements. The Government of India has realized that there is a need to devise a strategy that can exploit the full potential of such measures. Hence, a formal and systematic effort to capture various dimensions of both the demand-side and the supply-side innovation measures through the undertaking of a national innovation survey, which includes questions on the use of regulations, tax incentives, and the impact of soft loans, is being conducted (Krishna, 2011).

SCIENTIFIC AND TECHNOLOGICAL PLAN

United States

The contributions to science and technology and invention and innovation through most of the twentieth century by US government laboratories, such as Lawrence Livermore National Laboratory, Los Alamos National Laboratory,

Lawrence Berkeley National Laboratory, Sandia National Laboratories, Oak Ridge National Laboratory, Argonne National Laboratory, Brookhaven National Laboratory, Fermi National Accelerator Laboratory, Naval Research Laboratory, and Jet Propulsion Laboratory, along with those by US government agencies such as NASA, DARPA, NSF, NIH, NBS, and NIST, are well known and well documented. While these have played a huge role in the industrial and economic success of the United States for most of the twentieth century, the question remains, does the United States have a coordinated science and technology policy and does it allocate the necessary funding to keep the United States at the forefront of science and technology-based innovation and entrepreneurship in the twenty-first century?

US sentiment towards a coordinated government science and technology policy to support innovation and entrepreneurship is captured very effectively in the following excerpts from the National Academy of Sciences Report, "Rising to the Challenge, US Innovation Policy for the Global Economy" (Committee on Comparative National Innovation Policies: Best Practice for the 21st Century, Board on Science, Technology, and Economic Policy, Policy and Global Affairs, 2012):

> *Formulating policy to shore up competitiveness of the US is complicated by the fact that the US is one of the few industrialized nations whose policymakers have traditionally not thought strategically about the composition of the nation's economy.... Since World War II, U.S. science and technology policy has been conducted under the assumption that federally funded basic research will be translated by the private sector into commercial products and new U.S. industries.... But the popular mythology that the American economy has thrived for decades under solely a laissez-faire tradition and linear approach to innovation policy tends to discount both the complexity of innovation and the vigorous government role in the development and deployment of new technologies.... It is not just policies directly addressing the development and deployment of new technologies but also policies concerning tax, trade, intellectual property, education and training, and immigration, among others that play a role in innovation. In an age where Internet content is increasingly important to the economy, a broad range of skills is needed to secure American capabilities in innovation and competitiveness.*

Rather than try to summarize the state of affairs with a science and technology plan in the United States, we further quote the report that goes on to succinctly summarize the state of innovation policy in the United States and the challenges ahead:

> *In this highly competitive environment, the U.S. needs, once again, to devote policy attention and resources to the process of innovation because our future competitiveness as a nation is at stake. This commitment is needed if high paying jobs in sufficient numbers are to be created and if America's security is to be assured.*

*The U.S. must understand and urgently address the underlying factors that may be
weakening industries in which we might well compete. The world of innovation is
undergoing rapid and significant change, and America must change with it if the
nation is to continue to prosper. . . .*

*. . .But what exactly should a national innovation policy look like and aim to
achieve? In its essence, innovation is the alchemy of transforming ideas into new
goods, services, and processes. Fortunately, the United States remains very strong
in innovation as it is generally referred to—having ideas that have economic value
to the inventors and in many cases other social value. Yet to create substantial
value for the U.S. economy, policy must seek to achieve more than to encourage
discovery and invention. America's tremendous investments in research and
development cannot just be seen as a global public good. The fruits of innovation
should translate into new marketable products, companies, industries, and jobs—
and better living standards for Americans. There was a time when the proximity of
U.S. companies' production to U.S. researchers was sufficient to give U.S. companies a big advantage that made speed less critical. Modern information and
communications technologies have greatly reduced the significance of proximity,
and many countries are taking actions to increase the pace of innovation. Understanding how this process works—and how it can be advanced with public
policy—is no simple task.*

In the United States, a viable science and technology policy that spurs innovation and entrepreneurship and restores American competitiveness remains a
work in progress with significant challenges ahead, given the strongly divergent
views on the role of government in business and the resultant dysfunction and
political gridlock in Washington.

China

A large number of scientific programs are a very important display of Chinese
innovation policies. In the 1980s, the National Transformation Plan, the
National Key Technology Development Project, the Key Technologies R&D
Program, the National Key Laboratory Program, National High-tech R&D Program (863 program), and the National Torch Plan were put forward to promote
technology innovation. In the 1990s, more attention was paid to the use of science and technology policies to transform scientific and technological achievements into productivity. It was in this context that the National Key Science and
Technology Achievement Promotion Plan, National Science and Technology
Infrastructure Program and Production and Research Joint Development Project, and National Basic Research Program of China (973 program) were put
into place. Besides, Environment Building for S&T Industries and Mega-
projects of Science Research for the 10th Five-year Plan also played a great role
to promote innovation (http://www.most.gov.cn/kjjh/gjkjjh/).

A summary of the funds invested by the Chinese central government in main scientific and technological programs is shown in Table 5.1. Here, the three largest programs that the government invested in are the National Natural Science Fund, the Key Technologies R&D Program, and the Innovation Fund for Small Technology-based Firms. The three top programs with increasing investment are the State Key Laboratory Construction Program, the International S&T Cooperation Program, and the National Basic Research Program of China. And there is only one program, the S&T Basic Work program, where the investment decreased from ¥200 M in 2001 to ¥155 M in 2010.

India

India introduced four main policies to promote science, technology, and innovation. India's Scientific Policy Resolution of 1958 focused on fostering science and scientific research. The Technology Policy Statement of 1983 emphasized the need to attain technological competence and self-reliance. The Science and Technology Policy 2003 brought science and technology together for investment in R&D to address national problems and to create a National Innovation System. To further synergize science, technology, and innovation, India has declared 2010–2020 as the decade of innovation, and it aims to set up 14 national centers to achieve this goal.

A National Innovation Council has been constituted, which has been tasked to formulate a roadmap for innovations by creating a framework for evolving an Indian model of inclusive growth, develop and champion innovative attitudes and approaches, identify ways and means to scale and sustain innovations, facilitate innovations by SMEs, and encourage academic and R&D establishments for innovations. The council will also promote the setting up of state- and sector-specific innovation councils that will help implement strategies for innovation. The most recent Science, Technology and Innovation (STI) Policy 2013 envisions the involvement of the entire Indian scientific community, in both the private domain and the public domain in achieving *faster, sustainable, and inclusive development of people* through *science, technology, and innovation.* The aim of the policy, therefore, is to redefine innovation to go beyond formal R&D parameters and facilitate innovative solutions that lead to inclusive growth for the people and by the people. A strong and viable Science, Research and Innovation system for High Technology led path for India (SRISHTI) are the goals for the STI policy.

The policy also seeks the right sizing of gross expenditure on research and development by encouraging and incentivizing private sector participation in R&D, technology, and innovation activities. It aims to trigger an ecosystem for innovative abilities to flourish by leveraging partnerships among diverse stakeholders and by encouraging and facilitating enterprises to invest in innovation. It also seeks to encourage mechanisms for achieving gender parity in STI activities and to gain global competitiveness in select technology areas

TABLE 5.1 Appropriation for S&T by Central Government in the Main Programs of S&T (M yuan)

Item	2001	2005	2006	2007	2008	2009	2010
National Natural Science Fund	1598	2701	3620	4331	5359	6427	10381
National Basic Research Program of China (973 Program)	589	983	1354	1646	1900	2600	4000
Key Technologies R&D Program	1053	1624	2888	5423	5066	5000	5000
National Science and Technology Infrastructure Program	–	573	754	686	23	21	–
State Key Laboratory Construction Program	130	134	216	1600	2168	2917	2759
National Engineering Research Centers	50	60	84	86	–	103	105
S&T Basic Work	200	–	103	178	150	150	155
Spark Program	100	117	102	150	200	219	200
Torch Program	70	70	108	139	152	228	220
National New Products Program	140	140	139	140	150	200	200
Innovation Fund for Small Technology-based Firms	783	988	843	1256	1621	3484	4297
Agricultural Science and Technology Transfer Fund	400	300	300	300	300	400	500
International S&T Cooperation Program	100	180	300	300	400	500	1302
Special Technology Development Project for Research Institutions	158	186	200	250	250	250	250

Sources: China Statistics Year Book, 2002-2011

through international cooperation and alliances. India specifically endeavors to address the challenges of energy and environment, food and nutrition, water and sanitation, habitat, affordable health care, and skill building and employment through these efforts.

The following box outlines some of the prominent programs of the Government of India for promotion of innovation.

Technology Development and Demonstration Program (TDDP)
The DSIR under its plan scheme "Technology Promotion Development and Utilization" (TDPU) is promoting industry's efforts in technology development and demonstration of indigenous technologies and absorption of imported technologies so as to stimulate innovation in SMEs that are environment-friendly. Over 150 technologies supported under TDDP are from a variety of industries ranging from metallurgy; to electrical and electronics, instrumentation, and mechanical engineering; to earthmoving and industrial machinery; to chemicals, explosives, drugs and pharmaceuticals, and food processing. The total cost of these projects is Rs. 4 B and the government's share is around Rs. 600–700 M.

Technopreneur Promotion Programme (TePP)
TePP, a program jointly operated by the DST and DSIR from 1998, aims at promoting grassroots innovators such as farmers, students, housewives, scientists, engineers, doctors, and technicians who have an original idea or invention or knowhow to become technology-based entrepreneurs (technopreneurs).

New Millennium Indian Technology Leadership Initiatives (NMITLI)
The NMITLI is the largest R&D scheme that operates in partnership among R&D institutions, academia, and private industry with government finances playing a catalytic role. Forty-two R&D projects covering diverse areas, involving 287 partners with an estimated outlay of Rs. 3 B, have been implemented under this initiative.

Technology Development Board
In order to develop and commercially apply indigenous technology or to adapt imported technology to wider domestic applications, the Government of India provides financial assistance in the form of either equity capital or soft loans or grants through the Technology Development Board. This assistance is provided to industrial units, R&D laboratories, universities, and academic institutions.

Technology Parks
Technology parks enable interaction of groups of academic and research institutions and groups of industries and financial institutions to work in harmony to evolve new technologies starting from inventions. There are 45 software technology parks in existence set up by the Ministry of Information and Communication Technology (MICT).

Programs by Technology Information Forecasting and Assessment Council (TIFAC)
TIFAC under the DST has launched several schemes such as Relevance and Excellence in AChieving new heights in educational institutions (REACH), Sugar Production Technology Mission aimed at providing technology upgrade of selected sugar factories, Advanced Composites Mission for indigenous development of composite

products, and Fly Ash Mission supporting projects towards confidence building in fly ash disposal/utilization technology.

Pharmaceutical Research and Development Support Fund (PRDSF) Program
This program aims to facilitate new drug development and to stimulate skill development of human resources in R&D for drugs and pharmaceuticals and to enhance the nation's self-reliance in drugs and pharmaceuticals sector especially in areas critical to the national health requirement.

Instrumentation Development Program
National Instrument Development Board (NIDB) was constituted for capacity building and development of instruments in the country in areas such as Analytical Instrumentation, Sensors and Allied Instrumentation, Medical Instrumentation and Healthcare Systems, and Industrial Instrumentation.

Small Business Innovation Research Initiative (SBIRI)
The DBT through SBIRI supports high-societal-relevance projects ranging from high-risk, preproof-of-concept research to late-stage development in small- and medium-scale companies led by innovators with science background.

Other promotional programs
Several R&D projects have been initiated and/or supported by the Ministry of Information Technology through Technology Development Council, the National Radar Council, the National Microelectronics Council, and Electronic Materials Development Council. Funding R&D in Electronics in industry (FRIEND) is one more such initiative.

For peaceful applications of atomic energy and for generating technologies in atomic energy and nuclear energy, the Department of Atomic Energy has established horizontal linkages with industry. Power generation equipment and radio-pharmaceutical and radioimmunoassay kits for nuclear medicine are examples of such linkages. Several spin-off technologies from the department have been transferred to both private and public sectors in the areas of electronics, nuclear and radiation instruments, superconductivity, robotics, computers, lasers, electron beam welding, high vacuum and plasma systems, chemical and metallurgical processes, biosciences, etc.

The Department of Space has transferred over 200 technologies from 1983 to 1997, and through its Sponsored Research (RESPOND) program, the Indian space program has supported 300 research projects at 80 institutions, including universities, IITs, national laboratories, regional engineering colleges, and public sector industries. The Department of Space through its commercial venture "Antrix Corporation Ltd" transfers technology and provides consultancy services in India and export of space products and services.

The Ministry of Environment & Forests operates several research programs such as Man and Biosphere, Environmental Research Program, Action Oriented Research Programme for Eastern and Western Ghats, and Climate Change.

The Ministry of New and Renewable Energy, Department of Mines, and Ministry of Steel are other ministries that have instituted programs and initiatives to promote and support new technologies and R&D.

Source: *DSIR website.*

The following table, Table 5.2, gives an overview of the innovation budgets of the main departments and agencies of the Government of India as reported in a mini country report on India by INNO-Policy TrendChart with ERAWATCH. Except for the DST, the DSIR, and the DBT, formal announcements of innovation policy measures have not been made by government departments, although various departments and ministries are involved in innovation and commercialization of research-related activities. Individual innovation program

TABLE 5.2 Innovation Budgets of the Main Departments and Agencies of the Government of India

Name of the Organization	Number of Staff Responsible for Innovation Measures (% of Total)	Innovation Budget Managed	Estimated Share of Budget Earmarked for Specific Policy Measures
Department of Science and Technology (DST) http://www.dst.gov.in/	10%	15% of total budget	About 5% of total budget
Department of Scientific and Industrial Research (DSIR) http://dsir.nic.in/	12%	15% of total budget	About 10% of total budget
Department of Biotechnology (DBT) http://dbtindia.nic.in/index.asp	5%	20% of total budget	About 10% of total budget
Indian Space Research Organisation, Department of Space http://www.isro.org/	20%	25% of total budget	NA
Department of Atomic Energy http://www.dae.gov.in/	15%	NA	NA
Department of Telecommunications http://www.dot.gov.in/	10%	10%	3–4%

Continued

TABLE 5.2 Innovation Budgets of the Main Departments and Agencies of the Government of India—Cont'd

Name of the Organization	Number of Staff Responsible for Innovation Measures (% of Total)	Innovation Budget Managed	Estimated Share of Budget Earmarked for Specific Policy Measures
Ministry of New and Renewable Energy http://www.mnre.gov.in/	5%	20%	15%
Department of Information Technology http://www.mit.gov.in/	5%	20%	About 10%
National Innovation Foundation (NIF) http://www.nif.org.in/	40%	60%	About 25%
Ministry of Health and Family Welfare http://mohfw.nic.in/	3%	15%	10%

budget estimates are available for these departments, but an overall budget estimate for innovation is not available (Krishna, 2011).

Figure 5.1 gives a pictorial description of various government departments involved in R&D and innovation. Although the government has been playing a proactive role in R&D in India, it has to take steps to increase R&D efforts and the impact of public R&D expenditures and to strengthen commercialization of knowledge in order to fully exploit India's R&D potential.

Some of the actions suggested by Dahlman et al. (2007) and Krishna (2011) in this direction are:

(i) reviewing existing Early-Stage Technology Development (ESTD) programs so as to introduce measures to consolidate and expand such programs;
(ii) increasing resources for civilian research as most of the public R&D is not civilian-oriented;
(iii) providing more support for university R&D;
(iv) strengthening initiatives to commercialize publicly funded R&D by setting up a robust technology transfer mechanism for pubic R&D

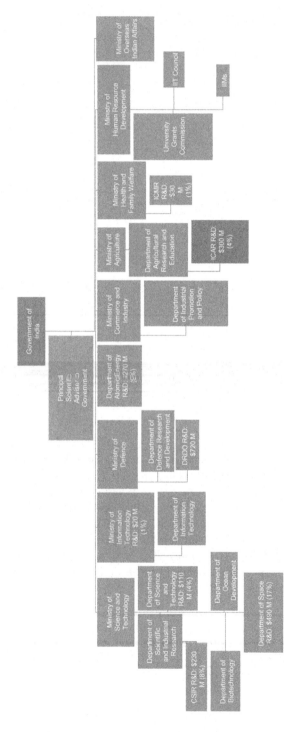

FIGURE 5.1 Key public institutions involved in R&D and R&D expenditure 2003–2004. *(Source: Dahlman et al. (2007).)*

institutions and for promoting mobility between public R&D labs, universities, and industry;
- (v) replicating the success of Software Technology Parks of India (STPI) and setting up more technology parks and incubators for other industries;
- (vi) creating an appropriate institutional environment for innovation within ministries and departments by increasing number of staff members devoted to innovation and related activities and implementing appropriate human resource development policies;
- (vii) introducing risk capital and venture capital funds for innovation across various R&D and S&T institutions;
- (viii) creating and supporting a global industrial partnership program.

INTERNATIONAL INNOVATION SYSTEM

International innovation linkages are being built in India in various ways. Several Indian entrepreneurs educated and employed in the United States have been able to create a cultural bridge between the East and the West by being able to navigate through the bureaucratic, linguistic, and logistical barriers that Western firms face in doing business in India (Ptak and Bagchi-Sen, 2011). There are no specific policy measures for internationalization of innovation policies, but the Ministry of External Affairs in consultation with the Prime Minister's Office plans most of the initiatives. Joint initiatives in cooperation with other countries (foreign participation, cross-border innovation support measures, and venture capital) are mainly confined to "big science" as part of the FP7[3] with EU and construction of nuclear plants with Russia, France, and the United States. Examples of such initiatives are the United States–India defense relationship for procurement and production, the US–India Bi-National Science and Technology Endowment for sponsoring joint research projects for industrial potential, the US–India Knowledge Initiative on Agriculture for raising agricultural productivity in India, and the Agreement on Civil Nuclear Energy Cooperation for creating more environmentally friendly energy technologies (Ptak and Bagchi-Sen, 2011). Most of the R&D links established by Indian institutions with the MNCs are "adaptive" rather than "creative" in nature. There is a lot of opportunity for India to build and consolidate more such linkages.

THE INFLUENCE OF RENT-SEEKING AND CORRUPTION

The phenomenon of rent-seeking in connection with monopolies was first formally identified in 1967 by Gordon Tullock. A simple definition of rent-seeking is spending resources in order to gain by increasing one's share of existing wealth, instead of trying to create new wealth. The net effect of rent-seeking is to reduce total social wealth, because resources are spent on existing wealth

---

3. 7th Framework Program for Research and Technological Development.

and no new wealth is created. From the view of the economy, this kind of activity uses scare resources to serve nonproductive targets and can cause nonproductive income to expel productive income.

China

After China's reform and opening up, on the one hand, forces of the free market economy continued to improve, and, on the other hand, the government continued to play a leading role in economic development. So, this type of a dual system helped propel innovation within enterprises but, at the same time, also was the cause of enterprises engaging in rent-seeking activity. Government had the right to intervene in the activities of the enterprise, but could not provide the public infrastructure required by a mature market and necessary for economic development. So, entrepreneurs had to buy such services by using unfair means. In the late 1990s, with improvement in ownership structure and increased anti-corruption activity, government's ability to control resources and its administrative approval authority were greatly limited. This greatly stimulated enthusiasm of entrepreneurs to engage in productive activities. But after 2000, government at all levels was involved in microeconomic activities, relying on its power of distributing resources, like the right to the use of land and the right to gain financial support. As a result, most projects were done primarily for window dressing, for maintaining an image, and for showcasing achievement for political reasons. In this environment, entrepreneurs who had cultivated cozy relations with government officials benefitted. For example, in many places, entrepreneurs spent a great deal of their time currying favors with local officials, rather than on technological innovation or product promotion. So, it is apparent that, in China, the opportunity for rent-seeking is huge, and it has been much easier for enterprises to prosper by taking advantage of policies rather than through innovation.

The negative impact of rent-seeking can be interpreted as follows. First, misuse of capital can lead to a paucity of funds for innovation. For example, during 2006–2007, the Chinese stock market and real estate markets were booming and were very profitable. Many nonfinancial enterprises invested their manufacturing capital into stocks, real estate, and futures resulting in a shortage of funds for innovation and production. Second, perceived unfairness in government support drives down the motivation to innovate. A number of companies in a few key industries received significant government support during their inception. This support took the form of capital, tax incentives, policy preference, and marketing and promotional support. Although these companies survived and grew quickly, they lacked innovation, because they did not have to struggle for survival, which often forces creativity and innovation in companies in an efficient, free market-driven economy. Companies without these privileges often lost because of this type of unfair competition from some of the larger companies. Also, since government support was readily available, some of these companies chose to imitate and be followers instead of leaders in innovation. This was driven by the fact that government's goal in supporting these companies was primarily their survival rather than support of innovation. So, essentially, the market was in a state of disorder and resources were not being allocated effectively to the most efficient enterprises, in order to ensure the survival of only the most efficient businesses (Liu, 2008).

India

In the case of India, in spite of a vibrant democracy, Indian politicians and bureaucrats enjoy high discretionary powers. Elected and nonelected officials in India have a vested interest in not granting independent powers to entities that are not inherently dependent on the government for their existence. This is a source of secrecy, delays, monopoly, abuse of bureaucratic discretion and power, and nontransparency. Businesses in India can only respond by acting illegally, and Indian businessmen and -women have shown a keen aptitude for independently finding devious routes to private profit at the expense of other firms. Petty corruption and harassment in urban areas, to where the rural poor migrate to seek economic improvement for their households, suppress the productive potential of labor. Moreover, major departments of public service in India are ridden with corruption that tends to deny access to education, medical services, justice, or protection to those without resources. All these factors impact economic growth adversely (Heston and Kumar, 2008).

Corruption has emerged as a national concern in India, and there is an overwhelming sense of how, if not dealt with efficiently, it might undermine India's visions of itself as articulated in VISION 2020 or India Shining campaign, at both the national and international levels. Various estimates of the size of the parallel economy in India range between 50 and 65% of the total economy. The state, the citizens, and the market are denouncing the widespread reach of corruption, and different groups are asking for strong measures against corruption in India (Nishant, 2012). Waldemar (2011) used a World Bank Enterprise Surveys from India with 1600 firms in 2005 and found that corruption, functioning as a bribery tax, diminishes the probability of new product introduction and has a negative impact on product innovation.

United States

This is an area where the United States has a decided advantage over China and India. As discussed earlier in the IPR section, a legal framework for respecting IP and hence the associated legal rent-seeking has long existed in the United States and has worked very well. Unfair rent-seeking through undue concentration of market power through monopolies that occur naturally or through mergers and acquisitions has been prevented in the United States through antitrust laws administered through the Federal Trade Commission (FTC) or the DOJ and is discussed in detail in a later chapter.

As discussed below, rent-seeking through corruption at various levels of government bureaucracies does not exist in the United States, in stark contrast to that in China and India. However, while it cannot be categorized as corruption, rent-seeking by industry sectors as well as by specific private enterprises, for financial gains of the sector or of the enterprise, sometimes at the expense of what might be construed as the "general good" of society at large, through what is politely known as "lobbying" in Washington DC has been and continues to be fairly common practice. However, this is the price of governing and living in a democratic society and a free market economy and in most instances far preferable to the constraints and shortcomings associated with an autocratic government or a centrally managed economy, which is typically characterized by far more inefficiency and plagued by corruption, and is discussed below.

The level of rent-seeking is closely tied to the institutional environment and the degree of control exercised by the government. These are reflected in the level of "voice and accountability," a measure of individual freedom and accountability, and the level of corruption. The level of voice and accountability in China, the United States, India, and the OECD are shown in Fig. 5.2. Note that in this measure, expressed as a percentile, a large number indicates a high degree of individual freedom and accountability. What is immediately obvious from the figure is the stark contrast in these numbers between those for China and those for the other regions shown.

In the case of China, the percentile rank was 12 in 1996, and that decreased to 5.2 in 2010. For the United States, the percentile rank also decreased a little, from 91.8 in 2002 to 87.2 in 2010. This percentile rank for India also decreased a little from 62 in 1996 to 59.2 in 2010. The OECD average percentile rank was the highest, at 92.1 in 1996 and 91.1 in 2010. In the above countries and regions, China had the lowest level in voice and accountability, and India was in the second to last place. Yet there was a significant difference in this measure between

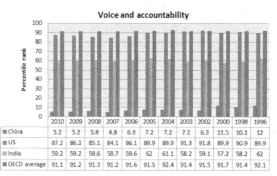

FIGURE 5.2   Voice and accountability in the United States, China, India, and the OECD. *(Source: http://info.worldbank.org/governance/wgi/sc_country.asp.)*

India and China—in 2010, the percentile rank of India was 17.5 times that of China—indicating a much higher level of individual freedom and accountability in India.

The level of corruption in China, the United States, India, and the OECD is shown in Fig. 5.3. In this measure, both India and China fare poorly in relation to the United States and the OECD countries. In China, the percentile rank was 43 in 1996 and reached its highest level of 50 in 2000. For the United States, the measure was at its highest at 92 in 2002 and at its lowest at 86 in 2010. This percentile rank in India decreased from its highest of 48 in 2006 to its lowest of 36 in 2010. The OECD fared quite well as well with levels comparable to those of the United States. Among the countries and regions in this chart, China and India show extremely high levels of corruption.

In summary, this chapter brings out some significant differences between China and India, on the one hand, in contrast to the United States on the other hand as it relates to the infrastructure of laws and regulations and the role of government institutions and their impact on innovation. A legal structure for the protection of IPR, while it still continues to evolve, has existed in the United States for a very long time and has played a key role through the industrialization of the United States as in other Western countries, whereas it is fairly recent in China and India and its success and impact are yet to be realized. While they played a role in earlier years, tax policies and government procurement for promotion of innovation in the United States as compared to that in China have not been very significant. In the case of India, the tax policies have been moderately effective in the targeted sectors.

In a broader context, there is more recent recognition in the United States for a comprehensive US policy that coordinates science and technology and innovation, if the United States is to regain its competitive edge in relation to China

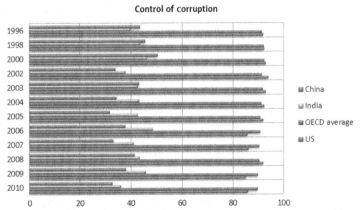

FIGURE 5.3 Control of corruption in the United States, China, India, and the OECD. *(Sources: http://info.worldbank.org/governance/wgi/sc_country.asp.)*

and India, where governments are heavily involved in shaping policies that affect innovation. The question for the United States, however, is given the political dysfunction and lack of consensus in Washington, does it have the political will to craft such a policy that will be acceptable to all involved and yet keep national interests in mind. Although the Indian government has been playing a proactive role in promoting innovation, the impact of its efforts is not optimal either in relation to the progress being made in this regard in China. This is because the approach of the Indian government has generally been paternalistic and directive rather than enabling (Rajan, 2006). A silver lining for the United States, however, is in the area of a fairly effective, efficient, mature, and sophisticated administrative and legal infrastructure free of corruption, for the most part—an area that is a significant malaise in China and India with the long-term potential of negating gains made in other areas.

REFERENCES

Acemoglu, D., Johnson, S., Robinson, J., 2001. The colonial origins of comparative development: an empirical investigation. Am. Econ. Rev. 5, 1369–1401.

Billings, B.A., 2003. Are US tax incentives for corporate R&D likely to motivate American firms to perform research abroad? Tax Exec. 7–8, 291–315.

Bozeman, B., Link, A., 1984. Tax incentives for R&D: a critical evaluation. Res. Policy 13, 21–31.

Bozeman, B., Link, A., 1985. Public support for private R&D: the case of the research tax credit. J. Policy Anal. Manage. 4, 370–382.

Chaudhary, A., Garner, P., 2007. Do governments suppress growth? Institutions, rent-seeking, and innovation blocking in a model of Schumpeterian growth. Econ. Polit. 19 (1), 35–52.

Chaudhuri, S., et al., 2010. Five Years into the Product Patent Regime: India's Response. UNDP.

China Youth Daily, May 5, 2004. http://zqb.cyol.com/gb/zqb/2004-05/05/content_866158.htm (accessed 05.05.04).

Committee on Comparative National Innovation Policies: Best Practice for the 21st Century, Board on Science, Technology, and Economic Policy, Policy and Global Affairs, 2012. Wessner, C.-W., Wolff, A.Wm. (Eds.), Rising to the challenge, U.S. Innovation Policy for the Global Economy. National Research Council, The National Academies Press, Washington, DC.

Coriat, B., Orsi, F., 2002. Establishing a new intellectual property rights regime in the United States: origins, content and problems. Res. Policy 31 (8–9), 1491–1507.

Dahlman, C., et al., 2007. Creating and commercializing knowledge. In: Dutz, M.A. (Ed.), Unleashing India's Innovation—Towards Sustainable and Inclusive Growth. The World Bank, Washington, DC, pp. 49–82.

Ding, X., Gao, Z., 2009. Economy Laws. China Business Publishing House.

Edler, J., Georghiou, L., 2007. Public procurement and innovation—resurrecting the demand side. Res. Policy 36 (7), 949–963www.sciencedirect.com.

Feng, J., Huang, S., 2009. An economic analysis of patent enforcement rate and its influential factors. Res. Inst. Econ. 4 (4), 21–39.

Geroski, P.A., 1990. Procurement policy as a tool of industrial policy. Int. Rev. Appl. Econ. 4 (2), S.182–S.198.

Gilbert, R., Shapiro, C., 1990. Optimal patent length and breadth. RAND J. Econ., Spring 21 (1), 106–112.

Hall, B.H., 1993. R&D tax policy during the eighties: success or failure. Working Papers in Economics E 93-1. The Hoover Institution, Stanford University.

Hall, R.E., Jones, C.I., 1999. Why do some countries produce so much more output per worker than others? Q. J. Econ. 1, 83–116.

Heston, A., Kumar, V., 2008. Institutional flaws and corruption incentives in India. J. Dev. Stud. 44 (9), 1243–1261.

Klemperer, P., 1990. How broad should the scope of patent protection be? RAND J. Econ. 21 (1), 113–130.

Krishna, V.V., December 2011. Mini country report/India. INNO Policy TrendChart and ERAWATCH.

Lee, J., Muro, M., 2012. Cut to invest—make the research & experimentation tax credit permanent. Brookings Metropolitan Policy Program.

Li, G., Zhou, X., 2003. Study on Support System for SME in China. Economic Science Press, Beijing.

Liu, X., 2002. On China's Policies to Promote SME Development. J. Nanjing Univ. (Philos. Humanit. Soc. Sci.) 39 (6), 134–142.

Liu, Q., 2008. Economic Analysis of Rent-seeking Behavior. Huazhong University Press, September.

Lu, L., Sheng, S., 2002. Tech SMEs: Environment and Countermeasures. China Economic Publishing House, Beijing.

Mani, S., 2008. Financing industrial innovations in India, how effective are tax incentives for R&D? In: Conference on Micro Evidence on Innovation in Developing Economies (MEIDE). UNU-MERIT.

Mowery, D., Rosenberg, N., 1979. The influence of market demand upon innovation: a critical review of some recent empirical studies. Res. Policy 8 (2), 102–153.

Mueller, J.M., 2006. The tiger awakens: the tumultuous transformation of India's patent system and the rise of indian pharmaceutical innovation. University of Pittsburgh School of Law Working Paper Series.

Nishant, S., 2012. Resisting revolutions: questioning the radical potential of citizen action. Development 55 (2), 173–180.

Niu, H., 2004. Tax incentives and SME risk investment. Chin. Circ. Econ. 2004, 3, 40–43.

Nordhaus, W.D., 1969. An economic theory of technological change. Am. Econ. Rev. 59 (2), 18–28.

North, D., Thomas, R., 1973. The Rise of the Western World. Cambridge University Press, Cambridge, UK.

Ptak, S., Bagchi-Sen, S., 2011. Innovation systems in emerging economies: the case of India. In: Cooke, P., Asheim, B., Boschma, R., Martin, R., Schwartz, D., Tödtling, F. (Eds.), The Handbook of Regional Innovation and Growth. Edward Elgar, Cheltenham, pp. 419–433.

Rajan, R., 2006. From paternalistic to enabling. Finance Dev. 43 (3), 54–56.

Ramasubramanian, 2009. Evolution of Intellectual Property Protection and Implications for India, http://www.altacit.com/pdf/evolutionofipprotection.pdf (accessed 31.01.13).

Research Team of Institute of Finance and Trade Economics, 2002. Analyses to China hi-tech patent application and innovation. Econ. Res. 7, 24–32

Rosenberg, N., Birdzell Jr., L.E., 1986. How the West Grew Rich: The Economic Transformation of the Industrial World. Basic Books, New York.

Rothwell, R., 1984. Technology based small firms and regional innovation potential: the role of public procurement. J. Public Policy 4 (4), 307–332.

Rothwell, R., Zegveld, W., 1981. Government regulations and innovation—industrial innovation and public policy, London. In: Rothwell, R., Zegveld, W. (Eds.), Industrial Innovation and Public Policy, London. Greenwood Press, Westport, CT, pp. 116–147.

Saha, R., 2006. Management of intellectual property rights. Department of Science and Technology and Director, Patent Facilitating Centre, TIFAC. http://www.pfc.org.in/workshop/workshop.pdf (accessed 12.02.13).

Sampat, B.N., 2006. Patenting and US academic research in the 20th century: the world before and after Bayh-Dole. Res. Policy 35, 772–789.

Surrey, S., 1969. Tax incentives: conceptual criteria for identification and comparison with direct government expenditures. In: Proceedings of the Tax Institute of America.pp. 20–21.

Tassey, G., 1996. Choosing government R&D policies: tax incentives vs. direct funding. Rev. Ind. Organiz. 11, 579–600.

Tassey, G., 2007a. Tax incentives for innovation: time to restructure the R&E tax credit. Technol. Transfer 32, 605–615.

Tassey, G., 2007b. The Technology Imperative. Edward Elgar, London.

Economics and Statistics Administration, United States Patent and Trademark Office and US Department of Commerce, 2012. Intellectual Property and the U.S. Economy: Industries in Focus.

The White House and the Department of the Treasury, 2012. The President's Framework for Business Tax Reform. U.S. Department of the Treasury.

Treasury Secretary of Ministry of Finance, 2002. The national government procurement was over ¥65.3 B in 2001. China Government Procurement.

Waldemar, F.S., 2011. New products and corruption: evidence from Indian firms. CES Working Paper. http://halshs.archives-ouvertes.fr/docs/00/59/50/48/PDF/11033.pdf (accessed 15.02.13).

Xiong, J., Chen, R., Yang, P., 2011. Research on USA government procurement policies to support domestic enterprises. China State Finance, 20, 65–67.

Zeng, G., 2001. Tax policy and enterprise technology innovation. Finance Trade Econ. 3, 34–39.

Zhang, J., 2007. A research on the opening of china government procurement market. Doctor Degree Paper. University of International Business and Economics, July, pp. 70, 77.

Zhang, H., Peng, C., Cheng, W., 2009. USA government science and technology policy and its implications for the economy. Forum Sci. Technol. China, 3, 7–15.

Zheng, C., 1986. The General Theory of Intellectual Property Law. Law Press Publishing.

Chapter 6

Demographics

Innovation is impacted by demographics in a number of ways: population size, age and gender, education level, and the level of immigration.

If we assume that useful inventions and innovations are rare, then small isolated societies will have low rates of invention and innovation. In small populations, complex technology will tend to be lost as a result of random loss or incomplete transmission (the Tasmanian effect). Large populations have more inventors and innovators and are more resistant to loss by chance (Richerson et al., 2009).

It is also commonly accepted that younger people are more likely to innovate than older people. Compared to older people, younger people can more quickly come up the learning curve of new technologies and are better able to grasp related knowledge. Besides, innovation is always accompanied by risk. Young people are not as encumbered by social and family responsibilities as their older counterparts and hence are in a position to take more risk. Research has found that older people especially those who are 50 and over prefer to use their innovation skills significantly less than those between ages 20–29 and 40–49 (Lerouge et al., 2005).

Level of education has a very important bearing on innovation as well. People with high levels of education have a higher likelihood of being innovative due to their advanced education and training. This is discussed in more detail in the next chapter.

With regard to immigration, immigrants can make direct contributions to research, and, in addition, immigration can boost innovation indirectly through positive spillovers on fellow researchers, the achievement of critical mass in specialized research areas, and the provision of complementary skills such as management and entrepreneurship (Hunt and Gauthier-Loiselle, 2009). Compared to a foreign-born population of 12% in 2000, 26% of United States-based Nobel Prize recipients from 1990 to 2000 were immigrants (Peri, 2007), as were 25% of founders of public venture-backed US companies in the 1990–2005 period (Anderson and Platzer, 2006) and 25% of founders of new high-tech companies with more than $1 M in sales in 2006 (Wadhwa et al., 2007).

In 2010, the world population was about 6.9 B, with about 26.8% below the age of 15 years, 65.6% between 15 and 64 years old, and 7.6% over 65 years old. In 2001, the population of the United States was 285.08 M and increased by 8.4% to reach 309.05 M by 2010, whereas the population of China increased by 4.6% from 2001 to 2009 going from 1.276 to 1.335 B, while the population of India increased by 17.5% from 1.03 to 1.21 B from 2001 to 2011. Male-to-female gender ratio in China is about 1.06 and 1.064 in India compared to that of 0.97 in the United States. The imbalance in both China and India is due to the preference for a male child, especially in rural areas (World Population Data Sheet, 2010).

A comparison of age distributions in China, India, and the United States is shown in Table 6.1. In the United States, the population of those under the age of 14 years decreased by 2.4% from 1980 to 2009, while in India, it decreased by 8.6% in the corresponding period, and in China, it decreased by 15.1% from 1982 to 2009. For the age group of 15–64, there was only a slight change of 1.2% in the United States, whereas in India, it increased by 7.3%, and in China, it increased by about 11.5%. The population of those over 65 increased by 1.6% in the United States reaching 12.9% of the overall population, and in India, it went up by 1.3% constituting 4.9% of the population, whereas in China, it grew by 3.6% but contributed to only 8.5% of the overall population.

These data suggest that while populations in both the United States and China are aging, it may be aging faster in the United States than in China. This may adversely affect the rate of innovation in the United States in the years to come. While this is not a serious problem in China today, this is likely to become a significant problem in the future, due to the low birth rate in China resulting from the one-child-only policy. In the case of India, most of its population is young, leading to growth and expansion in the labor force as a result of the past high-fertility cohorts (baby boomers) moving into prime working ages. Three forces responsible for the "demographic dividend" in India are (1) reallocation of resources from children to investing in physical capital, job training, technological progress, and stronger institutions; (2) rise in women workforce participation associated with declining fertility; and (3) savings receiving a boost because the incentive to save for longer periods of retirement increases as life expectancies increase (Bloom et al., 2010, Bloom, 2011 in Periyanayagam and Goli, 2012). Economists and demographers attribute India's current economic boom (measured by overall GDP growth) to the demographic dividend arising from the baby boomers of the 1970s and 1980s.

According to a projection by the United Nations, China's working-age population will reach a maximum in 2015, and then the percent of working-age people will start to decline (Fig. 6.1). In addition, the United Nations projects that China's proportion of elderly people over 60 will increase to nearly 28% by 2040, by which time over a quarter of the world's elderly population will live

TABLE 6.1 Change in China's Working-Age Population

Year	Ages 0–14 (%)				Ages 15–64 (%)				Ages 65 and over (%)			
	United States	China	India		United States	China	India		United States	China	India	
1980	22.6	–	39.58		66.1	–	56.86		11.3	–	3.56	
1982	–	33.6	39.29		–	61.5	57.11		–	4.9	3.60	
1990	21.7	27.7	37.96		65.9	66.7	58.26		12.7	5.6	3.79	
2000	21.4	22.9	34.71		66.2	70.1	61.06		12.4	7	4.23	
2003	21	22.1	33.43		66.6	70.4	62.13		12.4	7.5	4.44	
2004	20.8	21.5	33.00		66.8	70.9	62.48		12.4	7.6	4.51	
2005	20.6	20.3	32.58		67	72	62.84		12.4	7.7	4.58	
2006	20.4	19.8	32.16		67.1	72.3	63.19		12.5	7.9	4.65	
2007	20.3	19.4	31.76		67.1	72.5	63.53		12.6	8.1	4.72	
2008	20.2	19	31.36		67	72.7	63.86		12.7	8.3	4.78	
2009	20.2	18.5	30.97		67	73	64.18		12.9	8.5	4.85	

Sources: China Statistics Year Book (2011), United States Statistical Abstract (2012), and World Bank Data (2013).

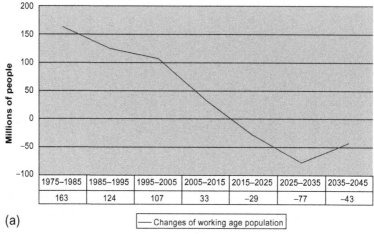

(a)

	1975–1985	1985–1995	1995–2005	2005–2015	2015–2025	2025–2035	2035–2045
	163	124	107	33	–29	–77	–43

— Changes of working age population

FIGURE 6.1   Change in China's working-age population (ages 15–59) by decade. *(Sources: United Nation Population Division, 2006; also, Bergsten et al., 2006.)*

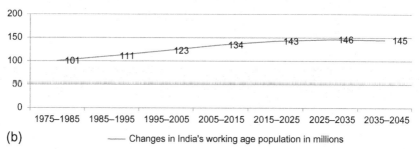

(b)

— Changes in India's working age population in millions

FIGURE 6.2   Change in India's working-age population (ages 15–64) by decade. *(Sources: Untied Nation Population Division, 2004 U.N. data, World Population Prospects: The 2004 Revision Population Database, http://esa.un.org/unpp, accessed January 24, 2006.)*

in China. The projected share of elderly in the population will begin to exceed that of the United States by 2030 (Bergsten et al., 2006). In the case of India (Fig. 6.2), the baby boomers of the current and last two decades are expected to drive the demographic dividend phase through the next three decades, possibly pushing India to the top slot in total GDP outcome during 2040–2050, overtaking Japan, China, and the United States. India will have the advantage of large human capital, as its working-age population will increase in the next 20 years. However, this projection may not be attainable if the quality of this young population is not improved (Periyanayagam and Goli, 2012).

With regard to the level of education, although China has made some progress in recent years, there is a big gap between China and the United States. Shown in Table 6.2 is the number of students per 100,000 of population at different education levels from kindergarten to higher education. The number of kindergarteners has not changed much from 1991 to 2010. The number of

TABLE 6.2 Number of Students at All Levels in China per 100,000 Inhabitants (Unit: Person)

Year	Higher Education	Senior	Junior	Primary	Kindergarten
1991	304	1355	3465	10,502	1907
1992	313	1365	3518	10,413	2072
1993	376	1448	3599	10,656	2190
1994	433	1293	3681	10,819	2219
1995	457	1610	3945	11,010	2262
1996	470	1780	4180	11,273	2208
1997	482	1905	4289	11,435	2058
1998	519	1978	4408	11,287	1944
1999	594	2032	4656	10,855	1864
2000	723	2000	4969	10,335	1782
2001	931	2021	5161	9937	1602
2002	1146	2283	5240	9525	1595
2003	1298	2523	5209	9100	1560
2004	1420	2824	5058	8725	1617
2005	1613	3070	4781	8358	1676
2006	1816	3321	4557	8192	1713
2007	1924	3409	4364	8037	1787
2008	2042	3463	4227	7819	1873
2009	2128	3495	4097	7584	2001
2010	2189	3504	3955	7448	2230

Source: China Statistics Year Book (2011).

primary students, on the other hand, continued to decrease from 1991 to 2010, which is affected by the population structure in China, once again caused by the birth plan policy. The number of junior students went up from 3465 per 100,000 in 1991 to 5240 in 2002 and then down to 3955 in 2010. The number of senior students and students in higher education increased substantially from 1991 to 2010, especially the latter number, which increased 6× during that period. In 2009, 7.12% of the sample people were illiterate, 30.1% had education at the

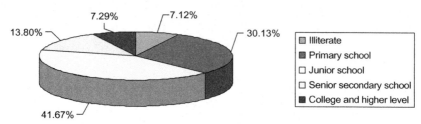

FIGURE 6.3 China's population distribution by education level. *(Source: Educational Statistics Yearbook of China 2010, derived from populations sampling in 2009.)*

Highest level of education attained by a person 25 years or older

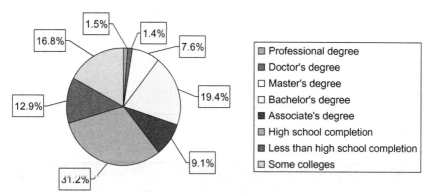

FIGURE 6.4 Population distributions by highest education level a person attained in the United States. *(Sources: Education at a Glance (OECD Indicators) (2010, 2011).)*

level of primary school, 41.7% graduated from junior school, 13.8% reached senior secondary level, and only 7.3% moved on to higher education (Fig. 6.3).

In the United States, only about 12% of the people who were 25–64 did not graduate from high school in 2001, 2005, and 2008 (Fig. 6.4).

In the case of India, overall literacy rate for population aged 7 years and above improved from 65% in 2001 to 74% in 2011. Enrolment of students shot up across all levels of education ranging from primary to higher education. However, the dropouts at primary level are still very high, and the decrease in the level of enrolment from one level to another is significantly large. Therefore, if India has to reap the demographic dividend, far-reaching policy and program initiatives to improve higher education in terms of both reach and quality will be required so that the growing youthful labor force is equipped with the necessary technical and functional skills. At the same time, policy measures will be needed to provide jobs for this burgeoning workforce (Bloom, 2011 in Periyanayagam and Goli, 2012).

According to Organisation for Economic Co-operation and Development (OECD) statistics, in 2009, in the overall 25–64-year-old population with

TABLE 6.3 Percentage of Population 25–64 Years Old in OECD and G20 Countries Who Completed High School or Attained Selected Levels of Postsecondary Education: Selected Years

Year	Completed High School	Vocational Degree	Bachelor's Degree
2001	87.7	9.0	28.3
2005	87.8	–	–
2008	88.7	9.6	31.5

Sources: United States Statistical Abstract (2012) and Education at a Glance (OECD Indicators) (2008, 2010, 2011).

tertiary education in OECD and G20 countries (Table 6.3), China's share was 12.1% and that of the United States was 25.8% (OECD Education at a Glance, 2011). In 2010, among Americans 25 or older, only 12.9% had less than a high school education, and 28.4% were awarded at least a bachelor's degree (Fig. 6.4). In China (Table 6.4), about 80% of the total population had less than a senior high level of education, and only 7.3% had college and higher level education, while in the United States, those numbers were 12% and 60%, respectively, and in India, they were 89% and 3% according to the 2001 census. A whopping 45.5% of Indians 25 years or older were illiterate and 92.9% of them had higher secondary or lower level of education and only 6.5% had a graduate or above qualification (Fig. 6.5). Obviously, there is a huge gap between the United States on the one hand and China and India on the other in literacy levels and levels of education.

In China, by the end of 2008, there were 3.85 M immigrants, accounting for only 0.29% of the total population. On the contrary, more and more people chose to emigrate. As shown in Table 6.5, China lost many students studying abroad. From 2000 to 2010, the average number of students studying abroad was 142,770, and the average number of students coming back after studies abroad was 47,050, that is, less than one-third returned to China (annual data in Table 6.5). The students who returned to China played an important role in Chinese innovation, because they were fluent in English, received top-notch education and experience in the United States, and understood how to conduct international business. For example, Robin Li was a student in the United States who returned to China and set up Baidu, which was better suited for the Chinese market than Google, since it was based on Chinese culture. But, on the flip side, China lost many well-educated and qualified people due to emigration.

According to the bilateral estimates of migrant stock in 2010 computed by the World Bank (Fig. 6.6), 11.36 M Indians are scattered around the world.

TABLE 6.4 Level-Wise Enrollment in Hundred Thousands in China

Year/Level	Primary (I–V)			Upper Primary (VI–VIII)			Secondary/Senior Secondary (IX–XII)			Higher Education		
	Boys	Girls	Total	Boys	Girls	Total	Boys	Girls	Total	Boys	Girls	Total
1950–1951	138	54	192	26	5	31	13	2	15	3.5	0.5	4.0
1960–1961	236	114	350	51	16	67	27	7	34	8	2	10
1970–1971	357	213	570	94	39	133	57	19	76	26	7	33
1980–1981	453	285	738	139	68	207	76	34	110	35	13	48
1990–1991	570	404	974	215	125	340	128	63	191	34	15	49
2000–2001	640	498	1138	253	175	428	169	107	276	54	32	86
2005–2006	705	616	1321	289	233	522	223	161	384	88	55	143
2006–2007	710	627	1337	298	246	544	229	169	398	96	60	156
2007–2008	711	644	1355	310	262	572	252	193	445	106	66	172
2008–2009[P]	700	645	1345	294	260	554	256	199	455	112	73	185
2009–2010[P]	708	648	1356	318	276	594	267	215	482	124	83	207
2010–2011[P]	705	648	1353	328	292	620	283	229	512	155	111	266

P, provisional.

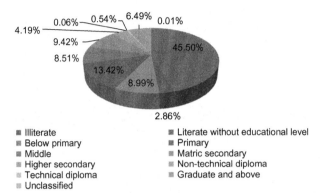

FIGURE 6.5   Higher level of education attained by a person above 25 years of age in India. *(Source: Computed from data of Office of Registrar General of India and Census Commissioner (2001).)*

TABLE 6.5 Number of Chinese Students Studying Abroad and Returning to China

Year	Number of Students Studying Abroad	Number of Students Coming Back after Study
2000	38,989	9121
2001	83,973	12,243
2002	125,179	17,945
2003	117,307	20,152
2004	114,682	24,726
2005	118,515	34,987
2006	134,000	42,000
2007	144,000	44,000
2008	179,800	69,300
2009	229,300	108,300
2010	284,700	134,800

Sources: China Statistics Year Book (2011) and World Bank Data (2013).

According to the OECD, highly skilled professionals account for 51.9% of the Indian diaspora (the corresponding figure for the Chinese diaspora is 39.6%). An analysis of the number of Indian students leaving to study overseas (Fig. 6.7) reveals that over the years, the trend has been increasing steadily with a major portion of them going to the United States. Many of the students in

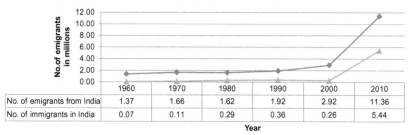

FIGURE 6.6 Bilateral estimates of migrant stocks for India. *(Source: The World Bank, http://databank.worldbank.org/data/views/variableselection/selectvariables.aspx?source=global-bilateral-migration.)*

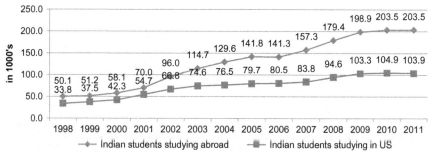

FIGURE 6.7 Indian students studying abroad. *(Source: UNESCO database on International students at tertiary level (ISCED 5 and 6) and http://opendoors.iienetwork.org/.)*

recent years leave with plans to return, and even if they do not return, they collaborate with Indians back in India. The old pattern of one-way flows of technology and capital from the core to the periphery is being replaced by a far more complex and decentralized two-way flow of skill, capital, and technology between differently specialized regional economies. Lower transaction costs associated with knowledge transfers in digital form are an important factor contributing to this trend (Bound, 2007).

These highly skilled immigrants who were once considered a "brain drain" have, therefore, now turned into an advantage for India as Indian ideas and culture have cross-pollinated with cultures overseas and have become an important source for providing intellectual, entrepreneurial, and capital investments in India. Indian innovation is now being driven to a significant extent by these transnational, nonresident Indians (NRIs). The NRI networks have been vital for a number of both start-up and more established companies, providing links to new sources of knowledge and finance in the United States and Europe. These networks help in piloting the entry of multinational companies as it takes an Indian to navigate and negotiate the vagaries of the Indian system.

Secondly, these networks have produced science leaders in that most scientists in top jobs in the best institutes studied and worked abroad. For example, while most PhD students graduating from elite institutions such as the Indian Institute of Science (IISc) in Bangalore leave the country for postdoctoral appointments or employment overseas, many return—some temporarily, while others more permanently—tempted back by new housing, tax breaks, and family connections (Adrian and Scoones, 2011). While this trend may facilitate innovation in India, many criticize it for the creation of hierarchy of science and innovation in that talent raised in India is seen always as inferior to that from abroad.

Thirdly, a new breed of the transnational entrepreneur is creating micro-multinationals—start-ups such as July Systems, Infinera, and InSilica—with sales, marketing, and brand based in the United States but with a back office and technical support in India (Bound, 2007). This circulation of brain and capital power has been in response to emerging private sector and lifestyle opportunities and proactive government measures in formulation of the necessary structures and investor-friendly environment.

The United States, on the other hand, has been a country of immigrants since its inception. From 2000 to 2010, the United States was home to more than 1 M legal immigrants every year except 2003 and 2004. Although the Chinese immigrants originally came to the United States as manual labor, primarily to build railroads, most recent Chinese immigrants to the United States have been knowledge workers. In the twentieth century, about 647,000 Chinese immigrants came to the United States, while the number greatly increased in the twenty-first century, and it was 591,711 in just the 10-year period from 2000 to 2009.[1]

Also, immigrants to the United States include many technical workers, as well as others either who have excellent education from their home countries or who come to the United States for advanced education and stay back. For example, in 2010, the total number of people who obtained permanent resident status was 1,042,625. Of these, approximately 14%, or 148,343, were people with employment-based preferences including priority workers (holders of H1B visa status), a category of workers frequently used by companies such as Google and others, professionals with advanced degrees or foreign nationals with exceptional ability, skilled workers and professionals, and sometimes unskilled workers, certain special immigrants who create employment in the United States (2010 Yearbook of Immigration Statistics, Office of Immigration Statistics). Besides, those students who travel to the United States for education contribute a significant amount to the economy. For example, according to the Association of International Educators, international students and their dependants contributed approximately $21.8 B to the US economy during the 2011–2012 academic year. This economic contribution international students make to the United States to support their education and their living

---

1. http://www.nationmaster.com/country/ch-china/imm-immigration; http://www.migrationinforma tion.org/feature/display.cfm?ID=685.

expenses was made by the National Association of Foreign Student Advisers (NAFSA) annual economic impact analysis. This number excludes any "multiplier effect," the contributions international students make by applying their education, skills, and training to the US economy. If this effect were considered, this contribution would be a lot higher.

In summary, while populations in both the United States and China are aging, it may be aging faster in the United States, due to the aging of the "baby boomer" generation, than in China, further driving the United States to be a nation more of consumers than producers, and this may adversely affect the rate of innovation in the United States in the years to come. This has the potential to create an increasing trend for immigration to the United States of technically skilled professionals or those willing to create innovative new business opportunities. While an aging population is not a serious problem in China today, this is likely to become a significant problem in the future, as China's working-age population will reach its peak in 2015, and then the percent of working-age people will start to decline. The projected share of elderly in the population in China will begin to exceed that of the United States by 2030. India, on the other hand, may have an advantage in this area, since most of its population is young, leading to growth and expansion in the labor force. However, while significant progress has been made over the years, levels of illiteracy are still very high and shares of population educated beyond high school are still very low in China and India compared with that in the United States.

The challenge for the United States, however, is that although it has a high percentage of population that has been through high school, the quality of this education in the United States may be declining relative to other industrialized nations. While China, and especially India, may have an advantage over the United States in terms of the sheer numbers of young population in the years to come, the quality of education and other opportunities available to these people needs to be examined more closely. In the past, the United States has been a magnet for attracting the "brain drain" from China and India, along with immigrants from other parts of the world. Contributions made by this immigrant population are an integral part of the history of innovation, the economy, and the social fabric of the United States. This is expected to continue at perhaps an even more vigorous pace in the future with the aging of the "baby boomer" generation in the United States. However, with the globalization of communication and travel, recent immigrant population in the United States is also contributing, to some extent, to innovation and economic transformations in the countries of their origins.

REFERENCES

Adrian, E., Scoones, I., 2011. The global redistribution of innovation: lessons from China and India. In: DIME Final Conference. Working Papers from the STEPS Centre, Maastricht.
Anderson, S., Platzer, M., 2006. American Made: The Impact of Immigrant Entrepreneurs and Professionals on U.S. Competitiveness. National Venture Capital Association.

Bergsten, C.F., Gill, B., Lardy, N.R., Mitchell, D., 2006. China: The Balance Sheet: What the World Needs to Know About the Emerging Superpower. Public Affairs pp. 46.

Bound, K., 2007. India: The Uneven Innovator. The Atlas of Ideas: Mapping New Geographies of Science. Demos, London.www.demos.co.uk.

China Statistics Year Book, 2011.

Education at a Glance (OECD Indicators), 2008, 2009, 2010, 2011.

Hunt, J., Gauthier-Loiselle, M., 2009. How much does immigration boost innovation? Discussion Paper Series IZA DP No. 3921.

http://www.migrationinformation.org/feature/display.cfm?ID=685. Also, immigrants to the 2010 Yearbook of Immigration Statistics, Office of Immigration Statistics, pp. 18 http://www.nationmaster.com/country/ch-china/imm-immigration.

Lerouge, C., Newton, S., Blanton, J., 2005. Exploring the systems analyst skill set: perceptions, preferences, age, and gender. J. Comput. Inf. Syst. 45 (3), 12–23.

Peri, G., 2007. Higher education, innovation and growth. In: Brunello, G., Garibaldi, P., Wasmer, E. (Eds.), Education and Training in Europe. Oxford University Press, Oxford.

Periyanayagam, A., Goli, S., 2012. Provisional results of the 2011 Census of India—slowdown in growth, ascent in literacy, but more missing girls. Int. J. Soc. Econ. 39 (10), 785–801.

Richerson, P.J., Boyd, R., Bettinger, R.L., 2009. Cultural innovations and demographic change. Hum. Biol. 81 (2), 211–235.

Untied Nation Population Division, 2006. 2004 U.N. data, World population prospects: the 2004 revision population database. http://esa.un.org/unpp (accessed 24.01.06).

United States Statistical Abstract, 2012.

Wadhwa, V., Saxenian, A.L., Rissing, B., Gere, G., 2007. America's new immigrant entrepreneurs. Kauffman Foundation report.

World Bank Data, 2013. http://data.worldbank.org/indicator/SP.POP.1564.TO.ZS/countries/IN?display=default (accessed 30.03.13).

World Population Data Sheet, 2010. Population Reference Bureau; http://www.prb.org/pdf10/10wpds_eng.pdf.

Chapter 7

Education and Universities

Chapter Contents

The general level of education in a country is an important factor that influences innovation. This is especially true in a knowledge-based economy, where the level of innovation is closely related to its intellectual capital, which in turn is tied to the level of education. Studies have found that some measures of human capital, such as secondary and higher education enrollment, the number of science and technology workers in the labor force, and per capita spending on education and science, are significantly related to the growth rate of the economy (Ding and Knight, 2008; Song et al., 2000; Yao and Zhang, 2001). The general level of education also depends on the investment a country makes in education at various levels, all the way from elementary, to high-school, to college and university levels. The number of colleges and universities, and the quality of these institutions, has a significant impact on the output and efficiency of education. Only top-notch institutions and universities attract excellent researchers and teachers and hence can create state-of-the-art learning and research opportunities for students. A country's human capital thus depends on the country's attitude towards education, its educational institutions, education policies, quality of education, and the skill level and dedication of its educators.

EDUCATION EXPENDITURES

China's ratio of education expenditures to GDP grew from 1992 to 2009, but it was still under 5% of GDP in 2009 (Fig. 7.1). In the United States, in 1995,

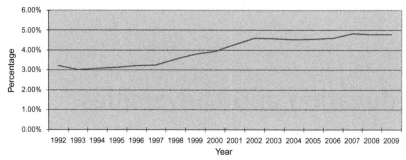

FIGURE 7.1   Ratio of educational expenditure to GDP in China. *(Source: China Statistics Year Book, 2011.)*

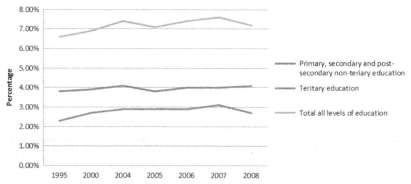

FIGURE 7.2   Ratio of educational expenditure to GDP in the United States. *(Sources: Statistical Abstract of the United States, 2012.)*

expenditures on primary, secondary, and postsecondary nontertiary education were about 3.8% of GDP, tertiary expenditure was about 2.3%, and the total expenditure at all levels was about 6.6%. These ratios did not change much until 2008 (Fig. 7.2).

Compared with the United States, China's education expenditure per student was very low, because China had a lower ratio, a lower GDP, but a much larger number of students. For example, in 2008, in the United States, the annual expenditure per student in preprimary education was $10,070; it was $12,097 for all secondary education, was $29,910 for all tertiary education, and was $14,923 for all primary to tertiary education. By contrast, in China, the annual expenditure per student in all tertiary education was $4550 in 2008, less than one-sixth of that of the United States, and it was $1593 for primary to tertiary education, only about one-tenth of that of the United States (OECD, 2011).

The expenditure on education as a percentage of GDP in the case of India is far less than that of the United States and China and has been hovering around 3–4% (Fig. 7.3). In the year 2009–2010, 41.8% of the total expenditure on

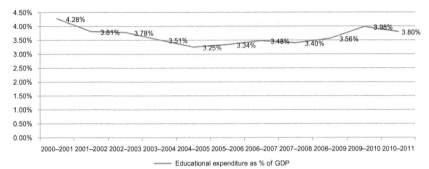

FIGURE 7.3   Education expenditure as % of GDP in India. *(Source: Ministry of Statistics and Program Implementation, Government of India.)*

education was spent on elementary education, and 25.6% was spent on secondary education, while 32.3% was spent on higher education and only about 0.3% was spent on adult education. In spite of a larger percentage of expenditure spent on elementary education, India will take at least another two decades to achieve 100% enrollment rate at the primary level. Besides, India faces an alarmingly high level of dropout at all levels of education and more so at the primary level to the extent of 44%. This significant difference among the three countries in even the very basic education obviously contributes to a paucity of educated people who could move on to become innovators, more in the case of India and to an extent in the case of China as well.

INSTITUTIONS AND UNIVERSITIES

Shown in Table 7.1 is the number of R&D institutions and institutions of higher education in China from 2005 to 2010. The number of R&D institutions shows a declining trend, which primarily was the result of a reduction in the number of institutions that were subordinated to the local level. While the number of institutions of higher education increased, the institutions in the field of natural science and technology and the institutions in the field of social sciences and humanities both had an upward trend and were almost equal in number in 2010. Figure 7.4 shows changes in the numbers of institutions of higher education in the United States from 1970 to 2009. In 1970, the total number of institutions of higher education was about 2500, and it was nearly 4500 in 2009, an increase of almost 80%. In the case of India, there has been an increase in both the number of R&D institutions and higher education institutions in all categories (Tables 7.2–7.4). As of 2010, there were 4288 R&D institutions in India. The share of various sectors in the total number of R&D institutions is the following: central government, 14.2%; state governments, 21.4%; higher education sector, 6.6%; private sector including scientific and industrial research

TABLE 7.1 Number of R&D Institutions and Higher Education Institutions in China

	Year					
	2005	*2006*	*2007*	*2008*	*2009*	*2010*
Number of R&D institutions						
Total number	3901	3803	3775	3727	3682	3696
Subordinated to central level	679	673	674	678	691	686
Subordinated to local level	3222	3130	3101	3049	3016	3010
Number of higher education institutions						
Total number	1792	1867	1908	2263	2305	2358
Natural sciences and technology	786	800	786	827	1003	970
Social sciences and humanities	815	843	840	869	954	963

Sources: China Statistics Year Book, 2011.

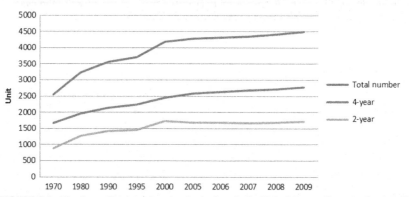

FIGURE 7.4 Numbers of higher education institutions in the United States. *(Sources: Statistical Abstract of the United States, 2012.)*

organizations, 53.7%; and public sector industry including state public sector, 4.5%. As for the total number of colleges, the number grew 2.6 times from 12,806 to 33,023 from 2001 to 2011, and the total number of universities grew 2.48 times from 256 to 634 during the same period.[1]

---

1. (http://www.nstmis-dst.org/).

TABLE 7.2 Number of Recognized Educational Institutions in India

Year	Universities, Deemed Universities, Institutions of National Importance	Research Institutions	College for General Education	Colleges for Professional Education (Eng. Tech., Arch., Medical, and Education College)	Other Colleges (Law, Mgmt., Agriculture, etc.)	Polytechnics
2001–2002	272	79	8737	2409	1926	1160
2002–2003	304	81	9166	2610	1982	1173
2003–2004	304	85	9427	2751	1991	1105
2004–2005	343	136	10,377	3201	2431	1171
2005–2006	350	140	11,698	5284	2513	1274
2006–2007	368	140	11,458	5728	2629	1296
2010–2011	634					

Source: Selected Educational Statistics Published by Ministry of Human Resource Development, Government of India.

TABLE 7.3 Enrollment in Higher Education According to Faculty and Stage

Year	Degrees		General Education Courses			Total
	PhD/M.Phil.	Arts	Sciences	Commerce		
2001–2002	53,119	3,858,475	1,597,637	1,633,693		7,089,805
2002–2003	65,357	4,198,804	1,770,281	1,678,317		7,647,402
2003–2004	65,525	4,252,067	1,851,506	1,755,328		7,858,901
2004–2005	55,352	4,241,507	1,689,504	1,587,285		7,518,296
2005–2006	36,019	4,209,248	1,809,602	1,612,171		7,631,021
2006–2007(P)	37,548	4,372,872	1,874,910	1,613,090		7,860,872
2007–2008	101,044	5,263,397	2,056,675	1,916,171		9,236,243

TABLE 7.4 Professional Education Courses

Year	Educ.	Eng./Tech./Polytechnic	Medicine	Agric.	Veterinary Science	Law	Others	Total
2001–2002	115,265	942,377	148,309	53,969	13,821	271,007	75,126	1,504,609
2002–2003	118,593	1,136,786	208,465	55,367	14,765	298,291	80,745	1,913,012
2003–2004	114,681	1,145,622	223,235	58,700	14,858	303,629	83,721	1,944,446
2004–2005	155,192	1,085,236	256,748	61,838	15,721	319,671	88,041	1,982,447
2005–2006	244,825	2,358,638	305,629					2,909,092
2006–2007	271,858	2,530,362	319,811					3,122,031
2007–2008	370,660	1,490,618	449,333	67,752	18,221	293,996	209,959	2,900,539

Note: Enrolment in open and distance learning has not been included.
Source: University Grants Commission, India.

Beyond just the number of research institutions and institutions of higher education, the quality of these institutions played an even more important role in promoting innovation. This is an area of huge difference between China and India on the one hand and the United States on the other. For example, from 2003 to 2011, 17 US universities were placed among the top 20 in the world, and the United Kingdom had 3 universities, while China had none. Among the top 100 universities, the United States had 53, while China and India had none. In the top 200, 300, 400, and 500 universities, the United States had 89, 110, 137, and 151 universities, respectively, while China only had 3, 13, 21, and 35 universities, respectively. India, on the other hand, had just one university—Indian Institute of Sciences—in the top 400 and 500 universities and none in the top 200 and 300 universities category. In 2011, among Chinese universities, only Tsinghua University was placed in the top 200, and that was between 151 and 200. Six universities including Fudan University, Nanjing University, Peking University, Shanghai Jiao Tong University, University of Science and Technology of China, and Zhejiang University were ranked between 200 and 300. Among the rankings in the top 300–500, China placed only 16 universities.[2]

According to the Times Higher Education World University Rankings 2012–2013 by Thomson Reuters, China had 2 universities (Peking University and Tsinghua University) in the top 100, 3 universities (Fudan University, University of Science and Technology of China, and Nanjing University) in the range of top 200–300, and 3 universities (Renmin University of China, Sun Yat, Sen University and Zhejiang University) in the top 300–400 range. The United States had 46 universities in the top 100 universities, 29 universities in the top 100–200 range, 18 in the top 200–300 range, and 18 in the top 300–400 range. In contrast to the United States and China, India had none in the top 200, 2 (Indian Institute of Technology Kharagpur and Indian Institute of Technology Bombay) in the top 200–300 range, and 1 (Indian Institute of Technology Roorkee) in the top 300–400 range.

Also, according to the Higher Education Evaluation and Accreditation Council of Taiwan (HEEACT) world university rankings from 2008 to 2010, in the top 20 universities by fields, the United States had 13 universities in the field of agriculture and environmental sciences, 17 in the field of clinical medicine, 9 in the field of engineering, computing, and technology, 14 in the field of life sciences, 14 in the physical and chemical fields, and 18 in the field of social sciences. By contrast, China only had 2 universities in the field of engineering, computing, and technology, which were Tsinghua university, ranking 5th in 2008, 6th in 2009, and 3rd in 2010, and Zhejiang university, ranking 38th in 2008, 24th in 2009, and 20th in 2010. When the universities were ranked by subjects, in the top 20 universities in 2010, the United States had 15 in physics including astronomy and space science, 10 in chemistry, 15 in mathematics, 14

2. http://www.shanghairanking.com/ARWU-Statistics-2011.html.

in geosciences, 11 in electrical engineering, 13 in computer science, 8 in civil engineering including environmental engineering, 13 in mechanical engineering, 4 in chemical engineering including energy and fuels, and 11 in materials science, while China only had 2 in chemistry ranking 16th and 17th; 1 in electrical engineering ranking 10th; 1 in computer science ranking 16th; 1 in civil engineering ranking 11th; 2 in mechanical engineering ranking 8th and 11th; 5 in chemical engineering ranking 8th, 10th, 13th, 16th, and 18th; and 1 in materials sciences ranking 5th. India did not have a single university in the top 20 universities by field.[3]

Much of India's problem in higher education has been the low intensity of R&D in the university sector. The university sector, comprising about 634 universities, has not been very effective in aiding innovation for the reason that no more than 20% of the universities are research-based universities. The ADB 2009 report on "India 2039" shows India's leading institutes of technology having a dismal performance in the number of patents granted.

CONTENT OF EDUCATION

In American primary schools, courses like mathematics, language, social studies, science, music, drawing, and sport are designed to provide a well-rounded education to the students. This phase of education not only is aimed to help students gain new knowledge but also is designed with an eye towards comprehensive development, including athletic ability, and communications and teamwork and social skills. Friendship, happiness, and individuality are far more important to students than just grades. As a result, many important personality traits such as honesty, self-confidence, compassion, justice, tolerance, and independence are built in this early phase and form the basis for later development.

In China, primary schools teach courses such as mathematics, Chinese, English, "moral cultivation," science, and art. While very different from American primary education, performance in certain subjects, especially math and Chinese language, is considered more important because it is taken as a standard to evaluate students' abilities. Also, some students attend some classes after school to improve their grades. Of course, some students can also attend classes in piano, dance, singing, the game of go, ping-pong, kung fu, etc. Although most students don't really like this, they do it only to appease their parents. In general, although lately there has been an increasing emphasis on quality education in China, getting very high scores in exams still takes priority due to the exam-oriented nature of the education system in China.

In India, there has been a major thrust in the last two decades on improving elementary education. However, the poor quality of the schools and their basic

3. http://en.wikipedia.org/wiki/HEEACT_%E2%80%93_Performance_Ranking_of_Scientific_Papers_for_World_Universities.

physical infrastructure often leads to children dropping out of the school system without learning. Besides, there are large educational inequalities among the various categories of population based on gender, urban or rural habitation, and social and economic strata, and these are visible in school enrolment, type of schooling, educational expenditures, and school performance. As a result, only about 54% of Indian children aged 8–11 are able to read a simple paragraph with even lower attainment for certain social classes of children. Arithmetic skills are even poorer. Teacher absenteeism and corporal punishment in schools remain rampant, and even private schools are not free from it.[4]

An emphasis on food, livelihood, and health guarantees is therefore simultaneously required to level the initial disadvantages of the poor in the educational sphere stemming from malnourishment, poverty, and health-related debility (Kumar and Kumar, 2012). There are 641,000 villages and 7936 towns in the country. Rough calculations reveal that 15 villages share a higher secondary school between them. Given the poor quality of government-run schools, education is being privatized at a rapid rate, leading to both increased enrolment in private schools and reliance on private tuition. Even among the poorest families or those with very low education levels, children in private schools have higher reading and arithmetic skills than those in government schools. With rapid privatization associated with the flight of middle-class families from government schools, there has been further deterioration of these schools and greater inequality between government and private school students, more in urban areas than in rural areas. These inequalities can be seen even in basic skills such as literacy, but the differences are vast when we consider advanced skills, such as knowledge of English or computer usage. Moreover, inequalities between women from different states are even greater than those between men. This digital divide may lead to widening income differences between regions in the years to come.

In secondary education, in the United States, textbooks are chosen by schools and teachers, and there is no standard across the country. In China, on the other hand, the same textbooks are used across the whole country, and textbooks chosen by schools are auxiliary. Comparing textbooks, American textbooks include inference steps, experimental tests, explanation of phenomena, and the introduction to various scientists. Chinese textbooks include theorems in mathematics, laws of physics, and formulas for chemical reactions. Also, there are big differences between the subjects taught and evaluation criteria.

In China, courses such as geometry, algebra, Chinese, English, chemistry, physics, biology, and history are all required courses and have very well-defined and fixed criteria for passing grades. The United States, by contrast, has a very flexible system that is based on collecting a required number of

---

4. http://ihds.umd.edu/IHDS_files/06HDinIndia.pdf.

credits, and students are free to choose curricula based upon their interests. In China, the college entrance examination is very important to every student, and their lives can take on significantly better trajectories if they can enter famous universities like Tsinghua University or Peking University. These students have to typically study very hard and have little to no time to do other things. In American high schools, students generally have six classes from Monday to Friday, which start usually at 7:30 in the morning and finish by 2:15 in the afternoon. While in China, students have at least had eight classes a day and had to study by themselves at school until 9 o'clock, and on weekends, they have to attend extra classes after school to improve their grades in these courses.

Chinese universities place a huge emphasis on memorizing or "cramming," with the goal of trying to develop a strong theoretical basis. But with this approach, students can lose their ability to be creative, innovative, curious, and entrepreneurial because their responses on exams are expected to conform to standard answers. American universities, on the other hand, tend to be very interactive, and students are expected to read before class, and teaching typically takes up only about one-third of the class time. Studying by themselves, looking for materials on the Internet and in the library, and discussing with others are the main methods of learning. So, Chinese students end up paying more attention to grades and improving their ability on their own, while American students pay more attention to communication and teamwork.

In the case of India, secondary education is institutionally diverse, with three national band 34 state and union territory boards. Each board has its own specified curriculum and school certificate examinations for Grades 10 and 12—rigor and pattern of examination also vary. The result is the lack of coordination and non-comparability of learning outcomes between states and over time, as measured by board examinations, a critical weakness in system accountability (World Bank, 2009, http://datatopics.worldbank.org/hnp/files/edstats/INDstu09b.pdf).

A comparison of Indian and international curricula in language arts, mathematics, and sciences highlights the issue of overemphasis on rote learning of facts as opposed to development of students' higher-order thinking skills. In addition, the sheer volume of facts that students are expected to master in order to succeed in examinations appears to exacerbate this problem, pointing to curriculum overload. Periodic curriculum reform to remain relevant has been slow to materialize in most Indian states. The quality of learning materials in secondary education, particularly of textbooks, is low. National and state boards differ widely in their approach to the organization of information and presentation of content in textbooks, with central board textbooks considerably better than state board textbooks. Textbook development remains a virtual monopoly of central institutions such that government schools and teachers lack choice and private publishers are excluded from the market; in those cases, there is little incentive to improve. The very limited availability of Information and Communication Technology (ICT) at the secondary level, in particular, limits teachers' ability to upgrade their subject-matter knowledge and students' ability to access essential learning materials, in addition to constraining the development of ICT-related skills and behaviors the youth need to succeed in the global knowledge economy. India lacks an effective quality assurance mechanism at the secondary level, for government, aided, and unaided schools.

As for higher education, India's talent pool in terms of young university graduates with 7 years or less of work experience is the largest worldwide. The number of institutions in higher education has increased, and nearly 42% of all enrolled students in 2010–2011 were studying sciences and engineering. However, higher education institutions suffer from large quality variation. At the higher end of the spectrum, there are some good institutions like the Indian Institutes of Technology (IIT), Indian Institutes of Sciences (IISc), Indian Institutes of Management (IIM), and National Institutes of Technology (NIT). The number of graduates and PhDs graduating from these institutions is not very high and is not adequate to fulfill industry needs. In addition, graduates from these top Indian science and engineering schools tend to head abroad to pursue their graduate studies where they frequently excel and decide to stay.

On the other hand, the quality of most other science and engineering colleges at the lower end is dismal. According to the 2005 Nasscom-McKinsey report, not more than 15% of graduates of general education and 25–30% of technical education are suitable for employment.[5] The education provided in many of these institutions is not relevant to current industry needs. Fresh graduates with undergraduate degrees have a low level of practical skills and thus are not directly employable. They require either on-the-job training or additional training after graduation. Eighty-six percent of the total workforce belongs to the unorganized sector, which is basically unskilled workforce. India has a massive task—a need for upgrading the skill set of this huge population. Since only a small number of universities and colleges are eligible for funding by the University Grants Commission, they are not monitored for quality by the National Assessment and Accreditation Council (NAAC). As a result, a vast majority of institutions have no quality control except for the little that is provided by university regulations and occasional university team visits.

DIFFERENT COLLEGE ENTRANCE EXAMS

Differences between college entrance exams also greatly influence the students' abilities at theoretical knowledge versus abilities at practical applications. In China, the college entrance exam is offered only once a year, and the test times for all courses are the same across the nation. Although some provinces can define their own set of questions, the topics are very similar. Exams generally fall into two categories: One is for students of science, and the other is for students of liberal arts. For the science-based student, exams commonly include

---

5. http://siteresources.worldbank.org/EDUCATION/Resources/278200-1121703274255/1439264-1193249163062/India_CountrySummary.pdf.

subjects such as Chinese, mathematics (for science), foreign language, physics, chemistry, and biology. For liberal arts students, the exam commonly includes subjects such as Chinese, mathematics (for liberal arts), foreign languages, history, politics, and geography. The score on this exam is very important, and it is almost the only standard to determine what university a student can join. Therefore, even if a student who may have been good throughout high school does not do well in this exam, she/he will not be able to go to their desired university. So, most students work very hard for as long as 3 years just to prepare for this exam.

In the United States, there is no unified national college entrance exam, since this is done at the state and local levels. However, Scholastic Assessment Test (SAT) hosted by the Educational Testing Service (ETS) produces and provides a uniform measurement for high-school students entering universities. There are two types of SAT exams: One is SAT-I and the other is SAT-II, although most schools typically use only SAT-I scores. The new SAT-I exam includes three parts: reading, mathematics, and writing for a total of 2400 points. SAT-II includes five parts: English, history and social studies, mathematics, science, and foreign language—a selection of almost 20 most commonly used foreign languages. Students can take the SAT exam multiple times—it is offered seven times a year—and the highest score is always considered. Universities, however, typically, like to select students with stable or increasing scores. American universities accept new students by evaluating them from various perspectives. Outside of the SAT score, school grades are the most important factor for university enrollment, carrying a weight of almost 30% of the total evaluation. The overall personality is another important factor, which can reflect the students' citizenship, leadership abilities, teamwork or communication skills, athletic abilities, innovation and research skills, or other special talents.

Due to differences in college entrance exams in China and in the United States, Chinese students always have textbook knowledge of math, physics, chemistry, history, biology, etc., but do not have the skills to use these in the real world. American students, on the other hand, appear to have less textbook knowledge but have stronger practical and social abilities.

In India, the wide variation in quality of higher education is a product of the differences in the entrance requirements among various colleges. Almost 98% of all entrance exam participants in IITs and IIMs are rejected due to capacity constraints. For example, 520,000 candidates appeared in IIT Joint Entrance Exams (IIT-JEE) in 2012 competing for 9647 seats.[6] The rejected 40% get admission anywhere in the world provided they pay for it. Over 150,000 students go overseas for university education every year.[7] On the other extreme,

---

6. http://en.wikipedia.org/wiki/Indian_Institute_of_Technology_Joint_Entrance_Examination#cite_note-10.
7. http://articles.economictimes.indiatimes.com/2008-03-17/news/27707365_1_indian-students-higher-education-professional-education.

the entry requirement for some of the remaining engineering colleges is just a mere passing grade in the 12th standard exam.

DIFFERENCES IN RELATIONSHIP BETWEEN TEACHERS AND STUDENTS

In China, the traditional relationship between teachers and students emphasizes the teachers' roles, and teachers are expected to control and manage the teaching process. In the classroom, it is somewhat of an "ask-answer"-type atmosphere, and the teachers' job is to give lectures and the students' job is to listen; that is, knowledge is passed to students by "feeding but not thinking." Students only passively accept what the teachers say in the classroom and almost ask nothing in class providing for very little interaction in the classroom. Another difference with the Chinese teacher–student relationship is position deference: That is, teachers are authoritative and dominant, and students are expected to be passive and conforming. So, the teachers will not acknowledge not knowing something and will try to answer any and all questions from students whether or not they know the answer. If the students, on the other hand, have questions, they will merely ask the teacher and not try to find the answer themselves. Also, there is a lot of emphasis on discipline in the classroom. While discipline is important, the rigid atmosphere is not conducive to motivate them to learn.

In the United States, the relationship between teachers and students is that of a "dialogue." In other words, communication is interactive and independent. In American classrooms, cooperation and interaction between teachers and students run through the teaching process, and teachers encourage students to express their own opinions and acquire knowledge through discussion and debate. In addition, teachers and students to a large extent are equal; that is, students will not just accept what the teachers say, and they are free to challenge and question the teachers' viewpoint. Lastly, American classrooms have a comfortable ambience. For example, desks and chairs are placed loosely and comfortably, and the teaching content and arrangement are organized by specific teaching and course needs. This kind of teaching environment and approach is very conducive to improving a student's thinking abilities, but it can have the drawbacks of a lack of discipline in the classroom and a potential for sacrificing academic rigor and theoretical foundations of the subject.

In general, Chinese students care far more about "results or answers," and they seem to lack curiosity and typically look for standard answers. Of course, this is not a problem created by the students, and is the result of the way exams are designed to test students. American students by contrast care far more about "process" and don't believe in standard answers. From this perspective, American students seem to have the ability to be more independent and capable of thinking and doing things on their own.

In India, like in most other countries in the East, lecturing is used as the predominant method of classroom instruction. The status of a teacher in ancient Indian culture is next to that of God in that a teacher is one who is venerable, flawless, and unquestionable. Therefore, traditionally, the best students were those who silently and without questioning listened to the sermons given by the teacher, and the best teachers were those who could make their students sit and listen throughout the session. Asking a question was supposed to be discourteous, and interactive teaching remained something restricted to a few elite institutions. When students gain knowledge from active participation in a course, real learning and critical thinking occur—but this is a relatively new idea in Indian educational philosophy and practice (Jangira, 1995).

However, since the late 1990s, thanks to the many empirical studies that have established beyond doubt the overarching merits of participatory learning coupled with the pressures of a globalizing educational environment, there has been a significant shift away from conventional lecturing to the more interactive learning styles (Chand, 2004). Concepts like "student-centered learning" and "teacher as facilitator" have started gaining momentum. There is, however, a huge scope for improvement in this area. This is due to the fact that mechanisms to evaluate the work of teachers are very shoddy, bureaucratic, and routine. Peer review of teachers and student evaluation of teachers are concepts almost unheard of within the teaching community.

Efforts to make teaching a joyful, creative, and fulfilling activity are nonexistent. The mix of ossified board functionaries and dull and bored teachers creates a situation in which—if one were to subtract what a student has "crammed" and if one were to concentrate on what a student has really learned—most of the student's real learning is primarily a product of their own hard work and that of his or her peers. Therefore, if the levels of student learning are to be upgraded, a lot of creative work needs to be done at reorienting teachers and the education bureaucracy—if the teachers do not enjoy their subject matter, their students cannot learn.

DIFFERENT RELATIONSHIPS BETWEEN ADMINISTRATIVE STAFF AND TEACHERS

In the United States, presidents of universities are appointed by the board of directors, and their primary job is raising funds for the university and recruiting excellent faculty and students and public relationship. They have little time to perform or manage research. Many universities have teaching affairs deans, or provosts, who are responsible for choosing the faculty, arranging courses, evaluating teaching quality, and setting research budgets. Most American universities engage tenure-track faculty with career-long academic employment and non-tenure-track faculty. The employment period of associate professors and above typically continues until retirement. Research universities also require faculty to perform research and publish academic articles and books. These are important criteria in the evaluation and promotion process. Because of this kind of evaluation process, some research faculty only pursue their own academic interests at the expense of teaching. But this problem is not very serious in the United States as the faculty's teaching abilities are also paid significant attention. Some studies have shown that over 50% of all faculty never publish a book, and 90% of the books are published by 30% of the faculty. Quality of publication is far more important than the number of publications, and 10 articles without innovative thought are less valuable than one article with breakout thinking. As a result, a healthy balance between teaching and research is maintained.

In China, presidents of universities are generally appointed by the government, and their jobs not only include financial budgets, research and teaching management, and faculty evaluation, but also some of them perform research to get academic recognition. However, presidents of Chinese universities are primarily administrators. Different departments take charge of specific jobs, and they can decide a faculty's destiny to a large extent. For example, evaluation and promotion standards are set by these departments, and sometimes, the rules may be randomly changed. Promotion criteria are mainly based on research ability, including numbers of qualified articles, books, research projects, research funds, and necessary awards, and these are indispensable. Teaching workload and teaching quality are also required, but they are not paid much attention. So, in many universities, faculty devote their time to research rather than teaching before the rules change again. Most faculty are therefore focused on quantity as opposed to quality of research output. As a result, academic corruption is increasingly becoming a serious problem.

In India, a large pool of scientists from the universities was absorbed into the research laboratories, and these laboratories have contributed significantly to indigenous growth models in space, atomic energy, and defense research. But this trend led to the delinking of teaching from research, which is one of the reasons for a lack of availability of good teaching faculty. In more recent times, the problem of shortage of teaching staff is because the best and the brightest who earlier became professors now opt for lucrative jobs in companies ranging from IT giants to investment banks. It was estimated that there is a shortage of around 40,000 teachers in higher education[8] (Herstatt et al., 2008). Besides, academia–industry linkage is missing, as most academic institutions are exclusively government-funded and are highly bureaucratic and industry has its own in-house R&D. Other institutions, which are not government-funded, have more funds but keep teaching and research separate. Without the capability of knowledge generation, knowledge dissemination is not effective for teaching faculty.

The shortcomings of the university-based research system include the following: there is very high teaching load coupled with administrative

---

8. http://unpan1.un.org/intradoc/groups/public/documents/apcity/unpan044014.pdf.

responsibilities hampering capacity to conduct research; there is acute shortage of manpower opting for teaching and research because of which most teachers are those who could not find other jobs; computing and experimental infrastructure are not up to the mark at least in state universities; academia–industry linkage in research is missing; and research is more incremental than disruptive in nature. Problems of interpersonal relationships, credit sharing, and more theoretical and less practical output are also common (Natarajan, 2006). The research-friendly environment in some of the better universities, such as—continuous availability of students; facilitation of objective inquiry resulting from the academic ambiance; productivity driven by peer pressure and the need for career advancement; potential to promote interdisciplinary research due to the availability of a large body of peers with a wide spectrum of specializations; the necessity to undertake sponsored research and consultancy which promotes R&D on problems actively pursued by national R&D agencies and industry; friendly rapport with international peers—promotes international collaboration. But these advantages do not prevail in all colleges and universities. As a result, many colleges and universities function more as degree-granting administrative entities rather than as centers of excellence.

CHALLENGES FOR THE UNITED STATES

The K Through 12 Education System

While the discussion based on education expenditures as a percent of GDP, education expenditures per student, and the number of universities and colleges would seem to suggest that the United States is doing very well, a number of studies (e.g., Peterson et al., 2011) over the last 10 plus years (Lagoria, 2005) suggest that there may be some serious problems lurking for the US educational system. These are especially true for the US kindergarten through the 12th grade education and more specifically for education in sciences, technology, engineering, and math (STEM). We once again quote Vint Cerf, "America simply is not producing enough of our own innovators, and the cause is twofold—(1) a deteriorating K-12 education system, and (2) a national culture that does not emphasize the importance of education and the value of engineering and science."

The United States led the world as recently as the 1980s but is now falling behind other industrialized nations in standardized tests—despite the fact that the United States spends more than most nations on a per student basis. The United States still has some of the very best K-12 schools and some of the very best students, but on the average, the performance of US students has been declining and students are performing poorly. The extent and severity of this decline have been a subject not only of great concern but also of much debate (Carnoy and Rothstein, 2013). These studies argue that ". . .because social class inequality is greater in the US than in any of the countries with which we can reasonably be compared, the relative performance of U.S. adolescents is better than it appears when countries' national average performance is conventionally compared..." This social class inequality problem is further exacerbated by an ever-widening income gap between the very rich, the middle class, and the very poor (Stone et al., 2013). Given this income inequality, challenges with student performance will be hard to overcome any time soon.

While one may debate the extent of this decline and the causes thereof, the United States needs to devote some serious attention and resources to the decline in its K-12 education, particularly in basic skills such as reading and math, and, in general, to STEM education to ensure that the huge amounts of money being spent on education are being spent effectively and efficiently.

The 2- and 4-Year Colleges and Universities and the Graduate School System

The K-12 system is the feeder system for the 2-year and the 4-year colleges in the United States. Any challenges with the K-12 system, such as the decline in the quality of STEM education, therefore, flow through into the nation's colleges. While the country continues to produce a stream of very bright students, the average quality of undergraduate students has declined, and with pressures to graduate students, there has been a steady inflation in grades over the years since the 1970s. College education that was once a privilege of the rich became a middle-class expectation (Reynolds, 2014) as a result of the GI Bill. There was a further ballooning of college enrollment that began in the 1970s as result of the US Congress passing legislation to make federally funded student aid, like Pell Grants, and low-interest Stafford student loans readily available. While all of this was very helpful in bringing college education within reach of the rapidly growing middle class, it burdened college students with huge loans that needed to be paid off after they got their degrees. This may be fine when the economy is doing well and jobs are aplenty but is a huge problem in poor economic times with shrinking job prospects. To make matters worse, with the availability of federally funded student grants and loans, the costs of this "credit-fueled" higher education system with bloated bureaucracies and sometimes overpaid tenured faculty, not quite subject to the pressures of the competitive free market private enterprise system, have been rapidly escalating. With rising costs and diminishing quality, the "value" of education provided by the 2- and 4-year US college system remains a matter of debate. See, for example, Collier (2013), "Students arrive woefully academically unprepared; students study little, party much and lack any semblance of internalized discipline; pride in work is supplanted by expediency; and the whole enterprise is treated as a system to be gamed in which plagiarism and cheating abound. The problems stem from two attitudes. Social preoccupations trump the academic part of residential education, which occupies precious little of students' time or emotions. Second, students' view of education is strictly instrumental and 'credentialist'. They regard the entire enterprise as a series of hoops they must jump through to obtain their 120 credits, which they blindly view as an automatic licensure for adulthood and a good job, an increasingly problematic belief."

As discussed in detail above, the United States still continues to have some of the best graduate schools and research universities anywhere, which probably are an envy of the world. Although federal funds for both fundamental research and applied research at universities have declined over the years, the quality of research in US universities, in general, continues to be very high. With a decline in corporate long-term research and development over the last roughly 50 years, discussed in more detail in the intrapreneurship chapter, the mantel of long-term R&D has been taken on more and more by the nation's universities. With the proliferation of the number of journals for publishing research papers, and the continued preponderance of the "publish or perish" academic culture, one might debate the quality of the articles published in these journals and their relevance to either the advancement of knowledge or the benefit to society at large. In this context, it may also be worthwhile to debate the role of the tenure-track system in US academia to explore whether it has outlived its usefulness in the fast-paced, global information-age, digital economy of the world. These two debatable issues notwithstanding a few of the top institutions, particularly on the two coasts, have done an outstanding job of not only emphasizing the quality of publications but also playing the role of a "mid-wife" in birthing new ventures out of university-based intellectual property—ventures that have gone on to become corporations with huge valuations and contributing enormously to the US and global economies. An area of concern for the United States, however, is the decline in the relative enrollment of domestic students, in comparison with those from other parts of the world, especially China, India, and South Korea. This decline in higher education among the US-born student population appears to be part of the broader cultural shift away from the importance of education towards other pursuits, discussed in the previous chapter.

In summary, there are significant differences in the quality and quantity of education provided in the United States, China, and India. US expenditures on a per student basis, in the K-12 grade range, are among the highest in the industrialized world, and the United States certainly spends a great deal more per student than do China or India. However, given the dismal performance of US school students in K-12 in standardized tests compared with their counterparts in other industrialized nations, the United States needs to take stock of the situation and do some serious soul searching about ways to improve the performance of these students despite the widening income gap and the apparent formation of a social dichotomy. China and India have a different set of problems for their K through 12 students, which have to do with (1) the sheer numbers of these students and the concomitant number and quality of teachers and financial resources needed to educate their students and (2) the methodology— memorization-based approach and an undue importance attached to grades.

The silver lining for the United States is in their colleges and universities, which have a disproportionately large representation among the best universities in the world compared especially with China and India. The challenge for the United States here is that the average quality of domestic students joining the undergraduate programs has been declining, while their superior graduate programs are increasingly being taken advantage of by international students rather than by domestic students.

REFERENCES

Carnoy, M., Rothstein, R., 2013. US Student Performance? Stanford Graduate School of Education and Economic Policy Institute. www.epi.org.

Chand, S., 2004. Development challenges for small open economies of the Commonwealth. In: Briguglio, Kisanga (Ed.), Economic Vulnerability and Resilience of Small States. Commonwealth Secretariat, London, pp. 302–314.

Collier, G.L., 2013. The Wall Street Journal, December 26, 2013.

Ding, S., Knight, J., 2008. Why has China grown so fast? The role of physical and human capital formation. University of Oxford, Department of Economics, Economics Series Working Papers, No. 414.

Herstatt et al., 2008. India's national innovation system: key elements and corporate perspectives. East-west Center Working Papers, No. 96.

Jangira, N., 1995. Rethinking teacher education. Prospects 25 (2), 261–272.

Kumar, Kumar, 2012. Status of enrolment at different levels of education. In: India Science and Technology: 2011–12. National Institute of Science, Technology and Development Studies (NISTADS). www.nistads.res.org. (accessed 24.09.12.).

Lagoria, C., 2005. CBS/AP. http://www.cbsnews.com/news/us-education-slips-in-rankings/.

Natarajan, R., 2006. The evolution of post graduate engineering education and research in India. Indian J. Tech. Educ. 29 (3), 48–61.

OECD, 2011. Education at a Glance 2011: OECD Indicators. OECD Publishing pp. 218.

Peterson, P.E., Woessmann, L., Hanushek, E.A., Lastra-Anadon, C.X., Fall 2011. Are U.S. students ready to compete? Educ. Next 11 (4), 50–59.

Reynolds, G.H., 2014. Degrees of value—making college pay off. The Wall Street Journal. January 4, 2014.

Song, S., Chu, G.S.-F., Cao, R., 2000. Intercity regional disparity in China. China Econ. Rev. 11, 246–261.

Stone, C., Trisi, D., Sherman, A., Chen, W., 2013. A guide to statistics on historical trends in income inequality. Center on Budget and Policy Priorities, December 5, 2013.

Yao, S., Zhang, Z., 2001. On regional inequality and diverging clubs: a case study of contemporary China. J. Comp. Econ. 29, 466–484.

Chapter 8

Industry and Market Structures, Industry and Regional Clusters

Chapter Contents

The state of industrial development in a country can reflect the level of technology and innovation in the country, because industrial development must be supported by related development in technologies. By the same token, industry can in turn also promote innovation. On the one hand, the financial benefits brought about by a new industry are a big motivation for enterprises to continue to innovate until the industry gradually matures. On the other hand, when financial benefits that can be derived from older industries begin to diminish, funds must flow to newer, less mature sectors and innovation in those fields flourishes.

The OECD, a leading advocate of cluster approaches to innovation policy, notes that clusters "represent a manageable system for governments to implement the National Innovation System (NIS) Framework by complementing horizontal policies with more targeted and customized policies" (OECD 1999, 2002). The key characteristics of clusters are the numerous linkages among geographically proximate firms through market and nonmarket interactions, as well as linkages with geographically proximate supporting firms and institutions, especially suppliers, business services, research institutions, and educational institutions (Davis et al., 2009). Opportunities to cooperate during the innovation processes with external partners become an important locational factor, which reduces risks and uncertainties and leads to collective learning (De Bresson and Amesse, 1991; Lakshmanan and Okumura, 1995; Malecki and Oinas, 1998). In addition, the spillover of technology between different enterprises within a cluster can further promote general innovation.

INDUSTRY AND MARKET STRUCTURES: THE UNITED STATES

The history of industry structure and its contribution to the US economy has gone through, and continues to go through, huge changes. The United States started out as an agricultural economy at its inception and continued to be primarily that through the nineteenth century, transitioning into an industry powerhouse by the 1950s. It stayed that way through the 1970s and 1980s and beyond that losing that industrial manufacturing edge first to the Japanese and then to the South Koreans and more recently to the Chinese (Johnston, 2012). This transition from an agricultural economy to an industrial economy and the subsequent decline of the manufacturing sector in favor of the services sector are shown in Fig. 8.1 (Bureau of Economic Analysis, National Income and Product Accounts; Gallman and Weiss, 1969; Johnston, 2012; Kendrick, 1961). Transition in the US industry structure since World War II is also evident by looking at the proportion of GDP by sector and also employment data in the United States in Figs. 8.2 and 8.3 (Pielke, 2013).

Another way to look at this change in industry structure in the United States is to look at the evolution of employment (Fig. 8.4) in tradable (goods and services that can be produced in one country and consumed in another or, as in tourism or education, consumed by people from another country) and nontradable sectors of the US economy (goods and services that must be produced and consumed in the same country) (Spence and Hlatshwayo, 2011).

The boundary between tradable and nontradable sectors is not fixed and can change over time. Examples of tradable goods and services include most manufactured products, many agricultural products, a growing set of business services and technical services, minerals, energy, and gas. The nontradable sector

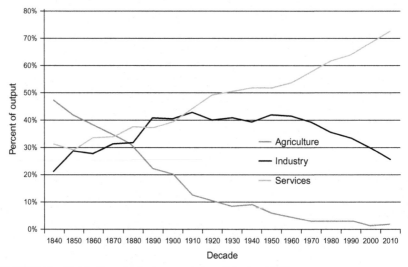

FIGURE 8.1 Distribution of output among sectors (Johnston, 2012).

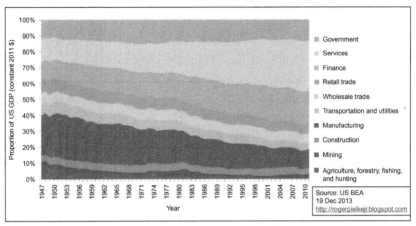

FIGURE 8.2 Proportion of US GDP by sector: 1947–2011 (Pielke, 2013).

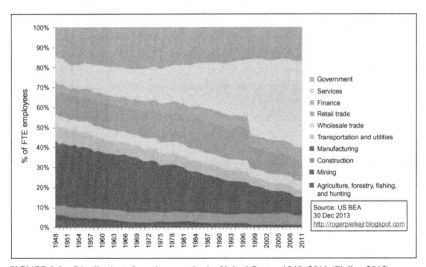

FIGURE 8.3 Distribution of employment in the United States, 1948–2011 (Pielke, 2013).

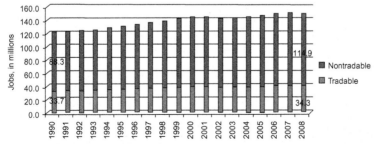

FIGURE 8.4 Evolution of employment in tradable and nontradable sectors (Spence and Hlatshwayo, 2011).

TABLE 8.1 Classification of Manufacturing Jobs (Spence and Hlatshwayo, 2011)

Manufacturing-I	Food, beverage, and tobacco production; textile, apparel, footwear, and leather goods
Manufacturing-II	Wood and paper products; petroleum and coal; basic chemical products; synthetic materials; nonmetallic mineral products; glass; and cement products
Manufacturing-III	Primary and fabricated metal products; heavy machinery; transportation equipment; computers and electronics; household appliances; semiconductors; and furniture production

Source: Summary of the North American Industry Classification System descriptors for manufacturing.

includes government, retail, health care, construction, hotels and restaurants, and most legal services (Spence and Hlatshwayo, 2011). Industry classification of tradable jobs is shown in Table 8.1, and the evolution of various tradable and nontradable jobs is shown in Figs. 8.5 and 8.6.

In summary, in the United States, nontradable jobs comprise about 80% of all jobs. The largest segments within those consist of jobs in the government, health care, retail, accommodation, and food services, followed by construction, other services, wholesale, and transportation. Only a very small segment of the nontradable jobs are manufacturing jobs, and these are in the category of Manufacturing-III. The remaining 20% of the jobs that are tradable are composed primarily of manufacturing jobs—Manufacturing-I, Manufacturing-II, and Manufacturing-III categories—and these have all been declining. The only tradable jobs that have been increasing are again in services—financial and insurance services, computer systems and related services, retail, engineering and architectural service, and other types of services. This has to be very concerning for the US economy, in general, and for innovation and entrepreneurship, in particular.

Apart from assessing the evolution of various sectors of the industry in terms of their contribution to the US GDP and employment levels, it is important to understand their contribution to innovation. As discussed earlier, an important factor to help encourage innovation is to protect intellectual property, which can come in the form of patents, trademarks, or copyrights. We look at the patent intensity in the United States (Table 8.2) and compare that later in the chapter to patent intensity in China and India.

INDUSTRY AND MARKET STRUCTURES: CHINA AND INDIA

The top 10 fastest-growing industries in China from 2005 to 2010 are shown in Table 8.3. The table shows that most of these industries are related to (1) developing natural resources, such as mining of ferrous and nonferrous metal ores

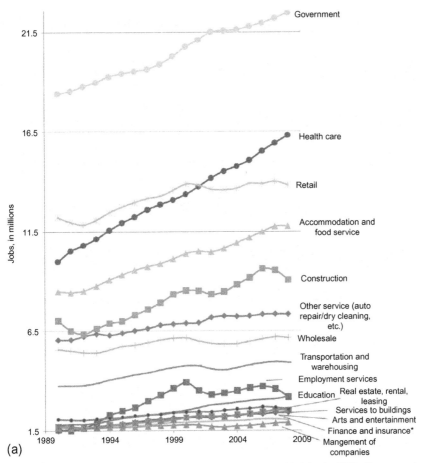

(a)

FIGURE 8.5 (a) Nontradable industry jobs greater than 1.5 M jobs in 1990 (Spence and Hlatshwayo, 2011).

Continued

and coal, and (2) manufacturing and processing industries, such as manufacturing transport equipment, special-purpose machinery, and food processing. So, currently, in China, the industries of mining, manufacturing, and processing not only have the highest growth rate but also are the most important parts of China's industrial economy. High-technology industries, such as new energy sources, biological and biochemical products, information and communications, computer manufacturing, and software development, on the other hand, are significantly smaller than other industries in China or in comparison with similar industries in the United States.

The top 10 industries in India in terms of growth in sales over 2006–2012 show that apart from retail trading and media broadcasting, infrastructure

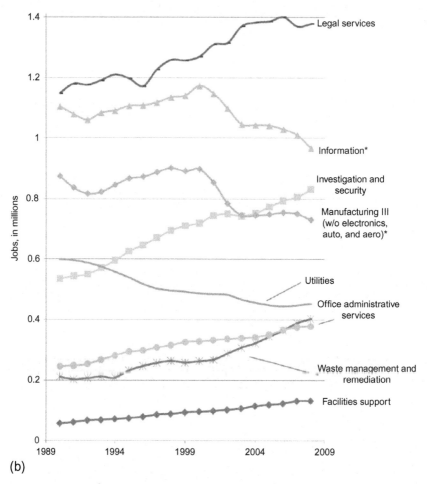

(b)

FIGURE 8.5—cont'd (b) Nontradable industry jobs less than 1.5 M jobs in 1990 (Spence and Hlatshwayo, 2011).

and construction sectors are the most booming sectors (Table 8.4). Similarly, the index of industrial production (IIP) *by usage* with 2004–2005 as the base year also indicates that consumer durables and goods followed by capital goods registered the highest growth rates in 2011–2012.[1] (Growth in usage of consumer durables and goods translates to growth in retail trading.) High-technology industries do not figure in either of these lists.

The top industrial sectors in China on the basis of return on new product development (the ratio of revenues from the sale of new product to development

1. Source: Database of Center for Monitoring Indian Economy.

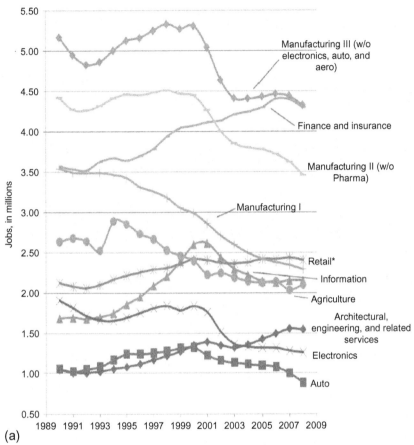

(a)

FIGURE 8.6   (a) Tradable industry jobs greater than 1.0 M jobs in 1990 (Spence and Hlatshwayo, 2011).

Continued

expenditures on new products) are shown in Table 8.5. Among all sectors, in 2010, the manufacture of tobacco had the highest return on the expenditures on new products (63 times). The processing of petroleum, coking, and processing of nuclear fuel was in second place, although the ratio declined greatly, from 42 times in 2008 to 19 times in 2010. Ratios for the manufacture of leather, fur, feather, and its products and the manufacture of transport equipment were higher than those in the other remaining sectors, both exceeding 20 times. None of these sectors except processing of nuclear fuel and the manufacture of communication equipment, computer, and other electronic equipment belong to the high-technology sectors (according to the criterion of High-technology industry defined by the statistics catalog of high-technology industry classifications,

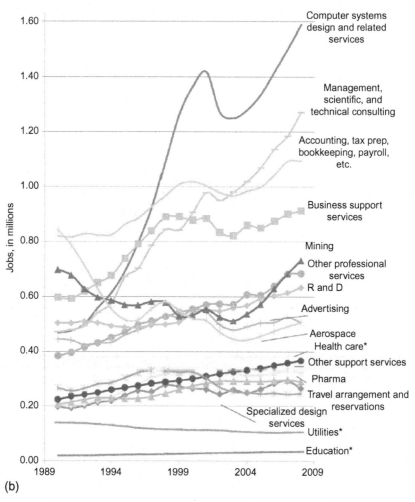

FIGURE 8.6—cont'd (b) Tradable industry jobs less than 1.0 M jobs in 1990 (Spence and Hlatshwayo, 2011).

China Statistics Yearbook on high technology industry). This, therefore, indicates that in China, the return of expenditures on new product development in high-technology industry is not very high. In other words, the level of innovation is not very high in these industries.

According to the study conducted by the National Knowledge Commission (NKC) on "Innovations in India" in 2007, innovation intensity (percentage of revenue derived from products or services that are less than 3 years old) has increased in the case of small and medium enterprises (SMEs), as compared to large firms. In the sample studied, more than 60% of the SMEs have innovation intensity greater than 20%, as compared to less than 25% of the large firms.

TABLE 8.2 Patent Intensity in the United States, FY 2004–2008 (Intellectual Property and the US Economy, Industries in Focus, Economics and Statistics Administration, and USPTO, US Department of Commerce, 2012)

	NAICS Code	Industry Title	Patents (Number)	Employment (1000 Jobs)	Patent Intensity (Patents/1000 Jobs)
Above mean	3341	Computer and peripheral equipment	54,416	196.1	277.5
	3342	Communications equipment	35,797	135.2	264.8
	3344	Semiconductor and other electronic components	50,088	448.7	111.6
	3343, -6	Other computer and electronic products	7744	71.4	108.5
	3345	Navigational, measuring, electromedical, and control instruments	42,415	441.3	96.1
	3251	Basic chemicals	12,109	150.9	80.2
	335	Electrical equipment, appliance, and components	23,503	433.0	54.3
	3254	Pharmaceutical and medicines	13,627	291.3	46.8
	3399	Other miscellaneous	12,717	339.2	37.5
	3253, -5, -6, -9	Other chemical products and preparation	10,322	318.1	32.4
	3391	Medical equipment and supplies	9716	303.2	32.0
	333	Machinery	37,105	1173.7	31.6
	3252	Resin, synthetic rubber, fibers, and filaments	2771	106.4	26.0

TABLE 8.3 Top 10 Increased Industrial Sectors in China (Only Including Industrial Enterprises Above Designated Size)

Sector	Increased Rate of Gross Industrial Output Value (%)					
	2006	2007	2008	2009	2010	2005–2010
Recycling and disposal of waste	61.24	62.05	67.15	26.90	59.72	785.21
Mining of ferrous metal ores	41.53	53.47	76.51	1.11	57.78	511.60
Production and distribution of gas	67.15	35.05	52.37	20.08	32.30	446.46
Mining and washing of coal	52.21	27.67	58.95	12.16	34.78	366.91
Manufacture and processing of nonferrous metals	107.18	39.39	16.18	−1.82	36.72	350.33
Mining of nonferrous metal ores	83.00	36.91	19.18	3.18	34.99	315.91
Manufacture of transport equipment	40.20	33.19	23.01	24.96	32.88	281.42
Manufacture of special-purpose machinery	36.54	33.18	37.10	15.58	28.46	270.17
Processing of timbers, manufacture of wood, bamboo, rattan, palm, and straw products	21.31	44.94	36.44	19.90	28.36	269.22
Processing of food from agricultural products	35.94	34.86	36.70	16.91	24.92	265.98

Industrial enterprises above designated size are those with annual revenue from principal business over 5 M yuan.
Sources: Calculated based on data from China Statistics Yearbook, 2006–2011.

TABLE 8.4 Industrial Sectors in India and Their Evolution

India: Y-o-Y % Change in Sales: 2006–2007 to 2011–2012

	2006–2007	2007–2008	2008–2009	2009–2010	2010–2011	2011–2012	Total
Retail trading	55.9	66.8	43.8	7.4	19.9	14.6	208.4
Commercial complexes	95.5	89.4	−34.2	20	28.4	1.5	200.6
Infrastructural construction	56.1	47.5	36.2	21.2	15.8	14.8	191.6
Media broadcasting	42	38	30.5	25.2	27.6	20.9	184.2
Industrial and infrastructural construction	38.5	46.2	38.1	17.5	13.3	17.1	170.7
Shipping transport infrastructure services	35.1	25.1	43.3	30.4	14.9	19.3	168.1
Real estate	76.2	76	−29.3	19	22.5	2.8	167.2
Production and distribution of films	58.9	85.5	8	−0.6	2.4	11.9	166.1
Construction and real estate	45.6	53.1	16.5	17.8	14.9	14.9	162.8
Other construction and allied activities	8.4	61.8	49.1	18.7	13.2	10.4	161.6

Source: Center for Monitoring Indian Economy.

TABLE 8.5 Top 10 Industrial Sectors of New Products Development in China (Including Large- and Medium-Sized Industrial Enterprises)

Sector	Ratio of New Products Sales Revenue to New Products Development Expenditure (Times)			
	Avg. (2008–2010)	2008	2009	2010
Manufacture of tobacco	59.03	57.59	56.81	62.69
Processing of petroleum, coking, processing of nuclear fuel	27.94	42.14	22.62	19.05
Manufacture of transport equipment	23.72	22.23	25.02	23.89
Manufacture of leather, fur, feather and its products	21.47	23.08	20.82	20.50
Mining of nonferrous metal ores	20.35	36.62	14.08	10.35
Processing of timbers, manufacture of wood, bamboo, rattan, palm, and straw products	18.82	17.00	21.08	18.38
Manufacture of communication equipment, computer, and other electronic equipment	17.72	17.90	15.66	19.61
Manufacture of paper and paper products	17.69	19.03	18.04	16.00
Manufacture and processing of nonferrous metals	17.49	19.74	14.84	17.88
Manufacture of textile	17.35	13.91	17.46	20.70

Sources: Calculated based on data from China Statistics Yearbook, 2009–2011.

A closer look at the components of innovation intensity reveals that with regard to introducing "new-to-the-world" innovations, large firms have been more successful than SMEs. A total of 42% of the large firms are highly innovative (firms that have introduced "new-to-the-world" innovations during the course of business in the last five years), whereas only 17% of SMEs belong to this category. Most of these innovations are more incremental than breakthrough in nature; 37.3% of large firms have introduced breakthrough innovation, while 76.4% have introduced incremental innovation, which may be an indication that large firms in India still have the mindset of incremental innovation as compared with breakthrough innovation (NKC, 2007).

It has also been found that large firms innovate to increase competitiveness, while SMEs innovate to increase market share. There is a clear indication that collaboration with universities and government R&D labs enhances firm innovativeness. According to this study, innovation intensity is higher for firms that collaborate, and the proportion of highly innovative firms is also higher. However, industry collaboration with universities and government R&D labs is not very common in India. In fact, more than half of the large firms and SMEs in this sample claim that the lack of cooperation among the three entities is an important barrier to innovation (NKC, 2007).

Innovation intensity for privately and publicly owned firms is significantly higher than that of government-owned firms. Firms with majority foreign ownership have greater innovation intensity than those with majority Indian ownership. In addition, 50% of the former and 43.5% of the latter are highly innovative. Innovation intensity for MNCs is significantly higher than for non-MNCs (average innovation intensity is 14% for MNCs, as compared to 9.38% for non-MNCs). However, 42% of non-MNCs are highly innovative, and 43% of MNCs are highly innovative. Firms other than public sector units that allocate funds specifically to innovation have higher innovation intensity. They are also more likely to be highly innovative. Firms with their primary market in India have higher innovation intensity than those with primary markets abroad. This shows that exposure to global competition may not lead to an increase in innovation intensity (i.e., in proportion to revenue earned from innovation in the last 3 years) but does lead to an increase in the likelihood of becoming highly innovative (i.e., in the propensity of firms to introduce "new-to-the-world" innovations) (NKC, 2007). As stated in Chapter 3, although the influx of foreign R&D centers has led to an increase in innovation in India, the spillover effects are limited as the efforts of foreign R&D investment in India have been focused so far more on meeting market demands of parent companies outside rather than in the local Indian market.

One can see from Table 8.6 that on the basis of corporate ownership in China, foreign-funded companies had the highest return on new product development and R&D spending, followed by companies that were jointly state-owned, and then joint ownership enterprises, while solely state-funded corporations had the lowest return on both new product development and R&D spending.

Analyzing patent applications accepted and granted in China by various categories based on international classifications, the largest number of patents granted was in the industrial and transportation sectors, over 20% of all patents every year. Patents granted in the personal use items category and in mechanical engineering were, respectively, in the second and third places. Among all categories, the largest increases in the number of patents granted were in physics and electricity, and the ratios were, respectively, 7.4 and 8.0 (Table 8.7).

TABLE 8.6 New Products Development and Production of Large- and Medium-Sized Industrial Enterprises in China by Registration Status

Status of Registration	Sale Revenue of New Products per Expenditure on R&D (Yuan)				Sale Revenue of New Products per Expenditure on New Products (Yuan)			
	2008	2009	2010	Avg. 2008–2010	2008	2009	2010	Avg. 2008–2010
State-owned enterprises	13.83	20.80	16.51	17.05	13.40	18.98	17.89	16.76
Joint ownership enterprises	21.26	18.04	16.71	18.67	38.19	20.08	18.57	25.61
State joint ownership enterprises	21.06	19.39	15.89	18.78	40.10	22.76	19.06	27.31
State solely funded corporations	13.53	12.71	11.96	12.73	12.94	12.03	11.45	12.14
Shareholding corporations	17.19	16.24	16.02	16.48	15.71	13.63	13.28	14.21
Private enterprises	18.44	17.33	19.67	18.48	13.50	15.00	15.80	14.77
Enterprises with funds from Hong Kong, Macao, and Taiwan	24.82	18.53	18.28	20.54	18.67	15.63	14.21	16.17
Foreign-funded enterprises	30.61	28.45	30.08	29.71	23.60	23.28	24.46	23.78

Sources: Calculated according to the data from China Statistics Yearbook, 2009–2011.

TABLE 8.7 Inventions and Utility Models of Patents Application Accepted and Granted by International Classifications (Pieces)

Item	Granted								
	2002	2003	2004	2005	2006	2007	2008	2009	2010
Total	78,957	106,060	119,983	132,654	165,441	217,984	270,381	332,291	479,582
Section A: Personal use items	16,165	20,075	23,159	25,744	32,910	41,692	48,730	55,401	86,350
Section B: Industrial and transportation	17,867	22,051	22,138	24,880	32,123	44,690	51,825	67,654	105,243
Section C: Chemistry and metallurgy	5804	8974	12,349	14,378	15,998	18,519	18,351	24,202	31,558
Section D: Textiles and paper making	1645	1893	2219	2432	3209	4292	4697	5418	8956
Section E: Fixed construction	6346	7958	8028	8955	11,511	14,715	17,358	19,677	31,952
Section F: Mechanical engineering	11,936	14,935	14,581	15,503	21,218	31,047	37,439	44,621	66,262
Section G: Physics	8955	14,301	16,944	18,415	23,123	29,810	43,097	51,229	66,633
Section H: Electricity	10,239	15,873	20,565	22,347	25,349	33,219	48,884	64,089	82,628

Classification refers to the classifying number of every patent assigned according to the technique theme of inventions and utility models of patents by the classification department of patent.
Designs patents are excluded in this table.
Sources: China Statistics Yearbook, 2003–2011.

Overall, the number of Indian patents granted has decreased in 2010 and 2011 (Table 8.8). Out of the total patents granted in India, the top three categories were mechanical (22.34%), chemicals (19.67%), and computer and electronics (10.63%) totaling 52.66% of the patents granted over the years 2006–2011.

INDUSTRY CLUSTERS

The United States

The role and importance of regional industrial clusters to economic growth have been well recognized since the 1980s (Lindqvist et al., 2013; Paytas et al., 2004; Porter, 1990; Turner et al., 2013). In the United States, the formation of high-technology clusters in the Silicon Valley area in California since the 1970s and along Route 128 in the Boston area and the impact they have had in value creation, employment generation, and US economic growth are legendary. Other clusters have sprung up in the United States since then—for example, in the telecom sector in the 1980s and 1990s in the "Telecom Corridor," Richardson, Texas and in the high-technology sector, in general, in Austin, Texas, and Research Triangle Park in North Carolina. There have been other clusters in the biotech and pharmaceutical sectors in other parts of the United States as well. In general, the formation of IP-intensive clusters in the United States is shown in the map in Fig. 8.7a and b (Intellectual Property and the US Economy, Industries in Focus, Economics and Statistics Administration, and USPTO, US Department of Commerce, 2012).

China

Geographically, China's industry clusters are located mainly in the areas of (1) Pearl River Delta, (2) southeast areas of Zhejiang province, (3) Yangtze River Delta, (4) Bohai Bay region, and perhaps a few other regions (see map of China). In the Pearl River Delta, typical industry clusters primarily include computer and related industries in the city of Dongguan, electronic information industry cluster in Huizhou city, home appliances industry cluster in Foshan, ceramic industry cluster in Shiwan Town, toy industry cluster in Shantou city, knitwear industry cluster in Chaoyang City, and lighting industry cluster in Zhongshan city. Zhejiang province had the best private economy where the philosophy of "one village owns one product" and "one county owns one industry" gradually became its unique characteristic. Industry clusters, including the

TABLE 8.8 Number of Patents Granted in India Under Various Fields of Inventions

	2001–2002	2002–2003	2003–2004	2004–2005	2005–2006	2006–2007	2007–2008	2008–2009	2009–2010	2010–2011
Chemicals	483	399	609	573	1140	1989	2662	2376	1420	1899
Drugs	320	312	419	192	457	798	905	1207	530	596
Food	36	67	110	67	140	244	154	97	72	84
Electrical	139	118	396	245	451	787	1067	1140	404	394
Mechanical	311	228	539	414	1448	2526	3503	3242	1024	1459
Computer/electronics				71	136	237	1357	1913	1195	892
Biotechnology				71	51	89	341	1157	449	165
General	302	255	401	278	497			1318	273	350
Other fields						869	2474	3611	801	1668
Total	1591	1379	2469	1911	4320	7539	15,316	16,016	6168	7509

Source: Various annual reports of the office of the controller general of patents, designs, trademarks including GIR and PIS/NIIPM (IPTI) accessed from http://www.ipindia.nic.in/

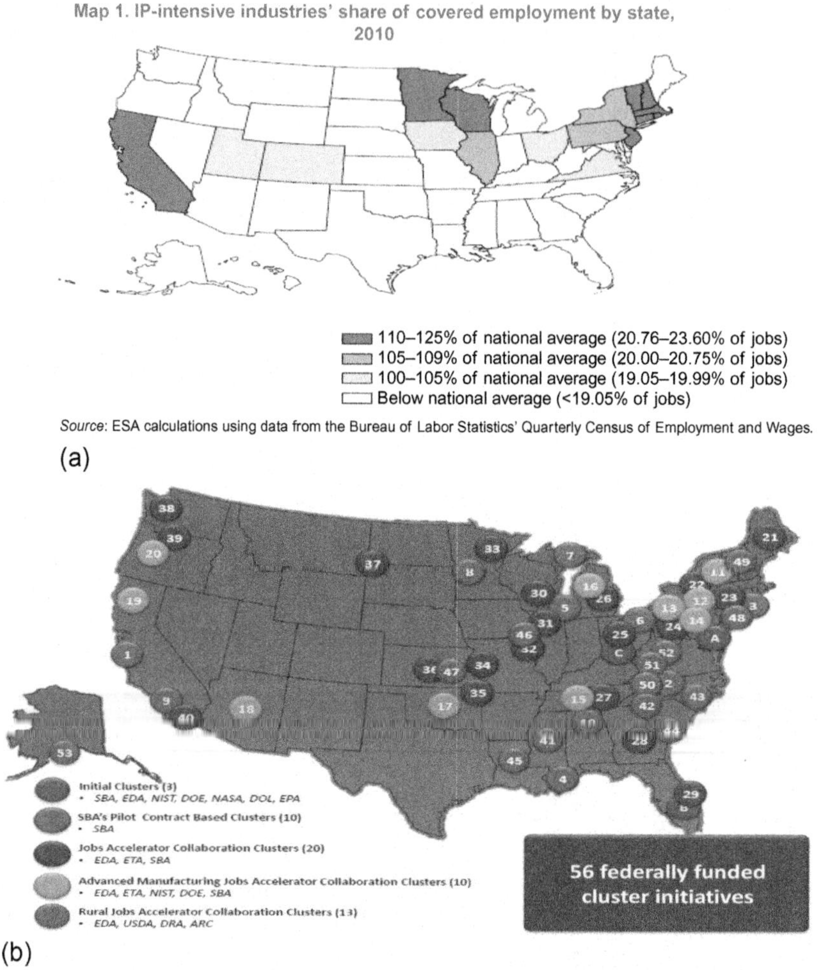

Map 1. IP-intensive industries' share of covered employment by state, 2010

■ 110–125% of national average (20.76–23.60% of jobs)
□ 105–109% of national average (20.00–20.75% of jobs)
□ 100–105% of national average (19.05–19.99% of jobs)
□ Below national average (<19.05% of jobs)

Source: ESA calculations using data from the Bureau of Labor Statistics' Quarterly Census of Employment and Wages.

(a)

Initial Clusters (3)
• SBA, EDA, NIST, DOE, NASA, DOL, EPA

SBA's Pilot Contract Based Clusters (10)
• SBA

Jobs Accelerator Collaboration Clusters (20)
• EDA, ETA, SBA

Advanced Manufacturing Jobs Accelerator Collaboration Clusters (10)
• EDA, ETA, NIST, DOE, SBA

Rural Jobs Accelerator Collaboration Clusters (13)
• EDA, USDA, DRA, ARC

56 federally funded cluster initiatives

(b)

FIGURE 8.7   (a) Intellectual Property and the US Economy, Industries in Focus, Economics and Statistics Administration, and USPTO (US Department of Commerce, 2012). (b) Federally funded cluster initiatives.

textile industry cluster in the city of Shaoxing, leather industry in Haining City, necktie industry in Shengzhou, hardware industry in Yongkang, low-voltage electrical products industry in Yueqing, and the socks industry in Zhuji, are very famous. In the Yangtze River Delta, industry clusters are due to the development of a regional industrial park.

Due to the proximity to Shanghai, some areas such as Suzhou, Ningbo, and their surrounding areas developed township enterprises earlier than other regions. Other industry clusters came later—for example, the high-technology industry cluster in Suzhou city and the garment industry cluster in Ningbo city.

In the Bohai region, Beijing, Shandong province, and Hebei province are the main centers. Zhongguancun high-technology industrial cluster in Beijing is representative of Chinese high-technology industry clusters. Also, the Shouguang fruit and vegetable industry cluster in Shandong, Wendeng craft textile industry cluster, Qinghe cashmere industry cluster in Hebei, Xinji leather industry cluster, Baigou luggage industry cluster, and Shengfang metal glass furniture industry clusters are all very well known in China. In addition to the abovementioned regions, new industry clusters are forming in other areas, such as the Wuhan optoelectronics industry cluster in the central region, Liuyang fireworks industry cluster in Hunan, Ganzhou rare earth material cluster in Jiangxi province, Huxian carton industry cluster in Shaanxi province, Jiajiang ceramic industry cluster in Sichuan province, Chongqing motorcycle industry cluster, Changchun automobile industry cluster in northeast China, optoelectronic information industry, and the Daqing petrochemical industry cluster. Guangdong, Zhejiang, Jiangsu, Fujian, and Shandong also account for a large proportion of China's industry clusters. Tables 8.9 and 8.10 show the regional distribution of pillar industries and industry clusters in China.

TABLE 8.9 Pillar Industries and Industry Clusters by Regions

Regions	Pillar Industries	Affiliated Industry Cluster
Northeast region	Agriculture	Agricultural industry cluster
	Construction industry Production and supply of electric power, heat power, and hot water Other services	Service industry cluster
	Metal smelting and processing industry	Metal industry cluster
Regions of Beijing and Tianjin	Metal smelting and processing industry	Petroleum industry cluster
	Other services	Service industry cluster
Northern coastal region	Machinery industry Construction industry Commerce industry Other services	Service industry cluster
	Manufacture of textile	Agricultural industry cluster
Eastern coastal region	Machinery and equipment repair Production and supply of electric power, heat power, and hot water Construction industry Other services	Service industry cluster
Southern coastal region	Metal smelting and processing industry Construction industry Other services	Service industry cluster
	Manufacture of wood and furniture Production and supply of electric power, heat power, and hot water	Electricity and coal gas industry cluster
Middle region	Metal smelting and processing industry Construction industry Other services	Service industry cluster
	Agriculture	Agricultural industry cluster
Northwest region	Manufacture of foods and tobacco Construction industry Commerce industry Other services	Service industry cluster

Continued

TABLE 8.9 Pillar Industries and Industry Clusters by Regions—Cont'd

Regions	Pillar Industries	Affiliated Industry Cluster
Southwest region	Agriculture	Agricultural industry cluster
	Coal mining industry	Electricity and coal gas industry cluster
	Metal smelting and processing industry Construction industry Other services	Service industry cluster

Source: Li (2007).

TABLE 8.10 Region Distribution of Different Industry Clusters

Industry Clusters	Mainly Distributed Regions
Information and communication technology (ICT) manufacturing cluster	Pearl River Delta, Yangtze River Delta, Bohai Bay Region, western regions primarily in Sichuan and Shanxi provinces
Media industry cluster	Southeast coastal region, e.g., Shanghai, Guangzhou, Hangzhou, Wuhan, Nanjing, northern region, e.g., Beijing, Shenyang and Changchun
Textile, apparel and leather, fur, feather manufacturing industry cluster	In the provinces of Zhejiang, Jiangsu, Fujian, Guangdong, Shandong
Nonmetallic manufacturing cluster	Eastern coastal region, e.g., Shandong, Zhejiang, Fujian and Guangdong
Machinery manufacturing cluster	Northeast region and eastern coastal cities
Appliances manufacturing cluster	Pearl River Delta, Yangtze River Delta, and Shandong Peninsula
Transportation equipment manufacturing cluster	Northeast region, middle region, southeast coastal region, Beijing-Tianjin region
Metal products manufacturing	In coastal areas of Zhejiang, Guangdong, Jiangsu, Shandong
Wood processing and furniture manufacturing cluster	In provinces of Zhejiang, Fujian, and Guangdong, Hebei, Hubei, Liaoning
Software and computer service cluster	In large cities, such as Beijing, Shanghai, Shenzhen, Nanjing, Chengdu, Jinan
Petroleum and chemical products industry cluster	Middle region, eastern coastal region
Food and beverage manufacturing industry cluster	Widely distributed in China

Continued

TABLE 8.10 Region Distribution of Different Industry Clusters—Cont'd

Industry Clusters	Mainly Distributed Regions
Stationery and sporting goods and handicrafts manufacturing cluster	Southeast coastal region, mainly in Guangdong, Zhejiang, Jiangsu, Fujian, Shandong
Modern service industry cluster	Beijing-Tianjin region, Yangtze River Delta, southern coastal region, western region
Metallurgical manufacturing cluster	Beijing-Tianjin-Tangshan region, northeast region, middle region
Pharmaceutical manufacturing cluster	Middle region, western parts of China, southeast coastal region

Source: http://www.chinadmd.com/file/scsxiiosirpwrvvuv33aoww6_1.html

India

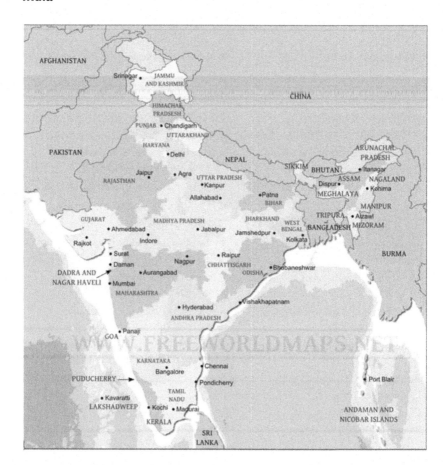

With an estimated over 6000 clusters, India (see map above) has probably mapped the highest number of clusters so far and has also been the pioneering country in various cluster development programs. In the late 1980s, cluster development was based on select thematic areas like technology upgrades and quality improvement and was supported by the then-Ministry of Small Scale Industries (MoSSI) and financial institutions like the Small Industries Development Bank of India (SIDBI) and the State Bank of India (SBI). It was only in 2002–2003 that cluster development programs, especially in the traditional manufacturing sector, gained noticeable momentum. In the past 5 years (2007–2012) alone, since the Department of Science and Technology (DST) has initiated a program exclusively for promoting innovation in MSME clusters, 24 cluster-based public schemes and major programs have been supported (Rao et al., 2013).

According to the Foundation of MSME Clusters, clusters in India are of six categories, namely, industrial, handloom, handicraft, information technology (IT), microenterprises, and services. The 1157 industrial clusters all over the country comprise product categories ranging from basic chemicals and chemical products; basic metal and alloy industries; electronics and electrical industries; food products; handloom and jute and other vegetable fibers; leather and leather fur; machinery and equipment, metal process and parts except machinery and equipment, nonmetallic mineral products, and other manufacturing industries; paper and paper products; printing and publishing; rubber, plastic, petrol, and coal products; textile products; transport equipment and parts; to wood and wood products.

There are 3094 handicrafts clusters all over the country with product categories ranging from appliqué, basketry, mat weaving and cane articles, carpets and durries, coconut shell, earthenware, folk painting, food products, forest-based products, glass, horn and bone, jewelry, leather, metalwork, musical instruments, natural fiber, nonmetallic mineral products, other decorative items, other manufacturing industries, to paper accessories.

Although there are 56 IT clusters in India, predominant among them are the clusters in Maharashtra, Karnataka, Andhra Pradesh, Tamil Nadu, and more recently in Gujarat.

The 54 clusters of microenterprises are in product categories such as basketry, mat weaving and cane articles, food products, forest-based, horn and bone, jewelry, leather, mechanical, metalwork, natural fiber, nonmetallic mineral products, paper products, plastics, pottery and clay, seashell craft, textiles, wooden products, and woodwork.

There are 566 handloom clusters and 50 services clusters spread throughout the country.

The National Innovation Council of India (NInC) has recognized that the most significant barriers for innovation in industry are skill shortages, lack of effective collaborations, insufficient capacity building, and inability to manage innovation successfully. To diffuse the innovation culture, NInC proposes to seed Cluster Innovation Centers (CICs) in industry clusters. This center will act as a networking hub/arm of the cluster, forge linkages between various stakeholders, initiate and assist innovation activities in the cluster, and work with the cluster and stakeholders to diffuse innovation as a solution for the needs of the industry and the society in general. To aid the CICs, the NInC also proposes to create an Innovation Toolkit, which will be a knowledge repository to be used by the CIC, cluster, and interested parties in general (Office of the Adviser to the Prime Minister on Public Information Infrastructure and Innovations, 2011).

In summary, this chapter compares the evolving industry structure and innovation intensity in the three countries, especially as it relates to patent generation in key industries, and also provides a comparison of industry cluster formations in the United States, China, and India. We present an overview of the evolution of the industry structure of the United States, as it led the way in transitioning from an agricultural economy to a manufacturing- and services-based industrial economy. Over time, various industries matured and the United States ceded its dominance in several industries to countries in the Far East, increasingly turning into a service-based economy. China and India on the other hand started the transition from an agricultural to an industrial economy only recently relative to the United States. Although China in recent years has become more of a destination for outsourcing of US manufacturing jobs, the manufacturing sector is not very innovative. Most of the innovative firms are either foreign-owned or from joint sector—not state-owned.

In India, the industrial growth is more prominent in infrastructure and retail sectors and not in high-technology sectors. With the recent efforts in cluster development in the MSME sector gaining momentum, the SME sector is proving innovative. However, with regard to introducing "new-to-the-world" innovations, the SME sector has a lot of catching up to do. Although government happens to be the highest R&D spender, the linkage between industry, university, and government R&D labs is missing. Government-owned firms have the least innovation intensity. Private sector companies, in general, and non-MNC companies specifically, are more innovative. The MNC firms have been focusing their R&D more on meeting market demands of parent companies elsewhere rather than in the local Indian market.

REFERENCES

Bureau of Economic Analysis – National Income and Product Accounts, http://www.bea.gov/national/Index.htm.

Davis, C.H., Creutzberg, T., Arthurs, D., 2009. Applying an innovation cluster framework to a creative industry: the case of screen-based media in Ontario. Innov.: Manage. Policy Pract. 11 (2), 201–214.

De Bresson, C., Amesse, F., 1991. Networks of innovators: a review and introduction to the issue. Res. Policy 20, 363–379.

Gallman, R.E., Weiss, T.J., 1969. The service industries in the nineteenth century. In: Fuchs, V.R. (Ed.), Production and Productivity in the Service Industries. Columbia University Press (for NBER), New York, pp. 287–352.

Johnston, L.D., 2012. History lessons: understanding the decline in manufacturing. MinnPost. http://www.minnpost.com/macro-micro-minnesota/2012/02/history-lessons-understanding-decline-manufacturing, February 22.

Kendrick, J.W., 1961. Productivity Trends in the United States. Princeton University Press, Princeton.

US Department of Commerce, 2012. Intellectual Property and the US Economy, Industries in Focus. Economics and Statistics Administration and USPTO, US Department of Commerce.

Lakshmanan, T., Okumura, M., 1995. The nature and evolution of knowledge networks in Japanese manufacturing. Pap. Reg. Sci. 74 (1), 63–86.

Li, M., 2007. Analysis of Spatial Distribution of Industrial Clusters in China. Nanjing Science and Technology University master degree paper. June, pp. 42-43.

Lindqvist, G., Ketels, C., Sölvell, Ö., 2013. The Cluster Initiative Greenbook, 2.0. Ivory Tower Publishers, Stockholm.

Malecki, E., Oinas, P., 1998. Making Connections – Technological Learning and Regional Economic Change. Ashgate, Aldershot.

National Knowledge Commission (NKC), 2007. Innovation in India. NKC, Government of India, New Delhi.

Office of the Adviser to the Prime Minister on Public Information Infrastructure and Innovations, 2011. Industry Innovation Clusters. Office of the Adviser to the Prime Minister on Public Information Infrastructure and Innovations, New Delhi.

OECD, 1999. Boosting Innovation: the Cluster Approach. Organisation for Economic Co-operation and Development, Paris.

OECD, 2002. Dynamising National Systems of Innovation. Organisation for Economic Co-operation and Development, Paris.

Paytas, J., Gradeck, R., Andrews, L., 2004. Universities and the Development of Industry Clusters. Prepared for Economic Development Administration, US Department of Commerce, Carnegie Mellon University, Center for Economic Development, Pittsburgh, PA.

Pielke, R. Jr., 2013. Blog December, 30th.

Porter, M., 1990. The Competitive Advantage of Nations. The Free Press, New York.

Rao, et al., 2013. Promoting Innovation Clusters in India. Foundation of MSME Clusters, New Delhi.

Spence, M., Hlatshwayo, S., 2011. The evolving structure of the American economy and the employment change. Working Paper, Council on Foreign Relations, Maurice R. Greenberg, Center for Geoeconomic Studies.

Turner, M., Monnard, A., Leete, L., 2013. The Evaluation of the U.S. Small Business Administration's Regional Clusters Initiative, Year Two Report, June 2013. http://www.chinadmd.com/file/scsxiiosirpwrvvuv33aoww6_1.html.

Chapter 9

Opportunity Areas for Innovation

Chapter Contents

Most discussions on innovation around the world have focused on improving efficiency and productivity in business in order to stay ahead of competition. However, there are a large number societal problems that need to be addressed through innovation, such as a large and widening gap between the rich and the poor; population growth, aging population, and associated healthcare needs; energy, water, and housing shortages; global climate changes; air and water pollution; and illiteracy and the need for improving the quality of education.

Promotion of innovation, beyond what occurs naturally anyway, therefore, needs to be driven by these major problems that a nation faces and needs to be built upon resources and capabilities specifically available in the country, taking into account their level of development and maturity. This chapter discusses various difficulties unique to the local contexts of China, India, and the United States and reviews the approaches being taken to address these problems.

CHINA

Challenges China Faces

A Large and Widening Gap Between the Rich and the Poor

China's GDP, as discussed earlier, is now the second largest in the world, second only to that of the United States. But China's GDP per capita is just about

$6000 in 2012, ranking 84th in the world (China Economic Net, 2013). China, therefore, is still a low-income country. More seriously, China has big inequalities between eastern and western China and between urban and rural areas (China Economic Net, 2013). Although incomes have greatly increased since China "opened up" to the West, the income gap between the developed regions, mainly in the east, and undeveloped regions, mainly in the west, continues to widen. For example, by the end of 2005, per capita annual disposable income of urban residents in Shanghai reached ¥18,645, while the per capita annual disposable income of urban residence in Xinjiang in the west was only ¥7990. So, the income of an urban residence in eastern China was about 2.3 times that of their counterparts in western China. In the same time frame, per capita net income of rural residents near Shanghai was ¥8248, while the per capita net income of rural residents in Guizhou in western China was only ¥1877, a ratio of about 4.4.

Furthermore, the income gap between the urban and the rural areas is growing. In 1978, the ratio of income between urban and rural areas was about 2.4, and it increased to 3.2 in 2005 and to 3.3 in 2006 ("The Rural Economy in 2007," Social Sciences Academic Press). These ratios are almost twice that of those in most countries, which is around 1.5, according to the World Bank (Ping, 2007).

China's income inequality is a fairly very serious issue. According to the UN Human Development Report in 2004, the Gini coefficient, which measures statistical dispersion in income distribution, reached 0.45–0.53 in China. This was significantly higher than the Gini coefficients in most developed nations, such as the United States, France, Japan, Britain, Germany, and South Korea, where it ranges between 0.3 and 0.4, which is considered to be a reasonable range. China exceeded that warning line. At the same time, China has a large number of poor people. In 2011, the Chinese government, in its efforts to alleviate poverty, decided to use the 2010 per capita rural net income of ¥2300 as the new national standard for defining the poverty line. This was a 92% improvement over the definition of poverty in 2009, which was ¥1196. According to this new 2011 standard, China's rural population considered to be in poverty increased from about 126.9 M to 128 M, accounting for roughly 13.4% of the rural population (Chinanews.com, 2012). Based on 2005 purchasing power parity (PPP), this new Chinese standard for defining poverty is $1.8 per capita per day, which is close to the median of low- and middle-income countries (Dr. Chen Shaohua, World Bank Development Economic Research Department, Chinese Economic Net, 2013). If one were to use this definition of the poverty line, as opposed to the 2011 Chinese government standard, then there are about 254 M Chinese people in poverty, instead of the 128 M claimed by the Chinese government (Chinanews.com, 2011). Historically, in most countries across the globe, large income disparities coupled with large populations in poverty have been a source of social unrest and political instability and upheaval.

Aging Population

In the twenty-first century, a large number of countries will be facing the challenges of an aging population, and China undoubtedly is one of them, as shown in Table 9.1. In 2008, the number of people of age 60 or over in China was about 160 M, accounting for 12% of the total population, getting up to 14.3% in 2012, and exceeding 200 M in 2013. It is estimated that this number will be more than 400,000 M by 2034 (China Securities Journal, 2013). China's aging population of 60 and over also contributed to a very large percentage of the aging population in the world, at 21.7%, and of Asia, at 40.1% (Ping, 2013).

Urbanization

After 1990, China began to accelerate its rate of urbanization. This rate, which from 1953 to 1990 had been only 7%, increased in the following 20 years, from 1990 to 2010, to 23% (Table 9.2). In spite of this rapid increase in urbanization, this rate in China was slower than that of most countries in the world. For example, as shown in Table 9.3, in 2008, China's urbanization rate was 45.7%, which was lower than that of all countries except India, and was about half of that of the United Kingdom.

TABLE 9.1 China's Aging Population (2008–2012)

	2008	2009	2010	2011	2012
Old ages 60 or over 60 (million)	159.89	167.14	177.65	184.99	193.90
Percentage to total population (%)	12.0	12.5	13.3	13.7	14.3

Sources: Chinese Civil Affairs Statistics Yearbook 2013.

TABLE 9.2 Rate of Urbanization in China

	1953	1964	1982	1990	2000	2005[a]	2008[a]	2010
Rate of urbanization (%)	13.26	18.30	20.91	26.44	36.22	42.99	45.68	49.68

[a]China Development Report 2009.
Sources: Six National Population Census.

TABLE 9.3 Rate of Urbanization in Main Countries in the World

	1970	1980	1990	2000	2008
World	36.0	39.1	43.0	46.7	49.9
Developed countries					
The United States	73.6	73.7	75.3	–	81.7
Japan	53.2	59.6	63.1	65.2	66.5
The United Kingdom	–	87.9	88.7	89.4	89.9
Germany	72.3	72.8	73.1	73.1	73.6
BRIC					
China	–	19.4	26.4	36.2	45.7
Russia	62.5	69.8	73.4	73.4	72.8
India	19.8	23.1	25.5	27.7	29.5
Brazil	55.8	67.4	74.8	81.2	85.6
Others					
South Korea	40.7	56.7	73.8	79.6	81.5
Malaysia	33.5	42.0	49.8	62.0	70.4
Mexico	59.0	66.3	71.4	74.7	77.2

Sources: China Finance Yearbook 2010.

Pressures to Transform the Manufacturing Sector

In recent years, the labels of "Made in China" have been seen all around the world, giving a strong indication of the rapid rise of the manufacturing sector in China. In 2008, Chinese manufacturing exports reached $1.37 T, accounting for 11.3% of worldwide manufacturing exports, and ranked number one among all countries. In 2010, China's manufacturing output was about $1.955 T, which represented 19.8% of global manufacturing output, and exceeded the US manufacturing share, of 19.4%.

According to the United Nations Industrial Development Organization, from 2000 to 2005, the average annual value added by China's manufacturing industry was 10.74%, which is not only higher than the average world growth rate of manufacturing (3.38%) but also higher than the growth rate of manufacturing in developing countries (6.74%). Although the ratio of China's value-added through manufacturing compared to that from the rest of the world gradually increased, Chinese manufacturing value-added per capita was very low. Based on year 2000 constant price, Chinese manufacturing value-added per capita was $303, which is only 32% of the world average level. In 2005, Chinese manufacturing value per capita reached $480, accounting for 46% of the world average level, and in 2010, it was $820 and at 78% of the world average level. Compared to developed countries, China's value-added per capita fell behind greatly. In 2010, it was only 14.8% of that of the United States ($5522), 17.6% of Germany ($4667), and 10% of Japan ($7994; Wenke, 2013).

In addition, Chinese manufacturing industry had less competition compared to that in other countries. For example, in 2009, China's R&D accounted for 1.52% of GDP, whereas the average level for OECD members was 2.29%. The contribution rate of science and technology to GDP in China was 20–30% lower than that in developed countries, and the rate for commercialization advancements in science and technology was 50–60% lower than that in developed countries (China Economic Information Net, 2010). Among the top 500 enterprises in the manufacturing sector in the world, the United States had a share of 45.6%, which accounted for 49% of the total market value, while China's share (including Hong Kong) was only 1.2%, accounting for only 0.7% of value (Yulun, 2010).

Energy Problem

Rapid economic development in China has been accompanied by greatly increased energy consumption. The structure of energy consumption from energy produced in various forms—coal, crude oil, natural gas, and hydropower—from 1980 to 2011 is shown in Fig. 9.1. In 1980, energy consumption was 6.03 hundred million tons of standard coal equivalent (SCE) and increased almost 5 × to 3.48 B tons of SCE in 2011. With regard to the consumption structure, consumption percentage of coal fluctuated around 70%; for crude oil, it ranged from 17% to 21%; and for natural gas and hydropower in 2011, it was 5% and 8%, respectively. From these data, it is clear that growth in China is heavily dependent on energy produced from coal. In spite of the huge energy consumption in China, energy efficiency was much lower than that in the United States. Energy efficiency in China was 0.86 in 2000 and by 2008 increased 74% to 1.5, compared to the energy efficiency in the United States of 4.21 in 2008, which was about 2.8 × that of China (Table 9.4).

Also, newer sources of energy developed relatively slowly in China and contributed only a small percentage to the overall energy usage. As shown in Table 9.5, the lowest contribution of new energy in China was 7.2% in 2000 and the highest was 9% in 2007, showing that there is no serious pursuit of newer energy in China. In comparison, that percentage in the US new energy was 21.41% in 2008, 2 × that of China.

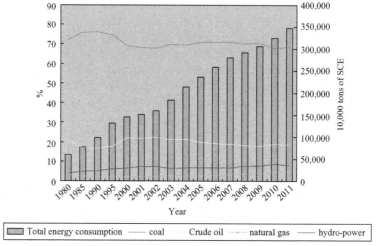

FIGURE 9.1 China's energy consumption and its structure (1980–2011).

Environmental Pollution

In recent years, China has faced increasingly serious environmental pollution. For example, in the winter of 2013, most cities in China often had very severe smog. In terms of the particulate matter index, PM-2.5, for the air in Harbin, for more than half of winter 2013, this index exceeded 200 µg/m³; for one-third of the winter, it was in the range of 100–200 µg/m³; and the index was under 100 µg/m³ for only a few days. Air quality in the major cities of China is shown in Table 9.6. The worst offending city was Lanzhou with its PM-10 index of 138 µg/m³. The city with the best index was Lhasa, Tibet, with its PM-10 index of 40 µg/m³. Of the 31 cities listed, in 10 cities, PM-10 indices are at or exceed 100 µg/m³, and only 8 cities have this index below 80 µg/m³.

By comparison, air quality in the United States is shown in Table 9.7, where particulates (PM-10) had a tendency to gradually decrease from 86.5 µg/m³ in 2001 to 68.5 µg/m³ in 2007. By contrast, in 2011, only three cities in China (Lhasa, Kunming, and Haikou) were able to achieve the PM-10 standard attained in the United States in 2007.

Addressing Unmet Needs in China

Given the above challenges faced by China, there are many unmet needs that must be addressed:

First, domestic consumption in China will keep increasing. This will be driven by income inequality, aging population, and increasing basic needs, such

TABLE 9.4 Output Value of Consumed Energy

Year	GDP in China (billion yuan)	GDP in the United States (billion dollar)	Chinese Energy Consumption (10 K tons of SCE)	US Energy Consumption (Btu $\times 10^{15}$)	Chinese Energy Efficiency ($/kg SCE)	US Energy Efficiency ($/kg SCE)
2000	9921.46	9817	138,553	98.98	0.86	2.9
2001	10,965.52	–	143,199	96.33	0.93	0
2002	12,033.27	10,470	151,797	97.86	0.96	3.13
2003	13,582.28	10,961	174,990	98.21	0.94	3.27
2004	15,987.83	11,686	203,227	100.35	0.95	3.41
2005	18,321.74	12,422	224,682	100.48	1	3.62
2006	21,192.35	13,178	246,270	99.88	1.08	3.86
2007	25,630.56	13,808	265,583	101.55	1.28	3.98
2008	30,067	14,265	285,000	99.3	1.5	4.21

Sources: Using data from China Statistics Yearbook 2009, China Energy Yearbook 2009, and US Statistical Abstract 2010 and foreign exchange rate from 2000 to 2008 published by the People's Bank of China.

TABLE 9.5 New Energy Percentages in the United States and China

		The United States	
Year	China	New Energy Percentage	Ratio of Renewable Energy to New Energy
2000	7.2	19.75	44.33
2001	8.2	18.57	39.85
2002	8.1	19.79	42.02
2003	7.3	20.03	43.71
2004	7.7	20.56	43.19
2005	7.9	20.92	43.99
2006	8.2	21.21	45.52
2007	9	21.34	44.56
2008	7.2	21.41	46.39

Sources: Zhijie Gao, Yukun Cao, 2012. Analysis of the Potential Development of Biomass Energy Industry in Heilongjiang Province under Carbon Economy. China Forestry Press, February, pp. 62–63.

TABLE 9.6 Ambient Air Quality in Major Cities in mg/m^3 (2011)

City	Particulate Matters (PM-10)	Sulfur Dioxide	Nitrogen Dioxide
Beijing	0.113	0.028	0.056
Tianjin	0.093	0.042	0.038
Shijiazhuang	0.099	0.052	0.041
Taiyuan	0.084	0.064	0.023
Hohhot	0.076	0.054	0.039
Shenyang	0.096	0.059	0.033
Changchun	0.091	0.026	0.043
Harbin	0.099	0.041	0.046
Shanghai	0.080	0.029	0.051
Nanjing	0.097	0.034	0.049
Hangzhou	0.093	0.039	0.058

Continued

TABLE 9.6 Ambient Air Quality in Major Cities in mg/m^3 (2011)—Cont'd

City	Particulate Matters (PM-10)	Sulfur Dioxide	Nitrogen Dioxide
Hefei	0.113	0.022	0.025
Fuzhou	0.069	0.009	0.032
Nanchang	0.088	0.056	0.038
Jinan	0.104	0.051	0.036
Zhengzhou	0.103	0.051	0.047
Wuhan	0.100	0.039	0.056
Changsha	0.083	0.040	0.047
Guangzhou	0.069	0.028	0.049
Nanning	0.073	0.026	0.033
Haikou	0.041	0.008	0.016
Chongqing	0.093	0.038	0.031
Chengdu	0.100	0.031	0.051
Guiyang	0.079	0.049	0.030
Kunming	0.065	0.037	0.044
Lhasa	0.040	0.009	0.023
Xi'an	0.118	0.042	0.041
Lanzhou	0.138	0.048	0.042
Xining	0.105	0.043	0.026
Yinchuan	0.095	0.038	0.030
Urumqi	0.132	0.079	0.068

Sources: China Statistics Yearbook 2012.

as food, daily supplies, education, medical services and facilities, community care, and in-home services for the elderly. Innovation will, therefore, be necessary in order to lower cost or to provide better products and services. For example, online shopping has already grown very rapidly in China. Taobao, the biggest platform for online shopping, is an example of one such company, whose online transactions broke the ¥35 B barrier on November 11, 2013, although its volume was only ¥19.1 B in 2012 (http://net.chinabyte.com/494/12772494.shtml). This will provide a big boost to innovation in the Internet

TABLE 9.7 National Ambient Air Pollutant Concentrations by Type of Pollutant: 2001–2007

Pollutant	Unit	Air Quality Standard[a]	2001	2002	2003	2004	2005	2006	2007
Carbon monoxide	ppm	[b]9	3.3	2.9	2.7	2.5	2.3	2.2	2.0
Ozone	ppm	[c]0.075	0.081	0.085	0.080	0.074	0.079	0.077	0.077
Sulfur dioxide	ppm	[d]0.03	0.0046	0.0043	0.0043	0.0041	0.0041	0.0037	0.0035
Particulates (PM-10)	µg/m³	[e]150	86.5	86.8	84.4	69.6	65.2	75.6	68.5
Fine particulates (PM-2.5) (annual average)	µg/m³	[f]15	13.2	12.7	12.3	11.9	12.9	11.6	11.9
Fine particulates (PM-2.5) (daily average)	µg/m³	[g]35	34.1	32.9	30.8	30.5	33.5	28.7	30.9
Nitrogen dioxide	ppm	[h]0.053	0.015	0.015	0.014	0.013	0.013	0.013	0.012

[a]Refers to the primary National Ambient Air Quality Standard.
[b]Based on the 8-h standard of 9 ppm.
[c]Based on the 8-h standard of 0.075 ppm. On March 12, 2008, the EPA revised the levels of primary and secondary 8-h ozone standards to 0.075 ppm.
[d]Based on the annual standard of 0.03 ppm.
[e]Based on the 24-h (daily) standard of 150 mg/m³. The particulates (PM-10) standard replaced the previous standard for total suspended particulates in 1987. In 2006, the EPA revoked the annual PM-10 standard.
[f]Based on the annual standard of 15 mg/m³. The PM-2.5 national monitoring network was deployed in 1999. National trend data prior to that time are not available.
[g]Based on the daily standard of 35 mg/m³. The PM-2.5 national monitoring network was deployed in 1999. National trend data prior to that time are not available.
[h]Based on the annual standard of 0.053 ppm.
Sources: US Statistical Abstract 2010.

finance and logistics industries. Similarly, services for the elderly also need to benefit from developments in Internet information video technologies, for example. Also, with increasing urbanization, innovation will be necessary to address issues created by pressures on housing and physical infrastructure.

Second, China will need to develop its own high-technology sector to replace the old, stagnating, and dying traditional industry sectors, which may be consumers of energy and materials, with low productivity and cost efficiency. Newer industries that are attracting a lot of attention in China, hence providing plenty of opportunities for innovation, are aircraft and aviation equipment, satellite and space applications, high-speed rail transportation, shipbuilding and marine engineering, robots and intelligent manufacturing equipment, and other advanced manufacturing sectors. China will need to transition from an emphasis on "Made in China" to "Created in China."

Third, there is increased emphasis on newer sources of energy. China's "Renewable Energy Development 'Twelfth Five-Year Plan'" points out that, by 2015, renewable energy, including hydropower, nuclear energy, wind energy, solar energy, biomass energy, and geothermal energy, will produce 460 M tons of SCE. Energy demand in China in 2020 is estimated to be 5 B tons of SCE, with 15% of this need being addressed by new energy sources. Also, the Chinese plan for automobiles states in the "Energy Saving and New Energy Automobile Industry Development Plan (2012–2020)," that, by 2020, China will produce 2 M pure electric and plug-in hybrid vehicles (Daily Economy News, 2013). Both of these areas provide opportunities for innovation in China.

Lastly, environmental protection is starting to gain increasing attention. With the recent onslaught of bad news on the environmental front, such as heavy smog, contaminated water, and industrial air and water pollution, increasing attention is being paid to multipollutant control and comprehensive recycling and disposal of solid waste. This also provides opportunities to innovate and develop products, services, and business models for air and water purification and more efficient energy consumption.

INDIA

Although economic development has been taking place at an increasingly fast pace, nearly half the world's population lives in acute poverty. Worldwide, over 4 B people form the "bottom of the economic pyramid" (BoP), a term coined to represent those earning less than $2 per day ($1500 per person/year in local purchasing power; office of the advisor to the Prime Minister, 2011).

India is an extreme "dual" economy. On one extreme, its recent economic growth has made it the world's third-largest economy in PPP terms, and its nuclear and space power and prominence in certain key economic sectors such as biotechnology, pharmaceuticals, automotive components, information technology (IT), software, and IT-enabled services are being recognized the world over.

At the opposite extreme, India is still a low-income, mainly rural, agrarian, and subsistence economy with an average per capita income of $1492 in 2012 (IMF ranking 139 among 182 countries), high illiteracy rates, and about a quarter of its population living below the national poverty line. The formal sector of the Indian economy employs only 11% of the workforce; the remaining 89% of the workforce is employed by the informal sector (Dutz and Dahlman, 2007).

Persistent poverty and unmet needs of the informal sector and the poor remain a huge challenge for India. The implications are limited access to basic services such as food, water, housing, health, and education to a large percentage of the population and spatial differences in growth. Big divides exist— between the west and the south on the one hand with the majority of new investments and the north and east on the other hand with relatively few; between urban areas where growth has taken off and the rural hinterlands that have stagnated, with a deep agrarian crisis affecting many regions; and last but not least the cultural gap between the treatment of men and that of women. These inequalities are manifesting themselves in the form of rural suicides, regular conflicts, protests, and unrest. With the global economic downturn, such discontent is also spreading to the urban areas, which have profited from the boom to date, as lower-skilled workers, very often women, are laid off as contracts end, when technology companies run out or when companies shut down due to a decrease in business volume with the United States and the West, in general.

In addition to the regional, social, and economic inequalities, there are disparities in the provision of basic amenities. Scientific Advisory Council to the Prime Minister (2010) in its report has highlighted the challenges in providing water, energy, and food as follows:

> Because of the vagaries of the monsoon, the nature of the hydrological cycle and the physiographical and geological attributes of the country the only replenishable water availability is finite and subject to unpredictable variability. Scientific analysis suggests that India's current water usage is already close to annual availability, and that this could lead to serious shortfalls over the next two decades. Furthermore, the physical and ecological integrity of India's water resource system is seriously jeopardized by rapid industrial and population growth. . ..
>
> Energy shortage is a chronic and serious problem in many parts of the country. Uncertainties in the availability and pricing of oil resources, increasingly serious concerns with climate change, difficult ecological and human displacement problems with large dams, and a host of other similar considerations have made it essential for us to take a more integrated view of energy problems. . .food security is associated with problems of water and energy resources that we have indicated above. A second green revolution is now needed. . ..

To sum up, in addition to the social and cultural problems alluded to earlier, the pressing economic challenges faced by India are energy and environment, food and nutrition, water and sanitation, habitat, affordable healthcare, skill building and employment, universal access to education, equity and social justice, and national security—internal and external (Ministry of Science and Technology, 2013 and a Scientific Advisory Council to Prime Minister, 2010).

Addressing Unmet Needs

Several innovative approaches have been proposed and applied by different communities and individuals to tackle these challenges.

The traditional top-down approach advocates provision of solutions to the poor by the government, nonprofit organizations, or business (Gupta, 2013). The celebrated bottom of the pyramid (BoP) approach on the other hand posits that over 4 B people, in India, China, and elsewhere, who live on less than $2 a day, present a market opportunity of $5 T in PPP (Prahalad, 2012). Prahalad (2012) argued that the BoP market is also a new source of radical innovation offering exciting opportunities for the creation of new products and business models by facilitating awareness, access, affordability, and availability. Prahalad and Mashelkar (2010) called this model the Gandhian innovation model, a frugal innovation model that overcomes lack of resources in such markets by developing strategies to create new products with few resources and sell them cheaply to more people or in other words a model that purports "more from less for more."

While the success of frugal innovation or Gandhian innovation model in a resource-scarce economy like India has its own merits, treating the poor merely as a sink of corporate goods and services will not work if there is a lack of appreciation of fundamental differences in the psychological, physical, and economic realities of the poor (Karnani, 2009). For example, if the BoP products and solutions assume that poorer people are doomed to live with pollution and unequal access to basic amenities such as water, sanitation, and power, the efforts may be counterproductive (Chattejee, 2009). Companies selling and marketing products that require no water, for instance, maybe perceived as "opportunistic" and disconnected from the larger issues of the society (Chattejee, 2009). Therefore, overemphasis of the role of private enterprise in such initiatives sometimes dilutes the legal, regulatory, and social roles of state in protecting the vulnerable poor (Karnani, 2009). e-Choupal, a widely acclaimed BoP IT initiative in agricultural markets in rural India created by ITC, a large private corporation, is an illustration of such a kind.

Varman et al. (2012) in their case study of e-Choupal found that the initiative excludes the socioeconomically underprivileged or subaltern groups that it claimed to serve and makes the relatively wealthy or privileged more active and entrepreneurial. This was because the public policy framework is unable to provide guidance for reducing the gulf between poverty alleviation and private gains inherent in the BoP initiative. Kurian et al. (2008) came up with a similar conclusion when they studied the impact of Akshaya kiosks public/private sector collaboration that aimed for rural development through access to information and computer literacy and financial viability through a sustainable business model. They found that these kiosks were used mostly by middle-class students and aspiring professionals, not by those who needed basic educational or e-governance services.

However, community-led enterprises have been successful in contributing to both local economic development and social development. In these enterprises, community acts corporately as both entrepreneur and enterprise in pursuit of the common good models of enterprise-led poverty alleviation (Peredo and Chrisman in Somerville and McElwee, 2011). Amul, Shri Mahila Griha Udyog Lijjat Papad, and Gram Mooligai Limited (GMCL) are examples of successful community-led enterprises in India that have helped in both social upliftment and economic upliftment of several poor people. Amul story or the white revolution as it is called in India transformed India into the largest producer of milk, significantly contributing to the country's growth trajectory (Office of Advisor to the Prime Minister, 2011). For a community-led enterprise to be successful, social capital and trust are required. There are instances where this model has not worked because of gaps between the common man, government, and the elite arising from the lack of social capital and trust (Lundahl, 2010).

An alternative approach for inclusive development is the grassroots innovation model. The Honey Bee Network is an example of this model. This network recognizes that poor people are not at the bottom of the knowledge, ethical, or innovation pyramids and that building upon grassroots innovations that emanate from this part of the pyramid can serve as a fundamental building block for societal transformation (Gupta, 2013). The network not only scouts and documents such innovations but also supports them through incubation, microventure capital, and building partnerships between formal and informal sciences. The network believes that by doing so, enterprise-led development can be achieved in a dignified and a mutually respectful manner.

India's challenges are so complex and diverse that the above models are not foolproof. While they are successful in certain circumstances, they have also failed in several cases. To make any innovation model effective, policy checks through which the promises of inclusivity are facilitated, monitored, and implemented are required.

Innovation in India has to play a role not only in finding affordable, quality services and products for people at the BoP but also in creating mechanisms and platforms to scale grassroots innovations to generate sustainable livelihood and employment. Challenges such as lack of housing, healthcare, and education will require innovations in processes, service delivery, design thinking, and human capital involving multiple stakeholders as well as stronger institutional infrastructure.

THE UNITED STATES

The United States faces some of the same problems as China, and to some extent as India, although to different degrees: (1) a large and widening gap between the rich and the poor, (2) an aging population, (3) resuscitation and growth of the declining manufacturing sector, (4) energy self-dependence, and (5) environmental pollution. Declining standards of education and the absence of a coordinated science and technology policy seem to be other problems that are significant challenges for the United States. However, the degree and severity of some of these challenges in emerging markets of China and India are far more daunting than those in a highly industrialized, modern economy, such as the United States. In some cases, given the dynamics, cost structures, and the price points affordable in emerging markets, innovations created in these emerging markets might find their way back to the United States, as examples of "reverse innovation."

While the United States has depended on the creativity, innovation, and entrepreneurial spirit of the private sector through most of its young history, the US government, as discussed earlier, has played a huge role in the past in advancing science and technology, which in turn has helped establish the United States as an industrial and economic superpower. Opportunity-driven innovation in the private sector will always happen in the United States, as evidenced by recent history and value created by private enterprise for the US economy, and will continue to happen in the future—opportunities that create value for the entrepreneur and for the society. However, very often, what is forgotten and "lost in translation" is the contribution made by the US government in funding the foundational work that later enabled private enterprise to benefit from it. US government investments usually do not have a short-time horizon for obtaining a return, usually taking decades to pay off—a much longer cycle than the 4-year political cycle of presidential and congressional elections, not infrequently heavily influenced by narrow industry-specific interest groups, operating as lobbyists and regional "pork-barrel" politics.

In a lot of ways, we are still reaping the benefits of US government investments made from the 1940s through the 1980s. Investments in research and development and innovation in the defense sector have certainly continued as they should. However, there is also a need for a coordinated US science and technology policy that encourages and supports research and development, invention, and innovation in other areas such as the ones mentioned below. This will also help spur investments by the private sector, as it did in the past, and will go a long way towards reestablishing US competitiveness in the future.

From an innovation and entrepreneurship perspective, therefore, we focus on those areas that provide the most fertile ground for new growth in the United States in the years to come that could benefit from a coordinated US government science and technology policy. Although not intended to be a comprehensive and all-encompassing list, we believe some of these areas are as follows:

1. Healthcare, telemedicine, biotechnology, and biomedical instrumentation
   This is the largest sector of the US economy at about $1.7 T, and a very large number of players are involved in the value chain and the ecosystem

for this sector. Also, as discussed earlier, among the three countries discussed in detail in this book, the United States has the fastest aging population who are now living longer. This sector affords a large opportunity for innovation and entrepreneurship.

2. Pharmaceuticals, biomolecular systems, and bioinformatics

    For some of the same reasons discussed above, this is another significant area for innovation and entrepreneurship. A much improved understanding of the human DNA and the functional and physical mapping of the human genes made possible by the Human Genome Project now enables discovery and development of new disease-specific pharmaceuticals and means for fighting new drug-resistant microbes.

3. Brain and neuroscience

    This appears to be the "last frontier" in understanding our own complexity as to who we are as human beings. What the Human Genome Project has done for understanding the human DNA, there is now a similar opportunity to understand the most complicated part of the human anatomy that defines us, who we are and why we are the way we are; to better understand human behavior and the link between feeling and being, thought and emotions, and the human "hardware and software"; and even potentially to understand what consciousness is.

4. Robotics, industrial automation, and increased focus on the manufacturing sector

    This has been a field that has been attracting a lot of attention in the last decade or two. With capabilities enabled by the progression along Moore's law, in the computing, storage, and communicating capabilities of semiconductor photonic chips, as well as in instrumentation, using control and feedback systems, highly functioning robots are very close to being realized for performing tasks that humans may rather not perform. The applications of these robots in dangerous tasks, as well as in the manufacturing sector for industrial automation, could further enhance productivity.

5. Nanotechnology-based new materials, devices, and technologies

    Advances in semiconductor technology have progressed along Moore's law over the last 50 plus years but may now be asymptotically reaching limits dictated by the laws of physics, limiting further scaling. However, this has driven research for materials and technologies on the nanometer scales. New materials have been discovered with very unique physical, chemical, or electrical properties that could further lead to entirely new types of materials devices and technologies. This is another area that is ripe for future innovation and entrepreneurship.

6. Energy, alternative energy, clean energy, utilities, and the energy physical infrastructure

    The US population today is approaching 350 M, and energy usage per person has been increasing over time. With such significant demands on energy usage, there is a need for new sources of energy—both traditional and new. Among the traditional sources, there is a need to further explore oil and gas, coal and shale, and cleaner forms of traditional energy, such as nuclear. Given the challenges of pollution and fossil fuel-driven global warming, there are opportunities to explore and develop newer and cleaner forms of energy—solar, wind, geothermal, and others. Along with sources of energy, for both mobile usage and fixed usage, the transmission and distribution network, and the energy grid in the United States, is aging and provides further opportunities for innovation and entrepreneurship.

7. Transportation infrastructure: roadways, high-speed rail, waterways, air traffic, and airports

   Most of Europe and Japan have had advanced, high-speed mass transportation railroad networks for several decades, and now, one of the most advanced, very high-speed rail networks is being built in China. This is an opportunity that has not been pursued in the United States in the past, due to the availability of an advanced road network and interstate highway system. Over the years, this was complemented by one of the world's most extensive and busiest air transportation networks. In the earlier years of its history, commerce and transportation in the United States were enabled by waterways and later an extensive rail network around and after the Civil War. Although these have been superseded by highway and air transportation infrastructures, investments in most of these areas for the most part are also somewhat dated. All of these areas provide opportunities for investments and innovation.

8. Information infrastructure: big data, big data analytics, fraud prevention, and cybersecurity

   The Internet and social media enabled by both advances in mobile wireless and fixed wire-line cable and optical networks close to infinite capacity, and increasingly smart endpoint devices, have driven an information explosion with an exponentially increasing number of bits and bytes and streams of ones and zeros floating around through space in the form of radio waves and through cables carrying both private information and non-private information. The "genie is out of the bottle" here and no reversal is expected in this trend. On the contrary, with content rapidly transitioning from pure data to data consisting of voice, audio, video, and now also high-definition (HD) and ultra-HD video, and in the future, potentially, 3D video, and the fundamental human need to connect with others, further continuation of the exponential rise in data is a foregone conclusion. This making information infrastructure—the information superhighway and broadband access—available to all strata of society has to be a priority.

   Data that describe users and their habits and patterns are being collected in the form of "metadata" and used by companies for marketing and commercial purposes—these are big data—and defining algorithms to discern patterns within those data for commercial use is termed big data analytics. Along with the availability of these massive amounts of data comes the need for privacy protection, fraud prevention, and, in general, maintaining security of the data. All fall within the general category of cybersecurity and at a corporate or national level become significant priorities, to prevent corporate or national espionage and to prevent cyberterrorism, which could potentially bring a nation's day-to-day activities to a standstill, since most commerce now depends so heavily on the information infrastructure. This area, just as it has in the recent past, will continue to be an area that will be driven by innovation and entrepreneurship.

9. The space program

The benefits accrued to the United States and the US economy—both psychological and physical—from the clarion call to "put man on the moon" are well known. The nation rallied and unified behind this vision, and when the mission was accomplished, the nation's psyche soared, filled with a sense of pride and accomplishment. Apart from these psychological benefits, the advances in technology needed to achieve that and funded by NASA flowed through the rest of the economy—new materials and technologies and devices that could be used in broader commercial applications. The work of NASA that followed and later of JPL to guide missions to other planets has yielded other dividends as well, along with increasing our knowledge of the universe we inhabit, and also laid the groundwork for potential commercial human travel to the moon and beyond. New private corporations are now pursuing commercial human travel with more advanced propulsion systems and transport vehicles, in another display of American innovation and entrepreneurship. Successes in these endeavors will encourage further investments in these areas.

10. Education infrastructure: schools, colleges, and universities

All of the areas discussed above are highly technology-driven and hence require advanced education in sciences, technology, engineering, and mathematics—the "hard skills," along with a good education in the social sciences to help develop the "soft skills" that are needed for comprehension and communication of complex concepts, as well as leadership and teamwork in large organizations, which typically is how complex projects get worked.

As discussed before, while these were areas of strengths for the United States until about the 1980s, there has been a gradual but perceptible and measurable decline in the interest in pursuing these areas and hence in these faculties, among the younger generations in the United States. This starts all the way from early education in the schools, which are the feeder systems for colleges and universities. While the US population has increased to 350 M with an accompanying increase in the population of young people, and the number of colleges and universities has also substantially increased over the same period, US students are not faring well in standardized tests in relation to their counterparts elsewhere, especially in other developed countries.

This has not been helped by the ever-widening income gap, a decline in the quality and rigor of education, rising costs of education, increasing debt burden for students who choose to pursue college and university education, and more importantly a cultural shift that seems to undervalue education in relation to other pursuits, such as sports and athletics and entertainment, as well as a regression in large parts of the country to a politicoreligious end of the spectrum that runs counter to well-known and well-established science. A common refrain by those who are in politics to address this problem has been as follows: we will allow an influx, an "insourcing," of skilled immigrants to come to the United States and be our future scientists and engineers and be our inventors and innovators. These are some of the same folks who do not bemoan the transition of the United States from a manufacturing economy to a service economy. While some of this is needed, and indeed necessary, to attract the best and brightest to come and devote their energies and talents to the United States, this cannot be a substitute for training those who are born and brought up in the United States.

The need for not only more investment but also more efficient use of the investments being made in this area, as well as innovative and creative ways to improve the quality and delivery of education, will be needed to reverse the downward trend in this area.

In summary, most discussions on innovation around the world have focused on improving efficiency and productivity in business in order to stay ahead of competition. However, there are a large number societal problems that need to be addressed through innovation, such as a large and widening gap between the rich and the poor; population growth, aging population, and associated healthcare needs; energy, water, and housing shortages; global climate changes; air and water pollution; and illiteracy and the need for improving the quality of education.

Promotion of innovation, beyond what occurs naturally anyway, therefore, needs to be driven by these major problems that a nation faces and needs to be built upon resources and capabilities specifically available in the country, taking into account their level of development and maturity. We discussed various difficulties unique to the local contexts of China, India, and the United States and reviewed the approaches being taken to address these problems.

REFERENCES

Chattejee, S., 2009, August. Selling to the Poor – Reflection, Critique and Dialogue. Retrieved July 8, 2013, from:http://warrington.ufl.edu/graduate/academics/pdb/docs/proposals/2009_SuparnaChatterjee.pdf.

China Economic Information Net, 2010. http://www.cei.gov.cn/default.aspx?tab=159 (accessed 18.10.10.).

China Economic Net, 2013. http://www.ce.cn/ (accessed 22.08.13.).

China Securities Journal, 2013. http://www.cs.com.cn/ (accessed 28.12.13.).

Chinanews Net, 2011. http://www.chinanews.com/ (accessed 15.04.11.).

Chinanews Net, 2012. http://www.chinanews.com/ (accessed 23.06.12.).

Daily Economy News, 2013. http://www.chinanews.com/ (accessed 31.12.13.).

Dutz and Dahlman, M.A., 2007. The Indian context and enabling environment. In: Dutz, M.A. (Ed.), Unleashing India's Innovation – Towards Sustainable and Inclusive Growth. The World Bank, Washington, DC, pp. 49–82.

Gupta, A., 2013. Tapping the entrepreneurial potential of grassroots innovation. SSIR 11 (3 (Summer)), 18–20 (Sponsored Supplement).

Karnani, A., 2009. Romanticizing the poor. SSIR 7 (1), 38–43.

Kurian, R., et al., 2008. *How to use technology to spur development*. Issues Sci. Technol. 24 (2 (Winter)), 73.

Lundahl, M., 2010. The failure of community-based entrepreneurship in Haiti. Int. J. Innov. Regional Dev. 2, 112–127.

Ministry of Science and Technology, 2013. Science, Technology and Innovation Policy 2013. Government of India, New Delhi.

Office of Advisor to the Prime Minister, 2011. Towards a More Inclusive and Innovative India – Creating a Roadmap for a Decade of Innovation. Office of Advisor to the Prime Minister, New Delhi.

Ping, L., 2007. Analysis on income inequality in china and countermeasures to resolve it. Special Zone Economy 9, 200–201.

Ping, L., 2013. Research on the Effect of Population Aging on Economic Growth in China, Shandong University doctor degree paper, April, p. 29.

Prahalad, C., 2012. Bottom of the pyramid as a source of breakthrough innovations. J. Prod. Innov. Manage. 29, 6–12.

Prahalad, Mashelkar, 2010. Innovation's Holy Grail. Harvard Business Review.

Scientific Advisory Council to the Prime Minister, 2010. India as a Global Leader in Science. Department of Science and Technology, Government of India, New Delhi.

Somerville and McElwee, 2011. Situating community enterprise: a theoretical exploration. Entrep. Reg. Dev. 23, 317–330.

Varman, et al., 2012. Conflicts at the bottom of the pyramid: profitability, poverty alleviation, and neoliberal governmentality. J. Public Pol. Marketing 31 (1), 19–35.

Wenke, C., 2013. Analysis on China manufacturing industry and its international competitiveness. Foreign Economic Relations & Trade (7), 7–10.

Yulun, L., 2010. A research on China current manufacturing and international comparison. J. North China Electric Power Univ. (Soc. Sci.) 3, 32–37.

Part II

Entrepreneurship

Chapter 10

Entrepreneurship

Chapter Contents

WHAT IS ENTREPRENEURSHIP?

As was the case in relation to the definition of the word innovation discussed previously, the word entrepreneurship may mean different things to different people, and there is no universally accepted definition of the word. Furthermore, the meaning of the term entrepreneur has evolved over time, since its earliest usage in the Middle Ages. Once again, as discussed previously, we refer back to the work of Joseph Schumpeter in the mid-twentieth century, who made significant contributions to the development of entrepreneurship.

An all-encompassing definition of entrepreneurship is that it is the process of creating value, by bringing together a unique combination of resources to exploit an opportunity. Key components of this definition are that it is a process where entrepreneurs create value where there was none before, by bringing together resources in a unique way, and that it is an opportunity-driven behavior. Entrepreneurship can occur in various contexts—start-up ventures, small firms, mid-sized firms, large conglomerates, nonprofit organizations, and public sector agencies. Thus, the words that are most commonly associated with entrepreneurship are starting, founding, and creating; new business and new venture; innovation, new products, and new markets; pursuit of opportunity; risk-taking, risk management, and uncertainty; and profit seeking and personal benefit (Morris et al., 2008). A narrower definition is that the essential act of entrepreneurship is new entry, the act of launching a new venture either by a start-up firm, or through an existing firm, or through internal corporate venturing—new entry is the central idea underlying the concept of entrepreneurship (Lumpkin and Dess, 1996).

Another definition of entrepreneurship is that it is the process of creating something new with value by devoting the necessary time and effort, assuming the accompanying financial, psychic, and social risks, and uncertainties and receiving the rewards of monetary and personal satisfaction. So how is entrepreneurship different from innovation? According to Peter Drucker, "Innovation is the specific function of entrepreneurship...it is the means by which the entrepreneur either creates new wealth producing resources or endows existing resources with enhanced potential for creating wealth." So, entrepreneurship and innovation are complementary. Entrepreneurship is about identifying new innovations in products, services, processes, or technologies and adapting these innovations to achieve greater competitiveness and enhanced performance or to create new business opportunities. Innovation is thus the core part of entrepreneurship and harnesses the creative energy and develops those ideas into realistic opportunities (Hisrich and Kearney, 2014).

Key dimensions of entrepreneurship are (1) the degree of innovativeness, (2) the degree of risk-taking, and (3) the degree of proactiveness. So, the degree of entrepreneurship is measured by these three factors. One can further analyze this factor by plotting the frequency of occurrence on the one axis and then plotting the degree of entrepreneurship versus the frequency at which this occurs to define the entrepreneurial intensity of an organization (Morris et al., 2008). This metric is very relevant in discussing corporate entrepreneurship, or intrapreneurship, which we will do in a later chapter.

A broad definition of an entrepreneur is someone who organizes, manages, and assumes the risk of a business or enterprise. Entrepreneurs create new ideas, new businesses, and new industries. Value is created by the entrepreneurs through their products or services both for the customers and for themselves and for their enterprise. They pursue these opportunities regardless of resources they initially control. They challenge existing assumptions and look to create value in more creative and innovative ways. They change ways in which business is conducted by identifying opportunities successfully and fulfilling societal needs. Entrepreneurs focus less on the current situation and more on what can be. To once again quote Joseph Schumpeter, "Entrepreneurs reform or revolutionize...they act with confidence beyond the range of familiar beacons to overcome resistance of tradition...their function does not involve essentially in inventing anything...it consists in getting things done." In this context, their most important assets are their intelligence, energy, experience, and creativity, not necessarily their money or material possessions.

THE ENTREPRENEURIAL PROCESS

As mentioned before, entrepreneurship is a process. Briefly, this process consists of six steps—(1) identifying the opportunity, (2) defining the business concept, (3) assessing the resource requirements, (4) acquiring the necessary resources, (5) implementing and managing the business concept, and (6) harvesting the venture (Morris et al., 2008). A similar approach to define the entrepreneurial process is discussed by Hisrich and Kearney and essentially consists of four steps not too dissimilar from the process above. This alternative process consists of (1) identifying and evaluating the business opportunity, (2) developing the business plan, (3) identifying the resources needed, and (4) starting and managing the enterprise.

In either approach, the most important and the most difficult part of the process is the first step—that of identifying and evaluating the business opportunity. This comes about through the entrepreneur's alertness to potential unmet needs of the customer and the ability to match that with a unique and superior solution from the entrepreneur. When these two come together, it creates a unique value proposition for the customer. This further needs to be subjected to several cycles of customer validation in order to confirm that "if you build it they will come." This is also the time to verify that the opportunity is real as opposed to perceived and understand the size and scope of the opportunity through market segmentation, market size analysis, and a take-to-market plan, thus being able to assess the risk versus reward of the opportunity. An initial analysis of this type then gives way to a more rigorous business concept validation and the development of a detailed business plan. This is then followed by determining the financial and human resources needed through the various phases of the project and then actually beginning the execution phase of the opportunity.

ENTREPRENEURSHIP: NEW VENTURES

Entrepreneurship has played very important roles in the United States, China, and India. By the end of 2009, small and medium enterprises (SMEs) registered with the Chinese administrative department of industry and commerce had reached 10.23 M, accounting for more than 99% of enterprises in China, more than 60% of GDP, more than 50% of tax revenue, 70% of import and export trade, and 80% of all jobs created in China (Zeng, 2010). In the United States, from 1965 to 1984, the level of employment grew from 71 to 103 M, an increase of 45%, and almost all of these jobs were created by entrepreneurial and innovative SMEs (Drucker, 1985). In the case of India, 29.8 M micro, small, and medium enterprises (MSME) employ 69 M people—the second largest workforce in the country after the agricultural sector—contributing 11.5% a year to GDP (International Financial Corporation (IFC) and Government of Japan, 2012). This clearly demonstrates the importance of entrepreneurship as a driving force for economic growth, as it not only increases productivity but also creates jobs.

Entrepreneurship entails commercialization of innovation and is driven not only by personal characteristics of entrepreneurial individuals but also to a large extent by the environment in which they operate.

As far as friendliness of business environment among the three countries is concerned, according to the "Doing Business 2013" report published by the World

Bank and International Financial Corporation, India ranks 132, the United States ranks 4, and China ranks 91 out of 185 countries in terms of ease of doing business based on various parameters, some of which are mentioned below.

Doing Business in the United States

- Starting a business: rank 13; 6 procedures; 6 days
- Dealing with construction permits: rank 17; 15 procedures; 27 days
- Registering property: rank 25; 4 procedures; 12 days
- Paying taxes: rank 16; 11 payments per year; 175 h/year
- Enforcing contracts: rank 6; 32 procedures; 370 days
- Resolving insolvency: rank 16, 1.5 years; recovery rate 87.5%.

Doing Business in China

- Starting a business: rank 151; 13 procedures; 33 days
- Dealing with construction permits: rank 181; 28 procedures; 270 days
- Registering property: rank 44; 4 procedures; 29 days
- Paying taxes: rank 122; 7 payments per year; 338 h/year
- Enforcing contracts: rank 19; 37 procedures; 406 days
- Resolving insolvency: rank 82, 1.7 years; recovery rate 35.7%.

Doing Business in India

- Starting a business: rank 173; 12 procedures; 27 days
- Dealing with construction permits: rank 182; 7 procedures; 67 days
- Registering property: rank 94; 5 procedures; 44 days
- Paying taxes: rank 152; 33 payments per year; 243 h/year
- Enforcing contracts: rank 184; 46 procedures; 1420 days
- Resolving insolvency: rank 116, 4.3 years; recovery rate 26%.

The above figures indicate that in terms of ease of doing business, India has a lot of catching up to do—as compared to China and the United States across all parameters.

In China, there is a lot of variability in friendliness of the business environment among various provinces. Table 10.1 shows the top and bottom five provinces that had the most friendly business environment, considering the following factors: permission to start a business, ability to register property and business, qualifying to obtain credit, and upholding and enforcing contracts. On the whole, Guangdong, Shanghai, Jiangsu, Fujian, and Shandong have better commercial environments, while Guizhou, Ningxia, Gansu, and Guangxi do not appear to have as friendly a business environment.

As in the case of China, India also has evidenced regional divergence in economic and entrepreneurial activity. The western region has the highest level of

TABLE 10.1 Ease of Doing Business in China: Top and Bottom Five Provinces

Rank No.	Starting a Business	Registering Property	Getting Credit	Enforcing Contracts
1	Zhejiang	Shanghai	Fujian	Guangdong
2	Jiangsu	Guangdong	Jiangsu	Jiangsu
3	Guangdong	Fujian	Guangdong	Zhejiang
4	Shandong	Shandong	Shandong	Shanghai
5	Shanghai	Jiangsu	Shanghai	Shaanxi
...	...	...	...	...
26	Ningxia	Shanxi	Xinjiang	Anhui
27	Anhui	Henan	Ningxia	Hunan
28	Guangxi	Guizhou	Shaanxi	Qinghai
29	Gansu	Gansu	Gansu	Yunnan
30	Guizhou	Guangxi	Guangxi	Gansu

Each province is represented by its capital city, and Hong Kong, Macau, Taiwan, and Tibet are excluded.
Resources: World Bank, Doing Business in China, 2008. Beijing: Social Sciences Literature Press, 2008, p. 38–9

economic activity followed by the northern and the southern regions, while Eastern India has the lowest level of economic and entrepreneurial activity. Regions with greater entrepreneurial development activity would have more success stories, have presence of informal networks to support entrepreneurship, exhibit more resilience to failure, benefit from informal learning from social channels of communication, and encourage entrepreneurial activity (Lavoie et al., 2000 in Goel et al., 2007). Together, they give rise to a positive spiral in favor of promoting entrepreneurship and entrepreneurial activity, thereby making the attitude towards entrepreneurs and entrepreneurship more positive in more developed regions. Goel et al. (2007) in their study partially substantiated this hypothesis and found that people from the more developed western and southern parts of India have a higher preference for entrepreneurship as a career option as compared to other parts of the country (Table 10.2).

FACTORS CONTRIBUTING TO ENTREPRENEURSHIP

We next address the question, what factors affect entrepreneurship in a given society? We use the Global Competitiveness Index (GCI) to understand the factors that impact the level of entrepreneurship in a country. GCI, prepared by the

TABLE 10.2 India: Regional Breakout of Registered Companies (2000)

Region	N	%
North	128,410	27.40
South	100,257	21.40
East	76,625	16.35
West	163,280	34.85
Total	468,572	100.00

Source: Indiastat.com

World Economic Forum for 2012–2013, measures the set of institutions, policies, and factors that set the sustainable current and medium-term levels of economic prosperity. It gives an overall score and ranking of competitiveness for 144 countries. These indices have been constructed using 12 factors or "pillars" of competiveness, grouped into three categories, or subindices—basic requirements, efficiency enhancers, and innovation and sophistication. The structure of these indices and subindices is shown in Fig. 10.1. Based upon the strength of

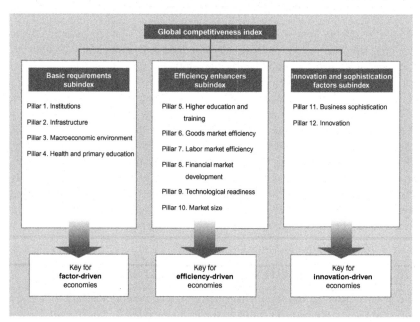

FIGURE 10.1 Structure of the GCI, 2012–2013, World Economic Forum.

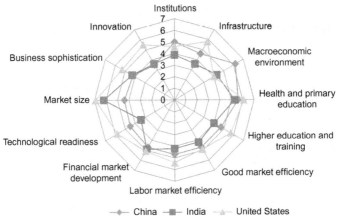

FIGURE 10.2 The local dynamics of competitiveness, GCI, 2012–2013, World Economic Forum.

these indices and subindices, the economy of a country can fall into one of three categories—factor-driven, efficiency-driven, and innovation-driven economies.

The radar diagram in Fig. 10.2 shows the scores of the three countries for each of the twelve factors or pillars. The United States ranks 7th out of 144 countries in the GCI, while China ranks 29th and India 51st. The overall GCI score for the United States is 5.5, while it is 4.8 for China and 4.3 for India. The United States is characterized as an "innovation-driven" economy, in this scheme, whereas China is described as "efficiency-driven" and India as "factor-driven." Both India and China need to catch up in almost all the input indicators as compared to the United States. Technologically, India seems to be lagging far behind the other two larger economies of the world, although in terms of market size it is ahead of China.

In summary, while innovation is associated with the idea of creating something new that is of value, and is a core aspect of entrepreneurship, entrepreneurship is generally associated with the notion of risk-taking, commercialization, and creation of value and wealth. Entrepreneurship depends on a number of characteristics that go beyond individual or personal characteristics. These characteristics relate to the environment in which the innovative or entrepreneurial individuals operate. By most commonly defined measures, the United States still provides an environment that is supportive of entrepreneurship, probably among the best in the world, and far superior to that provided by China and India, with China faring slightly better than India. We discuss these factors more in detail in the next few chapters.

REFERENCES

Drucker, P., 1985. Innovation and Entrepreneurship. Harper Business.

Goel, et al., 2007. Attitudes of the youth towards entrepreneurs and entrepreneurship: a cross-cultural comparison of India and China. J. Asia Entrep. Sustain.

Hisrich, R.D., Kearney, C., 2014. Managing Innovation and Entrepreneurship. SAGE Publications.

International Financial Corporation (IFC) and Government of Japan, 2012. Micro Small and Medium Enterprises finance in India—A Research Study on Needs, Gaps and Way Forward. International Financial Corporation (IFC) and Government of Japan.

Lumpkin, G.T., Dess, G.G., 1996. Clarifying the entrepreneurial orientation construct and linking it to performance. Acad. Manage. Rev. 21 (1), 135–172.

Morris, M.H., Kuratko, D.F., Covin, J.G., 2008. Corporate Entrepreneurship and Innovation. Thomson South-Western.

Zeng, K., 2010. On the Improvement of Legal Tax System to Incent SMEs in China. Inheritance & Innovation 10, 66–69.

Chapter 11

Personal Characteristics

Chapter Contents

The role played by personal traits of individuals has been the subject of entrepreneurship research for a long time (Gartner, 1985; Shane and Venkataraman, 2000). Personal traits are dispositional characteristics, meaning that they are relatively enduring preferences on a person's part for thinking or acting in a specific manner (Epstein and Brian, 1985). An entrepreneur is a person who habitually creates and innovates to build something of recognized value around perceived opportunities. Entrepreneurs are known to be individuals who make a significant difference, who are creative and innovative, who spot and exploit opportunities (Olakitan, 2011), and who typically confront risk of failure. Also, the need for achievement and internal locus of control (LOC) have been recognized as highly associated with entrepreneurship (Beugelsdijk, 2007; Korunka et al., 2003; Littunen, 2000; Rauch and Frese, 2000). Although entrepreneurs have some common characteristics, in general, cultural background can also impact entrepreneurial characteristics. For example, Davidsson et al. (2003) found that cultures that promote higher needs for autonomy, achievement, and self-efficacy enjoy higher firm formation (Lian-HW and Chiu).

INNOVATION ABILITY

Entrepreneurship is closely related to innovation. Without continuous innovation, new and emerging technological achievements would not exist, and a large number of new enterprises would never have been formed. While continuous and disruptive innovations are very important for the continued growth of well-established large- and midsize companies, innovation has played an even more important role in new start-ups. In the United States, innovation and entrepreneurship are closely related. US culture and market dynamics reward new businesses that are highly innovative, and significant new value creation has been associated with new innovative entrepreneurial companies.

In China, on the other hand, due to traditional social and cultural norms, individual independence is subjugated to social conformity, and this has hindered innovation to some extent. As a result of this, as well as due to the difficulties associated with starting a business, a lot more energy and attention are focused on this as opposed to that on innovation.

In India, studies have shown that Indian entrepreneurs are moderately innovative and there is a need to develop this trait in a concerted manner (Jain and Ali, 2012).

Technology transfer from universities and government research institutions is also very important for entrepreneurship. According to the Bay Area Council Economic Institute Report of 2011, in the United States, 38% of respondents agreed that they could get technology from government research centers, and in the case of India, the figure was 23%. Fifty percent of the respondents agreed that they could get technology from universities in the United States, while in India, the figure was 31%. In China, according to the same report, both proportions were at 12% (Benchmarking the Bay Area's Environment for Entrepreneur-Led Start-ups, 2011).

The above figures indicate that technology transfer to industry is far more successful in the United States than in China and India. In general, the nation that has a higher level of innovation will have a higher percentage of opportunity-driven activities. Fig. 11.1 shows improvement-driven opportunity activity level in the United States, China, and India according to the survey conducted by Global Entrepreneurship Monitor (GEM). This parameter indicates the percentage of those involved in early-stage entrepreneurial activity who (i) claim to be driven by opportunity as opposed to finding no other option for work and (ii) who indicate the main driver for being involved in this opportunity to be independent is to increase their income.

In the United States, it reached its highest level of 70% in 2005 and was at about 50% in 2011. The highest level for this metric in China was in 2005 and

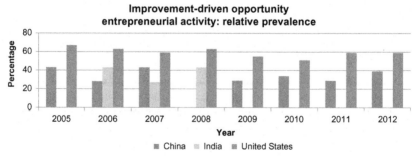

FIGURE 11.1   Improvement-driven opportunity entrepreneurial activity: relative prevalence. *(Source: GEM.)*

was about 40% and has since dropped to about 30% in 2011. The biggest gap between the United States and China in this area was over 30 points and that was in 2006 and the smallest gap was about 20 points in 2007. In the case of India, in 2006 and 2008, 43% of entrepreneurs were involved in entrepreneurship driven by opportunity. According to the report prepared by the National Knowledge Commission (2008) on "Entrepreneurship in India," market opportunity accounts for 19% of the total motivating triggers and idea-driven entrepreneurship accounts for 10% of the motivating triggers. The trend for opportunity-driven entrepreneurial activity is not as prominent as the other reasons for entrepreneurship in India.

PROPENSITY FOR RISK-TAKING

Chell et al. (1991) described a risk-taker as one "who in the context of a business venture, pursues a business idea when the probability of succeeding is low." High risk-taking is negatively associated with business success, but the relationship is small. According to Timmons et al. (1985), successful entrepreneurs take calculated risks, a position that suggests a nonlinear relationship between risk-taking and success.

In China, the predominant style of thinking is dialectic. Issues are analyzed and viewed from opposing perspectives. The approach takes into account interaction and interdependence between these opposing views and how they support and detract from each other to achieve an overall balance in the "system." Chinese are, therefore, broad thinkers and very "down-to-earth" and are always very well prepared before doing anything, as they strive "to seek a stable world." Despite external appearances to the contrary, throughout history, in spite of wars and revolutions and other upheaval, China has been striving to make progress towards achieving stability. In every historical period, stability has been the highest priority. Also, in addition to their desire for stability, the Chinese people lived in a relatively stable natural environment. Although China paid more attention to economic development after "it opened up" to the world in 1978, maintaining stability was still the most important consideration for China.

This, of course, is in stark contrast to the Americans who are very well known for their spirit of adventure, risk-taking, and seeking new opportunities. The American spirit of adventure is rooted in their immigrant ancestry and further strengthened by their exploration and development of the American Wild West in the mid-nineteenth century. In the United States, people believe that "You cannot stand still—if you are not moving, you are falling behind." This fundamental belief system inspired Americans generation after generation to look danger and new challenges in the eye and undertake bold new ventures. This very significant difference in the spirit of adventure between the Chinese and American cultures has a very strong influence on the different levels of entrepreneurship in the two countries.

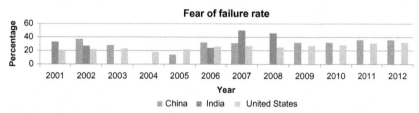

FIGURE 11.2   Fear of failure rate. *(Source: GEM.)*

As far as India is concerned, despite changes in the last 5–10 years, entre-preneurship and working in start-ups is considered very risky. Stigma attached to failure is a deterrent both for starting businesses and for recruiting talent for new ventures (Committee on Angel Investment and Early Stage Venture Capital, 2012).

Goel et al. (2007) in their empirical study found that Indians have a prefer-ence for a stable, well-paying job over a riskier pursuit like entrepreneurship. They further inferred that though entrepreneurship is seen as risky, the youth are positively inclined towards it.

In a study investigating obstacles to corporate entrepreneurship in China, Accenture reports aversion to risk-taking to be significantly higher than in other countries. Accenture reports that 83% of Chinese executives surveyed prefer not to take risk for fear of failure, in contrast to only 42% of executives on an average in the rest of the world. Unwillingness to take risk for fear of failure is one of the biggest obstacles for entrepreneurship in China. Most Chinese entrepreneurs start their businesses very cautiously after very carefully "dotting their i's and crossing their t's." Fig. 11.2 shows a comparison of fear of failure in China, India, and the United States. Though fear of failure in the United States has an increasing trend, it is much lower than in the other two countries. Shivani et al. (2006) conducted an empirical study of entrepreneurs in India and found that the respondents have low risk-taking propensity because of an overall high level of uncertainty in the environment.

INTERNAL LOCUS OF CONTROL

The concept of LOC from Rotter's (1966) social learning theory was tested with regard to the characteristics of entrepreneurs. Individuals who believe in control over their own lives are said to have an internal LOC (Kaufmann et al., 1996; Littunen, 2000), while individuals with an external LOC are those who believe in external forces, such as actions of other people, fate, luck, and chance or other factors that may be beyond their control (Dollinger, 1999; Kaufmann et al., 1996; Littunen, 2000). One can, therefore, expect that venture creators will have a high internal LOC rather than others in the general population. In most entrepreneur-ship studies, a high level of internal LOC has been associated with entrepreneurs and entrepreneurial activities (Kaufmann et al., 1996; Lee and Tsang, 2001).

People with different cultural backgrounds have different trends for LOC. Chiu (1986) found that Americans, in contrast to the Chinese, are more likely to ascribe success to internal control and failure to external control. Hsu (1981) contended that the American way of life is individual-centered and places a great deal of emphasis on self-reliance. If individuals are successful, their success is attributed to their own efforts or abilities. While the Chinese approach to life is situation-centered, this approach emphasizes the interdependence of individuals within a group. If individuals are successful, their success is attributed not only to their contributions but also to all those who are involved with them in that endeavor. Thus, in successful situations, the Chinese believe far more in an external LOC than their American counterparts. By the same token, in China, people are accustomed to expecting support from others when they encounter failure, whereas Americans may suffer alone, while pointing to external situations outside their control as the reason for their failure. So, essentially, when faced with failure, Chinese tend to be more internal than Americans. Although trends for LOC are different in the situations of success and failure, research indicates that the Chinese tend to report higher scores on externality than people in Western cultures (Chan, 1989; Hamid, 1994; Hsieh et al., 1969; Tseng, 1972). Hence, it appears that, in general, people in China have a lower level of internal LOC, which results in a lower level of entrepreneurship in China.

This impact of culture and social environment on the LOC, in various countries around the world, is also a function of time through different periods in the nation's history (Twenge, 2000; Twenge et al., 2004). In China, for example, since the onset of economic reforms in 1978, there have been great changes in the personal and professional lives of the Chinese (Turban et al., 2001). China has gradually moved from a completely centrally planned economy to increasingly more of a market economy; industries and knowledge have been developing; science and technology has taken a larger part in life than before; people are better educated. As incomes and related purchasing power improved, a new social class, the upper middle class, has arisen and continues to grow rapidly. All of the above contribute to individuals feeling more in control of their lives and the environment they live in. As a result, today's Chinese report a higher level of internal LOC. This suggests that the Chinese may be gradually changing from an external to an internal locus (Tong and Wang, 2006). This, in turn, may result in an increase in entrepreneurship in China.

Jain and Ali (2012) found that Indian entrepreneurs and intrapreneurs exhibit qualities that portray moderate internal LOC. Chattopadhyay et al. (2008) found that entrepreneurial success was high among those Indian entrepreneurs who had higher LOC. According to the report on "Entrepreneurship in India (2008)," "internal" factors (such as independence, challenge, and dream desire, i.e., the idea that "by nature, man cannot *but* be an entrepreneur") cumulatively account for the bulk of the total motivating triggers (42%) for entrepreneurship. Hence, Indian entrepreneurs appear to possess a moderate to high level of internal LOC.

VALUE OF ACHIEVEMENT

According to McClelland (1961), a high need for achievement generates a preference for challenging tasks of moderate difficulty rather than routine or very difficult tasks. This not only allows people to look for ways to improve their performance but also allows them to take personal responsibility and seek feedback with regard to their performance. Rauch and Frese (2000), by making a quantitative comparison between business performance and entrepreneurial performance, found that entrepreneurs have a significantly higher need for achievement when compared with other groups.

Indian entrepreneurs, according to Shivani et al. (2006), possess moderate levels of achievement orientation and managerial skills. With the easing of structural restrictions in India, as in China, younger Indians seem to be more motivated by their need for achievement. In fact, a 2007 global survey of 17 nations by the Swedish research and consulting firm Kairos Future (2007) reports that Indian youth (16–29-year-olds) are the happiest in the world.[1] For example, these youth strikingly exude more optimism about their future and their society's future. Additionally, work comes as a top priority for Indian youth, followed by a good career and higher status; these priorities exemplify values of both endurance and entrepreneurship.

In the United States, achievement is directly attributed to a person's ability. In other words, if a person can accomplish something difficult through their diligence, skill, experience, or perseverance, they will get credit for the accomplishment, and opinions of others are not very important. In China, on the other hand, achievement does not only mean that you need to do a good job but that you also need to be recognized by others. In other words, the so-called mianzi is very important. This means one's social status has to be taken into consideration as well. So, in a lot of situations, the Chinese will actually do things against their desire, because they are embarrassed to say "no" to their family members, friends, or acquaintances. At the same time, Chinese seem to attach a lot of importance to attention from media and government. Due to these factors—influence of society, or their "mianzi" or good reputation, as well as attention from media and government—it is very difficult for most entrepreneurs to make rational decisions. For example, from 2002 to 2010, the degree of media attention for entrepreneurship (Fig. 11.3) in China was over 70%, while in America, over the same period, it was well under 70%.

A case in point might be a comparison between the stories of Microsoft in the United States and the Giant Group in China. Bill Gates started Microsoft in 1975 with a start-up capital of $3000, with the specific purpose of making computer software. By the end of 1977, revenues from sales were about $3.8 M with a 2-year CAGR of 636%. But this significant accomplishment in a 2-year period

---

1. http://articles.timesofindia.indiatimes.com/2007-09-20/india/27973995_1_indian-youth-top-priority-survey.

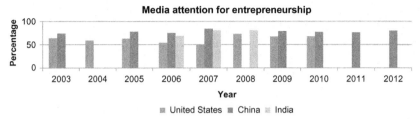

FIGURE 11.3   Media attention for entrepreneurship. *(Source: GEM.)*

did not draw any government recognition or significant media attention, and the founders of Microsoft could focus on running and growing the company without any distractions. The Giant Group in China, on the other hand, in spite of entrepreneurial beginnings very similar to Microsoft, ended up on a very different path and met with a completely different fate. In August 1989, Shi Yuzhu and three partners developed the M-6401 desktop publishing system for Chinese handwriting recognition computers and software with ¥4000 and began the entrepreneurial history of the Giant Group. In a period of less than 4 months, they were profitable to the tune of nearly ¥1 M. By the end of 1992, revenues from sales of the Giant Group were about ¥200 M with a net profit of ¥35 M and a CAGR of 500%. In 1993, sales revenues reached ¥360 M, and Shi Yuzhu was awarded the Special Grade Technology Prize by the city of Zhuhai. This was followed by many honorary titles, including "Outstanding Technology Entrepreneurs" and "China's Top Ten Reform Person." All this sudden and huge government and media adulation went to his head and impacted his business judgment. He made bad decisions, including the construction of the Giant Mansion, tying up the cash flow needed for his business. Giant Group business suffered and eventually filed for bankruptcy (Entrepreneur's Bottleneck: The Experience of Shi Yuzhu-the Bulgy "Mian Zi," 2003).

As far as India is concerned, there is a need to celebrate entrepreneurship so that more and more people choose entrepreneurship as a career option. This is because there is a tendency among Indians to choose a well-paying job over entrepreneurship as pointed out earlier. From this perspective, a higher percentage of people agreeing to the fact that there is a lot of media attention to entrepreneurship in India as measured by GEM in Fig. 11.3 augurs well for the country.

It was empirically established that youth find entrepreneurship to be a commendable pursuit when someone else chooses to pursue it. However, with regard to their own actions, they would prefer to possibly choose not to become an entrepreneur and they may not even wish to work for a small enterprise. Hence, several measures need to be taken to influence the attitude of youth so that entrepreneurship is chosen as a career path. In a country like India, this is even more challenging because of the disparities in developmental climates in different regions and variability in the perceptions of entrepreneurship depending on family backgrounds. Hence, there is a need for differentiated approaches.

Entrepreneurial efforts of those coming from nonbusiness family backgrounds need more support in order to attain success. Similarly in areas where developmental and entrepreneurial activities are low, a two-pronged strategy needs to be adopted. First, the necessary attitude and culture need to be nurtured through support activities. Second, incentives such as concessions and policies relevant to the region need to be introduced (Goel et al., 2007).

In summary, Americans are innovative and adventurous and have a higher LOC. Hence, they have lower fear of failure and have a higher propensity for risk-taking. The need for achievement is more self-driven. All these personal characteristics augur well for the spirit of entrepreneurship in the United States. Chinese, on the other hand, focus more on conforming to societal norms and are not opportunity-driven in their early entrepreneurial pursuits. They prefer stability as opposed to risk and fear failure. Their need for approval from society is high as a result of which they give more importance to media acclaim, which at times proves counterproductive to entrepreneurship. Hence, traditionally, Chinese do not have the requisite personality traits of an entrepreneur. But over the years, with China becoming increasingly market-oriented, the Chinese are becoming more enterprising. Indians, like the Chinese, are not very innovative, have lower propensity for risk-taking, and have a higher fear of failure. However, in recent years, entrepreneurship is being perceived, especially among the younger generation, as a worthwhile pursuit, and we are witnessing increasing levels of entrepreneurship.

REFERENCES

Benchmarking the Bay Area's Environment for Entrepreneur-Led Start-ups, 2011. A Bay Area Council Economic Institute Report, October.

Beugelsdijk, S., 2007. Entrepreneurial culture, regional innovativeness and economic growth. J. Evol. Econ. 17, 187–210.

Chan, D.W., 1989. Dimensionality and adjustment: correlates of locus of control among Hong Kong Chinese. J. Pers. Assess. 53, 145–160.

Chattopadhyay, et al., 2008. Entrepreneurial intention model-based quantitative approach to estimate entrepreneurial success. J. Small Bus. Entrep. 21 (1), 1–21.

Chell, E., Haworth, J., Brearley, S., 1991. The Entrepreneurial Personality: Concepts, Cases, and Categories. Routledge, London, New York.

Chiu, L.H., 1986. Locus of control in intellectual situations in American and Chinese school children. Int. J. Psychol. 21, 167–176.

Committee on Angel Investment and Early Stage Venture Capital, 2012. Creating a Vibrant Entrepreneurial Ecosystem in India. Planning Commission, Government of India, New Delhi.

Davidsson, P., Honig, B., 2003. The role of social and human capital among nascent entrepreneurs. J. Bus. Ventur. 18, 301–332.

Dollinger, M.J., 1999. Entrepreneurship: Strategies and Resources, second ed. Prentice-Hall, New Jersey.

Entrepreneur's Bottleneck: The Experience of Shi Yuzhu-the Bulgy "Mian Zi," 2003. China Technology Entrepreneurship, No. 12.

Epstein, S., Brian, E.J., 1985. The person-situation debate in a historical and current perspective. Psychol. Bull. 98, 513–537.

Gartner, W.B., 1985. A conceptual framework for describing the phenomenon of new venture creation. Acad. Manage. Rev. 10, 696–706.

Goel, A., et al., 2007. Attitudes of the youth towards entrepreneurs and entrepreneurship: a cross-cultural comparison of India and China. J. Asia Entrep. Sustainability 3 (1), 1–35.

Hamid, P.N., 1994. Self-monitoring, locus of control, an social encounters of Chinese and New Zealand students. J. Cross-Cultural Psychol. 25, 353–368.

Hsieh, Y.W., Shybut, J., Lotsof, E., 1969. Internal versus external control and ethnic group membership. J. Consult. Clin. Psychol. 33, 122–124.

Hsu, F.L.K., 1981. Americans and Chinese: Passage to Differences. University of Hawaii Press, Honolulu, HI.

Jain, R., Ali, S.W., 2012. Entrepreneurial and intrapreneurial orientation in Indian enterprises: an empirical study. South Asian J. Manage. 19 (3), 86–122.

Kaufmann, P.J., Welsh, D.H.B., Bushmarin, N.V., 1996. Locus of control and entrepreneurship in the Russian republic. Entrep. Theory Pract. 20 (1), 43–56.

Korunka, C., Frank, H., Lueger, M., Mugler, J., 2003. The entrepreneurial personality in the context of resources, environment, and the startup process—a configurational approach. Entrep. Theory Pract. 28 (1), 23–42.

Lee, D.Y., Tsang, E.W.K., 2001. The effects of entrepreneurial personality, background and network activities on venture growth. J. Manage. Stud. 38 (4), 583–602.

Littunen, H., 2000. Entrepreneurship and the characteristics of the entrepreneurial personality. Int. J. Entrepreneurial Behav Res. 6 (6), 295–309.

McClelland, D.C., 1961. The Achieving Society Paperback. D. Van Nostrand.

National Knowledge Commission (NKC), 2008. Entrepreneurship in India. Government of India, New Delhi.

Olakitan, O.O., 2011. An examination of the impact of selected personality traits on the innovative behaviour of entrepreneurs in Nigeria. Int. Bus. Manage. 3 (2), 112–121.

Rauch, A., Frese, M., 2000. Psychological approach to entrepreneurial success. a general model and an overview of findings. In: Cooper, C.L., Robertson, I.T. (Eds.), International Review of Industrial and Organisational Psychology. Wiley, Chichester, pp. 101–142.

Rotter, J.B., 1966. Generalized expectancies for internal versus external control of reinforcement. Psychol. Monogr 80 (1), 1–28.

Shane, S., Venkataraman, S., 2000. The promise of entrepreneurship as a field of research. Acad. Manage. Rev. 25, 217–226.

Shivani, S., et al., 2006. Socio-cultural influences on Indian entrepreneurs: the need for appropriate structural interventions. J. Asian Econ. 17 (1), 5–13.

Timmons, J.A., Smollen, L.E., Dingee, A.L.M., 1985. New Venture Creation. Irvine, Homewood, Ill.

Tong, J., Wang, L., 2006. Validation of locus of control scale in Chinese organizations. Pers. Individual Difference 41 (1), 941–950.

Tseng, W.S., 1972. On Chinese national character from the viewpoint of personality development. In: Li, Y.Y., Yang, K.S. (Eds.), The Character of the Chinese: An Interdisciplinary Approach. Institute of Ethnology, Academia Sinica.

Turban, D.B., Lau, C.M., Ngo, N.Y., Chow, I.H.S., Si, S., 2001. Organizational attractiveness of firms in the People's Republic of China: a person-organization fit perspective. J. Appl. Psychol. 86 (2), 194–206.

Twenge, J.M., 2000. The age of anxiety? Birth cohort change in anxiety and neuroticism, 1952–1993. J. Pers. Soc. Psychol. 79, 1007–1021.

Twenge, J.M., Zhang, L., Im, C., 2004. It's beyond my control: a cross-temporal meta-analysis of increasing externality in locus of control, 1960–2002. Pers. Soc. Psychol. Rev. 8, 308–319.

Chapter 12

Social and Cultural Factors

Chapter Contents

Cultural and social values affect the degree to which a society considers entrepreneurial activities acceptable and worthwhile. Researchers have recognized the significant impact of culture on entrepreneurship and have been studying it for decades (McGrath et al., 1992; Shane, 1993). Recently, Hayton et al. (2002) and others addressed this in a special issue of *Entrepreneurship Theory and Practice* devoted to the impact of culture on entrepreneurship. A majority of studies on culture and entrepreneurship have used Hofstede's cultural dimensions (Hayton et al., 2002). Researchers have hypothesized that the ideal entrepreneurial culture is high in individualism, low in uncertainty avoidance, low in power distance, and high in masculinity (Hayton et al., 2002; Hofstede, 1980). Shane (1993) found that uncertainty avoidance and power distance have a negative relationship, while individualism has a positive association with innovation.

A primary influence in Eastern culture is Confucianism (Pye, 1985; Ralston et al., 1997; Redding, 1990). Confucian values, followed later by similar values in Taoism and Buddhism, put strong emphasis on the importance of society, group, and hierarchical relationships. These values have influenced Eastern societies for several thousand years. In contrast, Judeo-Christian religions have been the primary influence in Western societies, notably in the United States. The primary contrast between Eastern and Western cultures is the relative focus on group, hierarchy, and harmony in Eastern societies and the emphasis on the individual, low power distance, and openness to change (Ralston et al., 1997) in the West.

POWER DISTANCE

Power distance indicates levels of authority in a hierarchical structure. In high power distance cultures, there is a significant amount of inequality between different levels. Those who are lower in the hierarchy are rarely involved in any significant decision-making. In this environment, position power is far more important than intelligence, diligence, or competitiveness, and a person's fate is usually determined by those in positions of authority, rather than by their own efforts or merits. As a result, most people in this environment just do their jobs and do what they are told, instead of taking initiatives and being creative, innovative, and entrepreneurial. This is typical of the Chinese work environment.

If one were to encapsulate the Indian attitude, it is paternalistic and hierarchical translating to acceptance of unequal rights between the power-privileged and those who are further down in the pecking order. Real power is centralized even though it may not appear to be that way and managers count on the conformance of their team members. Control is familiar and in fact perceived as a psychological security; communication is top-down and negative feedback is not passed up.

The United States, by contrast, is a society that is significantly less hierarchical and, hence, presents far more opportunities to entrepreneurs, and such activities are very prevalent. China scores at around 80 on the power distance scale, India scores 77, whereas the United States is at 40, while the world average is at 55.[1] Among the 56 countries or regions investigated, China ranks at 40 and the United States ranks at 5.

SOCIAL RELATIONS

In Chinese culture, people like to blend in. So, they abide by collective rules and strive for social acceptance. This is called "guanxi" in China. Even in formal institutions, informal channels are often far more effective, and they can be more developed than formal bureaucracy. Without such channels, a person cannot be very effective.

Traditional Chinese society is an agrarian society. Most Chinese, therefore, spent their entire lives in one place, where everyone knew everyone else (Xiaotong,1998). After the founding of New China, there was a period of about 10 years when people could move around freely and relocate. After 1958, however, the newly introduced household registration system severely limited population movements, and Chinese society reverted back to its original way of rural life. Family and social bonds are very strong in this type of society—a strong sense of obligation and responsibility that extends beyond the immediate family to friends, colleagues, acquaintances, and the society at large. The larger

---

1. http://geert-hofstede.com/india.html

this social network, the more likely an entrepreneur was to be successful in his or her business venture.

The United States has always been a nation of immigrants, representing a wide range of ethnicities and mixed races and cultures—the quintessential melting pot of cultures. In this society, it has always been acceptable to be different, and, in fact, the society is based on individualism and freedom of expression. The United States has never been a feudal system, unlike China, and early in its history evolved from being an agriculture-driven economy to a modern industrial society. Along with individual freedom, personal mobility and relocation to regions of opportunity within the country have been the hallmark of American society. Individuals were not tethered to the place they were born. People move and create new social structures and interdependencies where they relocate to and therefore are not as tradition- or history-bound as they are in Chinese society.

Indian society is divided into several religions, castes, languages, classes, ethnicities, etc. There is, in addition, a huge baggage of beliefs, attitudes, pride, and prejudices. Building bridges across cultural divisions has always been a challenge in Indian society (Sheth, 2010). Such divisions impact the entrepreneurial growth and sustained entrepreneurial success as mentioned in the previous chapter. Consequently, there is a need for designing appropriate structural changes to deal with this influence.

In fact, Shivani et al. (2006) found that caste influences the supply of entrepreneurs and the survival of an enterprise during difficult times although the caste in itself does not influence the level of success. In their study, they observed that entrepreneurs from higher strata of the caste system were better able to overcome difficulties due to the support that they generally received from their caste members, whereas for the low-caste entrepreneurs, there is a lack of such support because of which they are unable to continue in difficult situations. Hence, there are fewer entrepreneurs among lower castes.

Another interesting facet of Indian society is the impact of religion and spirituality. Indian society encompasses both spirituality and materialism, and they coexist in a functionally interdependent way. Shivani et al. (2006) found that Indian entrepreneurs believe that their religious functions, norms, practices, and God's power help them to be disciplined and give them the confidence to overcome difficulties. Therefore, religion is not a barrier to entrepreneurial success in India; rather, it is a source of internal strength for entrepreneurs.

With regard to materialism, there are huge levels of inequality in wealth and power and somewhere in the midst of this inequality is the rising middle class of India. With increasing consumerism, being on the rise, the middle class is aware of all the goods and services offered in the market. While some segments of the middle class can afford the desired goods and services, some other sections of this class cannot and therefore feel the pangs of relative deprivation or poverty. This relative deprivation or poverty is generating greed, false desires, and corruption leading to hostility towards the relatively better-provided. This coupled with changes in family structures and marital bonds has resulted in increasing frustration, giving birth to a new trend of antisocial entrepreneurship in the country (Sheth, 2010).

FAMILY CULTURE AND LEVEL OF TRUST

In China, the smallest social unit is the family. Harmony between family members is of paramount importance to most Chinese and oftentimes takes precedence over personal preferences. A person's identity, status, value, rights, obligations, and responsibilities are always tied to those of his or her family. Chinese families are very male-dominated. A Chinese father has a huge influence on his family, and his attitudes, values, and ideas have strong impact on the decisions and actions of his children. So, when a person wants to start a business, opinions of family members, especially the father, are very important. If most family members don't agree with them, they would most likely not proceed with the endeavor. This situation was very common at the beginning of the opening up of China. Many aspiring entrepreneurs chose to keep their "iron bowl," thus ensuring job security, and instead gave up their business dreams because their parents wanted them to avoid risk. However, with the changes in family structure, educational levels, and societal norms, a more open and accepting atmosphere is starting to evolve. So, while family bonds are still very strong, family members can be more open in discussions with parents, and parents are more accepting of their children's points of view and decisions. In the long run, this laid the foundation for increasingly more entrepreneurial behavior. Given the rugged individualism and, independence of thought, in general, this has not been an issue in the United States, and entrepreneurial spirit has flourished in the United States ever since its inception.

Many scholars researching factors affecting the level of trust found that the Chinese, in general, are not very trusting—no "universal trust"—and their level of trust stems only from kinship. The level of trust, mutual support, and help among family members is generally quite high. However, their attitude towards members outside the family, in general, is very different. As you go further and further outside the circles of kinship or friendship, the level of trust rapidly decreases. Relationships with outsiders generally begin with a level of distrust and a lack of concern for others and their rights and their business. The Chinese grow these circles of kinship by recognizing nominal kinship or by formally swearing others as brothers or sisters. This kind of trust has a great influence on entrepreneurship, and it is very common for the Chinese to start businesses only in partnerships with relatives and friends. Key positions with significant responsibility in enterprises are also generally held only by close relatives and friends. As a result, many businesses were not launched, or those that were launched failed due to such blatant nepotism. According to the Chinese People Entrepreneurship Report, 53% of entrepreneurs appointed their family members to financial positions, 25.3% appointed them to marketing positions,

19% appointed them to administrative positions, and 16.1% appointed them to technical positions. All in all, 71.7% of all entrepreneurs chose their relatives and friends to manage important departments, because of loyalty and trust.

Like in China, India has a family-oriented culture. Indian society is hierarchically structured starting from (1) extended family, followed by (2) class or caste (*jāti*), and then (3) the state (India itself). A person's duties or responsibilities are defined by his or her position in the structure and most importantly in the extended or joint family. Extended or joint family is again hierarchically structured by kinship position and gender. The family is defined in terms of male members descended lineally from common male ancestors, along with their respective wives, sons, and daughters. Relational concept of self for Indians, therefore, is defined more by self-to-other and other-to-self representations (Mascolo et al., 2004).

The implications for an entrepreneur in such a society are that the attitude towards entrepreneurship depends upon the family background and the extent of family support. Those from a business family background are more positively inclined towards entrepreneurship as a career choice (Goel et al., 2007) and to be more successful as entrepreneurs (Shivani et al., 2006). This is because of greater familiarity with entrepreneurship and better access to resources to start and run an enterprise. This is reflected by the fact that in India, 95% of the registered firms are family businesses.[2]

Some studies suggest that female entrepreneurs received less support than male entrepreneurs and hence were found to be less successful (Shivani et al., 2006). It is estimated that women entrepreneurs comprise only about 10% of the total entrepreneurs in India. This is likely due to the patriarchal structure of Indian society.

However, the National Knowledge Commission (NKC) (2008) found that two-thirds of the female entrepreneurs who responded in their study did not think that gender made a difference. But they did feel that there was a need for programs that could provide assistance to women entrepreneurs in obtaining finance, marketing support, counseling, and other core supports (such as functional day care centers and crèches). In general, there is lower participation of women in entrepreneurship, and women entrepreneurs could definitely benefit from more support from family and society at large.

As far as the level of trust is concerned, as in China, trust comes from kinship in India as well. Due to this culture, in family-owned organizations, which are the predominant form of business organization in India, key positions are held by family members.

The climate of trust in the United States is in stark contrast to that in China and India. Americans, in general, are more trusting—"universal trust." Americans, in general, therefore, are likely to hire the best person for the

---

2. Sir Adrian Committee Report "Family firms and their Governance—creating tomorrow's company from today's," Egon Zehnder International.

job, rather than hiring someone only on the basis of their relationship. As a norm, they are more trusting of others outside the circle of family and relatives or close friends.

As shown in Figs. 12.1 and 12.2, enterprise ownership rate in China is much higher than that in the United States in both new and established businesses. As opposed to the Chinese, Indians do not have a natural preference to own their own business. This is evidenced by the low rate of new business ownership as shown in Fig. 12.1. However, this is not true in the case of established businesses (Fig. 12.2). An interesting observation by the NKC study (2008) revealed that business families encourage their second and further generations to join or start businesses in the same field as opposed to a different field. As a result, established family businesses have experienced a higher growth rate in India. According to the PWC survey on family business (2012), growth of family businesses has been relatively strong in India (74% in India as compared to a global

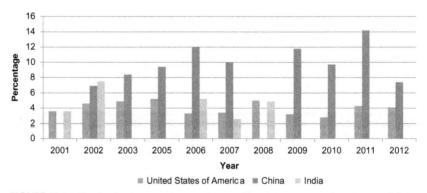

FIGURE 12.1   New business ownership rate. *(Source: Global Entrepreneurship Monitor (GEM).)*

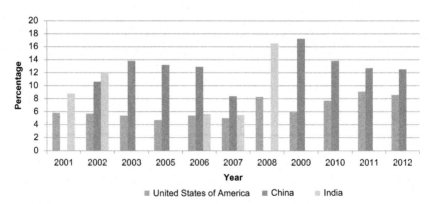

FIGURE 12.2   Established business ownership rate. *(Resources: Global Entrepreneurship Monitor (GEM).)*

average of 65%), and family businesses are very bullish with their growth goals. One in every three family businesses in the country aims to grow quickly and aggressively over the next 5 years. Also, 82% of family businesses pass on management to the next generation, which results in continuity of established businesses.

ACCEPTANCE OF FAILURE

As mentioned before, the Chinese are far more sensitive to public perception than the Americans, and "saving face" is very important to the Chinese. There is a lot of social stigma attached to failure in business—the entrepreneur feels guilty of letting down his family and the associated loss of social status. All the way from ancient times to today, the belief system that has prevailed is that somebody who has failed in entrepreneurship is a loser, and they must have done something wrong, and garners very little support and understanding from others in society. There is very little rational thought about success or failure in business. This has been a tremendous detriment for people who have aspired to start businesses, many of them giving up, without even trying.

Similarly, in India, the fear of failure is a major deterrent to entrepreneurship. It is considered to be a stigma. By contrast, failure is far more easily accepted in the United States, and it is well known that many entrepreneurs in the United States have failed many times before finally succeeding.

American culture on the other hand is low on power distance and high on individualism, mobility, and "universal trust"—all factors conducive to entrepreneurship. China has a high power distance culture with strong family and social ties. Traditional Chinese culture is not conducive to entrepreneurship although this may be gradually changing over time. India has a hierarchical, paternalistic, family-oriented, and patriarchal culture. Hence, attitude towards entrepreneurship varies depending on family background and family support. Those from a business family background are more positively inclined towards entrepreneurship. For entrepreneurship to thrive in India, there is a need to increase the social base by creating support systems across different family backgrounds, castes, and gender.

REFERENCES

Goel, A., et al., 2007. Attitudes of the youth towards entrepreneurs and entrepreneurship: a cross-cultural comparison of India and China. J. Asia Entrep. Sustain. 3 (1), 1–35.

Hayton, J.C., George, G., Zahra, S.A., 2002. National culture and entrepreneurship: a review of behavioral research. Enterp. Theory Pract. 26 (4), 33–52.

Hofstede, G., 1980. Culture's Consequences: International Differences in Work-Related Values. Sage Publications, Newbury Park, CA.

Mascolo, et al., 2004. Individual and relational conceptions of self in India and the United States. New Dir. Child Adolesc. Dev. (104), 9–26.

McGrath, R.G., Macmillan, I.C., Yang, E.A., Tsai, W., 1992. Does culture endure, or is it malleable? Issues for entrepreneurial economic development. J. Bus. Ventur. 7 (6), 441–458.

National Knowledge Commission (NKC), 2008. Entrepreneurship in India. Government of India, New Delhi.

Pye, L.W., 1985. Asian Power and Politics: The Cultural Dimensions of Authority. Becknap Press, Cambridge.

Ralston, D.A., Holt, D.H., Terpstra, R.H., Yu, K.C., 1997. The impact of national culture and economic ideology on managerial work values: a study of the United States, Russia, Japan and China. J. Int. Bus. Stud. 28 (1), 177–207.

Redding, S.G., 1990. The Spirit of Chinese Capitalism. Walter de Gruyter, Berlin.

Shane, S., 1993. Cultural influences on national rates of innovation. J. Bus. Ventur. 8 (1), 59–73.

Sheth, 2010. The social context of entrepreneurship. J. Entrep 19 (2), 99–108.

Shivani, et al., 2006. Socio-cultural influences on Indian entrepreneurs: the need for appropriate structural interventions. J. Asian Econ. 17 (1), 5–13.

Xiaotong, F., 1998. The Local China – Fertility System. Peking University Press, Beijing; pp. 6–11, 24.

Chapter 13

Entrepreneurial Training

Chapter Contents

RELEVANT EDUCATION

The United States

Since the mid-1970s, the US economy has transformed itself from a managed economy to an entrepreneurial economy (Drucker, 2002). Entrepreneurship education has also been emphasized in America. Many well-recognized universities such as Harvard University, the University of Chicago, Massachusetts Institute of Technology, and Stanford University established efforts in this field to help research, teach, and stimulate entrepreneurship. The evolution of entrepreneurial education can be traced as follows.

Entrepreneurship education has strong financial support. The National Science Foundation set up institutions to help implement the Small Business Innovation Research program to encourage researchers to become entrepreneurs and actively commercialize their innovations. In addition, entrepreneurship education is also supported by the social communities and business—for example, the Coleman Foundation, the National Federation of Independent Business, the Kauffman Foundation, and a host of others. Some of the largest players in supporting entrepreneurial activities and associated education have traditionally been the venture capital and angel investor communities.

Entrepreneurship education in this area is encouraged by formal and governmental organizations. Institutions that promote entrepreneurship education are mainly the Small Business Administration (SBA), Youth Entrepreneurs of Kansas, the Kauffman Entrepreneurship Center, and others. Also, many universities and colleges have established incubation and commercialization centers to facilitate creation of entrepreneurial venture based on student and faculty research. Many institutions of higher education have created structures to promote entrepreneurship. These are generally staffed by outstanding entrepreneurs who participate in teaching and/or in providing sponsorships. They function as think tanks, which have regular meetings to make suggestions for improving entrepreneurship education and family-owned enterprise research institutes, whose responsibilities include holding family enterprise seminars, as well as helping family enterprises.

The origin of this field can be traced back to the business management course at Harvard Business School in 1947 and has an established track record and maturity to create good curricula in most institutions that teach entrepreneurship (Yi, 2006). In 1977, there were about 70 universities that offered entrepreneurship courses, and by 1999, the number of universities teaching entrepreneurship was over 1000 (Yi, 2006). Entrepreneurship education resources in American universities include excellent teachers, good teaching environment, and excellent entrepreneurship courses. Courses cover various aspects of entrepreneurship ranging from operation of small businesses, management of high-tech enterprise, to improvement of innovation and management capabilities. For example, there are 15 entrepreneurship courses taught at Harvard University, 23 at the business school at the University of Chicago, and 17 at the School of Management at Stanford University (Shuancheng et al., 2010).

In addition, in order to cultivate an entrepreneurial spirit when people are young, entrepreneurship courses are also offered in primary and secondary schools. Also, in some instances, even community schools offer lessons in entrepreneurship to help people use their entrepreneurial knowledge and skills to start their own companies. It is important to note that a variety of entrepreneurial activities were held in most universities to reinforce entrepreneurship education to complement classroom courses. The first business plan competition was held at the University of Texas at Austin in 1983 (Yu, 2012), which was the origin of American business plan competition. At the present time, entrepreneurship centers established in universities annually hold business plan competitions and invite students to introduce their ideas for new products and services. The goal of these presentations is to obtain funding to help entrepreneurs launch their own companies. Many big companies, like Yahoo and Netscape, started this way.

China

China began its efforts in entrepreneurial education in 2002. Tsinghua University, Renmin University of China, Beijing University of Aeronautics and Astronautics, Heilongjiang University, Shanghai Jiaotong University, Xi'an Jiaotong University, Wuhan University, Northwest Polytechnic University, and Nanjing Economy College were chosen by the Department of Higher Education as pilot units to develop entrepreneurship education (Yao and LiHua, 2011). Chinese entrepreneurship education has three main components: entrepreneurship courses, entrepreneurship presentations, and entrepreneurship competition.

In contrast to American universities, there are far fewer entrepreneurship courses in China. One of the popular entrepreneurship programs is the Tsinghua University-Berkeley Global Technology Entrepreneurship Education Project. Courses in this joint program include core required courses, thematic elective courses, and a required practice project. Core required courses include technology entrepreneurship courses and lectures by global technology leaders; the thematic elective courses include industrial innovation and entrepreneurship, technology management, and intellectual property management; and in the required practice project, students are asked to complete an English-language business plan by participating in the start-up of an actual technology project. A few other courses, such as entrepreneurial spirit, venture capital, and entrepreneurial management, are offered in other universities. Students are also encouraged to engage in creative social practice, as well as in nonprofit entrepreneurship.

Entrepreneurship presentations and competitions are very popular in China. Some of these activities are organized by The Central Committee of the Communist Youth League, and they gave out awards to outstanding entrepreneurship graduates in more than 50 universities and colleges. Other competitions are organized by departments within various provincial governments or by universities. However, while these presentations are a source of great inspiration and motivation to students, they come across as superficial because they lack professional involvement and direction.

In China, business plan competitions are held at various levels: national, provincial (city), and college levels. Although many universities do not offer entrepreneurship courses, the concept of entrepreneurship is being gradually promoted to students. Among all business plan competitions, the one that is the most influential is the National Federation Challenge Cup Collegiate Business Plan Competition, which is cosponsored by The Communist Youth League Central Committee, China Association for Science and Technology, Ministry of Education, and National Student Federation. This event is gaining popularity with an ever-increasing number of students and universities attending. Winners at this event not only are honored but also receive material rewards. However, the biggest problem with this event is that most of the projects cannot be implemented into practice.

Entrepreneurship education in China has significant challenges. First, China began entrepreneurship education only as recently as 2002. As a result, it is low in gaining traction. Entrepreneurial education is still in the experimental phase and it cannot be widely implemented in most universities. Second, even among those universities that are developing entrepreneurship programs, the number of entrepreneurship courses offered is very limited and there is also a dearth of teachers with experience in this area.

India

In India, the need for a strong small-scale industry was felt only after the second five-year plan (1956–1961). Consequently, strategies were designed to develop entrepreneurs through training. For example, in the early 1960s, an idea called the Industrial Campaign took shape, enlarging itself through the years to become a countrywide movement presently known as the Entrepreneurship Development Program (Zhang, 2006).

Even at this stage, entrepreneurship did not become a part of curriculum in higher education. Universities did not consider entrepreneurship as a systematic body of knowledge worthy of being taught in institutions of higher education. It is only in recent times that higher education has begun to be perceived as a vehicle for promoting entrepreneurship (Zhang, 2006). The University Grants Commission developed a curriculum for the undergraduate level only as recently as in 2000 and circulated it to all universities and colleges for their consideration. Subsequently, a minuscule number of colleges have started basic entrepreneurship teaching. The All India Council for Technical Education (AICTE) has been promoting Entrepreneurship Development Cells (EDCs) in engineering and technology colleges. By a rough measure, there are about 50 EDCs supported by the AICTE. The Ministry of Micro, Small and Medium Enterprises (MSME) also supports, in a limited manner, the creation of EDCs in universities. The National Science and Technology Entrepreneurship Development Board (NSTEDB), of the Department of Science and Technology, is a major sponsor of EDCs, though they are focused on engineering and science colleges and universities. Thus far, they have sponsored close to 80 EDCs. NSTEDB has also been quite active in sponsoring entrepreneurship awareness programs, idea competitions, and business plan competitions.[1]

Besides, a number of management schools have been offering "entrepreneurship" as one of the electives. Only four or five business schools offer graduate programs in "entrepreneurship." Structured courses and programs on entrepreneurship are found lacking across most institutions. Entrepreneurship courses are similar to general business courses. Besides, business management education has no significant influence on entrepreneurial propensity. This has produced average managers but not very good entrepreneurs. The lack of industry and entrepreneurial experience of faculty has hampered the promotion of entrepreneurship at educational institutions (Committee on Angel Investment and Early Stage Venture Capital, 2012).

Even premier institutes in India lag global benchmarks in producing entrepreneurs. Less than 5% of courses start new ventures versus more than 10% in premier global schools (Committee on Angel Investment and Early Stage Venture Capital, 2012). Institutes such as the Indian School of Business, Hyderabad, NS Raghavan Center for Entrepreneurial Learning in IIM

---

1. http://ediindia.ac.in/e-policy/Doc/Draft-National-Entrepreneurship-Policy.pdf

Bangalore, and NMIMS are a few examples that have been proactive in encouraging and stimulating entrepreneurial drive in students.

Given the number of students, entrepreneurship infrastructure in educational institutions is quite inadequate. For example, of the 620 universities and over 33,000 colleges, only about 200 have EDCs. And not all cells are very active. Educational institutions also lack structured means of engaging the broader ecosystem of businesses, investors, mentors, and alumni to promote R&D, innovation, and entrepreneurship.[2]

The success of incubators run by educational institutions has also been mixed (Committee on Angel Investment and Early Stage Venture Capital, 2012). India has only about 115 technology business incubators as compared to 1300 incubators in the United States and Canada, 900 in Europe, over 800 in China, about 300 in South Korea, 200 in Japan, and 100 in a much smaller country like Taiwan. Of these 115, NSTEDB formed 70 incubators, while the remaining 40–45 incubators were formed by other public and private agencies including the MSME and Department of Information Technology. The Department of Scientific and Industrial Research also promotes incubation-based entrepreneurship through its Technopreneur Promotion Program.[3] However, successful incubators such as the CIIE of IIM Ahmedabad and Sine of IIT Mumbai are few and far between. This is because success is determined more by the motivation and quality of faculty involved in the incubator than by a robust and predictable operational and financial model. Despite the given pool of science and technology teachers in universities, scientists, researchers, and students with a background of science and technology, new technology venture ideas have not been forthcoming, due to the lack of appropriate strategic involvement by the ecosystem. Requisite infrastructure to take advantage of available scientific and technology-based resources has been lacking.

RELEVANT TRAINING AND CONSULTATION SERVICES

The United States

The US SBA also provides a variety of consulting services beyond just financial support. The Small Business Development Centers (SBDCs) run by the SBA are a cooperative effort between the government and universities, and they provide educational services for small business owners and aspiring entrepreneurs. SBDCs have been set up in each state, and there are literally several thousand of these across the country. Very often, these SBDCs are staffed by retired professional managers with a lot of experience, and they provide advice in the whole process from the start-up to the launch of the

2. Ibid.
3. Ibid.

214 PART | II Entrepreneurship

business. This advice is free, and some of these centers also provide training to the entrepreneurs for a nominal fee.

China

In 2001, a program called "START YOUR BUSINESS" (SYB) was officially launched in China by the China Labor and Social Security Ministry and International Labor Organization, with cities like Zhangjiakou, Baotou, and Jilin as pilots. By the end of 2004, more than 60 cities had introduced the SYB program to carry out technology and entrepreneurial training activities (Xiaoguo, 2005). Although the SYB program had a positive impact on promoting entrepreneurship in China, there are several shortcomings with the SYB program. On the one hand, this training is provided mainly to laid-off workers. As a result, the primary goal becomes finding a job, rather than starting a business. On the other hand, the content and skills provided in this training are adapted from foreign programs and are not directly relevant to conditions in China.

India

Collaboration and mentor networks are beginning to establish their presence in India. The Indus Entrepreneurs (TiE) and National Entrepreneurship Network are noteworthy examples. These are critical to ensure cohesive functioning of the ecosystem and enable access of resources (material and nonmaterial) to entrepreneurs. However, information availability through comprehensive portals is particularly lacking.

In conclusion, the United States has a long history of entrepreneurship education. Entrepreneurship education programs are well supported financially and institutionally. The quality and number of courses offered in the United States are far better than those in China and India. China and India are late starters in this field and are at a significant disadvantage. Entrepreneurship education in these countries is not very relevant in content due to lack of well-trained faculty and the requisite infrastructure.

REFERENCES

Committee on Angel Investment and Early Stage Venture Capital, 2012. Creating a Vibrant Entrepreneurial Ecosystem in India. Planning Commission, Government of India, New Delhi.
Drucker, P.F., 2002. The discipline of innovation. Harvard Business Review 80 (8), 95–103.
Shuancheng, W., Yang, C., Xiaoli, Z., 2010. Comparison of entrepreneurship education mode between China and US. Vocational Education Research 6, 62–63.
Xiaoguo, Z., 2005. Discussion on entrepreneurship training in China. China Technology Forum. September, No. 5.
Yao, L., LiHua, Z., 2011. Comparison of entrepreneurship curriculum between Chinese universities and American universities. Beijing Education 12, 73–74.

Yi, W., 2006. Comparison of entrepreneurship education in universities between China and US. Liaoning Taxation College J. 18(6).

Yu, F., 2012. A Comparative Study on Entrepreneurial Support System Between China and US. Zheng Zhou University master degree paper. May, p. 33.

Zhang, 2006. Entrepreneurship education within India's higher education system. The Asian Scholar. retrieved on January 31, 2014, http://www.asianscholarship.org/asf/ejourn/articles/zhang_1.pdf.

Chapter 14

External Environment

Chapter Contents

The presence of a competitive, monopoly-free market environment and a free market economy is a key external influence that supports entrepreneurship. Some entrepreneurship literature also indicates that market failures can play a crucial role in helping entrepreneurs exploit new opportunities (Dean and McMullen, 2007). In addition, to a large extent, opportunities for employment or lack thereof and policies supportive of entrepreneurship also play important roles in a person's motivation to start a business.

THE FREE MARKET ECONOMY AND COMPETITIVE ENVIRONMENT

The United States[1]

Market economy requires a fair and competitive environment so that potential abilities of competing parties can be expressed to the maximum extent. In order to promote a free market economy, the US government passed legislation to prevent the formation of monopolies. As early as 1890, the US government issued the first antimonopoly law—the Sherman Act. Thereafter, a series of laws were passed and policies were put in place to improve the competitive environment. A total of 90% of US firms are private. State-owned economy accounts for about only 1% of the total economy. The employees in state-owned enterprises also account for only 1% of total employment. Even this 1% is

---

1. Source: www.ftc.gov

mostly managed by private enterprises by way of rent or outsourcing. Cooperatives and unions also play a small part in the economy, and 90% of the economy is private (Dong, 2010). So, despite government efforts to the contrary, when there is a tendency towards monopoly power in the United States, that monopoly is the result of private enterprise and is spontaneously formed through market competition. Furthermore, with regard to numbers of enterprises, small- and medium-sized enterprises and nonmonopoly enterprises accounted for the vast majority. Above all, in the United States, "positive competition" is the basic principle of the free market economy, which in turn is a key driver for entrepreneurship.

In addition to this, the United States has had a very well-developed legal infrastructure for well over a hundred years, for allowing the forces of free market economy to play out and for a competitive environment to flourish. This dates back to state and federal policies in the 1880s, and the landmark Sherman Act of 1890 alluded to earlier as a "comprehensive charter of economic liberty aimed at preserving free and unfettered competition as the rule of trade." Further legislation was put in place by the US Congress in 1914, when it created the Federal Trade Commission (FTC) and passed two additional laws, the Federal Trade Commission Act and the Clayton Act. These three laws are the core antitrust laws still in effect today and provide the fundamental framework for a competitive economic environment. The basic objective of these laws has been "to protect the process of competition for the benefit of consumers, making sure there are strong incentives for businesses to operate efficiently, keep prices down, and keep quality up."

The Sherman Act outlaws "every contract, combination, or conspiracy in restraint of trade" and any "monopolization, attempted monopolization, or conspiracy or combination to monopolize." The Federal Trade Commission Act bans "unfair methods of competition" and "unfair or deceptive acts or practices." The Clayton Act addresses specific practices that the Sherman Act does not clearly prohibit, such as mergers and interlocking directorates (i.e., the same person making business decisions for competing companies). Section 7 of the Clayton Act prohibits mergers and acquisitions where the effect "may be substantially to lessen competition, or to tend to create a monopoly." As amended by the Robinson-Patman Act of 1936, the Clayton Act also bans certain discriminatory prices, services, and allowances in dealings between merchants. The Clayton Act was amended again in 1976 by the Hart-Scott-Rodino Antitrust Improvements Act to require companies planning large mergers or acquisitions to notify the government of their plans in advance. The Clayton Act also authorizes private parties to sue for triple damages when they have been harmed by conduct that violates either the Sherman or Clayton Act and to obtain a court order prohibiting the anticompetitive practice in the future (source: FTC, www.ftc.gov).

The responsibility for enforcing these antitrust laws rests with the FTC and the Antitrust Division of the United States, Department of Justice (DoJ). The two agencies complement each other in these roles, each with expertise in specific markets or industries. Over the years, these two agencies have played very vigorous roles in making sure that there is not an undue accumulation of market power in the hands of the bigger industry players. In fact, there are numerous examples of lawsuits brought by the FTC or the DoJ against large industry players to keep them from gaining monopoly or near-monopoly advantage in the marketplace, thus ensuring a "level playing field" for the smaller players in those industries.

In addition to the federal antitrust laws, the state attorney general can play an important role as well in antitrust enforcement on matters of particular concern to local businesses or consumers. They may also bring federal antitrust suits on behalf of individuals residing within their states or on behalf of the state as a purchaser. The state attorney general also may bring an action to enforce the state's own antitrust laws, as what happened in several states in 2013 in relation to the proposed American Airlines–US Airways merger.

The long-standing presence of this legal infrastructure, its evolution over the years to meet the changing environment, the very vigorous enforcement of these laws, and the guiding principles behind them have certainly made the United States the best example in the world of a truly free market economy.

China

China, by contrast, is not a free market economy and the level of monopoly power is very high, and more seriously, most of this monopoly power emanates from the government. In the list of top 500 Chinese enterprises in 2005, the top 10 are all large state-owned enterprises, such as China Sinopec, State Grid Corporation of China, China National Petroleum Corporation, China Mobile, China Life, and Industrial and Commercial Bank of China. These companies are all state-owned monopolies—large, central, state-owned enterprises. In the list of the Fortune Global 500 released by Fortune magazine, there were 54 Chinese companies in 2010 and 43 in 2009. China Petrochemical Corporation, the State Grid Corporation of China, and China National Petroleum Corporation reached the top 10, ranking no. 7, 8, and 10, respectively (Shangfeng, 2010). Huawei is the first Chinese private company to enter the Fortune Global 500, while the others are all state-owned enterprises. The large, central, state-owned enterprises have been given monopoly operating rights by the government by way of using public authority. Under the pretext of safeguarding national economic security, these monopolies have exclusive access to resources and also prevent competitors from entering markets. Most of their profits come from their highly preferential treatments as national companies. For example, market capitalization of the national power industry was ¥800 B, although the profits were only about ¥8 B per year. Only 10 of 31 provincial and urban subsidiaries of China Telecom were profitable, while the railway department had an industry-wide loss (Dong, 2010).

In order to change this situation, at the end of 2006, 24 supporting documents were issued concerning market access, and 200 local cases were filed by 31 provinces, municipalities, and autonomous regions to promote non-state-owned economic development. However, documents and files play a limited role in reality, because often, these rules can be overruled by other subsequent documents. For example, in 2005, "thirty-six articles about nonpublic owned" were issued, which was superseded, in 2006, by the document to "promote the adjustment of state-owned capital and the restructuring of state-owned enterprises," issued by the State Asset Regulatory Commission (Fanhe and Qian, 2006). In the latter file, it was indicated that the state-owned economy should have absolute control in industries including military, grid and electricity, petroleum, telecommunications, coal, civil aviation, and shipping industries. In 2007, the "2006 China's private economic development analysis report" was published by the National Federation, which showed that in the fields of postal services, telecommunications, radio and television, electricity, and finance, private enterprises were encouraged to enter.

However, this was difficult at a practical level due to significant barriers to entry such as capital requirements, technology capability, and relative professional qualifications. For example, in April 2006, the Ministry of Commerce stipulated the "Measures for the Administration of the Refined Oil Market" and required that companies engaged in oil and gas wholesale must have more than 10 gas stations and oil storage tanks with over 10,000 cubic meters. Most domestic private oil enterprises with ¥10 M in assets could not meet the above two requirements. If private enterprise wanted to enter the natural gas extraction industry, its registered capitalization needed to be ¥4 B (Dong, 2010). Similarly, the standard thresholds for market access in the fields of postal services, telecommunications, radio and television, electricity, petroleum, military, finance, insurance, transportation, water supply, gas supply, sewage treatment, and infrastructure are all set so high that private enterprises cannot enter those industries.

In the "Anti-monopoly Law of the People's Republic of China" passed in August 2007, the 7th article of Chapter One pointed out the importance of the state-owned economy to the security of the country and as a lifeline to the country's economy. The same article also offered protection to legally franchised monopoly companies and industries, as long as they operated legally. Here, the administrative-type monopoly of state-owned enterprises was provided legal protection. So, on the whole, although some official documents were generated to decrease the level of monopoly and increase competition, there were no significant changes in the way market forces operated. The level of monopoly activity was very high, and this, in turn, strongly decreased.

As far as competitive environment is concerned, China has issued many pieces of legislation to promote fair competition since 1993. In September 1993, the Anti-Unfair Competition Law of the People's Republic of China was passed, which described the penalties for unfair competitive actions and government's obligations to create a fair market economy. After that, a series of laws and governmental regulations were introduced to further enhance the Anti-Unfair Competition Law. In December 1993, provisions to prohibit bribes, kickbacks, and other unfair selling practices were released. In July 1995, provisions to prohibit counterfeiting of product brand names, packaging, and decoration were released. In January 1998, interim anticollusion provisions were published (Qinzhi, 2005). In addition, the Trademark Law of the People's Republic of China, the Advertising Law of the People's Republic of China, the Product Quality Law of the People's Republic of China, and the Law of the People's Republic of China on the Protection of Consumers' Rights and Interests were published to restrict anticompetitive practices.

Although many laws and provisions were put into place to foster a fair market environment, many problems remain. First, government provisions had a lower legal authority than government laws, and so, they played a very limited role in limiting unfair competition. Second, laws and provisions lacked clarity and specificity in defining penalties for violators and legal remedies for victims. In some cases, there was a complete absence of related regulations, or the punitive measures were completely ineffective because they were not severe enough. Lastly, government authorities, responsible for upholding and enforcing these laws and provisions, were highly fragmented, and their responsibilities were not clearly defined. When violations occurred, it was not clear which government department had the responsibility in that area or if they had an adequate level of authority or independence to enforce the legislation. Also, the standard mode of operation for relevant authorities was often surprise inspections rather than upholding the law on a day-to-day basis.

Furthermore, protection of local economic interests took precedence over ensuring fair competition. Local governments and authorities prioritized economic and social benefits of their regions over enforcing anticompetitive practices. Career advancement or otherwise of local officials depended on local economic development. These kinds of promotional practices made most local leaders merely pursue economic interests, and they connived in a multitude of illegal practices that undermined free market economics, caused environmental damage, and abused natural resources. In 2001, provisions to prohibit regional blocks of economic activities were issued by the State Council, where the prohibition of all forms of regional block behavior was further emphasized (Qinzhi, 2005). Local governments were prohibited from formulating provisions for implementing local blocks that hampered the establishment and improvement of national unity, fair competition, and a standardized and orderly market system. Although this document addressed the issue of local protectionism, this problem would not be totally solved as long as career progression of local officials also depended on regional economic indicators.

The lack of full market competition also negatively affected fair competition. In China, the market system is undeveloped, and there is lack of competition. At the same time, information asymmetry greatly increases consumers' cost to acquire more market or product information. This is aggravated by the fact that "moral hazard" cannot play an effective role in restricting the behavior of producers and sellers because the likelihood of being penalized and the size of the penalty are relatively small compared to the huge windfall they can receive through dishonest operation. There is no social credibility system to evaluate company or individual behavior and very little downside associated with being dishonest. Due to a confluence of the above factors, counterfeit products flooded the Chinese market. Even the most elementary level of trust that should exist between producers, sellers, and consumers disappeared. Original products cannot be protected because fake products have a cheaper price, and consumers cannot tell the difference between them. This, of course, negatively impacts entrepreneurial behavior, since fake products emerge in a very short time after original products come to market, thus taking the profit incentive away from the entrepreneur.

India

India, on the other hand, followed the mixed economy model where both public and private sectors coexisted. The earlier industrialization strategy of India was protectionist in nature, emphasizing import substitution and business regulation through licenses. It stressed the development of heavy industries and envisaged a dominant role for the public sector in the economy. However, it soon became clear that the actual results of this strategy were far below expectations.[2] Since the late 1980s, India started moving away from state-dominated commerce towards a market-oriented system.

With economic liberalization, post-1991, sectors that were the exclusive domain of public sector enterprises were opened to the private sector. Indian entrepreneurship received a big boost as a result. Figures 14.1 and 14.2 show the subsequent dominance by the private sector in almost all vertical sectors in terms of the sheer numbers of enterprises. In terms of the levels of investment, although the public sector still has an important role, this trend has been witnessing a slow decline. Some of the sectors in which the public sector continues to have a major share of output are coal, petroleum, telecommunications, power generation, and fertilizers. The Central Public Sector Enterprises (CPSEs) have complete monopoly in nuclear power generation (KPMG, 2012). In comparison to 1998–1999, however, the share of CPSEs in these industries has been significantly decreasing over the years (except power generation).[3]

On closer examination of the composition of businesses, one can observe that 20 years after India's process of liberalization began, state-owned

---

2. High level of legal protection to private interests of public servants leading to no accountability on the part of the public servants, weak enforcement of decisions by the government, and bureaucracy and red tape are reasons for failure of the public sector in India.

3. http://dpe.nic.in/sites/upload_files/dpe/files/survey1112/survey01/Overview. pdf#Disinvestment

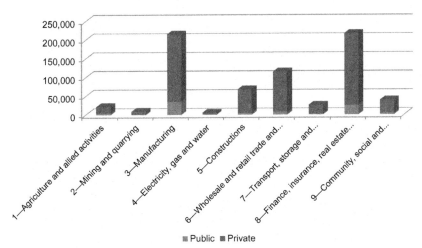

FIGURE 14.1   Number of public and private enterprises across sectors in India in 2009.

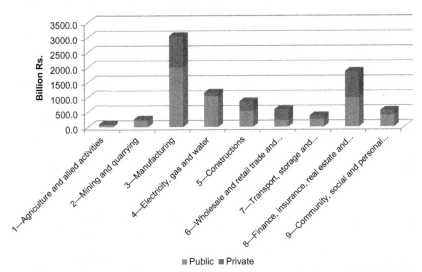

FIGURE 14.2   Paid-up capital of public and private enterprises across sectors in India in 2009. *(Source:http://mospi.nic.in/Mospi_New/site/India_Statistics.aspx?status=1&menu_id=43)*

enterprises and old conglomerates control a larger share of the Indian economy than the businesses that started after the reforms.[4] The micro, small, and medium enterprises (MSME), on the other hand, amounting to 29.8 M enterprises in various industries and employing 69 M people, have been able to contribute only 11.5% a year to India's GDP (International Financial Corporation (IFC) and Government of Japan, 2012).

---

4. http://world.time.com/2012/08/02/open-for-business-why-indian-entrepreneurs-need-a-hand/#ixzz2dxCFDUEW

This is because the Indian business environment is still "emerging" and suffers from several institutional voids. The large businesses have been able to build their wealth by "using economic power to secure neo-liberal policies" (Kshetri and Dholakia, 2011) and by crafting strategies to create appropriate systems to fill the institutional voids (Khanna and Palepu, 2010). The large family businesses that thrived before the 1991 liberalization because of government contacts, understanding of the bureaucratic system, close-knit joint family structure that fosters family values, teamwork, tenacity, and continuity have had to reorient themselves in the new, global, competitive environment. Those large family businesses that reoriented themselves succeeded, while others failed. For example, Tata Motors, a successful automobile corporation belonging to a huge Indian conglomerate, encountered several challenges in terms of underdeveloped capabilities such as market research providers, dealer network, consumer information providers, sources of capital for target customers, and vehicle service network. They had to build internal systems to fill the gaps in the institutional infrastructure and eventually emerged successful (Palepu, 2010). The small entrepreneurs characterized by MSME sector, however, find such dynamic growth constraining (see Box 14.1).

Palepu (2010) had proposed a framework of six factors to evaluate the extent of institutional voids present in a country. These factors are quality and presence of credibility of enhancers, information analyzers and advisors, aggregators and distributors, transaction facilitators, regulators, and other public institutions and adjudicators.

There are quite a few institutional voids in India if analyzed using the above framework (Table 14.1). India is the most populous democracy in the world. Yet its political system has become inherently "unaccountable, corrupt, and unhinged from the normal bench marks voters use to assess their leaders" (Huang (2008) in Dholakia and Kshetri (2011)). Multiparty coalition governments have brought about reforms in fits and starts. Court systems are overburdened and thus are characterized by procedural delays and red tape. Enforcement of laws is weak, resulting in delays in enforcement of contract (Dholakia and Kshetri, 2011). World Bank's Doing Business Report 2013 reported that it takes 1420 days to enforce a contract in India.

Bureaucratic barriers lead to longer times, higher costs, and reduced speed and flexibility for entrepreneurs to create and expand their ventures. Poor infrastructure and inadequate market linkages are further constraints. Suppliers are available in plenty but quality and dependability vary greatly. The retail segment is highly fragmented. The use of credit cards and financial cards is limited (Palepu, 2010). Only 11.9% of adults are covered by private credit registry, and 0% of them are covered by public credit registry (The World Bank and the International Finance Corporation, 2013).

India, however, has certain essential elements of democracy, which bodes well for entrepreneurship. For example, a vigorous and dynamic press, unfettered and open media, and vigilant nongovernment organizations have acted

BOX 14.1 Growth Constraints of MSME Sector

Many of the MSME firms are unregistered, unincorporated, largely informal, or in the unorganized sector as elaborated later in Chapter 16. The small firms stay small and unproductive and sometimes shrink in size but are not able to shut down. There are key challenges faced by these firms while starting up and at every level of growth. As pointed out in Chapter 10, according to the World Bank's Doing Business 2013 data, India ranks 132 out of 185 countries in ease of doing business. In order to start a business, after getting done with the initial procedures, entrepreneurs have to obtain a number of clearances when applying for building/occupancy permits and utility connections. These require separate visits to various authorities whose employees often inspect the site. It takes as long as 1.5 months to obtain an electricity connection in 7 out of the 17 benchmarked Indian cities. Many processes, especially at state level, remain complex, forcing companies to hire a consultant, thereby adding to the costs.

The MSME ecosystem needs an easier process of exit, where the claims of workers and financiers are quickly resolved and the assets of the failed firm put to better use. According to the World Bank (2009), across 17 Indian cities, the insolvency process takes on an average 7.9 years and costs 8.6% of the estate value (mostly due to attorney fees, newspaper publication costs, liquidator's fees, and preservation costs), and the recovery rate is only 13.7%. The process is slower even than in other South Asian countries where, in the same year, it took an average of 5 years, and creditors could expect to recover on average 19.9%. Low asset recovery in failed firms feeds into lower levels of financing for the Indian MSMEs. The government has tried to compensate for some of these impediments by offering MSMEs incentives and concessions. But schemes and interventions based on tightly defined classifications create an incentive structure that might prevent firms from growing. Service tax exemptions for firms with less than Rs 10 lakh revenue and exemption from central excise duty for firms with an annual turnover of less than Rs 1.5 crore are examples of these schemes. The jump from "small" to "medium" enterprise especially entails loss of several perks.

These firms have little incentive to invest in upgrading skills of largely temporary workers or in investing in capital equipment that could bring them into the tax net, so their productivity stays low. Low productivity gives them little incentive to grow, completing the vicious circle.

There are, however, many good practices and enabling regulations strewn over different cities of India, which, if standardized and adopted across the country, can improve the business climate enormously.

Source: *Economic Survey of India, 2012–2013.*

as checks and balances on politicians and companies (Palepu, 2010). Participative and collaborative processes have sometimes ensured a higher degree of influence in regulatory contexts in the country. Many new trade and professional associations and other organizations have played a key role in developing industries. India's National Association of Software and Services Companies is an example (Dholakia and Kshetri, 2011).

TABLE 14.1 Framework to Analyze Institutional Voids in a Country

Factors	Explanation
Credibility enhancers	Third-party certification of claims of suppliers or customers
Information analyzers and advisors	Collect and analyze information on producers and consumers in a given market
Aggregators and distributors	Provide low-cost matching and other value-added services for suppliers and customers through expertise and economies of scale
Transaction facilitators	Provide a platform for exchange of information, goods, and services. Provide support functions for consumer transactions
Regulators and other public institutions	Create and enforce the appropriate regulatory and policy framework
Adjudicators	Resolve disputes on regulations, laws, and private contracts

Source: Palepu (2010).

In essence, entrepreneurs who have been able to create their own internal systems or have been able to work through the inadequacies of the external environment have been successful in India, while others have remained small. As a result, India has the characteristics of oligopolistic capitalism where the benefits of economic growth are disproportionately appropriated by the wealthiest and have failed to trickle down to the poor. About 10 families control more than 80% of the stock in the country's largest corporations (Malhotra, 2009 in Kshetri and Nir, 2011). According to the Asian Development Bank, large Indian companies have won most of the lucrative government contracts, hold power over the country's natural resources, and have "privileged access to land."

According to the 2012 Gallup Poll, although more than 60% of the Indian population possesses personality traits to be an entrepreneur, only 16% of Indian adults report that they currently own a business. Of those, 22% say they formally registered their businesses. The lack of contextual support has been cited as a reason for the underutilization of latent Indian entrepreneurial talent (Yu and Tandon, 2012).

Given this backdrop, a new market-oriented draft competition policy has been formulated in India to reduce anticompetitive practices. The aim is to create a framework of policies to facilitate competitive outcomes in the market. The National Competition Policy is based on the principles of (a) fair market process, (b) institutional separation, (c) competitive neutrality, (d) fair pricing and inclusionary behavior, (e) third-party access to essential facilities, and

(f) advocacy and cooperation. Some of the initiatives to create a culture of competition and to involve all stakeholders include (a) reviewing existing policies, statues, and regulations that restrict competition, (b) carrying out competition impact assessment for proposed policies, (c) progressively diluting regulation as competition becomes more effective, (d) maintaining autonomous and independent anatomy of competition authority, and (e) incorporating competition clauses in various bilateral and regional trade agreements. The policy is yet to be approved by the government (Competition Committee—Directorate for Financial and Enterprise Affairs, 2012).

As for laws to restrict anticompetitive behavior, India was one of the first developing countries to pass such legislation in the form of the Monopolies and Restrictive Trade Practices (MRTP) Act, 1969, which enacted recommendations of the Monopolies Inquiry Commission. The MRTP Act was significantly amended twice—in 1984 and again in 1991. A high-level committee set up in 1999, known as the Raghavan Committee, recommended that the MRTP Act should be replaced by a modern competition law for fostering competition in markets and reducing anticompetitive practices in domestic and international trade.

The Competition Act, 2002, amended twice in 2007 and 2009, follows the philosophy of modern competition laws. The act prohibits anticompetitive agreements and abuse of a dominant position by enterprises and regulates combinations (acquisition, acquiring of control, and M&A), which cause or are likely to cause an appreciable adverse effect on competition within India. In addition, the Indian competition law mandates that Competition Commission of India (CCI) undertakes competition advocacy to promote competition, create awareness, and impart training about competitive issues. Sections 3 and 4 of the Competition Act, relating to anticompetitive agreements and abuse of dominance, were notified in May 20, 2009, while sections 5 and 6, relating to mergers and acquisitions, were notified with effect from June 1, 2011. Thus, Indian competition law has now fully come into force. While discharging its duties, the commission's objectives are to prevent practices that have an adverse effect on competition, promote and sustain competition in the market, protect interests of consumers, and ensure freedom of trade (Competition Committee—Directorate for Financial and Enterprise Affairs, 2012).

The competition law and policy is still evolving in India. The existing law is inclined more towards promoting competition than curbing monopolies. However, the gains of the law can be realized only with effective enforcement. There is the possibility for conflict between jurisdictions of the CCI and other regulators in other sectors like the Reserve Bank of India (RBI), the Telecom Regulatory Authority of India (TRAI), the Insurance Regulatory and Development Authority (IRDA), the Petroleum and Natural Gas Regulatory Board (PNGRB), and electricity regulators. This is definitely a challenge, one that requires answers at a policy level (Singh, 2011).

Employment Situation

The relationship between the lack of a job and self-employment has been shrouded in uncertainty (Audretsch and Roy Thurik, 2000, 2001). At the micro level, the risk of not having a job is likely to have a positive effect on the level of entrepreneurship through reducing the opportunity costs of self-employment. When there is little chance of finding paid employment, unemployed people are "pushed" into self-employment (EIM/ENSR, 1996).

Unemployment rates for the United States and China from 2002 to 2011 are shown in Fig. 14.3. In the United States, the unemployment rate in 2006 and 2007 was the lowest, at about 4.6%, and from 2009 to 2011 was very high, ranging from 9.28%, to 9.63%, to 8.95%. From 2002 to 2011, the urban registered, "official" unemployment rate in China was about 4%. But in reality, the unemployment rate was much higher than that. First, not everyone who lost his or her job registered with the relevant government department. Second, this rate only reflects unemployment in urban areas, but in China, over half the people live in rural areas, and there is huge hidden unemployment. Furthermore, due to the huge population of China, even with a small unemployment rate, the actual absolute number of unemployed people is very large.

China has very low per capita income, which places a huge survival burden on people, and as a result, a vast majority of them choose to own businesses. In 2010, China's per capita annual income was $4160, which was less than one-ninth of that of the United States at $39,937. The annual household income in 2005 and the projected annual household income in 2025 are shown in Table 14.3. According to these data, in 2005, 59% of the urban household income was below RMB 25,000 ($3019), while in 2025, households with income between RMB 40,000 and 100,000 are projected to be in the majority.

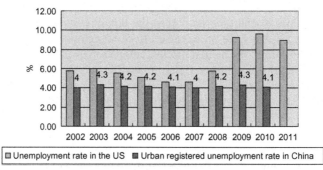

FIGURE 14.3   Unemployment rates for the United States and China from 2002 to 2011. *(Source: http://data.bls.gov/timeseries/LNS14000000 for US data (The annual unemployment rate is the average of monthly unemployment rate. The numbers for China urban registered unemployment rate are indicated in the figure because they are approximate.). China data source: Abstracted from National Bureau of Statistics of China; China City Statistical Yearbook 2005.)*

TABLE 14.2 Annual Household Income Status in China

Category	Annual Household Income (Real 2000 RMB)	Percentage of Urban Households in 2005	Percentage of Urban Households in 2025 (Projected)
Global	Over 200,000	Less than 1%	2%
Affluent	100,000-200,000	1	5
Upper aspirants	40,000-100,000	4	61
Lower aspirants	25,000-40,000	35	15
Urban poor	Below 25,000	59	16

In 2005, rural consumers accounted for 54% of national population but only 8% of national GDP. In 2000, 1 US $ = 8.28 RMB.
Sources: Abstracted from National Bureau of Statistics of China; China City Statistical Yearbook 2005; McKinsey Global Institute, From "Made in China" to "Sold in China: The Rise of the Chinese Urban Consumer, Nov 2006."

Urban households with annual income more than RMB 200,000 will account for only 2% of the households in 2025. RMB 200,000 is $24,155, which is lower than the per capita income in America in 2010[6] (Table 14.2).

At the same time, the labor cost in China is very low, which also motivated people to start their own businesses. As shown in Table 14.3, in 2003, the average hourly labor rate was $0.80, which was 3.66% of that in the United States. It was $1.27 in 2009, at 5% of that in United States. Given these factors, it is clear that there is strong motivation for people in China to start businesses.

The unemployment rate in India increased on a current daily status (CDS)[7] basis from 1993–1994 to 2004–2005 (Fig. 14.4). However, in 2009–2010, there was a decline in the unemployment rate. Despite negligible employment growth, the unemployment rate (CDS method) fell from 8.2% in 2004–2005 to 6.6% in 2009–2010 due to the "demographic dividend," as an increasing proportion of the young population opted for education rather than participating in

---

6. China data sources: http://web.worldbank.org/WBSITE/EXTERNAL/PROJECTS/EXTPOLI CIES/EXTOPMANUAL/0,,contentMDK:23208704~menuPK:51508133~pagePK:64141683~ piPK:4688102~theSitePK:502184,00.html

US data sources: U.S. Dept. of Commerce, Bureau of Economic Analysis, released March 2012.

7. Current Daily Status Unemployment (CDS): this refers to the number of persons who did not find work on a day, or on some days, during the survey week.

TABLE 14.3 Labor Cost Comparisons (Average Hourly Compensation Including Benefits for Production Workers)

	2003	2009 (Projected)
China	$0.80	$1.27
India	$1.12	$1.68
The United States	$21.86	$25.34

China data sources: http://web.worldbank.org/WBSITE/EXTERNAL/PROJECTS/EXTPOLICIES/
EXTOPMANUAL/0,,contentMDK:23208704~menuPK:51508133~pagePK:64141683~piPK:
4688102~theSitePK:502184,00.html
US data sources: U.S. Dept. of Commerce, Bureau of Economic Analysis, released March 2012.
Sources: Economist Intelligence Unit, Euromonitor, U.S. Department of Labor, and Boston Consulting Group.

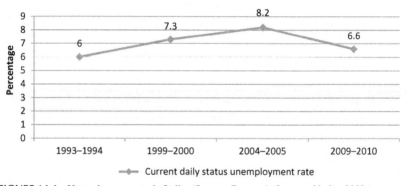

FIGURE 14.4 Unemployment rate in India. *(Source: Economic Survey of India, 2013.)*

the labor market. The total number of unemployed person days declined by 6.5 M, from around 34.5 M in 2004–2005 to 28 M in 2009–2010.

Among those who were employed, only about one in four Indian adults (26%) were employed full time for an employer other than self, in the first half of 2012, according to Gallup's[8] new Payroll to Population metric[9] (Fig. 14.5).

An analysis of the employment pattern shows that the job creation rate is much larger for small firms than for large ones; on the other hand, the job destruction rate is higher in large firms, with the result that the net employment rate in large firms is negative and strikingly smaller than in small firms. Unorganized-sector employment still constitutes more than 95% of overall

8. http://www.gallup.com/poll/158384/one-four-indians-steady-full-time-employment.aspx
9. The payroll to population rate measures the percentage of entire population that is employed full time for an employer.

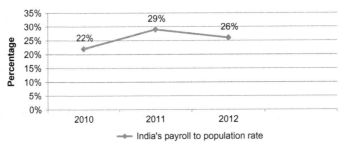

FIGURE 14.5 India's payroll to population rate.

industry employment; specifically within manufacturing, unorganized-sector employment comprises 70% of overall employment. "Informal" jobs within the formal sector have increased with little increase in productivity.

Strict labor laws seem to have hindered the growth of organized large-scale manufacturing. These large manufacturing firms have responded by (i) relying more on capital instead of labor, (ii) resorting to informal arrangements or limiting their scale in order to remain outside of the formal sector altogether, and (iii) hiring contractual labor (Ministry of Finance, 2013).

India's high rate of informality is a drag on its economic development and a source of considerable inequity. Productivity differences between workers in the formal and informal sectors are large (10 times in some cases). In addition to earning less, informal workers are also more vulnerable to violations of basic human rights such as reasonable working conditions and safety at work. Informality has been found to have a strong correlation with poverty in India (NCEUS 2009 in Ministry of Finance, 2013). Finally, persistently high levels of informality come at a significant fiscal cost in terms of forgone fiscal revenue.

The low level of per capita income reflects the effects of large levels of informality in employment. The per capita income of India was $1530 as compared with $5740 in China and $50,120 in the United States in 2012. Sixty-four percent of those employed in the informal sector come under the "self-employed" category and can be termed "necessity-driven" entrepreneurs.

Necessity-driven entrepreneurial activities were far more prevalent than innovation-driven entrepreneurial activities in both China and India. The figure below shows the percentage of population in the age range of 18–64 years, which was either a nascent entrepreneur or an owner-manager of a new business. The highest total early-stage entrepreneurial activity (TEA) in the United States was about 12% in 2005 and almost equaled the lowest rate in China. The highest TEA for India was 16% in 2002 but slowly tapered down to 11.5% in 2008. The TEA in China had an upward trend, with the highest rate of 24% in 2011, almost twice that of the United States, while India's TEA has been more or less the same as that of the United States (Fig. 14.6).

In China, the lowest necessity-driven entrepreneurial activity rate was 38% in 2007, a little higher than the highest rate in the United States, which was 37%

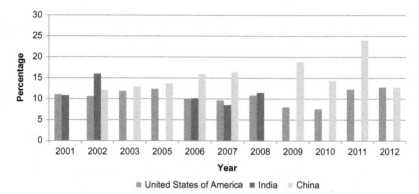

FIGURE 14.6   Total early-stage entrepreneurial activity. *(Source: Global Entrepreneurship Monitor (GEM).)*

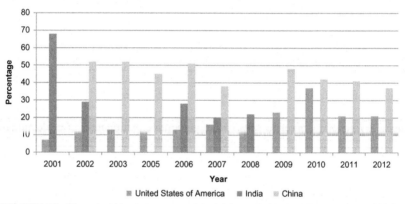

FIGURE 14.7   Necessity-driven entrepreneurial activity: relative prevalence. *(Source: Global Entrepreneurship Monitor (GEM).)*

in 2010. In the United States, the lowest rate was 11% in 2002 and it had an upward trend, and the average rate from 2002 to 2011 was about 18%. India started off with a very high rate of 68% in 2001, which decreased to an average of 24.75% during 2002–2008 (Fig. 14.7). These figures show that the overall entrepreneurial activity is low in India and almost 25% of this activity is driven by nonavailability of any other option for work.

SUPPORTIVE LAWS

The United States

In the United States, in order to strengthen employment and entrepreneurship training, a series of important bills were passed. In 1962, the Manpower Development and Training Act (Yuxuan, 2007) was enacted to improve job skills of the unemployed and the underemployed labor force with the funding coming jointly from the Department of Labor and the Department of Health, Education, and Welfare. The Vocational Education Law (Yuxuan, 2007) passed in 1963 emphasized diversified vocational education and strongly promoted reform of vocational education. These subsidies were intended for people with different social and demographic backgrounds—different age groups and different levels of education, including high school graduates, veterans, and people with disabilities. The Youth Employment and Demonstration Projects Act of 1977 implemented work-study cooperative education and improved cooperation between universities and companies (Maoxin, 2007).

The Job Training Partnership Act of 1982 was designed to improve employment status of disadvantaged (http://en.wikipedia.org/wiki/Job_Training_Partnership_Act_of_1982) young adults, dislocated workers, and individuals facing barriers to employment. Program components include on-the-job training, job search assistance, basic education, and work experience and improving participants' occupational skills. An experimental evaluation showed that participation in the Job Training Partnership Act increased levels of employment and training services.[10] The Worker Adjustment and Retraining Notification Act enacted in 1988 required employers of 100 or more full-time workers to give a 60-day advanced notice of a plant closing or a mass layoff to the appropriate local chief elected official so that training and help for unemployed workers could be arranged as soon as possible. The School-to-Work Opportunities Act of 1994 (the "School-to-Work Act," http://ada.ky.gov/stw_opp_act.htm) was designed to facilitate the creation of a universal, high-quality school-to-work transition system. The act used federal funds as venture capital to underwrite the initial costs of planning and establishing statewide systems that were maintained with other resources. These systems were set up to provide all students with opportunities to participate in programs that integrate school- and work-based learning, vocational and academic education, and secondary and postsecondary education.[11]

Since the Patent Law was enacted in 1790, the Trademark Law, the Copyright Act, the Anti-Unfair Competition Law, the Bayh-Dole Act, and the Stevenson-Wydler Technology Innovation Act were gradually passed. These laws protected the intellectual property of start-up businesses from all aspects so that they could quickly develop products and services. For example, the Bayh-Dole Act allowed universities and research institutions to own intellectual property rights of the projects sponsored by the government and supported entrepreneurial activities by researchers. Since then, entrepreneurial activities, the rate of patent filings, and the rate of commercialization of new technologies at American colleges and universities have increased three times.

---

10. http://www.childtrends.org/lifecourse/programs/JobTrainingPartnershipAct.htm
11. http://ada.ky.gov/stw_opp_act.htm

The US government also launched the Small Business Administration (SBA) in 1953 to provide support to entrepreneurs and small businesses by making government-backed guaranteed loans available to them through banks and other lenders. In 1982, the US government also launched a couple of other programs coordinated by the SBA, in order to help spur technological research in small businesses, Small Business Innovation Research (SBIR) program, and also to help commercialization of university-originated research, Small Business Technology Transfer (STTR) program, through public–private partnerships between publicly funded research at universities and private small businesses.

However, beyond creating these laws and regulations, infrastructure, and an environment supportive of entrepreneurship, in the United States, the actual act of entrepreneurship is driven by motivated individuals with very little intervention, by way of additional funding, training, or any other way by the government, whether federal, state, or local. Most value creation that has occurred in the United States through entrepreneurship has primarily been the work of the private sector.

China

In China, a few laws were also passed to promote entrepreneurship. In June 2002, the SME (small and medium enterprise) Promotion Law was adopted by the Standing Committee of the National People's Congress, which clearly stated that small and medium enterprises should be encouraged and supported by tax policy. In February 2005, a document entitled the *Several Opinions on Encouraging, Supporting and Guiding the Private and Other Non-public Economic Development* was issued by the State Council, which provided the policy basis for the establishment of SME development funds. Some of the policy basis consisted of the following recommendations. If high-tech enterprises needed government support, income tax rate could be reduced to 15%. If enterprises are small or barely profitable, income tax rate could be reduced to 20%. Venture capital firms investing in unlisted small- and medium-sized high-tech enterprises by way of an equity stake for 2 years or more could use 70% of the invested amounts to deduct current annual income tax. If 70% of invested funds were not sufficient, the rest of the income tax could be carried over for deduction in future years (Lirong, 2012). Although some progress was made to support entrepreneurs in China, there are still many shortcomings.

First, the SME Promotion Law is the only law set up for the development of small and medium enterprises, while all other laws and regulations are not aimed at supporting small and medium-sized businesses. Thus, there is not a complete system to support small- and medium-sized businesses. Second, in the current tax preference policies, small and barely profitable enterprises are defined on the basis of the number of employees and total assets of the enterprise, which narrows the number of eligible enterprises. Also, all these enterprises have the same income tax preference, so there is no preferential treatment for specific industries, in order to encourage entrepreneurship in those sectors. Third, except for the above-mentioned income tax preference, there are no other tax preferences for small- and medium-sized companies, such as sales tax preference, exempted or reduced income tax, or any other additional tax deductions.

India

In India, for employment training, the National Policy on Skill Development was formulated by the Ministry of Labour and Employment in 2009 to create a workforce empowered with improved skills, knowledge, and internationally recognized qualifications to gain access to employment and ensure India's competitiveness in the dynamic global labor market. The National Skill Development Corporation (NSDC) is a not-for-profit company set up by the Ministry of Finance. It is a pioneering public–private partnership (PPP) set up to facilitate the development and upgrade the skills of a growing Indian workforce through skills training programs.

For promotion of MSMEs, Micro, Small and Medium Enterprises Development (MSMED) Act was notified in 2006 to address policy issues affecting MSMEs and the coverage and investment ceiling of the sector. The Ministry of MSME was formed by merging the Ministry of Agro and Rural Industries (Krishi Evam Gramin Udyog Mantralaya) and Ministry of Small Scale Industries (Laghu Udyog Mantralaya). The MSMED Act seeks to facilitate the development of MSME enterprises and also enhance their competitiveness. It provides the first-ever legal framework for recognition of the concept of "enterprise," which comprises both manufacturing and service entities. It defines medium enterprises for the first time and seeks to integrate the three tiers of these enterprises, namely, micro, small, and medium.

The primary responsibility for the promotion and development of MSMEs is that of the state governments. However, the Government of India supplements the efforts of the state governments through various initiatives. The role of the Ministry of MSME and its organizations is to assist the states in their efforts to encourage entrepreneurship, employment, and livelihood opportunities and enhance the competitiveness of MSMEs in the changed economic scenario. The schemes and program undertaken by the ministry and its organizations seek to facilitate (i) adequate flow of credit from financial institutions; (ii) support for technology upgrades and modernization; (iii) integrated infrastructural facilities; (iv) modern testing facilities and quality certification; (v) access to modern management practices; (vi) entrepreneurship development and skill upgrades through appropriate training facilities; (vii) support for product development, design intervention, and packaging; (viii) welfare of artisans and workers; (ix) assistance for better access to domestic and export markets;

and (x) industry-cluster-based measures to promote capacity-building and empowerment of the units and their constituents.

The ministry and its two divisions, the Small and Medium-Sized Enterprises (SMEs) Division and the Agro and Rural Industry (ARI) Division, implement policies and various programs and schemes for providing infrastructure and support services to MSME through several of its interconnected organizations. These are the Office of the Development Commissioner, the National Small Industries Corporation (NSIC), the Khadi and Village Industries Commission (KVIC), the Coir Board of India, and three training institutes, namely, the National Institute for Entrepreneurship and Small Business Development (NIESBUD), the National Institute for Micro, Small and Medium Enterprises (NI-MSME), the Indian Institute of Entrepreneurship (IIE), and Mahatma Gandhi Institute for Rural Industrialization (MGIRI). The National Board for Micro, Small & Medium Enterprises (NBMSME), on the other hand, provides policy inputs to the ministry.

Also, a large number of ministries in the government, namely, Ministries of MSME, Finance, Commerce and Industry, Corporate Affairs, Law and Justice, Women and Child Development, Human Resource Development, Rural Development, Science and Technology, Food Processing Industries, Housing and Urban Poverty Alleviation, and Social Justice and Empowerment are engaged, directly or indirectly, in the promotion of entrepreneurship.

There are a plethora of policies such as the manufacturing policy, the competition policy, the industrial policy, the science and technology policy, and the national design policy that touch upon and have implications for entrepreneurship, directly and indirectly. But the focus on entrepreneurship remains fragmented and devoid of any strategy content.

Apart from the above-mentioned MSME policies, the Government of India is in the process of formulating a national entrepreneurship policy with the overarching aim to augment the supply of entrepreneurs. While the MSME policy focuses on existing enterprises or a group or cluster of enterprises, entrepreneurship policy focuses on individuals with an expectation that they would move towards entrepreneurship. This policy is being introduced with an objective of creating an ecosystem in India where opportunity-based innovative entrepreneurship germinates, sustains, and grows, leading to the creation of a more dynamic and entrepreneurial economy.

In summary, entrepreneurship in a given economy is strongly influenced by the environment external to the entrepreneur. More specifically, it is affected by the degree and vigor with which anticompetitive or antitrust legislation is enforced, the levels of employment especially as it relates to necessity-driven entrepreneurship, and a supportive legal infrastructure. In the United States, the free market economy and the supportive laws and legislations have been around for an extremely long time compared with those in China and India and have played a very significant role in value creation through entrepreneurship. In China and India, the legal framework has been evolving only within the last

20–30 years and still has a long way to go before reaching the level of sophistication that is seen in the United States. As of today, the Chinese market consists of predominantly state-owned monopolies with some emergence of competition localized to certain industries. In India, though private enterprise is growing in numbers, in terms of value, the market structure is more oligopolistic to the extent that about 10 families control about 80% of the stock of country's largest corporations.

While most entrepreneurship in the United States is driven by an eye towards value creation for the customer and for the enterprise through creatively searching for new opportunities, entrepreneurship in China and India to this point has been primarily necessity-driven, due to a lack of adequate employment opportunities for an increasingly burgeoning population.

REFERENCES

Audretsch, D.B., Roy Thurik, A., 2000. Capitalism and democracy in the 21st century: from the managed to the entrepreneurial economy. J. Evol. Econ. 10, 17–34.

Audretsch, D.B., Roy Thurik, A., 2001. What is new about the new economy: sources of growth in the managed and entrepreneurial economics. Ind. Corp. Change 19, 795–821.

Competition Committee—Directorate for Financial and Enterprise Affairs, 2012. Annual Report on Competition Policy Developments in India. Organization for Economic Cooperation and Development.

Dean, T.J., McMullen, J.S., 2007. Toward a theory of sustainable entrepreneurship: reducing environmental degradation through entrepreneurial action. J. Bus. Venturing 22, 50–76.

Dong, S., 2010. Comparison of market economy system between China and US. Special Zone Economy 8, 15–18.

EIM/ENSR, 1996. The European Observatory for SMEs: Fourth Annual Report. EIM Business and Policy Research, Zoetermeer.

Fanhe, K., Qian, M., 2006. On dilemma of market access for Chinese private enterprises – "virgin" phenomenon. Special Zone Economy 8, 109.

International Financial Corporation (IFC), Government of Japan, 2012. Micro Small and Medium Enterprises Finance in India – A Research Study on Needs, Gaps and Way Forward. International Financial Corporation (IFC) and Government of Japan.

Khanna and Palepu, 2010. Winning in Emerging Markets: A Road Map for Strategy and Execution. Harvard Business Press, Boston.

KPMG, 2012. Public Sector Enterprises – Unlocking Their True Potential. KPMG. http://www.kpmg.com/in/en/industry/publications/aima-pse.pdf.

Kshetri and Dholaki, 2011. Regulative institutions supporting entrepreneurship in emerging economies: a comparison of China and India. J. Int. Entrep. 9, 110–132.

Kshetri and Nir, 2011. The Indian environment for entrepreneurship and small business development. Studia Negotia 56 (4), 35–52.

Lirong, Z., 2012. Discuss on how to perfect the tax system for small and medium-sized enterprises in China. Forum, February, pp. 237–238.

Maoxin, L., 2007. USA manpower training and employment policy (1971–1982). Hist. Res. (1), 165.

Ministry of Finance, 2013. Economic Survey of India, 2012–13. Ministry of Finance, Government of India, http://indiabudget.nic.in/ (accessed 11.09.13.).

Qinzhi, C., 2005. Discuss on the fair market environment. Gansu Soc. Sci. (4), 67.

Shangfeng, X., 2010. Why Chinese monopoly enterprises bring so much disturbing? IT Time Weekly 79.

Singh, V.K., 2011. Competition law and policy in India: the journey in a decade. NUJS Law Rev. 4, 523–566.

The World Bank and the International Finance Corporation, 2013. Doing Business 2013 – Smarter Regulations for Small and Medium-Size Enterprises. The World Bank and the International Finance Corporation, Washington.

Yu and Tandon, 2012. India Lags Behind Other Asian Countries in Promoting Entrepreneurship. Gallup, Washington.

Yuxuan, W., 2007. On the American Policies of Manpower Training and Full Employment in the 1960s. Hebei Normal University master degree paper. p. 1.

Chapter 15

Infrastructure

Chapter Contents

Societies and civilizations have always depended on, to varying degrees, a common physical infrastructure to support human coexistence and interaction. In fact, the degree of advancement of the physical infrastructure may be correlated to the degree of social and cultural progress of a civilization. Physical infrastructure is, therefore, a leading indicator of the sophistication of a society, a civilization, or a nation. Given that entrepreneurship creates value for the entrepreneur, as well as, more importantly, for the target community whose unmet need is served by the product or service created by the entrepreneur and ecosystem, interaction among them is critical. This interaction is facilitated by the existence of a suitable physical infrastructure, which is thus a key contributing factor that enables entrepreneurship.

THE UNITED STATES

For over a hundred years, the United States has enjoyed one of the best physical infrastructures in the world. This has contributed to, and has also been the result of, the United States becoming the most dominant technological and economic power and, in many ways, the most advanced and sophisticated civilization of the twentieth century. This has consisted of one of the most advanced

(a) telecommunications networks, first via the telegraph, then the telephone and data networks, and now the Internet, first via copper and satellite and now fiber and wireless;

Innovation, Entrepreneurship, and the Economy in the US, China, and India

(b) media and entertainment systems and networks—print, as well as radio and television, and now the Internet, first over the air and now over copper, fiber, wireless, and satellite;

(c) surface transportation systems—railways and now roadways, bridges and tunnels, mass transit systems, and inland waterways and ports and seaports;

(d) aviation systems and air transportation networks—airlines and airports;

(e) energy and power systems—oil and gas field exploration and distribution networks, coal mines, coal-fired plants, nuclear power plants, and various other forms of energy generation, together with a very sophisticated and extensive transmission and distribution network, connected in a grid across the nation;

(f) utilities, such as drinking water reservoirs and distribution systems;

(g) dams for power generation and levees for flood control systems;

(h) wastewater, sewage, and solid and hazardous waste disposal systems; and

(i) national parks and public parks and recreation.

However, these investments were made over varying points in time in the twentieth century, and a vast majority of these are now somewhat dated. As with any other physical assets, these fixed assets have a finite useful life and need to be upgraded and updated with new investments and with the latest technology. That has not been happening in the United States to the degree necessary, and the infrastructure is now showing signs of aging. A number of reports are available that talk about the challenges of the gradually crumbling US infrastructure (American Society of Civil Engineers, ASCE, 2013; Galston, 2013; Reid, 2013; US Government Accounting Office, GAO, 2008; World Economic Forum, 2013). Without significant new investment, the US physical infrastructure that has propelled the United States to be the most dominant economic power of the twentieth century is in danger of falling behind that of the nations with which the United States will be competing economically and politically in the twenty-first century. This is especially true given that the United States spends roughly 2% of its gross domestic product (GDP) on infrastructure, compared with about 9% and 5% that China and India spend on infrastructure (Reid, 2013). While this may not have any immediate or near-term impact on entrepreneurship in the United States, it will be a longer-term concern. Vulnerability of this infrastructure to terrorist attacks, and ensuring the safety and security of this infrastructure, especially from cyber-attacks, continues to be an ongoing concern.

CHINA AND A COMPARISON WITH THE UNITED STATES

In the early days of reform and opening up of China, China's investment in infrastructure was very anemic, and as a result, infrastructure was in a very bad shape. In order to change that situation, from 1979 to 1989, investment funds were channeled into key industries. The total level of cumulative infrastructure investment in key basic industries amounted to ¥547.9 B, with an average annual growth rate of 10.7%. During this period, investment in culture, education, and healthcare also increased rapidly. The total cumulative investment in these areas was ¥83.9 B and had an average annual growth rate of 25.8%. From 1982 to 1989, in order to ease the bottleneck in raw materials, energy, transportation, and other basic industries and infrastructure, ¥248.6 B was cumulatively invested, accounting for 29% of the construction investment in the same period. Between 1998 and 2002, ¥660 B worth of treasury bonds was issued, of which ¥88.4 B was used in transportation, ¥101.5 B in urban infrastructure, ¥126.9 B in water conservancy facilities, and ¥62 B in rural power grids. From 2003 to 2007, the total investment in basic industries and infrastructure construction was ¥18.27 T, which was 1.6 times that invested from 1978 to 2002. In 2007, there were 143,971 projects in basic industries and infrastructure, and the total investment was ¥17.145 T. Infrastructure investment is also the highlight of economic and social development in the 12th Five-Year Plan. According to various estimates, during the 12th Five-Year Plan, fixed asset investment in city infrastructure will amount to ¥7 T. By the end of 2010, cumulative investment was about ¥4 T, and about half of the investment was used for transport infrastructure and urban and rural power grid construction (Li, 2011).

Figure 15.1 shows Internet usage in China from 2002 to 2011. In 2002, the number of people who had access to the Internet did not reach 100 M. With the development of high-speed Internet access, in 2011, more than 500 M people had access to the Internet, an increase of about four times in 9 years. Internet coverage rate was only about 7% in 2002 and reached 38% in 2011. In 2001, global Internet coverage rate was 30.2%, and China exceeded this level. Although the Internet

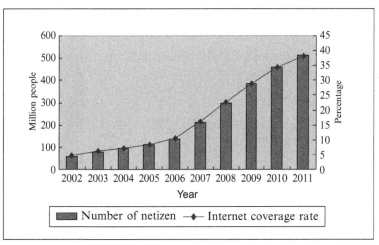

FIGURE 15.1   Internet development in China. *(Sources: The Statistical Report of China Internet Development, China Internet Network Information Center, January 2012 and January 2011.)*

quickly developed in China in recent years, over 800 M people still do not have access to the Internet. Furthermore, there is a serious imbalance in the development of the Internet. In big cities or developed provinces, Internet coverage rates are very high, while in small cities or developing provinces, Internet coverage rates were very low. For example, in 2011, in Beijing, the number of people with Internet access was about 13.8 M, with an Internet coverage rate of 70.3%, while in Guizhou province, the number of people with Internet access was only 8.4 M, at an Internet coverage rate of only 24.2%. While the Internet coverage rate in China has greatly increased, there is a big gap in coverage rates between China and the United States. By the end of June 2011, the population of the United States was 315.9 M, and only 6% of the population did not have access to fixed broadband meeting the speed benchmark (Table 15.1).

In China, most small and medium enterprises (SMEs) access the Internet and the percentage of Internet users has a positive correlation with the size of the enterprise. By the end of 2010, the proportion of SMEs using the Internet was 92.7%. Enterprises with 10 or fewer employees had the lowest ratio, at 83%. These same SMEs, with 10 or fewer people, have a lower rate of building their own website, at 27.8%, whereas enterprises with more than 500 employees have the highest rate of building their own website, at about 45% (Fig. 15.2).

The websites created by SMEs were used primarily (>90%) to provide contact information and to display products, whereas they were used very little (<50%) for providing online sales or for online services (as shown in Fig. 15.3). With regard to the usefulness of the website, most SMEs believed that the website was helpful only in displaying the company's products, and only 18% of them thought that the website was instrumental in bringing in orders (Fig. 15.4).

Figure 15.5 shows telephone usage in China from 2007 to 2011. In 2007, the number of people who used the telephone was about 900 M, and by the end of 2011, this number was over 1.2 B. In 2007, the proportion of cell phones was about 60%, and it was nearly 80% in 2011, increasing by almost 20 percentage points within 4 years.

With regard to transportation, China made huge progress, especially in the areas of construction of highways and navigable inland waterways. In 2000,

TABLE 15.1 Americans and Households Without Access to Fixed Broadband Meeting the Speed Benchmark

All Americans (Millions)	Americans Without Access (Millions/%)	All American Households (Millions)	Households Without Access (Millions/%)
315.9	19.0/6.0%	119.2	7.0/5.9%

Sources: Eighth Broadband Progress Report, Federal Communications Commission, Released: August 21, 2012.

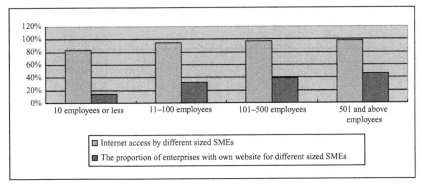

FIGURE 15.2 Internet usages by different-sized SMEs. *(Sources: The Statistical Report of China Internet Development, China Internet Network Information Center, January 2011.)*

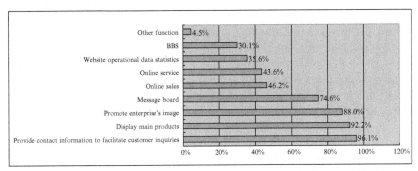

FIGURE 15.3 Types of website usage by SMEs. *(Sources: The Statistical Report of China Internet Development, China Internet Network Information Center, January 2011.)*

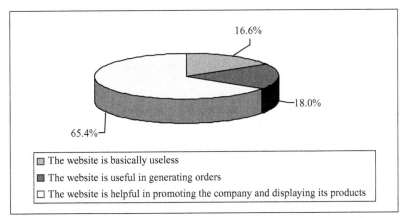

FIGURE 15.4 Assessment of website usage by SMEs. *(Sources: The Statistical Report of China Internet Development, China Internet Network Information Center, January 2011.)*

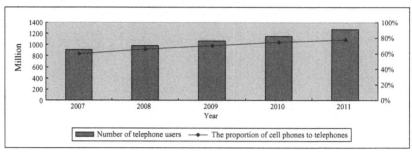

FIGURE 15.5   Number of telephone users in China. *(Sources: The Statistical Report of China Telecommunication Development, 2011.)*

railway operating mileage was 68,700 km, and it reached 91,200 km in 2010, an increase of 32.8% in 10 years. Highway mileage in 2000 was 1.403 M km, and it reached 1.871 M km in 2004, an increase of 33.3% within 4 years. From 2005 onward, highways included village roads, thus providing a further increase in highway mileage reaching 3.345 M km. By the end of 2010, this number increased further by 16.5% and reached 4.008 M km. With regard to inland waterways, there were no significant changes from 2000 to 2010, but the statistics indicator was changed in 2005—inland waterways to navigable inland waterways. There was a significant growth in navigable inland waterways. Also, there was similarly impressive growth in civil aviation. This was 1,503 M km in 2000 and reached 2.765 M km in 2010, an increase of 84% compared with 2000 (Table 15.2).

After 1998, especially after 2008, massive funds were invested in the transport infrastructure. By the end of 2010, the total mileage of the national road network reached 4 M km, the total railway mileage reached 91,000 km ranking second in the world, the total number of ports was 400, the number of new airports was 34, and the total number of all airports was 175. During the period of the "Eleventh Five-Year" Plan, investment in domestic airports and affiliated facilities reached ¥250 B, an amount that equaled the total cumulative investment of the previous 25 years. By the end of 2010, the number of commercial airports was 17, an increase of 33 airports in the previous 5 years. By the end of 2015, the number of domestic commercial airports is projected to be over 230, and these are expected to address 94% of the total national economic output, 83% of the population, and 81% of the county-level administrative units.

On March 21, 2012, the Twelfth Five-Year Comprehensive Transportation System Planning bill was passed by the State Council executive meeting, and the construction target for China's overall transportation system during the period of the "12th Five-Year Plan" was determined. An integrated transport network will be constructed in the form of a backbone consisting of a "five vertical and five horizontal" grid, with an expected completion of a rapid railway network and a highway network. The railway transport service is expected to

TABLE 15.2 Length of Transport Routes (Unit: 1000 km)

Year	Railway Operating Mileage	Highway Mileage	Inland Waterway Mileage	Civil Aviation Mileage
2000	68.7	1402.7	119.3	1502.9
2001	70.1	1698	121.5	1553.6
2002	71.9	1765.2	121.6	1637.7
2003	73	1809.8	124	1749.5
2004	74.4	1870.7	123.3	2049.4
2005	75.4	3345.2	123.3	1998.5
2006	77.1	3457	123.4	2113.5
2007	78	3583.7	123.5	2343
2008	79.7	3730.2	122.8	2461.8
2009	85.5	3860.8	123.7	2345.1
2010	91.2	4008.2	124.2	2765.1

From 2004, the inland waterway mileage being replaced by navigable inland waterway mileage.
From 2005, highway mileage included village roads, not comparable with historical data.
Sources: China Statistics Yearbook, 2011.

cover distribution centers for bulk goods, as well as cities with populations exceeding 200,000. Rural roads are expected to cover townships and villages. Shipping services are expected to be globally accessible, and 70% of high-grade inland waterways are expected to meet planning standards. Civil aviation network is further expected to expand and be optimized around 42 nationally integrated transport hubs (Jia, 2012).

Compared with China, US transportation construction has had almost no improvement since the time they were originally built. In fact, in some respects, despite the high quality and the expanse of the existing infrastructure when first set up, there are now signs of decrease, decline, and deterioration. Table 15.3 shows transportation status in the United States from 2000 to 2009, and it can be seen that except highway mileage, the mileages of class I rail, Amtrak, and navigable channels all decreased in 2009 compared with those in 2000. Similarly, the number of certified US airports decreased to 559 in 2009 from 651 in 2000.

In telecommunications construction, China's fixed asset investment was highest in 2009, at ¥377.3 B, and the lowest was ¥237 B in 2007. In 2011, this investment decreased ¥44.2 B compared with that of 2009 but increased ¥96.1 B compared with that of 2007 (Fig. 15.6).

TABLE 15.3 Transportation Status in the United States from 2000 to 2009

| | System Mileage Within the United States (Statute Miles) | | | | Number of |
Year	Highway	Class I Rail	Amtrak	Navigable Channels	Certificated US Airport
2000	3,936,222	99,250	23,000	26,000	651
2001	3,948,335	97,817	23,000	26,000	635
2002	3,966,485	100,125	23,000	26,000	633
2003	3,947,107	99,126	22,675	26,000	628
2004	3,981,512	97,662	22,256	26,000	599
2005	3,995,635	95,664	22,007	26,000	575
2006	4,016,741	94,801	21,708	26,000	604
2007	4,032,126	94,313	21,708	25,320	565
2008	4,042,778	94,082	21,178	25,320	560
2009	4,050,717	93,921	21,178	25,320	559

Certificated airports serve air-carrier operations with aircraft seating more than nine passengers. As of 2005, the Federal Aviation Administration (FAA) no longer certificates military airports.
Sources: National Transportation Statistics, U.S. Department of Transportation Research and Innovative Technology Administration.

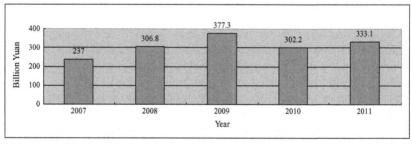

FIGURE 15.6   Investment in fixed assets in telecommunications in China. *(Source: The Statistical Report of China Telecommunication Development, 2011.)*

INDIA

India's infrastructure competitiveness as can be seen from Table 15.4 is far less as compared with China and the United States. Increased economic growth and population growth have put a massive strain on India's existing infrastructure. According to the World Economic Forum (2013), India is not providing access to some basic services to many of its citizens (e.g., only 34% of the population has access to sanitation). It is estimated that poor infrastructure in India reduces

TABLE 15.4 Infrastructure Competitiveness: India as Compared with China and the United States (2012–2013)

Key Indicators	India	China	The United States
	Rank Out of 144 Countries		
Infrastructure competitiveness	84	48	14
Quality of overall infrastructure	87	69	25
Quality of roads	86	54	20
Quality of railroad infrastructure	27	22	18
Quality of port infrastructure	80	59	19
Quality of air transport infrastructure	68	70	30
Available airline seat km/week, in M	3246.9 (rank 13)	11,685.5 (rank 12)	32,249.3 (rank 1)
Quality of electricity supply	110	59	33
Mobile telephone users/100 pop.	72.0 (rank 116)	73.2 (rank 114)	105.9 (rank 72)
Fixed telephone lines/100 pop.	2.6 (rank 118)	21.2 (rank 58)	47.9 (rank 15)
Individuals using Internet, %	10.1 (rank 119)	38.3 (rank 73)	77.9 (rank 20)
Broadband Internet users/100 pop.	1.0 (rank 101)	11.6 (rank 49)	28.7 (rank 17)
Intl. Internet bandwidth, kb/s per user	5.4 (rank 104)	2.7 (rank 119)	47.2 (rank 33)
Mobile broadband users/100 pop.	1.9 (rank 102)	9.5 (rank 69)	65.5 (rank 8)

Source: WEF, 2012–2013.

GDP growth by 1–2% p.a. (Singhala et al., 2011). Inadequate infrastructure is seen as the biggest impediment to doing business in India, as well as being the single biggest challenge to India's economic development (Singhala et al., 2011). The constraints in infrastructure affect small firms, start-ups, and SMEs more than large firms (Morris and Basant, 2005). With a population of over

1.2 B and an expected increase in urban population from 31.16% in 2011[1] to 45.6% by 2040,[2] India's infrastructure will witness significant additional pressures.

Although the Indian government has introduced several favorable policies and ensured relative transparency in the legal framework to attract investment from the private sector, including foreign investors, there are multiple challenges facing the infrastructure sector. For instance, according to the McKinsey report on "Financing and Investing in Infrastructure," India seems to be encountering hurdles in all the four important factors for successful implementation of planned targets in infrastructure investment, viz., creation of adequate projects for tender by government, uptake of available projects by private sector developers and cash contractors, financial closure and start of construction, and finally on-time execution of projects within budgets. In addition to this, recent poor macroeconomic forces, policy gridlock and political instability, delays in land acquisition and environmental clearances, high input costs, and structural and regulatory barriers for flow of domestic capital into infrastructure are hindering the growth of the sector (Maniar, 2013).

The end of the 11th Five-Year Plan saw India's missing targets in infrastructure development in sectors such as railways, ports, electricity, and airports while investing beyond the budgeted investment in others—the roads and telecom sectors (Table 15.5). Overall, Rs. 19.45 T was invested in Indian infrastructure between fiscal years 2007–2008 and 2011–2012, 95% of the projected Rs. 20.56 T.

Therefore, the need to significantly improve India's infrastructure has been recognized by the Indian government as a result of which the infrastructure sector continues to be a priority in India's 12th 5-Year Plan for 2012–2017 as in the 11th 5-Year Plan (Table 15.5). The GDP share of infrastructure investment is planned to increase to more than 10% by the end of the 12th Five-Year Plan (Table 15.6). This translates into an investment of $1 T in infrastructure projects, 50% of which is expected to come from the private sector (Department of Economic Affairs, 2012). Tables 12.5 and 12.6 show the breakup of these investments across various infrastructure sectors.

This investment, if it materializes, can propel India's economic growth to a higher trajectory. Recent developments in individual infrastructure sectors are as follows.

Roads

India boasts the third-largest road network in the world after the United States and China, with a total of 3,320,410 km of roadways, 1,517,000 km (45%) of which is paved. The majority of the country's freight is transported by road and

---

1. Census of India, 2011, www.censusindia.gov.in
2. United Nations Population Division, http://esa.un.org/unpd/wup/unup/p2k0data.asp

TABLE 15.5 11th Five-Year Plan Investment in Infrastructure in India (at 2006–2007 Prices)

Sector	Projected Investment (Rs. in trillion)	Actual Investment (Rs. in trillion)	Actual Investment as Proportion of Projected Investment (in %)
Electricity	6.66	6.35	95
Roads	3.14	3.62	115
Telecommunications	2.58	3.36	130
Railways	2.62	1.95	75
Ports	0.88	0.35	40
Airports	0.31	0.29	95
Others[a]	4.37	3.53	81
Total	20.56	19.45	95

[a]Others include irrigation, water supply and sanitation, storage, and oil and gas pipelines.
Source: High Level Committee on Financing Infrastructure (2012).

TABLE 15.6 12th Five-Year Plan Investment Projections in Infrastructure in India (at 2011–2012 Prices)

Sector	Projected (Rs. in trillions)	Project Investment as Proportion of Total Investment (in %)
Electricity	18.48	36
Roads	9.20	18
Telecommunications	8.84	17
Railways	4.57	9
Ports	1.61	3
Airports	0.71	1
Others[a]	8.05	16
Total	51.46	100

[a]Others include Mass Rapid Transit System (MRTS), irrigation, water and sanitation, storage, and oil and gas pipelines.
Source: High Level Committee on Financing Infrastructure (2012).

65% of total cargo is carried through roads. Although India has a relatively low vehicle density (2.5 vehicles per kilometer squared (km^2)) compared with other developing countries (4.06 in Brazil) and with developed economies (46.5 in the United States and 101.4 in the United Kingdom), 40% of the total road traffic is carried by India's national highways, which accounts for around 1.7% of the country's road network. Additionally, only 24% of India's national highways are four-lane. The road network within cities is a serious challenge. This leads to heavy congestion and quick wear and tear of the road network. Aware of this deficiency in the highway system, India's road building plan has been one of the flagship aspects of the country's road map for infrastructure; the 12th Five-Year Plan envisages the construction of more than 20 km of roads a day throughout the plan period (Business Monitor International, 2013).

Railways

India has railways totaling 64,015 km in length, approximately 82% of which is broad gauge (52,808 km). About 28% of the total railway system is electrified. India has the world's fourth-largest rail network after the United States, Russia, and China and is the second largest under single management. However, India's railway sector has suffered from several bottlenecks such as underinvestment, poor track record of completing projects on time and within budget, problems in land acquisitions and other clearances, improper planning, and coalition politics preventing timely approvals. Nevertheless, with the initiation of Eastern and Western Dedicated Freight Corridors, railways is projected as the second fastest-growing transport subsector, with annual average real growth of 7.8% anticipated between 2012/2013 and 2016/2017 (Business Monitor International, 2013).

Airports

The country has been developing its airport subsector, not only for the transport of goods but also for the accommodation of the growing numbers of international business travelers and tourists. India has 454 airports and airstrips, of which the state-run Airports Authority of India (AAI) owns and manages 97 airports and 28 civil enclaves at defense airfields. AAI handles around 40% of the total air traffic, while the remaining 60% is handled by five private airports at Delhi, Mumbai, Hyderabad, Bangalore, and Cochin. A total of 16 airports are designated as international airports as of October 2012. Under the 12th Five-Year Plan, India's airports are expected to need approximately INR675bn (US $13.86bn) in investment, nearly INR500bn (US $10.27 B) of which is likely to be from the private sector. This is part of a larger investment plan that envisions the establishment of connectivity to the six metropolitan cities (Bangalore, Chennai, Delhi, Hyderabad, Kolkata, and Mumbai) in the first stage followed by connectivity of metro cities with tier II and tier III cities. The airport sector is wrestling with problems like land acquisition and lack of regulatory clarity (Business Monitor International, 2013).

Ports

A major element of transport infrastructure within India—and an area that is expected to grow considerably—is India's ports. The country has 13 major ports and 187 minor ports along its extensive coastlines. The 13 major ports accounted for about 67% of the country's external sea trade and 569.9 M tons of cargo for the year ending March 2011. The most important ports are located at Chennai (Madras), Kochi (Cochin), Jawaharlal Nehru, Kandla, Kolkata (Calcutta), Mumbai (Bombay), Sikka, and Vishakhapatnam. India's rapidly expanding trade requirements are expected to put immense strain on the country's existing port infrastructure, with India's total port capacity standing at around 1.2 B tons in FY11/12. As of September 2012, India's Planning Commission is projecting cargo traffic to reach around 1.8 B tons by the end of FY16/17, with India needing a total capacity of 2.3 B tons to adequately manage this growth in cargo traffic (Business Monitor International, 2013).

The existing ports will also require major upgrades as they are currently not very efficient and completely mechanized. The roadblocks for the new projects are bureaucracy and strict cabotage rules (Business Monitor International, 2013).

Energy

The energy infrastructure sector in India is a major concern, with unreliable electric grid being a major operational challenge for industry. This supply gap is estimated to be an 11–13% shortfall during peak load times (Kumar, 2012). This has seen $250 B allocated to energy infrastructure over 2008–2012, including the Rajiv Gandhi Grameen Vidyutikaran Yojana program to provide electricity to all households and the Bharat Nirman program that includes electricity for rural communities (Singhala et al., 2011). By September 2012, total generation capacity stood at about 208,000 MW, and 87% of all Indian villages had been provided electricity, and 19.5 M below poverty line households were given free electricity connections (Maniar, 2013). With 67% of energy demands currently fuelled by coal (Maniar, 2013), investments in nuclear capacity and renewable energy capacity are being planned. In fact, the Indian government has set very ambitious targets for electricity generation, including 470 GW of nuclear power by 2050, 20 GW of solar power by 2022, and 20 GW of wind capacity by 2020 to realize the country's economic growth potential. The 12th Five-Year Plan foresees a capacity addition of 88,537 MW, with most of the new capacity additions coal-based (66,230 MW) and hydropower-based (9897 MW) (Business Monitor International, 2013).

Urban Infrastructure

With urban population on a continuous rise, the urban infrastructure is proving to be highly inadequate. The low capacity of Urban Local Bodies, limited financial resources, and multiple clearance channels have led to a mismatch in the demand and supply of urban services and development. While PPPs have been popular in solid waste management and sewage treatment plants, they have been scarce in urban transport due to high construction costs and capital requirements and long project tenures (Maniar, 2013).

Since water infrastructure is a weak area in India, the new National Water Policy in 2012 has been adopted to address the issues of water scarcity, management, and conservation (Business Monitor International, 2013). Jawaharlal Nehru National Urban Renewal Mission for cities with more than 1 M in population also has allocated resources for water supply (35%), sewage (25%), and drainage (14%) (Singhala et al., 2011).

Telecommunications

By October 2012, the wireless subscriber base in India had increased to 938 M, consisting of 596 M urban and 342 M rural subscribers. The number of wire line subscribers continued to decrease, with only 3.3% of all telecom subscriptions belonging to wire line services. This decline can be attributed to the relative affordability of wireless connections and the convenience with which they can be obtained. Overall telephone density or teledensity had increased to 77% in October 2012, while urban and rural teledensity had reached 161% and 40%, respectively (Maniar, 2013).

Internet

India has the third-largest base of Internet users in the world totaling 20 M. Given the current growth rate of Internet usage, by 2015, India is likely to have 330–370 M users, which will then be the second-largest user base and largest incremental growth in the world. Currently, the contribution of Internet to GDP is 1.6%. This is likely to go up to 2.8–3.3% provided the Internet infrastructure improves significantly. India rates poorly on Internet infrastructure and engagement—in terms of cost of access and usage, awareness and digital literacy, e-commerce platform, range of applications and services, ease of Internet entrepreneurship, and impact of e-governance. Internet-based applications are yet to scale up in agriculture, education, healthcare, and citizenship (Gnanasambandam et al., 2012).

While Indian entrepreneurs have devised innovative business models, Indian consumers, SMEs, and government sector have not leveraged ICTs and web technologies (Gnanasambandam et al., 2012).

In summary, physical infrastructure is a key factor that enables and facilitates entrepreneurship. The United States has had a decided advantage in relation to physical infrastructure compared with China or India, both of which are emerging economies compared with the United States, the most dominant economic power of the twentieth century. The United States continues to have this advantage over both these countries, and this is not expected to change in the near future. However, this is an area of concern for the United States, since the US physical infrastructure is aging and needs significant injection of new capital in order to stay competitive. This is especially true in relation to China, where huge investments are being made to rapidly build a very modern and advanced infrastructure, especially in the area of rail and air transportation. Other areas of infrastructure continue to lag behind in China and are expected to continue to present challenges for entrepreneurship in the near future. A significant and well-known concern for China is a disregard for environmental considerations and the resultant air and river water pollution. India on the other hand still lags behind significantly and despite recent increases in infrastructure investments faces huge challenges in all aspects of physical infrastructure. This is expected to significantly limit the efficiency and efficacy of entrepreneurship in India in the near and intermediate future.

REFERENCES

American Society of Civil Engineers, ASCE, 2013. America's Infrastructure Report Card.
Business Monitor International, 2013. India infrastructure report Q2 2013. BMI's Industry Report & Forecasts Series.
Department of Economic Affairs, Government of India, 2012. India – The Incredible Investment Destination. Department of Economic Affairs, Government of India, New Delhi.
Galston, W.A., 2013. Crumbling Infrastructure Has Real Enduring Costs. Brookings, USA. http:// www.brookings.edu/blogs/up-front/posts/2013/01/23-crumbling-infrastructure-galston.
Gnanasambandam, et al., 2012. Online and Upcoming: The Internet's Impact on India. Mckinsey and Company, USA Technology Media and Telecom Practice, www. mckinsey.com (accessed 14.06.13).
High Level Committee on Financing Infrastructure, 2012. Interim Report of High Level Committee on Financing Infrastructure. Secretariat for Infrastructure, Planning Commission, Government of India, New Delhi. http://infrastructure.gov.in/pdf/Interim_Report.pdf (accessed 13.06.13).
Jia, P., 2012. "Twelfth Five Year Plan": analysis China infrastructure industry. Bus. Res. 99 (4), 27–29.
Kumar, R., 2012. Issues in infrastructure development in India. In: Annual Conference of Chief Secretaries. Department of Administrative Reforms and Public Grievances, Ministry of Personnel, Public Grievances and Pensions, Government of India.
Li, G., 2011. Analysis of China's infrastructure investment and suggestions to improve it. China Securities and, Futures (11), 127.
Maniar, M., 2013. The Infrastructure Sector in India 2012 in "India Infrastructure Report – 2012 Private Sector in Education". IDFC Foundation.
Morris, Basant, 2005. Role of Small Scale Industries in the Age of Liberalisation. http://www.adb.org/ Documents/Reports/Consultant/TAR-IND-4066/Trade/morris-basant.pdf (accessed 14.06.13).

Reid, R., 2013. Special report. American Society of Civil Engineers (ASCE). http://www.asce.org/Content.aspx?id=25562.

Singhala, S., et al., 2011. The significance and performance of infrastructure in India. J. Property Res. 28 (1 (March)), 15–34.

US Government Accounting Office, GAO, 2008. Physical Infrastructure, Challenges and Investment Options for Nation's Infrastructure.

World Economic Forum, 2013. Global competitiveness report.

Chapter 16

Capital Availability

Chapter Contents

SOURCES OF BUSINESS FINANCING

The availability of capital to fund entrepreneurial ventures in terms of both amount and types of financing varies across the United States, China, and India. Figure 16.1[1] shows four categories of institutional financing that are available in each of these countries. The figure shows that the United States has strong equity and debt markets, while the domestic debt market and stock markets are not so vibrant in China. In the case of India, the domestic debt market is weak as compared with its stock market or private credit. This chapter explores the breadth and depth of financing available for entrepreneurial ventures across the three countries.

---

1. The four main variables that have been plotted in Fig. 16.1 are the following: Private and public bond market capitalization to GDP, which equals the total amount of outstanding domestic debt securities issued by private or public domestic entities divided by GDP, indicates the size of the domestic bond market. These two indicators thus measure the size of the market for public and private bonds relative to the real economy. Private credit by deposit money banks and other financial institutions to GDP indicates claims on the private sector by deposit money banks and other financial institutions divided by GDP. Stock market capitalization to GDP, which equals the value of listed shares divided by GDP, indicates the size of the stock market relative to the size of the economy.

Innovation, Entrepreneurship, and the Economy in the US, China, and India

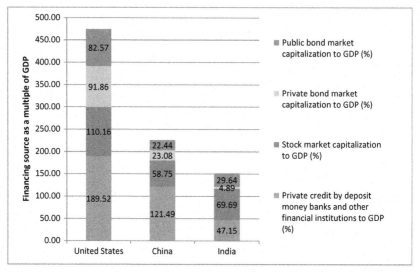

FIGURE 16.1 Sources of business financing—2011. *(Source: The World Bank Financial Development and Structure Dataset (http://econ.worldbank.org/WBSITE/EXTERNAL/EXTDEC/ EXTRESEARCH/0,,contentMDK:20696167~pagePK:64214825~piPK:64214943~theSitePK:469 382,00.html).)*

THE UNITED STATES

Financial Support from Government

In the United States, government financial support for small businesses is provided through the Small Business Administration (SBA).[2] SBA was founded in 1953 through a piece of legislation, viz., the Small Business Act. It has provided millions of loans, loan guarantees, contracts, counseling sessions, and other forms of assistance to small businesses. The three strategic goals of SBA are growing businesses and creating jobs, meeting the needs of today's and tomorrow's small businesses, and serving as the voice of small businesses.

Although the SBA provides financial assistance to entrepreneurs through many of its programs, the three most significant ones are Small Business Investment Company (SBIC), Small Business Innovation Research (SBIR), and Small Business Technology Transfer (STTR) programs.

The SBIC Program is a government-sponsored investment fund created in 1958 to bridge the gap between entrepreneurs' need for capital and traditional sources of financing. The program invests long-term capital in privately owned and managed investment firms licensed as SBICs. For every dollar an SBIC raises from a private investor, the SBA will provide two dollars of debt capital, subject to a cap of $150 M. Once capitalized, SBICs make debt and equity

---

2. http://www.sba.gov/about-sba-services/199

investments in small businesses, helping them grow. The program has so far invested \$3.13 B in 937 small businesses, 29% of which were in low- to moderate-income areas or in minority- or women-owned businesses. Well-known successful corporations such as Apple, Intel, FedEx, Staples, and Costco received financing from SBICs during their early stages of growth.[3]

The SBIR program is a highly competitive award-based program that enables small businesses to engage in federal research or research and development (R/R&D) that has the potential for commercialization. Federal agencies with extramural research and development (R&D) budgets that exceed \$100 M are required to allocate 2.8% of their R&D budget to these programs. Through these programs, the United States is able to tap the nation's entrepreneurial potential in meeting its R&D priorities.[4]

Modeled after the SBIR program, the STTR program was established as a pilot program by the Small Business Technology Transfer Act of 1992. It is a highly competitive program that reserves a percentage of federal R&D funding for awards to small businesses and US nonprofit research institutions. The program expands the public and private sector partnership to include joint venture opportunities for small businesses and nonprofit research institutions. Small business has long been the place where innovation and innovators thrive. But the risk and expense of conducting R&D can be beyond the means of many small businesses. Conversely, nonprofit research laboratories are instrumental in developing high-tech innovations. But frequently, innovation advances theory, rather than the development of innovative practical applications. The STTR program combines the strengths of both entities by introducing entrepreneurial skills to high-tech research efforts, thus enabling the transfer of technologies and products from the laboratory to the marketplace. The small business profits from the commercialization efforts, which, in turn, stimulates the US economy.[5]

The US SBA serves as the coordinating agency for the above programs. It directs their implementation, reviews their progress, and reports annually to Congress on their operations.

Venture Capital

Venture capital (VC) has enabled the United States to support its entrepreneurial talent and appetite in a big way by turning ideas and basic science into products and services. Although the US VC industry has been consolidating itself in the last few years as reflected in its reduced activity level, its impact on entrepreneurship and the US economy continues to be impressive. The activity level is roughly half of what it was at the 2000-era peak (Table 16.1).

3. http://www.sba.gov/content/sbic-program-overview-0
4. http://www.sbir.gov/about/about-sbir
5. http://www.sbir.gov/about/about-sttr

TABLE 16.1 Venture Capital Summary Statistics for the United States

	1992	2002	2012
No. of VC firms in existence	358	1089	841
No. of VC funds in existence	616	2119	1269
No. of principals	4996	14,541	5887
No. of first-time VC funds raised	13	25	43
No. of VC funds raising money this year	78	176	162
VC raised this year ($B)	4.9	15.7	20.1
VC under management ($B)	28.7	272.1	199.2
Avg. VC under management per firm ($M)	80.2	249.9	236.9
Avg. VC fund size to date ($M)	39.1	94.4	110.6
Avg. VC fund size raised this year ($M)	62.8	89.2	124.1
Largest VC fund raised to date ($M)	1775.0	6300.0	6300.0

Source: NVCA Yearbook (2013) (Data: Thomas Reuters, PricewaterhouseCoopers and National Venture Capital Association.).

The number of deals and the amount of money invested by the VC industry have been more or less stable over the last few years (Fig. 16.2a and b). However, with an investment level between just 0.1% and 0.2% of US gross domestic product each year in venture-backed companies, these companies employed 11% of the total US private sector workforce and generated revenue equal to 21% of US GDP. While the total employment and revenue for venture-backed companies contracted during the 2008–2010 downturn, both did so at lower rates than in the larger US economy.

This ability of VC-backed companies to outperform their nonventure counterparts—during good times and bad—flows from VC's focus on highly innovative, emerging growth companies. The US VC industry not only has spawned several life-changing technologies over the past half century but also has launched entirely new industries. Tables 16.2 and 16.3 give a snapshot of the vast impact the VC industry has on the US economy and its industry sectors.

In the year 2013, 55% of the total investments went into seed-stage and early-stage (Fig. 16.3) companies, underlining the major role of VCs in creation of new businesses. The investment trends indicate that of late, the VC industry has been channeling its investments more into software (37%) and biotechnology (15%) sectors (Fig. 16.4). The 500 largest public companies with venture roots increased their collective market capitalization by approximately $700 B, rising from $2.1 T in 2008 to $2.8 T in 2010 (MoneyTree™ Report, 2013[6]).

6. Data: Thomas Reuters, PricewaterhouseCoopers and National Venture Capital Association.

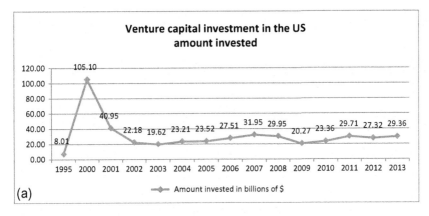

(a)

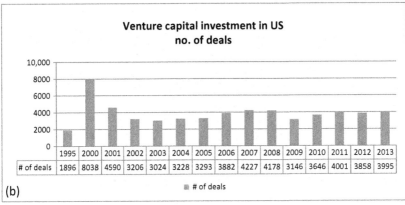

(b)

FIGURE 16.2   (a) Venture capital investment in the United States—amount invested. (b) Venture capital investment in the United States—no. of deals. *(Source: MoneyTree™ Report (2013).)*

TABLE 16.2 VC-Backed Jobs in Major Industry Sectors in the United States

Percent of VC-Backed Jobs in Major Industry Sectors
90% software
74% biotechnology
72% semiconductors/electronics
54% computers
48% telecom

TABLE 16.3 VC-Backed Revenue in Major Industry Sectors in the United States

Industry Sector	Revenue (%)	Amount ($ M)
Semiconductors/electronics	88	234.4
Biotechnology	80	161.6
Computers	46	402.3
Software	40	226.5
IT services	30	22.5

Source: IHS-NVCA (2011).

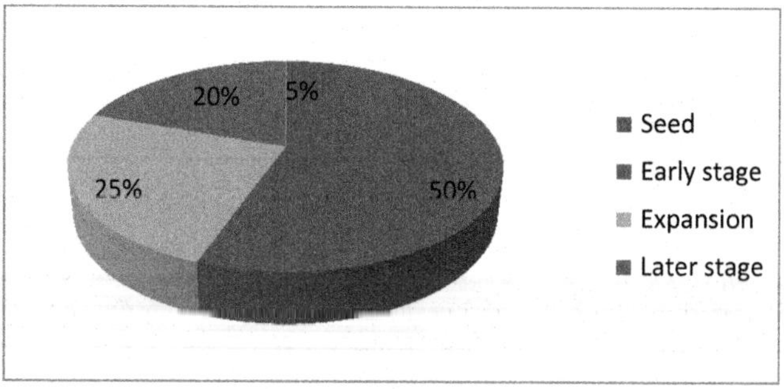

FIGURE 16.3 VC investments in the United States by stage of development—2013. *(Source: IHS-NVCA (2011).)*

Looking forward, VC's impact on the US economy will likely grow even larger. That's because many of the fastest-growing venture-backed companies in the United States today have yet to go public. IHS Global Insight research suggests that 92% of job growth for young companies occurs after their initial public offerings (IPOs). This fact underscores the importance of America's IPO market and of ensuring that our most innovative young companies can access the capital they need to grow (NVCA and IHS Insight, 2011).

Table 16.4 shows that around 50% of all IPOs in the United States have been venture-backed, explaining the ease of exit for VCs through the IPO route. In recent years, especially after the 2008 financial crisis, the IPO market has slowed down. However, in 2013, the total number of venture-backed IPOs went up again to 82, the second highest level since 2001.

Table 16.5 shows the total number of exits for the VC industry in the United States in the last 5 years. On an average, of the total first VC-funded companies over 1991–2000, 14% went public, 33% were acquired, 35% were still private, and the remaining 18% were known failures.

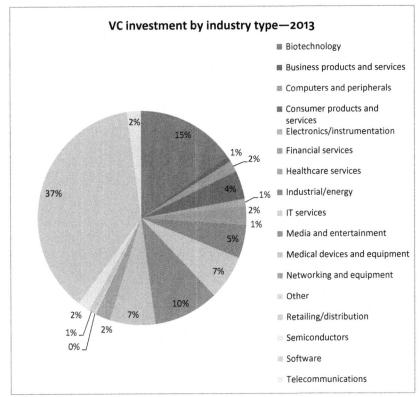

FIGURE 16.4   VC investment by industry type in 2013 in the United States. *(Source: Money-Tree™ Report (2013) (Data: Thomas Reuters, PricewaterhouseCoopers and National Venture Capital Association).)*

Stock Markets

The Securities and Exchange Commission (SEC) has about 18 national securities exchanges registered with it. Of these 18, the 2 main stock exchanges in the United States are the New York Stock Exchange and NASDAQ. The United States has a history of a vibrant primary and secondary stock market, which helps entrepreneurship to thrive in the country as mentioned earlier.

Moreover, the SEC is setting up a crowdfunding plan as part of a requirement in the "Jumpstart Our Business Startups (JOBS) Act of 2012." The law eases federal regulations on small businesses.

Crowdfunding is a way to raise money by asking many individuals to contribute funds, often in small amounts, to a specific business venture or cause. The contributions can be in small amounts, say $1, or large amounts such as in the thousands of dollars or even millions. Usually, crowdfunding takes place through the Internet.

TABLE 16.4 Number of Venture-Backed IPOs Versus All IPOs in the United States

Year	All IPOs	Venture-Backed IPOs
2000	347	238
2001	81	37
2002	76	24
2003	67	26
2004	188	82
2005	168	59
2006	167	68
2007	162	92
2008	24	7
2009	39	13
2010	104	68
2011	99	51
2012	113	49

Source: Reuter (2013).

TABLE 16.5 VC Exits in the United States

Year	No. of Exits Through the M&A Route	No. of Exits Through the IPO Route
2009	360	13
2010	543	70
2011	499	51
2012	488	49
2013	377	82

Source: http://www.nvca.org/index.php?option=com_content&view=article&id=344&Itemid=103

Debt Market

The United States has a thriving debt (bond) market amounting to $38.64 T in 2012. Corporate debt amounting to $9 T represents 23% of the bond market (Fig. 16.5). As mentioned at the beginning of the chapter, buoyant equity and debt markets support entrepreneurship in the United States.

CHINA

Compared with the United States, China has very little policy or government support for sponsoring entrepreneurship. Capital funds are set up by different ministries and commissions under the State Council or local governments. Some examples of such funds are the Torch Plan, SME Technology Innovation Fund, Agricultural Technology Transformation Fund, and SME International Marketing Fund, which play a role in helping start businesses. The main form of support provided to small businesses is low-interest or interest-free loans. Unlike in the United States, governmental funds in China are directly invested in the small businesses. But these funds have not been successful in stimulating other private funds to join in to help new businesses.

Venture Capital

In China, the VC industry began to develop in the 1980s. In 1985, the document on the reform of science and technology system was issued, which pointed out that VC should be established to support the quickly changing, high-risk

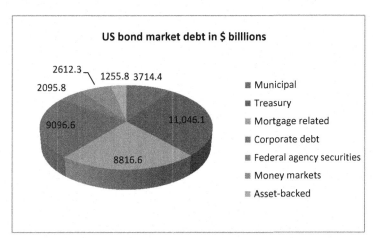

FIGURE 16.5   US bond market—2012. *(Source: The Securities Industry and Financial Markets Association (SIFMA) (www.sifma.org).)*

technology development. According to this document, the China New Technology Venture Investment Company was set up in 1985, which was the first foray of China in venture investment. In 1999, two reports were put forward that paved the way for development of the Chinese VC industry. One of them was on strengthening technological innovation, and industrialization was created by the CPC Central Committee, and the second one was on the establishment of a mechanism for risk investment. The number of Chinese VC companies substantially increased, from 26 in 1994 to 345 in 2006. The amount of investment was merely $5.13 B in 1995 but increased to $66.38 B in 2006. Although VC grew significantly, there were problems with sources of this fund, because 41% of the total VC funds came from corporations, 31% came from banks and insurance companies, and 17% came from the government. In reality, the government investment was far more than 17%, because the banks and insurance companies were mostly controlled by the government and most of the corporations were large and medium-sized state-owned or state-controlled listed companies (Xinling, 2008).

SME Board

In China, since the establishments of Shanghai and Shenzhen Stock Exchanges in 1990, China's securities market has been advancing step by step, with gradually improved market proficiency and growing market functions. The securities market has become an important component of the economy in China. One of the recent advancements in the market is the launch of the Small and Medium Enterprises Board (SME Board), which marked the beginning of the multitier capital market system in China. The SME Board was introduced by the Shenzhen Stock Exchange in 2004 to provide a direct financing platform for the SME with a prominent core business and high-tech contents. By the end of September 2004, the SME Board issued and listed 38 companies (Jianhua et al., 2005). The SME Board has witnessed continuous expansion in size. As of December 30, 2011, there were 646 companies listed on the SME Board with a total market capitalization of RMB 2.7 T (USD 428.6 B). Total IPO proceeds were RMB 558.8 B (USD 88.7 B). Total trading value stood at RMB 6.9 T (USD 1.1 T) in 2011.

INDIA

According to the report of the World Bank and the International Financial Corporation titled "Doing Business 2013," SME find it easier to obtain credit in the United States as compared with their counterparts in India and China, though India fares better than China on this count.

Although the "Doing Business 2013" rankings (Table 16.6) indicate that Indian entrepreneurs find it easier to get credit as compared with other entrepreneurs in other countries, NKC's survey of Indian entrepreneurs reveals that access to finance is one of the biggest limiting factors in achieving significantly

TABLE 16.6 Ranking Based on Comparison of Business Regulations for Domestic Firms in 185 Economies

	China	India	The United States
Getting credit (rank)	70	23	4
Strength of legal regulations (0–10)	6	8	9
Depth of credit information (0–6)	4	5	6

Source: The World Bank and the International Finance Corporation (2013).

higher levels of entrepreneurial growth in India. The role of banks, VCs, and angel investors continues to be highly underexploited for the advancement of entrepreneurial activities in India.

NKC's survey (Fig. 16.6) found that the majority of the entrepreneurs were self-financed and nearly half of the self-financed entrepreneurs borrowed start-up money from family or friends owing to strong sociocultural support systems in Indian family setup. Nearly a third of these entrepreneurs invested their own savings into the start-up, while money from an existing family business helped only about one-fifth of the self-financed entrepreneurs.

A comparison of the source of the start-up funding of Indian entrepreneurs with Bay Area entrepreneurs reveals (Table 16.7) that VC, angel investor, bank credit, and credit cards constitute major sources of funding in the Silicon Valley. Personal or family loans constitute only 24% of sources of funding.

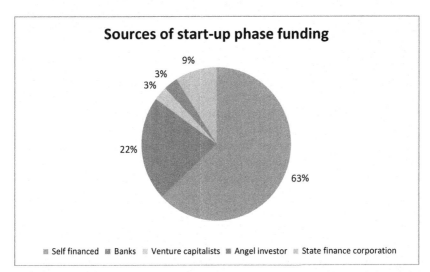

FIGURE 16.6 Sources of start-up-phase funding in India. *(Source: National Knowledge Commission (2008).)*

TABLE 16.7 Breakout of Start-up Funding—Bay Area Entrepreneurs

Type	Number	%
Personal/family loans	13	24
Venture (traditional)	11	20
Bank debt	9	16
Credit card	9	16
Angel seed capital	8	15
Venture (corporate)	2	4
Lease/receivables finance	1	2

Source: Bay Area Council Economic Institute (2011).

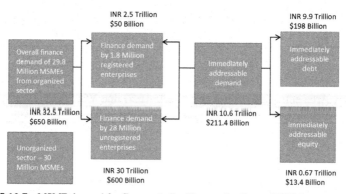

FIGURE 16.7 MSME demand for finance: India. *(Source: Intellecap (2013).)*

According to a report on micro, small, and medium enterprise (MSME) finance in India (International Financial Corporation and Goverment of Japan, 2012), of the overall MSME finance demand of INR 32.5 T ($650 B), 14% or INR 92 T ($4.6 B) is self-financed in the form of equity, and 22%, that is, INR 7 T ($140 B), is financed from debt. Sixty-four percent of the demand or INR 20.9 T ($418 B) is addressed by informal sources such as family, friends, family business, and informal institutional sources comprising money lenders and chit funds (Fig. 16.7).

A further examination of the finance demand shows that out of INR 32.5 T or $650 B, only INR 10.6 T or $211.4 B can be immediately addressed.

The current nonaddressable demand, that is, INR 20.9 T or $418 B (64% of total demand addressed by informal sources), comprises (a), in the debt market, new enterprises, sick enterprises, voluntary exclusions, and enterprises with poor financial records and (b), in the equity market, micro and small enterprises that have legal structures such as proprietorship and partnership. Considerable efforts by way of policy and building market and business models are required to gradually transform the above demand and make it financially viable (IFC and Government of Japan, 2012).

Some of the interventions that can help transition the MSMEs into lucrative financing opportunities for the financial sector include (a) increasing awareness among entrepreneurs about how access to formal sources of finance can benefit the growth of their business, (b) incentivizing entrepreneurs to increase financial transparency and plan their financial requirements better, (c) creating an effective policy environment to revive sick enterprises and make them financially viable, (d) providing incubation support to early-stage enterprises, and (e) increasing the enterprise knowledge on various low-overhead legal structures available to them. Expansion in the level of formal finance to the MSME sector could unlock enormous potential for the sector's growth and corresponding contribution to GDP (IFC and Government of Japan, 2012).

Equity Demand

The total equity demand in the MSME sector, including both addressable and nonaddressable demands, is estimated at INR 6.5 T or $130 B, which comprises entrepreneur's equity of INR 4.6 T or $92 B as explained above and INR 0.58 T ($11.6 B) of early-stage equity—defined here as equity required by those enterprises that have an operational history of one year or less—and the balance equity demand being growth-stage equity to the tune of INR 1.32 T ($26.4 B) (IFC and Government of Japan, 2012).

Debt Demand and Supply

It is estimated that of the total debt demand of INR 26 T ($520 B) in the MSME sector, at least 38% or INR 9.9 T ($198 B) is the size of the viable demand that can be addressed by the formal financial sector in the near term. Most of the total demand is fulfilled by informal sources, and 95% of the informal sources amounting to INR 23.2 T ($464 B) come from noninstitutional sources such as family, friends, and family business (IFC and Government of Japan, 2012). Access to debt from formal sources is constrained for small and early-stage firms in India. Banks and financial institutions are wary of lending to these firms due to the lack of robust credit ratings and collateral. Such institutions rarely use innovative solutions like venture debt, hybrid instruments, and factoring. The skills and culture required to lend without collateral (which is the case with most emerging businesses) are found lacking in the banking system. While schemes such as the credit guarantee scheme by SIDBI have been very useful, they are unable to address this gap completely (Committee on Angel Investment and Early Stage Venture Capital, 2012).

Angel Investing and VC

The venture capitalists (VC) define early-stage investments as the first or second round of institutional investments into companies that are less than 5 years old and not part of a larger business group, and investment amount is less than $20 M and in some cases $10 M. Growth-stage investments according to the VC industry are the third/fourth round funding of institutional investments or the first/second round of institutional investments for companies 5–10 years old or spin-outs from larger businesses, and investment amount is less than $20 M.

India lags in early-stage investing in a big way. Angel investors drive significant early-stage investments in countries with high entrepreneurial activity. Apart from capital, angel investors also provide mentoring and network access to entrepreneurs. They play a critical role in scaling up businesses to make them attractive for institutional investors such as VC funds. Angel investing is just beginning in India. Despite a growing population of high-net-worth individuals, angel investments are at a nascent stage in India with less than 500 angel investors and investments of around INR 1 B (about $22 M) in 2011, in around 50 deals as compared to Canada—where angels invested INR 20 B ($390 M). Most investments are accomplished through angel groups such as Indian Angel Network and Mumbai Angels. This is around 7–8% of the total annual early-stage investing—negligible in contrast to over INR 1 T (approximately $27B) of VC and angel investing in the United States annually, of which around 75% comes from angels. It is noteworthy to mention that angel investing is already beginning to show some success in India (Committee on Angel Investment and Early Stage Venture Capital, 2012).

Early-stage venture investing is also inadequate. Annual investments are around INR 12 B ($2.4 B) as against INR 290 B ($6.3 B) in the United States and INR 30 B ($7 B) in China. Around 90% of the early-stage venture funds in India come from offshore sources rather than from domestic investors (Committee on Angel Investment and Early Stage Venture Capital, 2012).

The reason for a lag in early-stage investing is because early stage as a distinct class of investments is not formally recognized in India. Multiple regulations hinder establishment of domestic venture funds that can access domestic capital for venture investments. Angel investors are hampered by issues such as inefficient financial structures for investments and exits. Extensive procedures and compliance requirements for M&A and restrictions on IPOs, along with regulations on liquidation, are key deterrents to exits for VC investors. Debt providers too do not feel encouraged to specifically allocate funds to emerging businesses for reasons explained earlier. VC funds are also severely restricted from providing debt. The government also acts as a provider of funds, especially through grants and seed funding programs such as Technopreneur Promotion Programme (TePP), proof of concept funds, and Technology Development Board. However, these are often available after extensive paperwork, slow processing, and inconsistent procedures followed by different departments (Committee on Angel Investment and Early Stage Venture Capital, 2012).

However, it is estimated that early-stage investments could increase to around INR 140 B ($3 B) annually in the next 10 years as both the number of funds and the propensity to invest increase with a larger entrepreneurial base. The total VC investments including all stages of investing totaled INR 555.42 B only as of December 2012. A significantly large portion of these funds is offshore funds as mentioned earlier—these funds arguably have a limited understanding of the local environment, in terms of both markets and working with local regulations, and thus tend to focus more on growth-stage capital. Fund raising is much lower than global benchmarks. Over the last 5 years, domestic funds that focus on early-, growth-, and late-stage VC investing raised around INR 270 B in India, whereas funds in China raised around INR 2 T or more than two times as a percentage of cumulative GDP in that period (Committee on Angel Investment and Early Stage Venture Capital, 2012).

VC investments in India seem significantly biased towards services, especially technology and e-commerce (Fig. 16.8). These investments have however already started showing success (Committee on Angel Investment and Early Stage Venture Capital, 2012).

Exits of VC and Private Equity (PE) Investments

A comparison of the exit mechanisms of VC/PE industry in India vis-à-vis China reveals that M&As have been more prominent in India, while IPOs were more common in China (Table 16.8).

SME Exchanges

In order to increase the avenues of equity financing for MSMEs and provide potential exit opportunities for investors, the government and regulators have

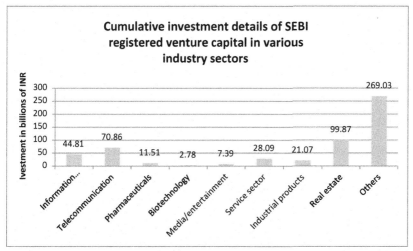

FIGURE 16.8   VC investments in various industry sectors in India. *(Source: http://www.sebi.gov. in/cms/sebi_data/attachdocs/ArchDec2012.html.)*

TABLE 16.8 Exit Channels—China and India 2000–2010

	VC	PE	Buyouts
China			
No. of companies with entry and exit details	476	212	14
IPO	72%	63%	21%
M&A	28%	37%	79%
India			
No. of companies with entry and exit details	160	123	7
IPO	34%	33%	14%
M&A	66%	67%	86%

Source: Prahl et al. (2011).

facilitated the formation of the SME Stock Exchange. Both the Bombay Stock Exchange and the National Stock Exchange have set up SME exchanges. As of June 2013, 24 scrips were listed on BSE SME exchange. Although setting up of the SME Stock Exchanges is a step in the right direction, the cost of initial public offer, valuation concerns, and limited deal flows may continue to present challenges for equity investors.

In summary, the United States has very strong equity and debt markets, while the domestic debt market and stock markets are not so vibrant in China. In the case of India, the domestic debt market is weak as compared with its stock market or private credit. We explored the breadth and depth of financing available for entrepreneurial ventures across the three countries. In the United States, financial support is available from the US government through the SBA. More importantly, VC and angel investor communities are very well developed in the United States, and VCs have played a key role in the genesis of what are now major US and global corporations.

Compared with the United States, China has very little policy or government support for sponsoring entrepreneurship. Unlike in the United States, governmental funds in China are directly invested in small businesses. But these funds have not been successful in stimulating other private funds to join in to help new businesses. In China, the VC industry began to develop in the 1980s. Although VC funds have grown in China in recent years, most of the sources of these funds are either the government or large corporations. Major stock exchanges were established in China in the 1990s, and an exchange was set up for small and medium enterprises very recently and has been growing rapidly. Although SME find it easier to obtain credit in the United States as compared with their counterparts in India and China, India fares better than China on this count. In spite of that, access to finance is one of the biggest limiting factors in achieving significantly higher levels of entrepreneurial growth in India. The role of banks, VCs, and angel investors continues to be highly underexploited for the advancement of entrepreneurial activities in India.

REFERENCES

Bay Area Council Economic Institute, 2011. Benchmarking the Bay Area's Environment for Entrepreneur-Led Start-Ups – Bay Area Council Economic Institute Report. Bay Area Council Economic Institute, San Francisco.

Committee on Angel Investment and Early Stage Venture Capital, 2012. Creating a Vibrant Entrepreneurial Ecosystem in India. Planning Commission Government of India, New Delhi.

Intellecap, 2013. Providing Venture Debt to MSME Sector in India. http://intellecap.com/sites/default/files/publications/10_Intellecap_MSME%20Report.pdf, Intellecap (accessed 24.06.13.).

International Financial Corporation (IFC) and Goverment of Japan, 2012. Micro Small and Medium Enterprises Finance in India – A Research Study on Needs, Gaps and Way Forward. International Financial Corporation (IFC) and Goverment of Japan.

Jianhua, J., Shuzhen, W., Guiqin, L., 2005. Discuss on the establishment of second board market. Soc. Sci. Nanjing, 11, pp. 32.

National Knowledge Commission (NKC), 2008. Entrepreneurship in India. Government of India, New Delhi.

National Venture Capital Association (NVCA), and IHS Insight, 2011. Venture Impact: The Economic Importance of Venture-Backed Companies in the US.

Prahl, et al., 2011. Private Equity Exits in China and India. INSEAD Global Private Equity Initiative.

Reuters, T., 2013. NVCA Yearbook – 2013.

Xinling, Z., 2008. Study on the Development of Risk Investment Under Different Culture. Minzu University of China master degree paper. pp. 18–20, 23–25.

Chapter 17

Intrapreneurship

Chapter Contents

Intrapreneurship, corporate entrepreneurship, and corporate venturing are terms used to describe entrepreneurial behavior inside established medium-sized or large corporations (Pinchot and Pellman, 1999).

There are a lot of *similarities* between new venture or start-up entrepreneurship and corporate entrepreneurship. They both involve opportunity recognition and definition; require a unique business concept that takes the form of a product, service, or process; are driven by an individual champion who works with a team to bring the concept to fruition; require that the entrepreneur be able to balance vision with managerial skill, passion with pragmatism, and proactiveness with patience; involve concepts that are most vulnerable in the formative stage and that require adaptation over time; entail a window of opportunity within which the concept can be successfully capitalized upon; are predicated on value creation and accountability to a customer; find the entrepreneur encountering resistance and obstacles, necessitating both perseverance and an ability to formulate innovative solutions; entail risk and require risk-management strategies; find the entrepreneur needing to develop creative strategies for leveraging resources; involve significant ambiguity; and require harvesting strategies (Hisrich and Kearney, 2012; Morris et al., 2008).

There are also significant *differences* between start-up entrepreneurship and intrapreneurship. In the former, the entrepreneur takes the risk, whereas in the latter, the company assumes all risks, other than career risk for the intrapreneur; in the former, the entrepreneur owns the innovative idea or the business concept, and in the latter, the company owns the idea as well as any intellectual property surrounding the concept; in a start-up, the entrepreneur starts out owning all or much of the business, and in corporate entrepreneurship, the intrapreneur may have none to very little equity in the internal venture; potential rewards for a start-up entrepreneur are in principle unlimited, and so is the potential downside of failure, whereas in corporate entrepreneurship, there are clear limits on the financial rewards the intrapreneurial team can receive, but the downside is limited as well, since failures can be absorbed by the company (Morris et al., 2008).

A start-up entrepreneur is more vulnerable to outside influences, but an intrapreneur is more insulated from outside influence; a start-up entrepreneur can be quite independent although backed by a strong team, while the intrapreneur is typically very interdependent on many others with whom he or she needs to share credit; a start-up entrepreneur has a lot of flexibility in changing course, but an intrapreneur's ability to maneuver can be limited by company rules and procedures and bureaucracy; start-up entrepreneurs can make decisions quickly, while corporate entrepreneurs have to deal with long approval cycles; start-up entrepreneurs have very little security, no safety net, and very few people to talk to, but intrapreneurs have job security, dependable benefit packages, and an extensive network, internal and external contacts they can bounce ideas off; start-up entrepreneurs have limited resources, while the intrapreneur has access to finances, R&D, production facilities for trial runs, an established sales force, an existing brand, distribution channels that are in place, existing databases and market research resources, and an established customer base; as a result, a start-up has limited initial scope and scale, whereas a corporate venture has the potential for rapidly increasing in scope and scale (Morris et al., 2008).

Intrapreneurship thus refers to encouraging corporate employees to create new businesses by using a company's funds and other resources. Stopford (1994) stressed that with regard to intrapreneurship or new business creation within the corporation, there are three key aspects: first, it is about creating the new business within an existing organization; second, it is about organizational transformation and update of activities within an existing organization; and, third, it is about activities needed to change the rules of competition within the industry.

Antoncic and Hisrich (2001) defined the meaning of intrapreneurship to consist of four dimensions: first, it means a new business that is related to current products or markets. Second, it means innovation, which includes research and development of new products, new services, new technology, or new processes. Third, it means self-renewal, which comes from strategic reconstruction, organizational restructuring, and change. Fourth, it means leadership thinking, which refers to executives' initiative, aggressive, and risk-taking thinking to seek new business opportunities or enhance competitive performance. Intrapreneurship is also helpful in exploring potential talent, in establishing mechanisms for encouraging innovation, in cultivating entrepreneurial culture, and in supporting the company's sustainable development. Besides, intrapreneurship has the potential to result in more successful outcomes than external start-up entrepreneurship. There are statistical data that indicate that the success rate for start-up entrepreneurship is only 20%, while given the support of a parent company, the success rate for intrapreneurship can reach as high as 80% (Jiangtao and Haowei, 2012).

In order to facilitate intrapreneurship, companies can proactively undertake certain steps.

First, tolerance of failure should be fostered and risk taking and trial and error should be encouraged. With a good idea and a good business plan, the biggest concern for intrapreneurs is the risk of failure. If in addition to a low salary and limited financial upside, if intrapreneurs are also faced with huge penalties for failure or job loss, then that would discourage intrapreneurship.

Second, an open platform for information exchange should be set up. Early intrapreneurial ideas usually come in a flash to those close to the issues, but intrapreneurship is a continuous innovation process, which requires cross-functional cooperation from a number of different organizations—marketing, finance, production, human resources, development, and others. No matter how good an idea is, it will usually run into difficulties, which can stall execution and could even result in complete failure. This can be prevented through experience-based careful planning and execution. Through the information exchange, such as, job rotation, intrapreneurs can broaden their overall experience base, thus improving the chances of successful outcomes for intrapreneurial projects. Intrapreneurship can and should also be guided by a company's strategies and goals. With regard to the choice of an intrapreneurial business, employees need to be familiar with the subject matter and related fields and policies. Also, the company should have fair policies for providing internal resources and professional guidance to assist intrapreneurs as they try to access internal or external resources.

Third, companies need to develop effective performance appraisal systems. This is an area of one of the biggest differences between start-up entrepreneurship and corporate entrepreneurship. Intrapreneurs, especially those who are well established in the company and are at the higher end of the compensation spectrum, have a higher opportunity cost than entrepreneurs just starting out. So, the performance evaluation for them should be different from those who have no intrapreneurial intentions. For example, intrapreneurs, in the average intrapreneurial cycle, should be allowed to maintain their position and primary salary, so that they can devote themselves worry-free to creating the new business, along with some upside potential tied to the success of the new business.

Fourth, full authority should be given to maintain independence of the new business. Senior management not only needs to have policies supportive of intrapreneurship but also needs to be flexible and be able to make decisions and provide feedback rapidly, with very few intervening levels in the approval cycle. For intrapreneurs, a comfortable working atmosphere and cooperation from other internal organizations are both very important. Only when the intrapreneurs have the necessary freedom to create the new business, will they be able to use the resources at their disposal effectively to meet their creative needs. It is also important to involve early on the business unit that is expected to be the target host organization for the new business, in order to ensure the ultimate success of the business.

Fifth, when the new venture is still a fledgling business, it needs to be protected. Commercialization of new technologies takes time, and the average period for a new business to become profitable is about 8 years. So, during the early years, different metrics need to be used to measure success, and these need to be different from those used for assessing traditional businesses. In addition, when these intrapreneurial projects begin to mature, there is always the possibility that some of these new ventures are spun out of the parent company. It is, therefore, important, at the very outset of the intrapreneurial efforts, to properly establish the relationship between the parent company and the new business—for example, relative allocation of assets and capital, profit distribution, and equity buy-back must be well defined from the very beginning.

THE UNITED STATES

The role of corporate innovation and entrepreneurship in the US economy has gone through a lot of changes over the last few decades. In the last 50 or so years, start-up entrepreneurship has become far more common, but before that, corporate entrepreneurship was the more dominant mechanism for new business creation, and the corporate world needs to get back to innovation and new venture creation far more effectively than is generally being done today. Prior to the last 50 or so years, most innovation and entrepreneurship in the United States came out of laboratories and new business creation operations within venerable, world-class corporations.

Examples of such organizations in the high-tech fields of electronics, optics, computing, and telecommunications were AT&T Bell Labs at various locations in New Jersey; IBM Research Labs in Yorktown Heights, NY, or in San Jose, CA; GE Research Labs in Schenectady, NY; RCA David Sarnoff Research Center in Princeton, NJ; Xerox Research Center in Webster, NY, and in Palo Alto, CA; Kodak Research Labs in Rochester, NY; and other corporate labs such as those at Motorola, Texas Instruments, and a number of others. There are examples of 3M and Procter and Gamble in the industrial and consumer products sectors. Examples of significant corporate innovation and entrepreneurship prior to the last 50 years can also be found in other sectors, such as aviation, automotive, chemicals, defense, pharmaceuticals, and oil and gas. Some of these companies were far more effective at transforming inventions and R&D investments into innovations in the marketplace and successful businesses. Those among these companies that, in spite of a successful innovation and entrepreneurship track record, were eventually not very effective in corporate entrepreneurship for a wide variety of reasons ultimately paid a hefty price in terms of losing their dominant position and in some cases disappear altogether as independent companies.

Although the corporate graveyard has been littered by some of these marquee companies that were unable to eventually effectively nurture and harness corporate entrepreneurship, there are examples of companies, such as, 3M and Procter and Gamble, which have been able to sustain that spirit through various corporate and macroeconomic ups and downs. There are examples of other "'corporate elephants' who have learnt to dance" and transform themselves, such as IBM and GE, under the leaderships of Lou Gerstner and Jeff Immelt, through, along with other corporate initiatives, instituting new methodologies and systems for corporate entrepreneurship, such as IBM's EBO (Emerging Business Opportunities) and GE's IB (Imagination Breakthrough) programs. These have been chronicled in a number of Harvard Business Review cases (e.g., Bartlett et al., 2008; Garvin and Levesque, 2005), and IBM's EBO system was modeled after the work of Baghai et al. (1999) of McKinsey and Co. Most other large corporations, such as HP, Lucent, Xerox, and Microsoft, have also experimented with and employed various models for corporate venturing in the 1990s and 2000 and beyond, and a number of cases and articles have been published about them as well.

However, despite this very rich and long history of intrapreneurship in the United States prior to the last 50 years, over the last 50 years, it has had a checkered past going up and down with the equity markets (Chesbrough, 2000). Typically, during economic downturns this activity was one of the first to be either cut entirely or scaled back. In fact, in the 1960s and 1970s, 25% of Fortune 500 companies had corporate venturing programs, and a large number of these were disbanded in the late 1970s. Interest in corporate entrepreneurship grew in the 1980s due to the growth in the private venture capital market but declined again during the market crash of 1987. Corporate venturing again came into vogue during the go-go days of the dot-com and telecom bubbles in the 1990s, until the market downturn and the bursting of these two bubbles in 2002.

A survey of 3000 global executives conducted by the Boston Consulting Group (BCG) finds that 43% consider corporate entrepreneurship to be among their top three priorities and 23% consider it to be their top priority (BCG, Hisrich and Kearney, 2012, 2013). The same study also finds that over a 2-year period from 2006 to 2008, satisfaction with the return on investment on innovation decreased from 52% to 43% and spending on innovation decreased from 72% to 63%. In another study conducted in 2010 by the consulting arm of Ernst & Young found that most corporate executives recognize the importance of intrapreneurship, but most have difficulty determining how to go about it.

In addition to financial considerations, attempts at intrapreneurship over the last 50 years have been stymied by the fact that approaches to corporate entrepreneurship have evolved over time, and there are a large number of models for how to go about pursuing such efforts, various models effective in various situations. One of the other challenges in the last 50 years has been the proclivity for the low-hanging but less rewarding fruit of incremental innovation, rather than pursuing disruptive (Anthony et al., 2008; Christensen 1997; Christensen et al., 2004; Dyer et al., 2011) or strategic (Govindarajan and Trimble, 2005, 2010) innovation with the potential for higher longer-term returns. Methodologies for these approaches to corporate entrepreneurship have been expounded by these authors and their colleagues through their extensive research and writings on the subject.

Some of the most intriguing approaches to, and probably the new standard for, corporate innovation and entrepreneurship are those pursued by the "new age" high-tech and software companies, especially, the likes of Google, Apple, Amazon, Salesforce.com, and others. Their success in innovation and intrapreneurship through their unique approaches to them—their innovation not only in processes, products, and services but also in their business models and also their unique cultures—is reflected in the rapid growth of their valuations and the ubiquity of the usage of their products and services. These companies demonstrate that being big and established, although only recently, is not necessarily an impediment to intrapreneurship—on the contrary, they demonstrate that to continue to be successful, companies need to demand intrapreneurship and a corporate culture that supports it.

CHINA

In China, from 2001 to 2012, the top 10 enterprises were all state-owned, and China National Petroleum Corporation, State Grid Corporation of China, and China Petroleum & Chemical Corporation held the top 3 spots in most of those years. Also, China Construction Bank Limited Corporation, Industrial and Commercial Bank of China Limited Corporation, Agricultural Bank of China Limited Corporation, China Mobile Communications Corporation, China Life Insurance (Group) Company, and Bank of China Limited Corporation often appeared in the top 10 list. Generally, the top 10 enterprises were the result of very little competition, so they did not have any huge pressure for supporting intrapreneurship. With regard to private enterprises, those that frequently appeared in the top 10 from 2003 to 2012 were Jiangsu Shagang Group Limited Corporation, Huawei Investment & Holding Co. Limited, Suning Electrical Appliance Group, Legend Holdings Limited Corporation, Wanxiang Group, and Jiangsu Yurun Food Group Limited Corporation. In contrast to state-owned enterprises, since these companies face competitive pressures, they have a lot more motivation to support intrapreneurship (Top 500 Enterprises, 2001–2012, Fortune China).

In China, corporate entrepreneurship has mainly taken the form of (a) businesses created internally within the company and (b) businesses formed externally and managed outside the company. (a) Internally created businesses include both businesses resulting from new business ideas that have gone through internal business incubators and newly created business divisions of existing businesses. (b) Externally formed businesses consist of spinouts, mergers, and joint ventures. In practice, different companies have taken different ways to corporate entrepreneurship, but most fall within the forms discussed above. Although most companies used their own approach to corporate entrepreneurship, we discuss approaches to intrapreneurship in three specific companies as representative examples of intrapreneurship in China—Huawei, Giant Network Productions, and China Telecom.

Case 1: Intrapreneurship at Huawei (Wubao and Rongwei, 2011)

Huawei was established in 1988 as a private high-tech enterprise that designs, manufactures, sells, and services communications products. In 1992, Huawei made an important breakthrough in its technology and got their first-generation product, C & C08 A-type central office digital PBX, which established Huawei as a telecommunications equipment supplier with competitive ability. In 1994, sales reached ¥800 M and Huawei began to grow rapidly. In just 4 years, in 1998, sales grew 10 times to ¥8.93 B, and for the first time, Huawei captured the top spot in the market for central office digital PBX.

Around 2000, the Chinese economy was in a state of transition. Market economy in China was not mature, and the reforms that followed made the business environment very dynamic and uncertain. With the overall downturn in the global telecommunications market in that time frame and more serious competition, China's telecommunications industry faced a serious downturn. Given this environment, Huawei introduced business process reengineering and began delayering management layers, facilitating the process for introducing intrapreneurship.

In the second half of 2000, Huawei introduced internally "guidelines for intrapreneurship," which encouraged senior employees to get involved in all aspects of intrapreneurship in all noncore business areas, including potentially spinning out noncore technologies. As a result of this policy, many senior staff chose to start their own businesses. The goals of Huawei's intrapreneurship initiative can be summarized by saying that (a) it provided senior employees opportunities to become entrepreneurs and (b) it enabled the formation of collaborative groups across the company, allowing Huawei to grow rapidly.

After "guidelines for intrapreneurship" was published, Li Yinan chose to become an entrepreneur, and he set up Gangwan Networks Limited Corporation, which was a distributor of Huawei at that time. As Gangwan Networks began to grow, venture capital was invested in Gangwan, and it became more than a distributor. It started building network equipment needed for broadband IP, thus benefiting from technology advances, which it could not do previously as only a distributor of products. By 2004, in this product category, Gangwan was leading Huawei by at least 6 months.

In November 2003, Huawei established a joint venture with 3COM, Huawei 3COM, a US maker of telecom products. After the establishing of Huawei

3COM, competition between Huawei 3COM and Gangwan was very fierce. In 2004, although Huawei 3COM increased sales revenues by 80%, it was not very profitable. During roughly that same time frame, Gangwan reached revenues of 1.2 B yuan in 2004, an increase of 20% over 2003. Huawei and Gangwan announced that they had reached an agreement to merge, and with this, Gangwan gave birth in Huawei's intrapreneurship. Once they were finally fully merged, intrapreneurship became a very important part of Huawei culture.

With regard to intrapreneurship, Huawei conforms to the following rules: first, Huawei's R&D and innovation are centered on customers' needs, with both new and old graduates and engineers permitted to do R&D; second, Huawei endorses "outside technology used inside," and this principle is widely used. At Huawei, patents are not a goal, but are a way to design cost-competitive products. As new products are developed, Huawei emphasizes the importance and need for improving current products and technologies, instead of brand new inventions. Huawei obtains its technology through cooperating with partners or purchasing from others. Huawei's cooperation with Tsinghua University and merging with 3COM are examples that reflect this approach. Finally, the strategy of "grasp the core, loose the peripheral" was adopted. Intrapreneurship, thus, is an important way to fulfill Huawei's need for backward integration, which implies that Huawei's core businesses are at the center of the alliance and other businesses arising out of intrapreneurship are in supportive roles.

Case 2: Intrapreneurship at Giant Network Corporation (Liping and Naiqiu, 2010)

Shanghai Giant Network Technology Co. Limited is an entertainment business mainly engaged in developing online games. With changing consumer needs, Giant Network faced increased competition, and its core business was under siege. In order to pursue new opportunities, in 2009, Giant Network launched intrapreneurial initiatives. Giant Network's intrapreneurship activities can be characterized as change in strategic direction, organizational change, and execution.

As Giant Network began its intrapreneurial efforts, change in strategic direction was the first step. On January 13, 2009, Giant Network announced "Win with Giant," which aimed to invest in external online gaming entrepreneurial teams—instead of internal teams—especially in those teams that had good ideas but lacked funds. For those external entrepreneurial teams that joined this program, Giant Network would provide capital, technology, and team support. Once the venture was successful, the entrepreneurial team would receive up to 20% of the profits. With the "Win with Giant" program, Giant Network was able to integrate the best small and medium enterprises engaged in online gaming, to gain a very significant competitive advantage in terms of resources needed for innovation. Giant Network thus transformed itself from a company doing its own independent online game development to essentially the preferred operating platform for online gaming.

Giant Network's organizational changes were carried out gradually, and these internal and external changes benefitted its intrapreneurship efforts. With regard to external organizational changes, by June 2010, Giant Network had absorbed five outstanding teams. In February 2009, Giant Network began its internal organizational changes. The plan of "Win with Giant" was promoted within the company, and employees were encouraged to come up with creative new ideas, to set up teams, and to independently develop new projects. In June 2009, Giant Network published an ownership reform program, which had at its core the notion of ownership by employees in their idea and the resulting company. The idea here was that when a new project succeeded, it would be set up as a new company, and Giant Network would own 51% of the equity and the project team would own the remaining 49%. This plan addressed compensation and the resultant motivation challenges typically associated with entrepreneurship. The newly launched company was also self-managed by the employees who went with the new company.

Execution at Giant Network emphasized, encouraged, and internally promoted originality, creativity, and bold risk taking as personality characteristics that were needed to discover new businesses and pursue new opportunities. Intrapreneurship with a focus on execution provided comprehensive support to entrepreneurial teams earlier than competitors, through rapid decision making and an action orientation, once the intrapreneurial opportunities related with key businesses had been identified. It sent a clear message to everyone that Giant Network wanted to be a leader instead of a follower.

Giant Network made an online gaming entrepreneurship platform when it built the online gaming operational platform. This integrated intrapreneurship and fostered entrepreneurship. The most prominent feature of intrapreneurship at Giant Network is the execution associated with "fostering entrepreneurship."

Case 3: Intrapreneurship at China Telecom (Jiangtao and Haowei, 2012)

In February 2012, China Telecom officially launched its hundred million yuan program to encourage employees to be intrapreneurial. Intrapreneurial teams were formed with each team consisting of at least three members over a 2-year period, with fifty to one hundred thousand yuan invested in each team at the outset. As a state-owned enterprise, China Telecom has done a great deal to increase R&D in the field of mobile Internet service. The goal of the intrapreneurial teams was to improve China Telecom's competitive position in the mobile Internet business.

In terms of intrapreneurship, compared with private or public enterprises, state-owned enterprises need to pay far more attention in the following areas.

First, intrapreneurial enthusiasm among employees will need to be fully evoked and stoked. As a state-owned monopoly, China Telecom can be very profitable. Employees can, therefore, receive very good salaries, profit sharing, and benefits. This high compensation can become a disincentive and an invisible barrier to intrapreneurial behavior. In contrast to Huawei's private sector job, for example, if a person finds a job in China Telecom, it means he or she gets a "golden bowl," that is, he or she has little chance of losing that job, while collecting healthy benefits and compensation along the way. In this system, it is very easy for employees to lose their intrapreneurial spirit, which is not very high to begin with. Intrapreneurship in this environment will need a strong appeal to the conscientiousness of these employees and an extraordinary effort at fostering an entrepreneurial spirit. Also, based on the specific situation, old compensation system and advancement and promotion policies will need to be changed to ensure that intrapreneurship is rewarded.

Second, effective supervision of invested funds and fair and thorough assessment of intrapreneurs and intrapreneurial projects will be necessary. Because of its state-owned status, China Telecom is less sensitive than private enterprises to the efficiency of capital utilization. This means that special attention will need to be paid to monitoring the finances and financial risk associated with intrapreneurial projects in order to avoid financial disaster. Furthermore, intrapreneurial projects will need to be carefully assessed for their feasibility, market demand, technical support, risk-mitigation measures, and potential benefits. Overall intrapreneurial strategy and business plan will also need to be thoroughly vetted by an expert team to ensure good guidance of the intrapreneurial activity. In addition, it will be important to ensure that intrapreneurs have high levels of integrity and company loyalty, excellent leadership and risk-management abilities, and good communication and interpersonal skills.

Finally, an open information platform will need to be set up. Internal to the company, full and open information exchange will help employees stay informed about the various intrapreneurial projects. This will help raise intrapreneurial enthusiasm and excitement, improve internal vitality, and enhance employee identification with the organization. Also, this will help early identification and resolution of problems with intrapreneurial efforts. Outside the company, a good mechanism for information release to the general public will help increase awareness of the company and new directions the company is pursuing.

In conclusion, Chinese private enterprises have strong efforts underway to be intrapreneurial. As discussed earlier, there are many routes to corporate venturing. Performing corporate venturing by enlisting the help of external resources, rather than creating new business as entirely relying upon internal resources, is the approach preferred and chosen by many Chinese companies. Although state-owned enterprises are beginning to recognize the importance of intrapreneurship, they are still in the very early stages, and they will still need a lot more patience, practice, and experience.

INDIA

Indian organizations are yet to institute many systems and procedures required for supporting innovations and, therefore, intrapreneurship. Although some organizations have formal R&D departments or divisions, R&D is treated merely as a ritual rather than as part of a proactive innovation strategy. In a qualitative analysis of innovation processes and intrapreneurship in Indian public sector organizations, Manimala et al. (2006) found that these organizations had the following organizational constraints that impeded innovation and intrapreneurship:

- Absence of failure-analysis systems (100%)
- Lack of patenting initiatives (97%)
- Lack of recognition for innovations in noncore areas (94%)
- Poor handling of change management (90%)
- Informal team formation (81%)
- Low emphasis on dissemination and commercialization (77%)
- Inadequacy of rewards and recognition (65%)
- Procedural delays (58%)
- Poor documentation and maintenance of records (58%)
- Easy access to foreign technologies (55%)
- Unclear norms on linking innovations with career growth (48%)
- Lack of recognition for contributions by support functions (45%)
- Ambivalent support from the immediate supervisor (39%)
- Inadequate systems for the promotion and management of ideas (35%)
- Lack of facility for pilot testing (29%).

Similarly, Anu (2012) observed that in Indian organizations, the costs of failure are high, while the rewards of success are low. Appropriate incentive systems to promote intrapreneurship are not widespread. Other impediments to intrapreneurship are reluctance to change or organizational inertia and organizational hierarchies that disempower people creating narrow career paths. These qualities hinder creativity and foster myopic thinking (Anu, 2012).

However, with changing times, there are a few examples of organizations that have overcome such constraints and have promoted entrepreneurial cultures. For example, software subsidiaries of multinationals have encouraged high levels of subsidiary initiative by adopting approaches different from their counterparts in developed countries (Krishnan, 2006). Since a number of multinationals have come to India in a relatively short span of time and local companies also offer a number of challenging jobs, competition for manpower is intense, and this makes the task of retention of manpower particularly difficult. In particular, manpower retention in technical roles is a challenge as the more ambitious employees move to managerial jobs that carry higher compensation and allow movement up the corporate ladder. While multinationals are able to attract talent, thanks to their brand, reputation, compensation, and the lifestyle that the compensation allows, retention is indeed a challenging task. Distinctive features of the Indian environment for these subsidiary managers are the following:

- The pressure of retaining and motivating engineers with multiple career options

- Pressures from the media and wider societal expectations as they relate to nationalist ambitions in terms of indigenously developed products (newspapers in India give considerable coverage when multinational subsidiaries located in India develop identifiable products or cutting-edge technologies in India)
- A desire on the part of their local employees to control their own destinies, given the prevailing belief among the young that "India's time has come," and their perception that they have unlimited opportunities to take advantage of.

In order to cope with such challenges, Indian subsidiaries are given high levels of autonomy in that some multinational parents are allowing subsidiaries to chart their own course in return for dilution of a part (or whole) of their stake in the subsidiary. Based on this trend, Krishnan (2006) found that parent–subsidiary relationship in India is changing from "Loyalty for Security in the MNC" model to "Competitiveness for Growth Opportunities" model (see Fig. 17.1).

Examples of intrapreneurship in India have been documented by several authors (Kamath, 2006; Seshadri and Tripathy 2006; Teltumbe, 2006). Both public and private sector organizations have been able to address some of the challenges faced by them by promoting entrepreneurial approaches in their organizations.

A case in point is the 40-year-old Tata Refractories Limited (TRL) that turned around from the brink of disaster in the late 1990s using innovative and intrapreneurial initiatives (Kamath, 2006). As part of the famous Tata group, the company adopted the "Tata Business Excellence Model"—a holistic initiative encompassing all aspects of a business starting from vision and

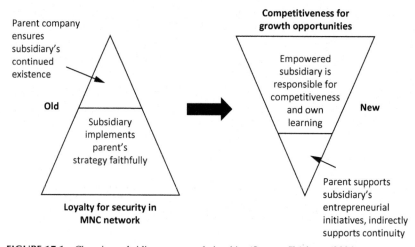

FIGURE 17.1   Changing subsidiary–parent relationship. *(Source: Krishnan (2006).)*

strategy to operational challenges, customer satisfaction, and human resource issues. This entailed modernization of factories in order to achieve state-of-the-art operations, business expansion for products with potential, managing demand–supply gaps, and setting up new units based on strategic analysis. In order to achieve these objectives, a large number of changes in all facets of management were introduced. Management involved all stakeholders including employees in the change process. The company embarked on an intense program of human resource development for both executives and workers to enhance skill sets for operations and maintenance of equipment and to improve managerial capabilities. This led to an increased awareness of the issues facing the company and sharing of the company vision among employees. Employees in turn were receptive to change management even when it affected them personally. Thus, by reinventing and instilling intrapreneurial attitudes among employees, TRL was able to come out of the crisis (Kamath, 2006).

Similarly, Tata Steel Limited has recognized that creating an innovative and intrapreneurial organization is the first step in the long journey of success in today's turbulent times. For example, when Tata Steel Limited wanted to set a cold rolling mill (CoRM) in 1997, it did not have a strong in-house project implementation team. Hence, it recruited Mr. R. P. Singh, who had extensive experience in project management positions in various public sector steel plants, as the head of the new CoRM project. When he took charge, he aimed at creating a world record in completion of the project in terms of both time and cost. His team initially looked at his plans with polite amusement and at times disagreed with him outright. Gradually, he was able to garner the support of his 400-strong CoRM team. He changed the mind-set of his team by introducing several initiatives that included "creating a new way of thinking; changing work habits; comprehensive research on the subject, situation, requirement, and necessary resources; providing a project road map to team members; developing stretch targets for individuals in the team through a process of patient dialogue with team members; meticulous planning; close review and monitoring of the project; and the creation of a system and culture which resulted in fewer failures. Most importantly, he succeeded in creating a pervasive sense of 'ownership' and 'intrapreneurship' among the team members energized by a powerful collective vision of 'creating a world record in project implementation of the CoRM'" (Seshadri and Tripathy, 2006).

By June 1999, Tata Steel Limited completed the project successfully under Singh's leadership in a world record time of 26½ months and at the lowest project cost of Rs. 16 B while ensuring world-class quality. The company had managed to beat all earlier records set by several other giants in the industry including Bethlehem Steel of the United States, POSCO of S. Korea, Siam United Steel of Thailand, and Baoshan Iron & Steel of China in implementing similar CoRM projects (Seshadri and Tripathy, 2006).

Subsequent to the setting up of CoRM, Mr. Singh and his team took up the task of revamping Blast Furnace-F in 110 days with a project cost of Rs. 2.1 B as against an estimated shutdown time of 150 days and an estimated cost of Rs. 5 B.

Another example of intrapreneurship in Tata Steel Limited is that of Mr. Nandji Pandey who took over as the chief executive of the run-down Merchant Mill (MM) in 1997. When Mr. Pandey took charge, the top management found no merit in making any further capital investments in reviving the mill and, therefore, had decided to sell off the assets to any willing buyer. Mr. Pandey set about motivating his team of officers and workers, encouraging them to come up with their best ideas so that they could run the plant without additional capital expenditure. The team came up with several ideas and implemented them systematically without requiring any significant incremental investment. Whatever minor investments were needed for implementing these ideas came from the revenue budget of the mill. Eventually, the plant turned around. After the successful turnaround of MM, Pandey was given charge of another comatose 70+-year-old company, Indian Steel and Wire Products Ltd., Jamshedpur, that had recently been taken over by Tata Steel Limited. Pandey's entrepreneurial efforts ensured that the company achieved its rated capacity within a few months of its takeover.

The above examples also exemplify the fact that for intrapreneurial efforts to flourish in an organization, there has to be a strong backing by the top management. In the above cases, the organization had taken several measures to promote intrapreneurial behavior.

Another instance of promotion of intrapreneurship by an organization is that of HCL Technologies. Mid-level managers in HCL Technologies go through a training program called the "Emerging Leaders Program" delivered by Harvard Business Publishing to help HCL develop intrapreneurial talent. As a result of the Emerging Leaders Program, HCL is actively developing talent from within its organization and has enhanced company loyalty and morale. Participants have acquired a new understanding of core leadership competencies, and HCL has cultivated a sustainable community of leaders.

As opposed to the above examples, Bharat Petroleum Corporation Limited (BPCL) followed a different approach. Project management teams at BPCL decided to create an antithetical paradigm of a subculture within an established organization entirely on their own without top management blessing (Teltumbe, 2006). The typical culture of project teams, in BPCL, did not entail any communication across teams. Project teams from the southern part of the country decided to break this norm, transcend stereotypes, and achieve excellence. They decided to learn from each other by creating communication channels across teams. The requisite change was, consequently, modeled using cybernetics principles, which relied on small teams bound together by multiple information and feedback loops within a new cultural paradigm. The relative isolation of the project department from the mainstream was used to create this paradigm of open, supportive, entrepreneurial, and "fun- and action-oriented" culture.

New artifacts, values, and assumptions substituted the old. This resulted in an open, excellence-oriented culture where everyone was treated as an equal and there was constant ongoing communication facilitating continuous learning and improvement. Team spirit was deeply internalized, and each person had an opportunity to excel at both strategy and intrapreneurship. Project management results established new industry benchmarks. Top management was informed about this experiment only after it was successfully completed.

India is bestowed with an artisan culture—rich in skills and knowledge—a requisite condition for innovation. However, Indian organizations have several obstacles that hinder innovation and intrapreneurship. To compete in today's dynamic environment, which is replete with rapid changes in technology and enhanced competition, Indian organizations have to make conscious efforts to promote corporate entrepreneurship and innovation. While some of the private and public sector organizations and software subsidiaries of MNCs have been able to stimulate entrepreneurial culture in their organizations, others need to follow suit.

In summary, there are a lot of similarities between start-up entrepreneurship and corporate entrepreneurship, or intrapreneurship, and there are also some significant differences. While start-up entrepreneurship has played a huge role in the economic development of the United States through its early history, especially after the Civil War, corporate entrepreneurship was the dominant mechanism for technology-based innovation until about the 1970s. During this period, most significant innovations came through the efforts of major US corporations and their corporate labs. However, since about the 1970s, the intensity of corporate innovation has waxed and waned with the ups and downs of the US economy. This torch for innovation has been carried, to a large extent, in the United States by start-up ventures, very many of which have grown into giant corporations in their own rights and some of them have succeeded in maintaining their innovation and intrapreneurial culture. However, there is still a significant need for established corporations to show a steady commitment to pursue intrapreneurial activities with greater intensity.

In China and India by contrast, corporate entrepreneurship is quite nascent. In China, especially, the situation is fairly unique since a vast majority of large enterprises are state-owned, which have not felt any compelling need for corporate entrepreneurship in the past. That is beginning to change and intrapreneurship in state-owned enterprises is in the very early stages. In private enterprises, however, a strong movement is underway to promote intrapreneurship using various routes to accomplish those objectives. Similarly, in India, systems and procedures have not been in place to promote entrepreneurship within corporations. In recent years, however, there are a few examples of organizations, which have overcome challenges of the past and have promoted entrepreneurial cultures. The most compelling examples of these are software subsidiaries of multinationals, which have been able to encourage entrepreneurial cultures within their subsidiaries in India.

REFERENCES

Anthony, S.D., Johnson, M.W., Sinfield, J.V., Altman, E.J., 2008. The Innovator's Guide to Growth – Putting Disruptive Innovation to Work. Harvard Business Press.

Antoncic, B., Hisrich, R.D., 2001. Intrapreneurship – constructive refinement and cross-cultural validation. J. Bus. Venturing 16 (5), 495–527.

Anu, L., 2012. In: Fostering intrapreneurship – the new competitive edge. Conference on Global Competition & Competitiveness of Indian Corporate, 18–19 May. Indian Institute of Management, Kozhikode, Kozhikode.

Baghai, M., Coley, S., White, D., 1999. The Alchemy of Growth – Practical Insights for Building the Enduring Enterprise. Perseus Publishing.

Bartlett, C.A., Hall, B.J., Bennett, N.S., 2008. GE's Imagination Breakthroughs: The Evo Project. Harvard Business School, June 30, 2008, 9-907-048.

Chesbrough, H., 2000. Designing Corporate Ventures in the Shadow of Private Venture Capital. Calif. Manage. Rev. 42 (3 (Spring)), 31–49.

Christensen, C.M., 1997. The Innovator's Dilemma. Harvard Business School Press.

Christensen, C.M., Raynor, M.E., 2003. The Innovator's Solution. Harvard Business School Press.

Christensen, C.M., Anthony, S.D., Roth, E.A., 2004. Seeing What's Next. Harvard Business School Press.

Dyer, J.H., Gregersen, H.B., Christensen, C.M., 2011. The Innovator's DNA. Harvard Business School Press.

Ernst & Young, 2010. Igniting Innovation – How Hot Companies Fuel Growth from Within.

Top 500 Enterprises (2001–2012). Fortune China http://www.fortunechina.com/.

Garvin, D.A., Levesque, L.C., 2005. Emerging Business Opportunities at IBM. Harvard Business School, February 28, 2005, 9-304-075.

Govindarajan, V., Trimble, C., 2005. 10 Rules for Strategic Innovators – From Idea to Execution. Harvard Business School Press.

Govindarajan, V., Trimble, C., 2010. The Other Side of Innovation – Solving the Execution Challenge. Harvard Business School Press.

Hisrich, R.D., Kearney, C., 2012. Corporate Entrepreneurship – How to Create a Thriving Entrepreneurial Spirit Throughout the Company. McGraw Hill.

Hisrich, R.D., Kearney, C., 2013. Managing Innovation and Entrepreneurship. Sage Publications.

Jiangtao, W., Haowei, S., 2012. Central enterprises try entrepreneurship, can they make a breakthrough? Market. Manage. Rev. (May), 50.

Kamath, C.D., 2006. A case study in intrapreneurship: the turnaround at Tata Refractories Limited. Vikalpa 31 (1), 117–121.

Krishnan, R.T., 2006. Subsidiary initiative in Indian software subsidiaries of MNCs. Vikalpa 31 (1), 61–71.

Liping, W., Naiqiu, L., 2010. Discuss on intrapreneurship – take giant network as an example. Enterprise Management (7), 43–46.

Manimala, M.J., Jose, P.D., Thomas, K.R., 2006. Organizational constraints on innovation and intrapreneurship: insights from public sector. Vikalpa 31 (1), 49–60.

Morris, M.H., Kuratko, D.F., Covin, J.G., 2008. Corporate Entrepreneurship and Innovation. Thomson South-Western, Mason, OH.

Pinchot, G., Pellman, R., 1999. Intrapreneuring in Action – A Handbook for Business Innovation. Berrett-Koehler Publishers, San Francisco.

Seshadri, D.V.R., Tripathy, A., 2006. Innovation through intrapreneurship: the road less traveled. Vikalpa 31 (1), 129–132.

Stopford, J.M., Baden-Fuller, C.W.F., 1994. Creating corporate entrepreneurship. Strategic Manage. J. 15 (7), 521–536.

Teltumbe, A., 2006. Entrepreneurs and intrapreneurs in corporations. Vikalpa 31 (1), 61–71.

Wubao, Z., Rongwei, R., 2011. Enhancing corporate competence with intrapreneurial strategy: a case study of Huawei's intrapreneurship activity. J. South China Univ. Technol. (Soc. Sci. Ed.) (8 (August)), 24–32.

Part III

Impact on the Economy

Chapter 18

Impact on the Economy

Chapter Contents

ROLE OF INNOVATION AND ENTREPRENEURSHIP IN THE ECONOMY

Having discussed innovation and entrepreneurship at great length and having considered various factors that contribute to and are conducive to innovation and entrepreneurship, we now look at the impact of innovation and entrepreneurship on the economy and, more specifically, on economic growth. As indicated before, both innovation and entrepreneurship are important factors that contribute to economic growth.

ECONOMIC GROWTH

The study, both theoretical and empirical, of long-run economic growth has become a major area of research since the 1990s. The foundations for economic growth were laid by the works of classical economists, such as Smith (1776), Ricardo (1817, 1821), Malthus (1798), and, in later years, Ramsey (1928), Young (1928), Knight (1944), and Schumpeter (1934). This was followed by the works of Harrod (1939) and Domar (1946), both of whom attempted to integrate the work of John Maynard Keynes (1931) with aspects of economic growth. Then came the contributions of Solow (1956, 1957) and Swan (1956). Further contributions were made to the "neoclassical" growth theory by Debreu (1954), Arrow (1962), Arrow (1968), Arrow and Enthoven (1961), Arrow and Kurz (1970), Cass (1965), and Koopmans (1965). More recently, a number of authors—Acemoglu (2009), Aghion and Howitt (2009), Barro and Sala-i-Martin (2004), Jones (1995, 1999, 2001, 2002), Klenow and Rodriguez (1997), Romer (2006), and Romer (1986, 1987, 1990)—have contributed massively to this field through extensive research and through books by several of them. While the contributions of these authors and others to the field of economic growth are extensive and comprehensive and account for a wide range of factors that contribute to economic growth, and some of the work attempts to explain convergence versus divergence in growth rates across nations, we will focus entirely on the impact of innovation and entrepreneurship on economic growth.

However, before delving further into the impact of innovation and entrepreneurship on economic growth, it may be beneficial to go back and look at the Solow growth model, which is the foundational work, on which a vast majority of the later models and enhancements are based. In the Solow model, also sometimes known as the Solow-Swan model, the aggregate output of an economy, $Y(t)$ at time t, is represented by a function, the production function, $F(t)$, with aggregate units of physical capital, $K(t)$, and aggregate units of Labor, $L(t)$, as *inputs* to this production function, so that

$$Y(t) = F[K(t), L(t)] \tag{18.1}$$

A few key properties of this aggregate production function are that (1) it exhibits constant returns to scale—an increase by a specific factor in both inputs results in an increase of output F by the same factor; (2) it also exhibits diminishing marginal products to the accumulation of capital or labor with increase in either input—that is, the slope of the production output as a function of inputs decreases as inputs increase; and (3) as a function of time, it cannot explain sustained economic growth, that is, growth in $Y(t)$. This is where the Solow "residual" is invoked and is attributed to growth in "technology." The growth rate, λ, in the Solow residual is postulated to explain the growth rates that cannot be explained by growth in factor inputs of physical capital and labor (Weitzman, 1996) and is *exogenously* determined for most applications. A vast majority of the growth in most cases is indeed contained in this λ, which is usually unknown and is essentially a fitting parameter, in accounting for empirically observed economic growth.

Advances in economic growth theories since the Solow model have been attempts to go inside this "black box" (Weitzman, 1996) of the residual in order to determine λ *endogenously* by accounting for other factors after accounting for exogenous savings rates added to the Solow-Swan model, such as the accumulation of knowledge, improvements in technology, technological spillovers, and improvements in human capital through education.

The most common example of a production function used to represent the Solow model considering only capital and labor as inputs is the Cobb-Douglas production function:

$$Y(t) = AK(t)^{\alpha}L(t)^{1-\alpha}, \quad 0 < \alpha < 1 \tag{18.2}$$

where A, which represents technology, is held constant, or there is no technological progress.

If we now relax the assumption that A is constant, and instead, let it be a function of time, so that we have $A(t)$ as part of the production function, then $A(t)$ captures the growth that is not explained by an increase in capital and labor, and we have

$$Y(t) = A(t)K(t)^\alpha L(t)^{1-\alpha}, \quad 0 < \alpha < 1 \tag{18.3}$$

The challenge of developing a theory where long-run growth is endogenous, as opposed to exogenous, is addressed by exploring ways to eliminate the long-run tendency of capital to experience diminishing returns. The way that is accomplished is by thinking of capital to consist of both physical capital and human capital. Here, human capital is used to represent the stock of skills, education, competencies, and other means of enhancing productivity of labor.

With the inclusion of human capital, $H(t)$, as an additional input, the Solow model in one version takes the form

$$Y(t) = F[K(t), H(t), AL(t)] \tag{18.4}$$

With the Cobb-Douglas version of the production function, the equation becomes (Mankiw et al., 1992)

$$Y(t) = K(t)^\alpha H(t)^\beta [AL(t)]^{1-\alpha-\beta}, \quad 0 < \alpha < 1, 0 < \beta < 1, \alpha + \beta < 1 \tag{18.5}$$

The framework discussed thus far would be considered part of "classical" economic theory. Here, in the Solow growth model, savings rate, that is, the ratio of income minus the current consumption to income, is considered exogenous and fixed. This precludes optimal behavior of customers and does not reflect the reality of how consumers and the economy respond to interest rates, tax rates, and other measures of the economy. Preferences of consumers for utility of consumption today versus utility of savings for consumption in the future are driven by their desire to optimize this perceived utility. Similarly, firms produce goods, pay wages for labor input, and pay for the cost of capital used in producing output. Firms, in turn, have the objective to optimize present profits while also investing in the future growth of the business. This optimization of consumer and firm behavior through the use of optimization theory is a further enhancement of the Solow model and is the Ramsey-Cass-Koopmans model (Cass, 1965, 1972; Koopmans, 1965; Ramsey, 1928). This model is consistent with the Arrow-Debreu dynamic general equilibrium model and is considered to be part of "neoclassical" economics (Acemoglu, 2009; Arrow, 1962, 1968; Debreu, 1954, 1959, 1974; Heer and Maussner, 2004; Wickens, 2008). Economic growth is then modeled using advanced mathematical and numerical optimization techniques (Acemoglu, 2009; Anderson et al., 1987), such as the optimal control theory (Acemoglu, 2009; Arrow, 1962, 1968; Brandimarte, 2006; London, 2005, 2006; Sethi and Thompson, 2006), dynamic programming, and stochastic dynamic programming (Acemoglu, 2009; Brandimarte, 2006).

It may be worthwhile to pause for a moment here and explore how technology, in general, and innovation, in particular, are addressed in the framework discussed thus far. The goal still is to be able to (1) explain sustained economic growth that is observed in most economies across the globe and (2) explain that growth endogenously, as opposed to ascribing it to exogenous factors. Implicit in the first of these goals is also that our objective is to have a situation where the production function does not exhibit diminishing returns to inputs of production and, therefore, can support sustained economic growth.

The simplest of such a situation is where we allow $\alpha = 1$ in Eq. (18.2), resulting in

$$Y(t) = AK(t) \tag{18.6}$$

This is known as the *AK model of endogenous growth*. There is sustained growth as indicated in Eq. (18.6), although there is no technological progress. The AK model can be further enriched by considering the capital to consist of both *physical capital and human capital*, as alluded to before. A model where the physical capital and human capital are both inputs to the production function and are generated by different production functions, the latter driven by education, is called the *two-sector AK model* and further explains endogenous growth (Aghion and Howitt 2009).

However, another perspective is that this accumulation of capital cannot be sustained in the long run and must eventually encounter a significant decline in the rate of return (Barro and Sala-i-Martin, 2004), hence the need to look to technological progress, which includes advances in methods of production and types of and qualities of products, to escape from diminishing returns in the long run.

Economic growth models are thus further "endogenized" by explaining technological progress and *process innovations* (Acemoglu, 2009) through conceptual discussions and modeling-related discussions of the economics of R&D, monopoly power, innovation incentives, etc. Another model used to explain technological change is known as the *product varieties model* (Romer, 1986, 1987, 1990), where growth is driven by *product innovations* instead of process innovations—by expanding the varieties of products rather than expanding the variety of inputs. These outcomes are somewhat similar to the models based on knowledge accumulation and technology spillovers developed *by increasing returns for growth with externalities* (Romer, 1986, 1987, 1990).

Another model that addresses technological progress, innovations, and R&D expenditures in the context of their contribution to economic growth is the *Schumpeterian growth model* (Aghion and Howitt, 2009) and focuses on quality-improving innovations that render old products obsolete and thus involves a force that Schumpeter called "creative destruction." In contrast to the product varieties model, which might be thought of as *"incremental"* innovations in the quality of existing products through a continuing series of refinements in goods and services, the Schumpeterian model may be thought of as one that creates *"disruptive"* new innovations that result in dramatically new kinds of products or services or processes for production or business models and displaces existing ones.

A further enhancement to endogenous technology and innovation models for economic growth accounts for differences in frequencies and degrees of innovation in various sectors and factors of production. This is done by considering *directed technological change* (Acemoglu, 2009), which endogenizes the direction and bias of new technologies that are developed and adopted, as opposed to the evolution of aggregate technology.

One shortcoming of the above approaches to addressing technological progress is that the technology stock of a society is determined by its own stock of R&D. However, as Acemoglu pointed out, many countries not only generate technological know-how from their own R&D but also benefit from the technological advances made by other countries. As a result, technology adoption and patterns of technology diffusion become very important and must be accounted for in explaining technological progress of a country.

General-purpose technologies are those technologies that have an impact on multiple sectors of the economy and hence noticeable macroeconomic effects, are generally underperforming when first introduced and only gradually improve productivity, and are also drivers for secondary innovations (Bresnahan and Trajtenberg, 1995). These can cause long-term accelerations and decelerations in economic growth and have also been modeled (Aghion and Howitt, 2009).

A common thread in the above framework is that these approaches focus on the production function to generate the *output* and factor *inputs* into the production function, such as physical capital, labor, human capital, knowledge accumulation, technology progress, and R&D. In this "neoclassical" framework, optimal control theory and optimization, dynamic programming, stochastic dynamic programming, etc. are then used to model economic growth consistent with the general equilibrium theory.

Equilibrium implies a "steady-state" condition, which may occur in the long run, and hence, these approaches may be well suited to address growth in the economy at a "macro" level in steady-state conditions. This then begs the question, do these models adequately represent the highly dynamic situation that prevails when new innovations or entrepreneurial initiatives occur? Furthermore, R&D activities do not necessarily result in innovation and entrepreneurship; in fact, very few of them do, and R&D investments may not necessarily capture the level of these activities. One might even argue whether R&D activities are the cause or the result of entrepreneurial opportunities (Holcombe, 1998). It may be reasonable to consider R&D as a factor that causes technological change and also improves the level of knowledge and knowledge externalities, as well as human capital, thus helping increase returns.

Innovation and entrepreneurship is a complex process that is affected by a number of factors that we have discussed in previous chapters. Economic growth theory based on the foundations of the Solow model must necessarily make a lot of simplifying assumptions to address the issues brought up in the previous sections, which might be thought of as "economic development theories" as opposed to "economic growth theories" based on the recent classifications of these two areas (Nobel Symposium on Growth and Development, September 2012).

Further considerations in the adoption, diffusion, and survival of innovations and entrepreneurial initiatives are the roles played in these highly nonequilibrium-type conditions by network effects on the demand-side and supply-side externalities, positive feedback, path dependence and lock-in, and self-reinforcing and self-organizing mechanisms (Arthur, 1989, 1990, 1997; Haken, 1983; Arthur et al., 1987; Katz and Shapiro, 1994; Schoder, 2000).

Also, as pointed out by Aghion and Howitt and others, there is a dichotomy in approaches to addressing (1) macroeconomic policy (budget and trade deficit, taxation, money supply, exchange and interest rates, etc.), which is used to stabilize the economy in the short-run, and (2) long-run economic growth, which is either taken to be exogenous or assumed to depend only on structural characteristics of the economy, some of which are discussed in the previous chapters. In essence, in all of these discussions, it appears that macroeconomic policy is decoupled from long-run economic growth.

We first discuss this in the next chapter, and then in the following chapter, we propose an approach to modeling the impact of innovation and entrepreneurship.

REFERENCES

Acemoglu, D., 2009. Introduction to Modern Economic Growth. Princeton University Press.

Aghion, P., Howitt, P., 2009. The Economics of Growth. The MIT Press.

Anderson, P.W., Arrow, K.J., Pines, D., 1987. The economy as an evolving complex system. In: The Proceedings of the Evolutionary Paths of the Global Economy Workshop, September, 1987, vol. 5. Santa Fe Institute, Studies in the Sciences of Complexity, Sante Fe, New Mexico.

Arrow, K.J., 1962. The economic implications of learning by doing. Rev. Econ. Stud. 29 (June), 155–173.

Arrow, K.J., 1968. Applications of control theory to economic growth. In: Dantzig, G.B., Veinott, A.F. (Eds.), In: Mathematics of Decision Sciences, American Mathematical Society, Providence, RI.

Arrow, K.J., Enthoven, A.C., 1961. Quasi-concave programming. Econometrica 29 (October), 779–800.

Arrow, K.J., Kurz, M., 1970. Optimal growth with irreversible investment in a Ramsey model. Econometrica 38 (March), 331–344.

Arthur, B.W., 1989. Competing technologies, increasing returns, and lick-in by historical events. Econ. J. 99, 116–131.

Arthur, B.W., 1990. Positive feedbacks in the economy. Sci. Am. 262 (2), 92–99.

Arthur, B.W., 1997. Increasing Returns and Path Dependence in the Economy. The University of Michigan Press.

Arthur, B.W., Ermoliev, Y.M., Kaniovski, Y.M., 1987. Path-dependent processes and the emergence of macro-structure. Eur. J. Oper. Res. 30, 294–303.

Barro, R.J., Sala-i-Martin, X., 2004. Economic Growth. The MIT Press.

Brandimarte, P., 2006. Numerical Methods in Finance and Economics, A MATLAB-Based Introduction. Wiley.

Bresnahan, T., Trajtenberg, M., 1995. General purpose technologies: engines of growth. J. Econom. 65, 83–108.

Cass, D., 1965. Optimum growth in an aggregate model of capital accumulation. Rev. Econ. Stud. 32, 233–240.

Cass, D., 1972. On capital over accumulation in the aggregate neoclassical model of economic growth: a complete characterization. J. Econ. Theory 4, 200–223.

Debreu, G., 1954. Valuation equilibrium and Pareto optimum. Proc. Natl. Acad. Sci. U.S.A. 40, 588–592.

Debreu, G., 1959. Theory of Value. Wiley, New York.

Debreu, G., 1974. Excess demand functions. J. Math. Econ. 1, 15–23.

Domar, E.D., 1946. Capital expansion, rate of growth, and employment. Econometrica 14, 137–147.

Haken, H., 1983. Advanced Synergetics—Instability Hierarchies of Self-Organizing Systems. Springer-Verlag.

Harrod, R.F., 1939. An essay in dynamic theory. Econ. J. 49 (June), 14–33.

Heer, B., Maussner, A., 2004. Dynamic General Equilibrium Modeling—Computational Methods and Applications. Springer.

Holcombe, R.G., 1998. Entrepreneurship and economic growth. Q. J. Austrian Econ. 1 (2), 45–62.

Jones, C.I., 1995. R&D-based models of economic growth. J. Polit. Econ. 103, 759–784.

Jones, C.I., 1999. Growth: with or without scale effects. Am. Econ. Rev. 89, 139–144.

Jones, C.I., 2001. Was an industrial revolution inevitable? Economic growth over the very long run. Adv. Econ. 1 (2), 1–45, Article 1.

Jones, C.I., 2002. Introduction to Economic Growth. W.W. Norton and Company.

Katz, M.L., Shapiro, C., 1994. Systems competition and network effects. J. Econ. Perspect. 8 (2), 93–115.

Keynes, J.M., 1931. Essays in Persuasion. Norton, New York.

Klenow, P.J., Rodriguez, A., 1997. Economic growth: a review essay. J Monetary Econ. 40 (3), 597–618.

Knight, F., 1944. Diminishing returns from investment. J. Polit. Econ. 52 (March), 26–47.

Koopmans, T.C., 1965. On the concept of optimal economic growth. In: The Econometric Approach to Development Planning. North-Holland, Amsterdam, pp. 225–295.

London, J., 2005. Modeling Derivatives in C++. Wiley.

London, J., 2006. Modeling Derivatives Applications in MATLAB, C++ and Excel. FT Press.

Mankiw, G.N., Romer, P., Weil, D.N., 1992. A contribution to the empirics of economic growth. Q. J. Econ. 107, 407–437.

Malthus, T., 1798. An Essay on the Principle of Population. Pickering, London 1986.

Nobel Symposium on Growth and Development, 2012. Institute for International Economic Studies, 50th Anniversary, Stockholm University, September 3–5, 2012.

Ramsey, F., 1928. A mathematical theory of saving. Econ. J. 38, 543–559.

Ricardo, D., 1817. On the Principles of Political Economy and Taxation. Cambridge University Press; 1951.

Ricardo, D., 1821. The Principles of Political Economy. J.M. Dent 1912.

Romer, P.M., 1986. Increasing returns and long-run growth. J. Polit. Econ. 94, 1002–1037.

Romer, P.M., 1987. Growth based on increasing returns due to specialization. Am. Econ. Rev. 77, 56–62.

Romer, P.M., 1990. Endogenous technical change. J. Polit. Econ. 98, 71–102.

Romer, D., 2006. Advanced Macroeconomics. McGraw-Hill Irwin.

Schoder, D., 2000. Forecasting the success of telecommunications services in the presence of network effects. Inf. Econ. Policy 12, 181–200.

Schumpeter, J., 1934. The Theory of Economic Development. Harvard University Press.

Sethi, S.P., Thompson, G.L., 2006. Optimal Control Theory. Springer.

Smith, A., 1776. An Inquiry into the Nature and Causes of the Wealth of Nations. Random House, New York 1937.

Solow, R.M., 1956. A contribution to the theory of economic growth. Q. J. Econ. 70, 65–94.

Solow, R.M., 1957. Technical change and the aggregate production function. Rev. Econ. Stat. 39, 312–320.

Swan, T.W., 1956. Economic growth and capital accumulation. Econ. Rec. 32, 334–361.

Weitzman, M.L., 1996. Hybridizing growth theory. Papers and Proceedings of the 108th Annual Meeting of the American Economic Association. Am. Econ. Rev. 86 (2), 207–212.

Wickens, M., 2008. Macroeconomic Theory—A Dynamic General Equilibrium Approach. Princeton University Press.

Young, A., 1928. Increasing returns and economic progress. Econ. J. 38 (December), 527–542.

Chapter 19

General Macroeconomic Framework

As discussed in the last chapter, theories of economic growth address long-run trends in the economy. In order to understand changes in the economy in the short term, one must consider a broader macroeconomic framework. The question is, do the short-term and long-run trends need to be decoupled from each other?

The field of macroeconomics began after the Great Depression of the 1930s and has evolved along two schools of thought (Mankiw, 2006): (1) the Keynesian school (Hicks, 1937; Keynes, 1931; Klein, 1946; Modigliani, 1944; Samuelson, 1948, 1988), which later evolved through the various waves of "new-Keynesian" thinking in the 1970s and 1980s, and (2) the classical school of Smith (1776), Ricardo (1817, 1821, 2006), and Marshall (1890), which later evolved into the "neoclassical" school (Friedman 1957, 1968; Friedman and Schwartz, 1963; Lucas, 1976, 1980; Lucas and Sargent, 1979; Phelps, 1968) through its various waves in the late 1960s and 1970s and other waves in the 1980s, with the real business cycle (RBC) theory (Kydland and Prescott, 1982; Long and Plosser, 1983; Mankiw, 1989), ultimately serving as examples of the dynamic general equilibrium theory (Arrow, 1962, 1968; Arrow and Enthoven, 1961; Arrow and Kurz, 1970; Debreu, 1954, 1959, 1974). The former was better suited to address short-run dynamics of the economy, especially the impact of monetary and fiscal policies through the famous IS-LM model (Hicks, 1937), and the latter better suited for the long run, although adjustments were made over time through technology and other shocks to the economy through the RBC model to explain short-run fluctuations.

There were attempts in the early evolution of these two schools to reconcile the two views and propose a combined "neoclassical-Keynesian synthesis." However, it was the late 1990s before a consensus view emerged and has been called "the new neoclassical synthesis" (Goodfriend and King, 1997). Several authors have written extensively about these two approaches through landmark papers and books—Mankiw (2010), Heer and Maussner (2004), Romer (2006), Wickens (2008), and Woodford (2003). This new synthesis combines the dynamic stochastic general equilibrium theory of the neoclassical model with the IS-LM theory of the Keynesian models (Mankiw, 2010).

This combined view is discussed below following Mankiw. We represent the macroeconomic framework in a large comprehensive seven-equation model that combines classical and Keynesian theory, as described by Mankiw (2010):

$Y = C(Y - T) + I(r) + G$ $+ NX(\varepsilon)$	IS curve: goods market equilibrium
$M/P = L(i/Y)$	LM curve: money market equilibrium
$NX(\varepsilon) = CF(r - r^*)$	Foreign exchange market equilibrium
$i = r + E\pi$	Relationship between real and nominal interest rates
$\varepsilon = eP/P^*$	Relationship between real and nominal exchange rates
$Y = \overline{Y} + \alpha(P - EP)$	Aggregate supply
$\overline{Y} = F(\overline{K}, \overline{L})$	Natural level of output

These seven equations determine the equilibrium values of the *seven endogenous* variables: output Y, the natural level of output $\overline{Y}$, the real in-country interest rate r, the nominal interest rate i, the real exchange rate ε, the nominal exchange rate e, and the price level P. The *exogenous variables* that influence these endogenous variables include taxes T; consumption $C(Y - T)$, indicating that C is a function of $(Y - T)$; investment $I(r)$, where investment I is a function of the real interest rate r; government purchases G; net exports $NX(\varepsilon)$, where the net exports NX are a function of the real exchange rate ε; money supply M; capital flow $CF(r - r^*)$, which is a function of the difference between real in-country and world interest rates; the capital stock K; the labor force L; the world price level P^*; and the world interest rate r^*. There are also two expectation variables: the expectation of future inflation $E\pi$ and the expectation of current price level formed in the past EP. The parameter α is a measure of the responsiveness of the demand for goods and services to the real interest rate.

This general set of equations with suitable assumptions results in the Mundell-Fleming model that can be used to describe open economies, that is, the economic dynamics associated with the flow of goods and services and also capital between countries. The model is thus an open economy equivalent of the closed-economy IS-LM model. The Mundell-Fleming model applies to small economies, since the borrowing or lending by a small economy does not affect world interest rates, and hence can borrow or lend as much as it wants and its interest rate equals the world interest rate. With additional manipulation, the model can be extended to large economies with free capital flows and floating exchange rates and independent monetary policy like the United States and India and to large economies with independent monetary policy, but with fixed exchange rates and restricted international flows of capital in and out of the country like China. We will not digress here into those discussions.

Another point of note here is that the equations discussed above and the IS-LM model and the Mundell-Fleming model, as well as the discussion about the

AD-AS model to follow, can also be investigated using a causal framework developed by Wyatt (2004) using linear systems control theory techniques such as signal flow graphs, block diagrams, and transfer functions (Golnaraghi and Kuo, 2010), techniques commonly used in engineering. However, in the interests of looking at long-term economic growth and factors contributing to it, we will defer this discussion to another time.

Before getting into a discussion about the long term, we further look at short-run fluctuations. We further follow Mankiw and recast the above equations into a dynamic model of aggregate demand and aggregate supply (AD-AS) model, where various variables at time t are given as follows:

$Y_t = \overline{Y_t} - \alpha(r_t - \rho) + \varepsilon_t$	The demand for goods and services
$r_t = i_t - E_t\pi_{t+1}$	The Fisher equation
$\pi_t = E_{t-1}\pi_t + \phi(Y_t - \overline{Y_t}) + \upsilon_t$	The Phillips curve
$E_t\pi_{t+1} = \pi_t$	Adaptive expectations
$i_t = \pi_t + \rho + \theta_\pi(\pi_t - \pi_t^*) + \theta_Y(Y_t - \overline{Y_t})$	The monetary-policy rule

The variables and parameters in this dynamic AD-AS model are as follows:

Endogenous variables

Y_t	Output
π_t	Inflation
r_t	Real interest rate
i_t	Nominal interest rate
$E_t\pi_{t+1}$	Expected inflation

Exogenous variables

$\overline{Y_t}$	Natural level of output
π_t^*	Central bank's target inflation rate
ε_t	Shock to the demand for goods and services
υ_t	Supply shock: shock to the Phillips curve

Predetermined variable

π_{t-1} previous period's inflation

Parameters

α	The responsiveness of the demand for goods and services to the real interest rate
ρ	The natural rate of interest
ϕ	The responsiveness of inflation to output in the Phillips curve
θ_π	The responsiveness of the nominal interest rate to inflation in the monetary-policy rule
θ_Y	The responsiveness of the nominal interest rate to output in the monetary-policy rule

The above five equations can be simplified into two equations, the dynamic aggregate demand curve and the dynamic aggregate supply curve, shown below:

$$Y_t = \overline{Y_t} - \left[\frac{\alpha\theta_\pi}{(1+\alpha\theta_Y)}\right](\pi_t - \pi_t^*) + \left[\frac{1}{(1+\alpha\theta_Y)}\right]\varepsilon_t \qquad (9.1)$$

$$\pi_t = \pi_{t-1} + \phi(Y_t - \overline{Y_t}) + \upsilon_t \qquad (9.2)$$

In any period t, these equations together determine two endogenous variables: inflation π_t and output Y_t. The solution depends on five other variables that are exogenous or determined prior to period t. These exogenous or predetermined variables are the natural level of output $\overline{Y}_t$, the central bank's target inflation rate π_t^*, the shock to demand ε_t, the shock to supply v_t, and the previous period's rate of inflation π_{t-1}.

Taking these five exogenous variables as given, the economy's short-run equilibrium is given by the intersection of the dynamic aggregate demand curve and the dynamic aggregate supply curve represented by Eqs. (9.1) and (9.2) above. Short-run dynamics of the economy caused by shocks to the demand or supply curves can be analyzed by studying changes in the intersection of these graphs and numerically simulating the above equations.

The *long-run equilibrium* represents the normal state around which the economy fluctuates. It occurs when there are no shocks ($\varepsilon_t = v_t = 0$) and inflation has stabilized ($\pi_t = \pi_{t-1}$). The above equations result in

$$Y_t = \overline{Y}_t$$

$$r_t = \rho$$

$$\pi_t = \pi_t^*$$

$$E_t \pi_{t+1} = \pi_t^*$$

$$i_t = \rho + \pi_t^*$$

In long-run equilibrium, output and the real interest rate are at their natural values, inflation and expected inflation are at the target rate of inflation, and the nominal interest rate equals the natural rate of interest plus target inflation. The long-run equilibrium reflects the classical dichotomy referred to earlier between short-term behavior and long-term behavior of the economy and monetary neutrality of the classical models. The equations show that long-run output Y_t and the real interest rate r_t do not depend on monetary policy, and the long-run dynamics of the AD-AS model are similar to those discussed in the classical models.

So, now, the question is how are we accounting for the impact of innovation and entrepreneurship in the short- or long-term dynamics of the economy, beyond the approaches discussed in the previous chapter?

REFERENCES

Arrow, K.J., 1962. The economic implications of learning by doing. Rev. Econ. Stud. 29 (June), 155–173.

Arrow, K.J., 1968. Applications of control theory to economic growth. In: Dantzig, G.B., Veinott, A.F. (Eds.), Mathematics of Decision Sciences. American Mathematical Society, Providence, RI.

Arrow, K.J., Enthoven, A.C., 1961. Quasi-concave programming. Econometrica 29 (October), 779–800.

Arrow, K.J., Kurz, M., 1970. Optimal growth with irreversible investment in a Ramsey model. Econometrica 38 (March), 331–344.

Debreu, G., 1954. Valuation equilibrium and Pareto optimum. Proc. Natl. Acad. Sci. U.S.A. 40, 588–592.

Debreu, G., 1959. Theory of Value. Wiley, New York.

Debreu, G., 1974. Excess demand functions. J. Math. Econ. 1, 15–23.

Friedman, M., 1957. A Theory of the Consumption Function. Princeton University Press.

Friedman, M., 1968. The role of monetary policy. Am. Econ. Rev., March 58 (1), 1–17.

Friedman, M., Schwartz, A.J., 1963. A Monetary History of the United States, 1867-1960. Princeton University Press.

Golnaraghi, F., Kuo, B., 2010. Automatic Control Systems. Wiley.

Goodfriend, M., King, R., 1997. The new neoclassical synthesis and the role of monetary policy. In: Bernanke, B.S., Rotemberg, J.J. (Eds.), NBer Macroeconomics Annual. MIT Press, pp. 231–283.

Heer, B., Maussner, A., 2004. Dynamic General Equilibrium Modeling—Computational Methods and Applications. Springer.

Hicks, J.R., 1937. Mr. Keynes and the 'Classics'. Econometrica 5 (2), 147–159.

Keynes, J.M., 1931. Essays in Persuasion. Norton, New York.

Klein, L.R., 1946. Macroeconomics and the theory of rational behavior. Econometrica, April 14 (2), 93–108.

Kydland, F., Prescott, E.C., 1982. Time to build and aggregate fluctuations. Econometrica, November 50 (6), 1345–1371.

Long, J.B., Plosser, C., 1983. Real business cycles. J. Polit. Econ., February 91 (1), 39–69.

Lucas Jr., R.E., 1976. Econometric policy evaluation: a critique. Carnegie-Rochester Conf. Ser. Public Policy 1, 19–46.

Lucas Jr., R.E., 1980. The Death of Keynesian Economics: Issues and Ideas. University of Chicago Winter, pp. 18–19.

Lucas Jr., R.E., Sargent, T.J., 1979. After Keynesian macroeconomics. Federal Reserve Bank Minneapolis Q. Rev., Spring 3 (2), 1–16.

Mankiw, G.N., 1989. Real business cycles: a new Keynesian perspective. J. Econ. Perspect., Summer 3 (3), 79–90.

Mankiw, G.N., 2006. The macroeconomist as scientist and engineer. J. Econ. Perspect. 20 (4), 29–46.

Mankiw, G.N., 2010. Macroeconomics. Worth Publishers.

Marshall, A., 1890. Principles of Economics. Macmillan, London 1949.

Modigliani, F., 1944. Liquidity preference and the theory of interest and money. Econometrica, January 12 (1), 45–88.

Phelps, E., 1968. Money wage dynamics and labor market equilibrium. J. Polit. Econ., July/August 76 (4, pt. 2), 678–711.

Ricardo, D., 1817. On the Principles of Political Economy and Taxation. Cambridge University Press 1951.

Ricardo, D., 1821. The Principles of Political Economy. J.M. Dent 1912.

Romer, D., 2006. Advanced Macroeconomics. McGraw-Hill Irwin.

Samuelson, P.A., 1948. Economics: An Introductory Analysis. McGraw-Hill, New York.

Samuelson, P.A., 1988. Keynesian economics and harvard: in the beginning. Challenge: Mag. Econ. Aff. 31 (July/August), 32–34.

Smith, A., 1776. An Inquiry into the Nature and Causes of the Wealth of Nations. Random House, New York 1937.

Wickens, M., 2008. Macroeconomic Theory—A Dynamic General Equilibrium Approach. Princeton University Press.

Woodford, M., 2003. Interest and Prices. Princeton University Press.

Wyatt, G.J., 2004. Macroeconomic Models in a Causal Framework. En Exempla Books.

Chapter 20

An Economic Model

Chapter Contents

A MODEL FOR ECONOMIC GROWTH WITH INNOVATION AND ENTREPRENEURSHIP

Before we discuss a new model, it may be worthwhile to revisit and briefly review how technology, innovation, and entrepreneurship have been addressed in the literature to this point. To begin with, "technology" was used in the Solow model as a "catchall" to explain that part of economic growth that was not explained by increases in capital and labor. The thought was that this technology changed over time exogenously and contributed to economic growth, as well as offset the dampening effect of diminishing returns (Acemoglu 2009; Aghion and Howitt, 2009; Barro and Sala-i-Martin, 2004).

Efforts to "endogenize" this technology contribution took the paths of innovation-based growth models: (a) the product variety model due to Romer (1986, 1987, 1990) where innovation causes productivity growth by creating new, but not necessarily improved, varieties of products using labor, as the only R&D input into the Cobb-Douglas production function, what may essentially be thought of as incremental innovation, and (b) Schumpeterian growth theory due to Aghion and Howitt, where quality-improving innovations render old products obsolete and involve the force that Schumpeter calls creative destruction, which may essentially be thought of as disruptive innovation. In a further enhancement of this model, a hybrid neoclassical/Schumpeterian model, capital accumulation and technological progress are both treated endogenously in the same model. However, in either case, innovations enter the model through the Cobb-Douglas production function as factor inputs to production and are considered to be the result of R&D investment. Furthermore, in order to make the math tractable, a number of simplifying assumptions need to be made.

Innovation, Entrepreneurship, and the Economy in the US, China, and India

307

We also referred previously to directed technological change (Acemoglu, 2009) and general purpose technologies (Aghion and Howitt, 2009), both of which can be labor augmenting in that they effectively improve productivity of labor through technological change. Within the framework discussed thus far, R&D is undertaken by combining other factor inputs to produce technological change, which is essentially equated to innovation, and this, in turn, further improves the productivity of labor. This may, in general, be true, but there are other issues that must be considered, when considering the impact of innovation and entrepreneurship.

It is well known in science, engineering, business of technology, and business, in general, that the terms research, R&D, inventions, technology, innovation, and entrepreneurship have very specific meanings, somewhat different from the context in which they are discussed in economic growth modeling by academic economists. Investment in research and R&D may result in inventions, and perhaps innovations, but may not necessarily lead to commercially viable entrepreneurial opportunities. One might even argue that entrepreneurial opportunities are the cause of R&D investments rather than the result of R&D investments (Holcombe, 1998). By the same token, innovation, and especially entrepreneurship, may not require huge investments in R&D or technological innovation—what they require, of course, are viable and sustainable business opportunities that need to be acted upon. In fact, most entrepreneurial opportunities are created as a result of past entrepreneurship and specialized knowledge known to the entrepreneurs (Harper, 1996; Hayek, 1945; Holcombe, 1999, 2003; Kirzner, 1973, 1979; Kirzner, 1985). Also, the more entrepreneurial activity an economy, or a region of the economy, exhibits, the more new entrepreneurial opportunities it creates.

The impact of entrepreneurship on the economy has also been studied extensively by Baumol (1968, 1986, 1990, 1993). Extensive work to understand the role of entrepreneurship in the economy, especially as it relates to collecting empirical data, has also been carried out by Audretsch and Acs and their colleagues (Acs and Armington, 2006; Acs and Audretsch, 2010; Acs et al., 2004, 2013; Audretsch, 1995, 2007; Audretsch and Thurik, 2001; Audretsch et al., 2006), and we discuss that further in the next chapter. The relationship between entrepreneurship and economics has also been written about extensively by Simon Parker (Parker, 2004, 2009). However, in what follows, we approach the relationship between entrepreneurship and economics from a different perspective and address it a manner similar to approaches used in sciences and engineering.

While it is important to recognize the importance of physical and human capital, knowledge externalities, and increasing returns, as the present models of economic growth do, it is equally important, if not more so, to explicitly emphasize the role of innovation and entrepreneurship in economic growth. These factors are essential ingredients, but the process that determines when and how innovations and entrepreneurial opportunities arise, and which of these survive, is not a deterministic process. "Schumpeter's discussion of entrepreneurship flows from his vision of economic growth as a spontaneous, revolutionary, and discontinuous process, implying that the motive forces of growth are exogenous to his model of growth" (Holcombe, 1998).

Further, it is important to recognize that, as discussed in the previous two chapters, economic growth theory and macroeconomic theory, in general, assume equilibrium. This is clearly implied in the terms general equilibrium, dynamic general equilibrium, and ultimately dynamic stochastic general equilibrium. There are many interpretations of what this equilibrium really means (Hahn, 1984; Hayek, 1949; Holcombe, 1999; Kirzner, 1979; Lewin, 1997; Stiglitz, 1994) and whether the concept of equilibrium is even relevant in economics (Kaldor, 1972). Certainly, given the complex nature of innovation and entrepreneurship, their impact on the economy cannot be modeled as equilibrium processes. Also, the theories of the previous two chapters, with the complexity of the problems being addressed at a macro level, have to make a lot of simplifying assumptions to make the problem even somewhat manageable. Innovation and entrepreneurship certainly are influenced by a large number of factors, as discussed in previous sections, very few of which lend themselves to be treated quantitatively. Perhaps, there are alternative nonequilibrium approaches that can be deployed to describe the occurrence of innovation and entrepreneurship, drawing inspiration from the modeling of similar phenomena that occur in the physical sciences.

At a "macro"-level, one can view innovation and entrepreneurship as occurring spontaneously as a result of "micro"-level random processes under nonlinear, nonequilibrium conditions. The activity level or the intensity level of these stochastic processes is influenced by the factors that affect innovation and entrepreneurship and have been discussed qualitatively in the first two sections of this book. These random processes are then subject to a wide range of phenomena, such as positive and negative nonlinear feedbacks from these factors and their role in self-reinforcing or self-rejecting mechanisms, direct and indirect network effects caused by demand- and supply-side externalities and their role in innovation diffusion and adoption, positive and negative returns to adoption and their relation to critical mass and its relevance to stable or unstable positions in adoption, path dependency in the evolution of an innovation, and its role in locking in the innovation. A number of authors have written extensively about these topics (Arthur, 1989, 1990, 1997; Arthur et al., 1987; Schoder, 2000; Weidlich, 1991; Weidlich and Braun, 1992; Katz and Shapiro, 1994; Witt, 1997). These self-organizing complex systems result in a manner analogous to the physics of nonequilibrium processes, work pioneered by Prigogine and Nicolis (1977) and Prigogine and Stengers (1984), and also in the related field of the physics of cooperative phenomena, whose application in a wide range of situations has been described using a common mathematical framework, in a field called "synergetics" and expounded by Haken (1983).

Haken (1975) pointed out that these types of systems that consist of a large number of subsystems cannot be analyzed by merely decomposing the system into its subsystems and randomly superimposing the effects on the subsystems.

The reason for that is these subsystems can interact and cooperate with each other, in a manner that is either self-reinforcing or self-rejecting. When they self-reinforce, they can explain characteristic changes in the system as a whole, for example, transition from one state to another or from a disordered to an ordered state. Examples of such phenomena in physical systems, especially in solid-sate and laser physics, are the transition of a laser from an incoherent to a coherent state (Graham and Haken, 1970; Haken, 1964a,b; Lamb, 1964; Scully and deGiorgio, 1970); of a ferromagnet from an unmagnetized to a magnetized state, or to various degrees of magnetization, which is described by the well-known Ising model; or of a system going into a superconducting state below a critical temperature, which is described by the Ginzburg-Landau model and later also by the Bardeen-Cooper-Schrieffer theory of superconductivity— as well as a number of other physical and nonphysical systems not in equilibrium. Interestingly, the behavior of such nonequilibrium systems is also analogous to the behavior of systems in equilibrium as they go through phase transitions. These models have also been applied to nonlinear wave interactions in physics, for example, nonlinear optics, excitons in crystals, and solitons in fibers, and to biological (interacting systems of neurons) and sociological systems.

Most systems referred to above consist of an extremely large number of subsystems, and thus, the description of the system as a whole in terms of the behavior of individual subsystems is usually an impossible task. Instead, a relevant macroscopic parameter is chosen to describe the system as a whole, and the concept of the order parameter is introduced. This is typically used in phase-transition theory and is useful in describing nonequilibrium systems. In the case of ferromagnets, for example, the macroscopic quantity magnetization acts as an order parameter and is zero in the unmagnetized or disordered state and is one when the ferromagnet is fully magnetized, or the ordered state. Temperature of a system similarly is a macro-level parameter that is a measure of the activity level of a system. The time constants associated with these order parameters are usually very long compared to those for the subsystems. The macro parameter, the order parameter, acts on the individual subsystems to "drive" or "order" the associated subsystems and governs their behavior. The subsystems themselves create feedback loops and organize the behaviors of the subsystems and can result in self-reinforcement and hence self-organization. These systems, at either the microscopic or the macroscopic level, described by the order parameter, can be treated with a statistical description, with some causal forces that tend to increase the order or "coherence" among the subsystems and some fluctuating or stochastic processes, which tend to increase the disorder. The formalism typically used to model these situations is that of Markov processes and stochastic differential equations.

Analogous to the nonlinear, nonequilibrium phenomena in physical systems described above, one can think of the impact of innovation and entrepreneurship on the economy as a nonlinear, nonequilibrium process. The various factors that were discussed qualitatively in the previous sections and chapters can be thought of as the subsystems of the system. The interaction among these "micro"-level subsystems can be self-reinforcing leading to innovation and entrepreneurship at a "macro"-level. The degree of this self-reinforcement at the "micro"-level among the various factors discussed in previous book chapters can lead to a "mesoscopic"-level, or firm-level, behavior that can be thought of as an order parameter, described as the degree of entrepreneurship, E_i, at a firm level, very analogous to the degree of magnetization of a ferromagnet. Any single instance of entrepreneurship, say, a successful new venture, is then described by E_i, a "mesoscopic" order parameter that measures the entrepreneurial intensity at the firm level. The degree and frequency of this occurrence of entrepreneurship (E_i), as evidenced by the number (n_i) of sustainable new firms created in a given economy, are further affected by the factors discussed in previous chapters, giving rise to a macroeconomic parameter, E, which is a measure of how conducive all the qualitative factors are in supporting entrepreneurship in the economy. This parameter E can be thought of as an "order parameter" for innovation and entrepreneurship in a given economy, which results from the nonequilibrium, nonlinear processes at work among all the qualitative factors discussed previously, and as a measure of the "temperature" of the innovation and entrepreneurship level, or the intensity level of innovation and entrepreneurship in a given economy.

As discussed above, these systems can be treated using Markov processes and stochastic differential equations, consisting of Brownian motion or the Wiener process of diffusion, or the generalized Wiener process with drift, also known as the Ito process. The stochastic differential equation associated with Brownian motion is also known as the Langevin equation, and the probability density function associated with that is the Fokker-Planck equation, and these two are related to each other through the Feynman-Kac formula. It can be shown that three types of processes—jump processes, diffusion processes, and drift processes—naturally fall out from Markov processes under the right differentiability and continuity conditions (Gardiner, 1983; Van Kampen, 1981).

While jump diffusions in Markov processes appear quite naturally through stochastic differential equations, we introduce them in our treatment in a somewhat "phenomenological" manner—by adding them to the traditional equilibrium models rather than developing a truly nonequilibrium model, which will be deferred to future work. In the present approach, the net effect of the innovative and entrepreneurial efforts that survive through the abovementioned highly nonlinear, nonequilibrium processes is to have a positive change and may be looked upon as a positive "jump," in the output of the economy. This is to be contrasted with a "shock" to the economy (Bloom, 2009), where after a positive or negative shock to the economy, the economic output changes temporarily and then reverts back, after a suitable length of time, determined by the nature and size of the shock, to its natural equilibrium level as discussed previously. The impact of these positive jumps to the economy from any one individual innovation or entrepreneurship event (e.g., new firm or new business creation within an existing firm) may be small (E_i, as indicated earlier), but the cumulative effect of these (E, as indicated earlier) is to increase the output of the economy over time.

The model we propose here augments the existing growth models, which address economic growth due to improvements in factor inputs, with the impact of innovation and entrepreneurship modeled using cumulative jumps, and borrowing "jump diffusion," which is characterized by a Poisson process, from their use in finance (Ait-Sahalia, 2004; Ait-Sahalia and Jacod, 2011, 2012; Hanson and Westman, 2002; Kou, 2008; Merton, 1976, 1992) and now also in macroeconomics (Posch, 2009), in addition to the standard Brownian motion or Wiener process with drift or the Ito process.

We start with the production function in the augmented Solow model with human capital:

$$Y(t) = F[K(t), H(t), A(t)L(t)] \tag{20.1}$$

Assuming a Cobb-Douglas production, Eq. (20.1) becomes

$$Y(t) = K(t)^{\alpha} H(t)^{\beta} [A(t)L(t)]^{(1-\alpha-\beta)} \tag{20.2}$$

With a little algebra, this can be shown to be the same as

$$\frac{dY}{Y} = \alpha \frac{dK}{K} + \beta \frac{dH}{H} + (1-\alpha-\beta)\frac{dA}{A} + (1-\alpha-\beta)\frac{dL}{L} \tag{20.3}$$

To this expression, we add to the right-hand side drift, diffusion, and jump diffusion terms:

$$\frac{dY}{Y} = \left\{ \alpha \frac{dK}{K} + \beta \frac{dH}{H} + (1-\alpha-\beta)\frac{dA}{A} + (1-\alpha-\beta)\frac{dL}{L} \right\} + \mu' dt + \sigma W(t)$$

$$+ d\left(\sum_{i=1}^{N(t)} (V_i - 1) \right) \tag{20.4}$$

where μ' is the standard drift term, $W(t)$ is the Wiener process with a variance of σ^2, $N(t)$ is a Poisson process with rate λ, and $\{V_i\}$ is a sequence of independent identically distributed nonnegative random variables, with all sources of randomness entering through $N(t)$, $W(t)$, $V(t)$ assumed to be independent.

Recognizing that $\frac{dX}{X} = d\ln X$ and denoting $\ln X$ by lower case x, where X is any of the variables above, we can rewrite the above equation as

$$y(t) = \{\alpha k(t) + \beta h(t) + (1-\alpha-\beta)a(t) + (1-\alpha-\beta)l(t)\} + \mu' dt + \sigma W(t)$$

$$+ d\left(\sum_{i=1}^{N(t)} (V_i - 1) \right) \tag{20.5}$$

Each of the jumps in the jump diffusion process may be thought of as the impact (E_i) on the economy, the "mesoscopic" order parameter introduced earlier, from a single new firm, or a single new business, that has been created in an economy. The cumulative effect of these new ventures on the economy is then the "macro"-level order parameter, E, introduced earlier, and is reflected through the amplitude, frequencies, and the type of distribution function— whether Poisson or some other—the jump diffusion processes follow. The parameters in the above equation can be determined using maximum likelihood estimation to provide an estimate for the entrepreneurial intensity levels of a given economy.

In summary, in this chapter, we propose that processes such as innovation and entrepreneurship are nonlinear and nonequilibrium processes, in analogy with processes in the physical sciences. We refer to approaches and models that have been used to mathematically describe such processes in physical and now also in nonphysical systems. The qualitative factors that have been discussed in previous chapters (Chapters 1 through 17) are "micro"-level subsystems of the larger system, the economy (Chapters 18 through 20). These subsystems interact among themselves cooperatively to create "mesoscopic" effects at the firm level and cumulatively across the economy to have a "macro"-level effect. In lieu of a truly nonequilibrium model, we treat the effects of innovation and entrepreneurship as jump diffusions that augment the traditional equilibrium models. The net cumulative effect of these jumps is economic growth. The intensity level or the activity level of this jump diffusion is determined by the net effect of all the qualitative parameters discussed in previous chapters. The intent of future work would be to build on this approach to treating the impact of innovation and entrepreneurship on economic growth. The next chapter, Chapter 21, reviews what empirical data are available to assess the degree of entrepreneurship, as well as other relevant macroeconomic data, in these regions of the world.

REFERENCES

Acemoglu, D., 2009. Introduction to Modern Economic Growth. Princeton University Press.
Acs, Z.J., Armington, C., 2006. Entrepreneurship, Geography, and American Economic Growth. Cambridge University Press.
Acs, Z.J., Audretsch, D.B. (Eds.), 2010. Handbook of Entrepreneurship Research. second ed. Springer.
Acs, Z.J., Audretsch, D.B., Braunerjelm, P., Carlsson, B., 2004. The knowledge filter in endogenous growth. Discussion Papers on Entrepreneurship Growth and Public Policy, Max Planck Institute for Research into Economic Systems, pp. 1–38.
Acs, Z.J., Szerb, L., Autio, E., 2013. The Global Entrepreneurship and Development Index. Edward Elgar Publishers.
Aghion, P., Howitt, P., 2009. The Economics of Growth. The MIT Press.
Ait-Sahalia, Y., 2004. Disentangling diffusion from jumps. J. Financ. Econ. 74, 487–528.
Ait-Sahalia, Y., Jacod, J., 2011. Testing whether jumps have finite or infinite activity. Ann. Sci. 39 (3), 1689–1719.
Ait-Sahalia, Y., Jacod, J., 2012. Analyzing the spectrum of asset returns: jump and volatility components in high frequency data. J. Econ. Lit. 50 (4), 1007–1050.

Arthur, B.W., 1989. Competing technologies, increasing returns, and lick-in by historical events. Econ. J. 99, 116–131.

Arthur, B.W., 1990. Positive feedbacks in the economy. Sci. Am. 262 (2), 92–99.

Arthur, B.W., 1997. Increasing Returns and Path Dependence in the Economy. The University of Michigan Press.

Arthur, B.W., Ermoliev, Y.M., Kaniovski, Y.M., 1987. Path-dependent processes and the emergence of macro-structure. Eur. J. Oper. Res. 30, 294–303.

Audretsch, D.B., 1995. Innovation and Industry Evolution. MIT Press.

Audretsch, D.B., 2007. Entrepreneurship Capital and Economic Growth. Oxford Rev. Econ. Policy 23 (1), 63–78.

Audretsch, D.B., Thurik, R., 2001. Linking entrepreneurship to growth. OECD Science, Technology Industry Working Papers, pp. 1–34.

Audretsch, D.B., Keilbach, M.C., Lehmann, E.F., 2006. Entrepreneurship and Economic Growth. Oxford University Press.

Barro, R.J., Sala-i-Martin, X., 2004. Economic Growth. The MIT Press.

Baumol, W.J., 1968. Entrepreneurship in economic theory. Am. Econ. Rev. 58 (2), 64–71.

Baumol, W.J., 1986. Productivity growth, convergence, and welfare: what the long-run data show. Am. Econ. Rev. 76 (5, December), 1072–1085.

Baumol, W.J., 1990. Entrepreneurship: productive, unproductive, and destructive. J. Polit. Econ. 98 (5, pt. 1, October), 893–921.

Baumol, W.J., 1993. Formal entrepreneurship theory in economics: existence and bounds. J. Bus. Ventur. 8, 197–210.

Bloom, N., 2009. The impact of uncertainty shocks. Econometrica 77 (3), 623–685.

Gardiner, C.W., 1983. Handbook of Stochastic Methods for Physics, Chemistry and the Natural Sciences. Springer.

Graham, R., Haken, H., 1970. Laserlight—first example of a second order phase-transition far away from thermal equilibrium. Z. Phys. 237, 31–46.

Hahn, F.H., 1984. Equilibrium and Macroeconomics. MIT Press.

Haken, H., 1964a. Theory of coherence of laser light. Phys. Rev. Lett. 13 (11), 329–331.

Haken, H., 1964b. A nonlinear theory of laser noise and coherence. Z. Phys. 181, 96–124.

Haken, H., 1975. Cooperative phenomena in systems far from thermal equilibrium, and in non-physical systems. Rev. Mod. Phys. 47 (1), 67–121.

Haken, H., 1983. Advanced Synergetics—Instability Hierarchies of Self-Organizing Systems. Springer-Verlag.

Hanson, F.B., Westman, J.J., 2002. Jump-diffusion stock return models in finance: stochastic process density with uniform-jump amplitude. In: Proceedings of the 15th International Symposium on Mathematical Theory of Networks and Systems, 12 August 2002.7 pages (invited paper).

Harper, D.A., 1996. Entrepreneurship and the Market Process: An Inquiry into the Growth of Knowledge. Routledge, London.

Hayek, F.A., 1945. The use of knowledge in society. Am. Econ. Rev. 35 (September), 519–530.

Hayek, F.A., 1949. Economics and knowledge. In: Hayek, F.A. (Ed.), Individualism and Economic Order. Routledge and Keegan Paul, London.

Holcombe, R.G., 1998. Entrepreneurship and economic growth. Q. J. Austrian Econ. 1 (2), 45–62.

Holcombe, R.G., 1999. Equilibrium versus the invisible hand. Rev. Austrian Econ. 12, 227–243.

Holcombe, R.G., 2003. The origins of entrepreneurial opportunities. Rev. Austrian Econ. 16 (1), 25–43.

Kaldor, N., 1972. The irrelevance of equilibrium economics. Econ. J. 82 (328), 1237–1255.

Katz, M.L., Shapiro, C., 1994. Systems competition and network effects. J. Econ. Perspect. 8 (2), 93–115.

Kirzner, I.M., 1973. Competition and Entrepreneurship. University of Chicago Press.

Kirzner, I.M., 1979. Perception, Opportunity, and Profit: Studies in the Theory of Entrepreneurship. University of Chicago Press.

Kirzner, I.M., 1985. Discovery and the Capitalist Process. University of Chicago Press, Chicago.

Kou, S.G., 2008. Jump diffusion models for asset pricing in financial engineering. In: Birge, J.R., Linetsky, V. (Eds.), Handbook in OR & MS, vol. 15. pp. 73–116.

Lamb Jr., W.E., 1964. Theory of an optical maser. Phys. Rev. 134, A1429–A1450.

Lewin, P., 1997. Hayekian equilibrium and change. J. Econ. Methodol. 4, 245–266.

Merton, R.C., 1976. Option pricing when underlying stock returns are discontinuous. J. Financ. Econ. 3, 125–144.

Merton, R.C., 1992. Continuous Time Finance. Wiley.

Parker, S.C., 2004. The Economics of Self-employment and Entrepreneurship. Cambridge University Press.

Parker, S.C., 2009. The Economics of Entrepreneurship. Cambridge University Press.

Posch, O., 2009. Structural estimation of jump-diffusion processes in macroeconomics. J. Econom. 153, 196–210.

Prigogine, I., Nicolis, G., 1977. Self-organization in Non-equilibrium Systems. Wiley.

Prigogine, I., Stengers, I., 1984. Order out of Chaos: Man's New Dialogue with Nature. Flamingo.

Romer, P.M., 1986. Increasing returns and long-run growth. J. Polit. Econ. 94, 1002–1037.

Romer, P.M., 1987. Growth based on increasing returns due to specialization. Am. Econ. Rev. 77, 56–62.

Romer, P.M., 1990. Endogenous technical change. J. Polit. Econ. 98, 71–102.

Schoder, D., 2000. Forecasting the success of telecommunications services in the presence of network effects. Inf. Econ. Policy 12, 181–200.

Scully, M., deGiorgio, V., 1970. Analogy between the laser threshold region and a second-order phase transition. Phys. Rev. A2, 1170–1177.

Stiglitz, J.E., 1994. Whither Socialism? MIT Press.

Van Kampen, N.G., 1981. Stochastic Processes in Physics and Chemistry. Elsevier.

Weidlich, W., 1991. Physics and social science—the approach of synergetics. Phys. Rep. 204 (1), 1–163.

Weidlich, W., Braun, M., 1992. The master equation approach to nonlinear economics. J. Evol. Econ. 2, 233–265.

Witt, U., 1997. Lock-in vs. critical masses—industrial change under network externalities. Int. J. Ind. Organiz. 15, 753–773.

Chapter 21

Entrepreneurship Indices Relevant Macroeconomic Data

Chapter Contents

The ultimate goal of a model, such as the one proposed in the previous chapter or eventually the one that is truly a nonequilibrium model to describe the economy, would be to be able to relate *GDP growth rate* to *key macroeconomic parameters* and a *macro-level parameter that accounts for the intensity level of innovation and entrepreneurship in the economy*. As discussed in the previous chapter, this macro-level or system-level parameter, E, would be the result of nonlinear or nonequilibrium interactions among the "micro"-level or subsystem-level parameters, which have been described qualitatively in earlier sections and chapters and are the factors that contribute to innovation and entrepreneurship.

While empirical data on GDP and key macroeconomic parameters such as those in the equations in the previous chapter have generally been available for most countries, including the three of interest in this book (Appendix 1), the challenge has been to obtain empirical data that can be used to measure the entrepreneurial intensity of a country. As mentioned in the last chapter, our search for this empirical data led us to the extensive work in this area by Audretsch and Acs and their colleagues (Acs and Armington, 2006; Acs and Audretsch, 2010; Acs et al., 2004, 2013; Audretsch, 1995, 2007; Audretsch and Thurik, 2001; Audretsch et al., 2006) and the work of Alfaro and Charlton (2006), Alfaro and Chari (2009), and Ghani et al. (2011a, 2011b).

Empirical data for these three countries that we list below and have been also used elsewhere in earlier chapters are drawn primarily from the following sources:

- Global Entrepreneurship and Development Index (GEDI)—Zoltan Acs and Laszlo Szerb (http://cepp.gmu.edu/research/geindex/)

- Global Entrepreneurship Monitor (GEM)—The GEM Project (http://www.gemconsortium.org/)
- Global Competiveness Index (GCI)—The World Economic Forum (http://www.weforum.org/reports/global-competitiveness-report-2013-2014)
- Global Innovation Index (GII)—Cornell University, INSEAD, and WIPO (http://www.globalinnovationindex.org/content.aspx?page=GII-Home)
- Index of Economic Freedom—The Heritage Foundation (www.heritage.org)
- Doing Business ranks—IFC, International Finance Organization (http://www.doingbusiness.org/reports/global-reports/doing-business-2014)
- The Kauffmann Index—data for the United States—Ewing Marion Kaufmann Foundation (http://www.kauffman.org/what-we-do/research/kauffman-index-of-entrepreneurial-activity).

GEDI DATA

We begin with Tables 21.1–21.3 constructed for these three countries drawing from GEDI data—*GEM Data*.

All GEM data are survey data expressed in percentage terms (Fig. 21.1 and Tables 21.4–21.6).

Table 21.7 provides the rankings of these three countries among the 142 countries in the GII report. Fig. 21.2 below provides graphs for the actual scores for the GII index and the subindices. Detailed data for each of the subindices are presented in Appendix 1.

Additional details on the above data are available in Appendix 2.

DATA FROM THE HERITAGE FOUNDATION

The Heritage Foundation measures *economic freedom* based on *10 quantitative and qualitative factors*, grouped into *4 broad categories, or pillars*, of economic freedom:

1. *Rule of law* (property rights and freedom from corruption)
2. *Limited government* (fiscal freedom and government spending)
3. *Regulatory efficiency* (business freedom, labor freedom, and monetary freedom)
4. *Open markets* (trade freedom, investment freedom, and financial freedom).

Each of the 10 economic freedoms within these categories is graded on a scale of 0–100. A country's overall score is derived by averaging these 10 economic freedoms, with equal weight being given to each. More information on the grading and methodology can be found in the appendix on their website—www.heritage.org (see Figs. 21.3 and 21.4).

Our search for empirical data on innovation and entrepreneurship resulted in the sources of data listed above. We have provided some of the most relevant data

TABLE 21.1 Variables Used for Constructing Entrepreneurial Attitude Index (GEDI) (2013)

Institutional Variable	China	India	United States	Individual Variable	China	India	United States	Pillars	China	India	United States
Market agglomeration	0.51	0.30	1.00	Opportunity recognition	0.46	0.66	0.37	Opportunity perception	0.42	0.34	0.69
Tertiary education	0.26	0.15	0.97	Skill perception	0.41	0.61	0.61	Start-up skills	0.19	0.16	1.00
Business risk	0.33	0.50	1.00	Risk acceptance	0.68	0.53	0.67	No fear of failure	0.33	0.38	0.85
Internet usage	0.36	0.07	0.78	Know entrepreneurs	0.83	0.77	0.20	Networking	0.50	0.09	0.47
Corruption	0.23	0.21	0.70	Career status	0.65	0.67	0.60	Cultural support	0.27	0.25	0.70

TABLE 21.2 Variables Used for Constructing Entrepreneurial Ability Index (GEDI) (2013)

Institutional Variable	China	India	United States	Individual Variable	China	India	United States	Pillars	China	India	United States
Economic freedom	0.29	0.14	0.88	Opportunity motivation	0.35	0.59	0.64	Opportunity start-up	0.16	0.13	0.67
Tech absorption	0.53	0.64	0.81	Technology level	0.11	0.05	0.54	Technology level	0.09	0.05	0.56
Staff training	0.52	0.46	0.75	Educational level	0.31	0.46	0.81	Quality of human resources	0.28	0.40	0.87
Market dominance	0.68	0.66	0.80	Competitors	0.15	0.42	0.92	Competition	0.17	0.37	0.89

TABLE 21.3 Variables Used for Constructing Entrepreneurial Aspiration Index (GEDI) (2013)

Institutional Variable	China	India	United States	Individual Variable	China	India	United States	Pillars	China	India	United States
Technology transfer	0.49	0.40	0.91	New product	0.67	0.17	0.41	Product innovation	0.65	0.17	0.62
GERD	0.34	0.18	0.66	New tech	0.28	0.57	0.33	Process innovation	0.21	0.21	0.47
Business strategy	0.51	0.48	0.76	Gazelle	0.43	0.05	0.47	High growth	0.55	0.07	0.74
Globalization	0.37	0.26	0.65	Export	0.14	0.07	0.78	Internationalization	0.08	0.03	0.64
Venture capital	0.53	0.50	0.65	Informal investment	0.26	0.04	0.41	Risk capital	0.29	0.04	0.53

Constructed from data sourced from www.thegedi.org

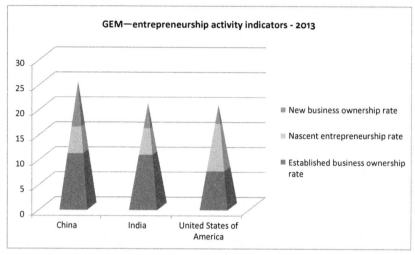

FIGURE 21.1   Entrepreneurship activity comparisons constructed from the GEM data (2013).

on innovation and entrepreneurship indices and for some of the qualitative factors that lead to innovation and entrepreneurship that we have discussed in previous sections. As we begin our future work to bridge the model proposed in the previous chapter to appropriate parameters that represent innovation and entrepreneurship, we may use some of the indices discussed in this chapter or create new indices that might be more appropriate to the model we have proposed.

In summary, in this section, we have provided a review of economic growth theory in Chapter 18. We traced the evolution of growth theory from the early years and through the work of Robert Solow. We reviewed how technology and innovation have been addressed in increasingly more complex models that have attempted to "endogenize" the impact of technological change and innovation, as they relate to the long-run "steady state" of the economy and associated economic growth.

In Chapter 19, we provided an overview of a general macroeconomic framework that reviews approaches that have been taken to bring together the two major schools of thought—the Keynesian and the classical—into a common economic framework. This approach shows how the short-term and long-term dynamics of the economy relate to each other, with the latter being described by the models discussed previously in Chapter 18. All of these models are described by equilibrium economic models and most generally by dynamic stochastic general equilibrium models.

In Chapter 20, we propose that processes such as innovation and entrepreneurship are nonlinear and nonequilibrium processes, in analogy with processes in the physical sciences. We refer to approaches and models that have been used to mathematically describe such processes in physical and now also in nonphysical systems. The qualitative factor that has been discussed in previous chapters

TABLE 21.4 Select Indicators for Entrepreneurship Activity Levels

Country	2001	2002	2003	2004	2005	2006	2007	2008	2009	2010	2011	2012	2013
Established business ownership rate													
China	–	10.6	13.8	–	13.2	12.9	8.4	–	17.2	13.8	12.7	12.5	11
India	8.8	12.1	–	–	–	5.6	5.5	16.5	–	–	–	–	10.7
United States	5.8	5.7	5.4	5.4	4.7	5.4	5	8.3	5.9	7.7	9.1	8.6	7.5
Nascent entrepreneurship rate													
China	–	5.8	4.6	–	5.6	4.4	6.9	–	7.4	4.9	10.1	5.4	5.2
India	6.9	9	–	–	–	5.2	6	6.9	–	–	–	–	5.1
Untied States	8.1	7.1	8	7.4	8.8	7.4	6.5	5.9	4.9	4.9	8.3	8.9	9.2
New business ownership rate													
China	–	6.9	8.4	–	9.4	12	10	–	11.8	9.7	14.2	7.4	8.9
India	3.6	7.5	–	–	–	5.2	2.6	4.9	–	–	–	–	4.9
United States	3.6	4.6	4.9	4.8	5.2	3.3	3.4	5	3.2	2.8	4.3	4.1	3.7

Constructed from data sourced from http://www.gemconsortium.org/key-indicators

TABLE 21.5 Select Indicators for Entrepreneurship Attitudes and Perceptions

Country	2001	2002	2003	2004	2005	2006	2007	2008	2009	2010	2011	2012	2013
Perceived capabilities													
China	–	36	38	–	23	36	39	–	35	42	44	38	36
India	40	42	–	–	–	62	73	58	–	–	–	–	56
United States	61	57	54	54	52	51	48	56	56	60	56	56	56
Perceived opportunities													
China	–	27	32	–	21	31	39	–	25	36	49	32	33
India	31	42	–	–	–	52	71	58	–	–	–	–	41
United States	35	37	31	34	32	24	25	37	28	35	36	43	47
Entrepreneurial intention													
China	–	27.5	29.5	–	45.5	24.7	31.5	–	22.6	26.9	42.8	20.4	14.4
India	–	30	–	–	–	31.3	49.7	32.9	–	–	–	–	22.8
United States	–	9.2	9	8	9	7.1	8.2	6.9	6.9	7.3	10.9	12.5	12.2
Entrepreneurship as a desirable career choice													
China			73	–	74	69	69	–	66	70	73	72	70
India			–	–	–	67	67	67	–	–	–	–	61
United States			63	58	59	51	50	63	66	65	–	–	–

Constructed from data sourced from http://www.gemconsortium.org/key-indicators

TABLE 21.6 Select Indicators for Entrepreneurship Aspirations

Country	2001	2002	2003	2004	2005	2006	2007	2008	2009	2010	2011	2012	2013
Growth expectation of early-stage entrepreneurial activity: relative prevalence													
China	27	27	21		20	33	36		26		–	27	
India	9	7				15	12	7					8
United States	27	36	29	25	37	32	31	36	27	29	32	30	30
New product early-stage entrepreneurial activity													
China		15	30		41	52	73		61		60	–	38
India	–	21				54	29	23					38
United States	–	45	38	37	39	39	49	40	37	32	45	47	45
International orientation early-stage entrepreneurial activity													
China		–	3		3	3	8		3		1	–	
India	–	–				15	8	5					6
United States	–	–	11	15	21	15	15	17	13	12	13	12	11

Constructed from data sourced from http://www.gemconsortium.org/key-indicators

TABLE 21.7 Tables Constructed from GII Data: GII Ranks

	2008–2009			2009–2010			2011			2012			2013		
	China	India	United States	China	India	United States	China	India	United States	China	India	United States	China	India	United States
Global Innovation Index	37	41	1	43	56	11	29	62	7	34	64	10	35	66	5
Institutions	56	44	17	92	73	18	98	94	15	121	125	17	113	102	17
Human capital and research	38	28	1	87	38	5	56	104	13	84	131	22	36	105	6
Infrastructure	48	76	10	71	108	12	33	63	14	39	78	14	44	89	17
Market sophistication	46	39	3	60	32	3	26	45	4	35	46	2	35	49	2
Business sophistication	49	50	1	46	41	2	29	84	15	28	75	9	33	94	2
Knowledge and technology outputs	28	23	6	17	70	14	9	60	5	5	47	11	2	37	7
Creative outputs				79	78	18	35	38	24	56	34	33	96	65	19

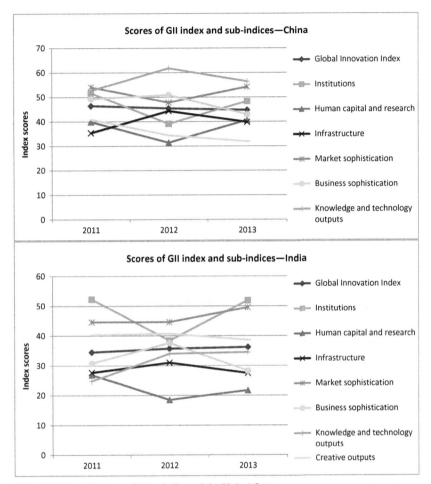

FIGURE 21.2   GII scores: China, India, and the United States.

(Continued)

is the "micro" level of the larger system, the economy. These subsystems interact among themselves cooperatively to create "mesoscopic" effects at the firm level and cumulatively across the economy to have a "macro"-level effect. In lieu of a truly nonequilibrium model, we treat the effects of innovation and entrepreneurship as jump diffusions that augment the traditional equilibrium models. The net cumulative effect of these jumps is economic growth. The intensity level or the activity level of this jump diffusion is determined by the net effect of all the qualitative parameters discussed in previous chapters.

In this chapter, we have shared the results of our search for suitable empirical data to represent the intensity level of innovation and entrepreneurship in a given economy, in our case China, India, and the United States.

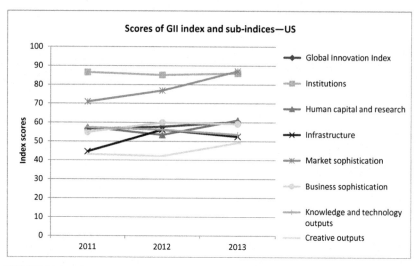

FIGURE 21.2 (Continued)

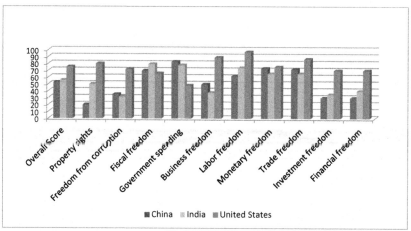

FIGURE 21.3 Index of Economic Freedom (2014). *(Source: Constructed from data sourced from www.heritage.org.)*

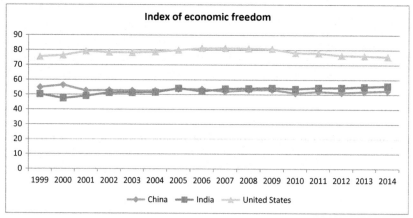

FIGURE 21.4 Index of Economic Freedom: overall score from 1999 to 2014. *(Source: Constructed from data sourced from www.heritage.org.)*

The intent of future work would be to build on the model and approach we have proposed here and relate them to suitable empirical data in order to assess the impact of innovation and entrepreneurship on economic growth.

REFERENCES

Acs, Z.J., Armington, C., 2006. Entrepreneurship, Geography, and American Economic Growth. Cambridge University Press.

Acs, Z.J., Audretsch, D.B. (Eds.), 2010. Handbook of Entrepreneurship Research, second ed. Springer.

Acs, Z.J., Audretsch, D.B., Braunerjelm, P., Carlsson, B., 2004. The knowledge filter in endogenous growth. Discussion Papers on Entrepreneurship, Growth and Public Policy, Max Planck Institute for Research into Economic Systems, pp. 1–38.

Acs, Z.J., Szerb, L., Autio, E., 2013. The Global Entrepreneurship and Development Index. Edward Elgar Publishers.

Alfaro, L., Chari, A., 2009. India transformed? Insight from the Firm level—1988–2005. NBER Working Paper 15448. http://www.nber.org/papers/w15448.

Alfaro, L., Charlton, A., 2006. International financial integration and entrepreneurship. International Monetary Fund. https://www.imf.org/external/. . ./alfaro.pdf.

Audretsch, D.B., 1995. Innovation and Industry Evolution. MIT Press.

Audretsch, D.B., 2007. Entrepreneurship capital and economic growth. Oxford Rev. Econ. Policy 23 (1), 63–78.

Audretsch, D.B., Thurik, R., 2001. Linking entrepreneurship to growth. OECD Science, Technology Industry Working Papers, pp. 1–34.

Audretsch, D.B., Keilbach, M.C., Lehmann, E.F., 2006. Entrepreneurship and Economic Growth. Oxford University Press.

Ghani, E., Kerr, W.R., O'Connell, S.D., 2011a. Promoting entrepreneurship, growth, and job creation. In: Ghani, E. (Ed.), Reshaping Tomorrow. Oxford University Press, Oxford, UK.

Ghani, E., Kerr, W.R., O'Connell, S.D., 2011b. Spatial determinants of entrepreneurship in India. NBER Working Paper, 17514. http://www.nber.org/papers/w17514.

Part IV

Conclusions

Chapter 22

Conclusions and Thoughts about the Future: The United States, China, and India

Chapter Contents

We close with our conclusions from this work and our thoughts and qualitative assessments about the future of innovation and entrepreneurship and its impact on economic growth and the economies of the United States, China, and India. A lot has been written about these three countries, especially about the "rise" of China and India in relation to the United States. However, most of these books have not focused on the role of innovation and entrepreneurship. What has been written about innovation and entrepreneurship in these two countries very recently, given the recent growth in their economies, is either very anecdotal or very prescriptive and, in some cases, highly romanticized narratives of entrepreneurship in these countries.

The first of these is a book edited by McKinsey & Company (2013). It is a book about India, which in the words of the editors, "brings together leading thinkers from the around the world to explore the challenges and opportunities faced by one of the most important and least understood nations on earth. . .." The book provides very engaging reading with over 70 individual perspectives each from a different vantage point.

The next of these edited by Li (2013) is focused on two specific concepts in the context of these two countries—(a) *disruptive innovation*, a concept pioneered primarily by Clayton Christensen, and (b) *bottom of the pyramid*, a concept pioneered by C.K. Prahalad, in 2009.

The book by Khanna (2011) is elegantly written in a very engaging, entertaining, easy-to-read, "conversational," personal style resorting mainly to "on-the-ground stories." Instead of using "hard data," the book makes concrete and specific points using stories and anecdotes and associated qualitative analysis by the author.

The book by Eichengreen et al. (2010) is again another well-organized edited book, rich in data with charts and graphs and figures, written primarily from an economic and trade perspectives. The book starts out discussing the economies of China and India and the roles they play in the global economy, trade, and export patterns of these two countries and then gets into contrasting these two countries in their development experiences and the challenges they face in sustaining growth in the future. The book discusses economic issues without requiring the reader to delve into complex mathematics.

The book by Bardhan (2010) is also a very well-written, easy-to-read book for a nonacademic reader written in a data-rich but a nonmathematical, political-economic perspective. As the author indicates in the preface, "this is a short book on two large countries, focusing on the economic development in the past quarter century (a miniscule segment of their long history). It is not about their now considerable impact on the global economy, which gets most of the attention in the Western media; it is more about what has happened to the lives of people inside those countries and under what structural constraints...the deliberate focus in the book is on long-term institutional and political-economic issues...avoiding the minutiae of analytical or empirical details, it tries with broad-brush strokes to portray the overall contours in a relatively coherent exercise in comparative political economy meant for general readership...."

The book by Gupta and Wang (2009) is another good book on the subject, but this time from the perspective of a business strategist. In the words of the authors, "The central premise underlying the book is that being present in China and India, is not the same as getting China and India right...very few CEOs grasp the magnitude and pace of change and the multifaceted nature of the new reality. Fewer still have figured out what these developments mean for the future architecture of their company. Some of the most common mistakes are viewing China and India solely from the lens of offshoring and cost reduction, building marketing strategies that are centered around just the rich cities and the top 5–10% of the population, underestimating the ambitions and capabilities of emerging competitors, and treating these two countries as peripheral rather than core to their company's global strategy." This excerpt from the preface of the book is truly indicative of the "spirit" of this book. It is meant to be more of a book on advisory to corporations planning to do business in China and India and provides some data and charts, depending on a large number of stories, cases, and anecdotes to make those points.

Another book on the subject of China and India is the one by Sharma (2009)—an excellent book, written from the point of view of a political scientist. The book talks about the evolution of these two countries from the 1950s onward. It briefly covers economic evolution during this period and then addresses social and political evolution and the evolution of economic and financial reforms. The roles of these countries as they embrace globalization, strategies, and recent patterns of their relationships with other countries, especially the United States, and with respect to each other constitute the bulk of the book. The book then concludes with a discussion about the challenges and opportunities these countries face in the future.

The approach we have taken in this book is to look at China and India through the lens of innovation and entrepreneurship and their impact on the economy. We chose to delve far more thoroughly into the fundamentals of the factors that drive innovation and entrepreneurship in China and India and compared them with their state in the United States. Our motivation for this study was driven by a number of questions. While innovation and entrepreneurship have driven the United States to its present status as the most dominant economic power of today, can the United States continue on that path? China and India used to be dominant economic powers several centuries ago, when the United States was not even on the map or was not very heavily populated. With the rise of the West, and due to a number of social and political reasons, these two nations lost their economic clout, and their economies were dwarfed by Western economies. While both these countries have shown significant growth in recent decades, can that growth be sustained? If we believe in the premise that innovation and entrepreneurship are indeed vital for the long-term growth of a country, can these two nations exhibit that? *That brought us to the question of what are the factors that are important for innovation and entrepreneurship to thrive? We looked at how these factors compare between the United States, China, and India, looked at the evolution of these factors in the past, and assessed the pointers they give us about the future, and hence about the likelihood for continued growth in these economies. These assessments are what we have summarized in the following pages in this chapter.*

In that context, we want to compare our conclusions with the views of Josef Joffe, of Stanford University, in *The Myth of America's Decline—Politics, Economics, and a Half Century of False Prophecies* on the one hand versus the starkly contrasting, almost diametrically opposing views of Robert D. Atkinson, of the National Innovation and Competitiveness Strategy Advisory Board, and Stephen J. Ezell in *Innovation Economics—The Race for Global Advantage* (2012); those of Thomas Friedman and Michael Mandelbaum in *That Used to be US: How America Fell Behind in the World It Invented and How We Can*

Come Back (2011); and those of Steven C. Currall et al. in *Organized Innovation—A Blueprint for Renewing America's Prosperity* (2014) on the other.

INNOVATION DEFINED, IMPORTANCE OF INNOVATION, FACTORS CONTRIBUTING TO INNOVATION

We began our work by defining innovation as a process for creating and introducing something new, novel, or advanced with the intention of creating value or benefit value to both the customer and the user and value to the entrepreneur and the enterprise and of course value to the society or the economy at large. Innovation is a process that begins with a new idea and concludes with market introduction. Innovation is important because it results in new business creation, which in turn drives economic growth. We then examined in detail various factors that affect innovation specific to each of these three countries, and we discuss below our conclusions regarding how these three countries fare in regard to these factors.

HISTORY

In order to assess the role history plays in innovation, we looked at the historical GDP of China, India, and the United States and how the roles have reversed in the last couple of centuries. We believe having had a history of innovation does provide a perspective on the intrinsic nature of a culture and its people and a potential proclivity towards reverting to that behavior under the "right circumstances." We, therefore, traced the role of technology and innovation in the phenomenal rise of China and India in the distant past and examined the factors that obstructed innovation in later years, which resulted in the subsequent decline of these economies. We briefly compared that with the history of innovation in the United States over the last 200 years. We discussed the history of innovation in the United States only briefly, since a lot has already been written about it and is fairly well known, and spent most of the effort discussing the history of innovation in China and India, since not much about it is known nor has been written about in the West.

China started off as an economy with significant inventive capabilities but subsequently witnessed a decline due to the then prevalent political, ideological, and social conditions. The opening up of the economy in 1978 gave a boost to science, technology, and innovation in the country and set the stage for ensuing growth and progress in China. India, on the other hand, had a rich science, technology, and innovation base to start with. The period of European dominance, particularly British rule, adversely impacted the economy and its superiority in science, technology, and industrial development. After India's independence from the British, it went about building a strong science and technology infrastructure. While some of its efforts were fruitful, it did not result in building significant innovative capabilities in the industrial sector. The link between science and technology with industry was missing and the resultant economic performance was unstable. In spite of its very brief history, about 200 years, the United States has been phenomenally successful in contrast to China and India, in advancing and commercializing science and technology. The history of these countries brings to light the bearing that the political environment and ideology that a country espouses and develops over a period of time has on its innovative capabilities. *This has certainly been a huge plus for the United States in relation to China and India in the recent past.*

ECONOMY

There are at least three measures of the economy that can be considered in relation to technological innovation—R&D expenditures, FDI, and patenting. With regard to these three indicators, China and India have greatly improved in recent years but still lag behind the United States. In R&D expenditure, while China and India spent far more than before, China's R&D expenditure is not structured to encourage sustainable innovative ability. Besides, some of the R&D work carried out by universities and institutions appears to be low on efficiency, since they appear to be disconnected from market demand. In India, the government has the most prominent share of R&D spending, and most of its efforts are not directed towards commercial activities. Business sector R&D and patenting have shown improvements, and the incremental effects are more pronounced in certain sectors, such as ICT and pharmaceuticals, although investments made in these sectors are far less than those in the United States and in China. The recent influx of FDI into R&D spending and the resultant growth in foreign R&D centers have contributed to an increase in patenting activities in China and India. However, while the number of patents applied for and granted has grown fast in China and India, these are still outnumbered by the number of US patents, and also the quality of these patents is far inferior to those filed in the United States. *Again, this is another strong positive for the United States.*

CULTURE

Compared with Chinese and Indian cultures, traditional American culture is very conducive to innovation. However, winds of mainstream cultural change in the United States that have affected its ability to innovate in recent years may be a reason for future concern.

Chinese culture has the characteristics of relatively higher power distance and bureaucracy, more collectivism and uncertainty avoidance, high reluctance to openness and acceptance of change, ambiguous opinions about achievement, and higher levels of femininity—all of which have greatly hindered, in recent years, the nurturing of an innovative spirit. The barriers to innovation in Indian culture range from high power distance exhibiting itself in a strong need for control, individualism demonstrated by poor teamwork, high uncertainty avoidance leading to weak strategic outlook, achievement culture driven more by philosophical and intellectual pursuits rather than an action orientation and physical work, to moderate levels of masculinity affecting the degree of experimentation. Since 95% of Indian organizations are family-owned, their ability to innovate and adapt to new technologies is also a major challenge by virtue of their ownership structure and management style. *This is certainly another huge plus for the United States at this time in relation to China and India, although it could be an area of concern for the United States in the future without efforts to stimulate the culture of innovation.*

LAWS AND RULES AND ROLE OF GOVERNMENT AND INSTITUTIONS

There are some significant differences between China and India, on the one hand, and the United States, on the other hand, as it relates to the infrastructure of laws and regulations and the role of government institutions and their impact on innovation. A legal structure for the protection of intellectual property rights, while it still continues to evolve, has existed in the United States for a very long time and has played a key role through the industrialization of the United States as in other Western countries, whereas it is fairly recent in China and India and its success and impact are yet to be realized. While they played a role in earlier years, tax policies and government procurement for the promotion of innovation in the United States as compared with that in China have not been very significant. In the case of India, the tax policies aimed at promoting innovation have been moderately effective in certain targeted sectors. There is also a problem of accountability of these incentives.

In a broader context, there is more recent recognition in the United States for a comprehensive US policy that coordinates science and technology and innovation, if the United States is to regain its competitive edge in relation to China and India, where governments are heavily involved in shaping policies that affect innovation. *This is also an area of huge opportunity for the United States in terms of a more concerted and comprehensive policy for coordinating science, technology, and innovation to complement activities in the private sector—an opportunity for both the United States and India, given the role already being played by the Chinese government and the strong gains being made in China as a result of these efforts. Without significant efforts in this area, the advantage in this area in the future may be shifting to China.* The question for the United States, however, is given the political dysfunction and lack of consensus in Washington, does it have the political will to craft such a policy that will be acceptable to all involved and yet keep national interests in mind? Although the Indian government has been playing a proactive role in promoting innovation, the impact of its efforts is not optimal either in relation to the progress being made in this regard in China. This is because the approach of the government has been paternalistic and directive rather than enabling (Rajan, 2006).

A silver lining for the United States, however, is in the area of a fairly effective, efficient, mature, and sophisticated administrative and legal infrastructure free of corruption, for the most part—an area that is a significant malaise in China and India with the long-term potential of negating gains made in other areas. *This is again an area that is a huge plus for the United States. Widespread corruption and the presence of significant size parallel economies are huge challenges in China and, especially, India.*

DEMOGRAPHICS

While populations in both the United States and China are aging, population may be aging faster in the United States, due to the aging of the "baby boomer" generation, than in China, further driving the United States to be a nation of more consumers than producers, and this may adversely affect the rate of innovation in the United States in the years to come. This has the potential to create an increasing trend for immigration to the United States of technically skilled professionals or those willing to create innovative new business opportunities. While an aging population is not a serious problem in China today, this is likely to become a significant problem in the future, as China's working-age population will reach its peak in 2015, and then, the percent of working-age people will start to decline. The projected share of elderly in the population in China will begin to exceed that of the United States by 2030. India, on the other hand, may have an advantage in this area, since most of its population is young leading to growth and expansion in the labor force. However, while significant progress has been made over the years, levels of illiteracy are still very high, and shares of population educated beyond high school are still very low in China and India compared with that in the United States.

The challenge for the United States, however, is that although it has a high percentage of population that has been through high school, the quality of this education in the United States may be declining relative to other industrialized nations. While China, and especially India, may have an advantage over the United States in terms of the sheer number of young population in the years to come, the quality of education and other opportunities available to these people need to be examined more closely. In the past, the United States has been a magnet for attracting the "brain drain" from China and India, along with immigrants from other parts of the world. Contributions made by this immigrant population are an integral part of the history of innovation, the economy, and the social fabric of the United States. This is expected to continue at perhaps an even more vigorous pace in the future with the aging of the "baby boomer" generation in the United States. However, with the globalization of communication and travel, the recent immigrant population in the United States is also contributing, to some extent, to innovation and economic transformations in the countries of their origins. *From the standpoint of demographics of age, the United States and China are both aging, and strictly from an age perspective, the advantage here may go to India. However, both China and India have huge challenges with literacy levels and the quality of education of the workforce in general. The United States may continue to have an advantage here because the problem in the United States is likely to be addressed in the future, as it has been in the past, through a greater influx of suitably qualified immigrants.*

EDUCATION AND UNIVERSITIES

There are significant differences in the quality and quantity of education provided in the United States, China, and India. US expenditures on a per student basis, in the K through 12 grade range, are among the highest in the industrialized world, and the United States certainly spends a great deal more per student than does China or India. However, given the dismal performance of US school students in K through 12 in standardized tests compared with their counterparts in other industrialized nations, the United States needs to take stock of the situation and do some serious soul-searching about ways to improve the performance of these students despite the widening income gap and the apparent formation of a social dichotomy. China and India have a different set of problems for their K through 12 students, which have to do with (1) the sheer number of these students and the concomitant number and quality of teachers and financial resources needed to educate their students and (2) the methodology—memorization based approach and an undue importance attached to grades.

The silver lining for the United States is in their colleges and universities, which have a disproportionately large representation among the best universities in the world compared especially with China and India. The challenge for the United States here is that the average quality of domestic students joining the undergraduate programs has been declining, while their superior graduate programs are increasingly being taken advantage of by international students rather than by domestic students. *Once again, the United States still has a definite advantage here, in relation to China and India. However, this is an area that needs to be addressed in the United States—improved STEM education in schools, regardless of income disparities, and greater incentives and encouragement for domestic students to pursue meaningful, relevant, and affordable college and university education.*

INDUSTRY AND MARKET STRUCTURES, INDUSTRY AND REGIONAL CLUSTERS

We compare the evolving industry structure and innovation intensity in the three countries, especially as it relates to patent generation in key industries, and also provide a comparison of industry cluster formation in the United States, China, and India. We present an overview of the evolution of the industry structure of the United States, as it led the way in transitioning from an agricultural economy to a manufacturing- and service-based industrial economy. Over time, various industries matured and the United States ceded its dominance in several industries to countries in the Far East, increasingly turning into a service-based economy. China and India on the other hand started the transition from an agricultural to an industrial economy only recently relative to the United States. Although China in recent years has become more of a destination for outsourcing of US manufacturing jobs, the manufacturing sector is not very innovative. Most of the innovative firms are either foreign-owned or from joint sector—not state-owned.

In India, the industrial growth is more prominent in infrastructure and retail sectors and not in high-tech sectors. With the recent efforts in cluster development in the MSME sector gaining momentum, the SME sector is proving innovative. However, with regard to introducing "new-to-the-world" innovations, the SME sector has a lot of catching up to do. Although the government happens to be the highest R&D spender, the linkage between industry, university, and government R&D labs is missing. Government-owned firms have the least innovation intensity. Private sector companies, in general, and non-MNC companies specifically are more innovative. The MNC firms have been focusing their R&D more on meeting market demands of parent companies elsewhere rather than in the local Indian market.

This is also an area that the United States has had a distinct advantage historically. The concern for the United States in this area has to be the transformation that it has gone through from a manufacturing to a service economy and its resulting strong dependence on other countries for manufactured goods. China and India are certainly gaining in this area in specific sectors.

OPPORTUNITY AREAS FOR INNOVATION

Most discussions on innovation around the world have focused on improving efficiency and productivity in business in order to stay ahead of competition. However, there are a large number of societal problems that need to be addressed through innovation, such as a large and widening gap between the rich and the poor; population growth, aging population, and associated health-care needs; energy, water, and housing shortages; global climate changes; air and water pollution; and illiteracy and the need for improving the quality of education.

Promotion of innovation, beyond what occurs naturally anyway, therefore, needs to be driven by these major problems that a nation faces and needs to be built upon resources and capabilities specifically available in the country, taking into account their level of development and maturity. We discussed various difficulties unique to the local contexts of China, India, and the United States and reviewed the approaches being taken to address these problems.

Certainly, there are huge societal problems as they relate to fundamental human needs in both China and India that could benefit from innovation targeted in those areas. Innovative approaches are being tried in India, but with mixed results. While these are not as significant today in the United States, there are certainly areas of opportunity in the United States that could benefit from focused and targeted innovation beyond the innovation that naturally occurs in the United States.

ENTREPRENEURSHIP

While innovation is associated with the idea of creating something new that is of value, and is a core aspect of entrepreneurship, entrepreneurship is generally associated with the notion of risk-taking, commercialization, and creation of value and wealth. Entrepreneurship depends on a number of characteristics that go beyond individual or personal characteristics. These characteristics relate to the environment in which the innovative or entrepreneurial individuals operate. We discuss these in detail below. *By most commonly defined measures, the United States still provides an environment that is supportive of entrepreneurship, probably among the best in the world, and far superior to that provided by China and India, with China faring slightly better than India.*

PERSONAL CHARACTERISTICS

Americans are innovative and adventurous and have a higher locus of control. Hence, they have lower fear of failure and have a higher propensity for risk-taking. The need for achievement is more self-driven. All these personal characteristics augur well for the spirit of entrepreneurship in the United States. Chinese, on the other hand, focus more on conforming to societal norms and are not opportunity-driven in their early entrepreneurial pursuits. They prefer stability as opposed to risk and fear failure. Their need for approval from society is high as a result of which they give more importance to media acclaim, which at times proves counterproductive to entrepreneurship. Hence, traditionally, Chinese do not have the requisite personality traits of an entrepreneur. But over the years, with China becoming increasingly market-oriented, the Chinese are becoming more enterprising. Indians, like the Chinese, are not very innovative, have lower propensity for risk-taking, and have a higher fear of failure. However, in recent years, entrepreneurship is being perceived, especially among the younger generation, as a worthwhile pursuit, and we are witnessing increasing levels of entrepreneurship. *Again, the advantage here goes to the United States, in relation to China and India.*

SOCIAL AND CULTURAL FACTORS

American culture is low on power distance and high on individualism, mobility, and "universal trust"—all factors conducive to entrepreneurship. China has a high power-distant culture with strong family and social ties. Traditional

Chinese culture is not conducive to entrepreneurship although this may be gradually changing over time. India has a hierarchical, paternalistic, family-oriented, and patriarchal culture. Hence, attitude towards entrepreneurship varies depending on family background and family support. Those from a business family background are more positively inclined towards entrepreneurship. For entrepreneurship to thrive in India, there is a need to increase the social base by creating support systems across different family backgrounds, castes, and gender. *The United States does not have the constraints that China and India have in this regard.*

ENTREPRENEURIAL TRAINING

The United States has a long history of entrepreneurship education. Entrepreneurship education programs are well supported financially and institutionally. The quality and number of courses offered in the United States are far better than those in China and India. China and India are late starters in this field and are at a significant disadvantage. Entrepreneurship education in these countries is not very relevant in content due to lack of the well-trained faculty and the requisite infrastructure. *The United States is in a very strong position here.*

EXTERNAL ENVIRONMENT

Entrepreneurship in a given economy is strongly influenced by the environment external to the entrepreneur. More specifically, it is affected by the degree and vigor with which anticompetitive or antitrust legislation is enforced, levels of employment especially as relates to necessity-driven entrepreneurship, and a supportive legal infrastructure. In the United States, the free market economy and the supportive laws and legislation have been around for an extremely long time compared with those in China and India and have played a very significant role in value creation through entrepreneurship. In China and India, the legal framework has been evolving only within the last 20–30 years and still has a long way to go before reaching the level of sophistication that is seen in the United States. As of today, the Chinese market consists of predominantly state-owned monopolies with some emergence of competition localized to certain industries. In India, though private enterprise is growing in number, in terms of value, the market structure is more oligopolistic to the extent that about 10 families control about 80% of the stock of the country's largest corporations.

While most entrepreneurship in the United States is driven by an eye towards value creation for the customer and for the enterprise through creatively searching for new opportunities, entrepreneurship in China and India to this point has been primarily necessity-driven, due to a lack of adequate employment opportunities for an increasingly burgeoning population. *Again, this is an area with a huge advantage going to the United States.*

INFRASTRUCTURE

Physical infrastructure is a key factor that enables and facilitates entrepreneurship. The United States has had a decided advantage in relation to physical infrastructure compared with China or India, both of which are emerging economies compared with the United States, the most dominant economic power of the twentieth century. The United States continues to have this advantage over both these countries, and this is not expected to change in the near future. However, this is an area of concern for the United States, since the US physical infrastructure is aging and needs significant injection of new capital in order to stay competitive. This is especially true in relation to China, where huge investments are being made to rapidly build a very modern and advanced infrastructure, especially in the area of rail and air transportation. Other areas of infrastructure continue to lag behind in China and are expected to continue to present challenges for entrepreneurship in the near future. A significant and well-known concern for China is a disregard for environmental considerations and the resultant air and river water pollution. India on the other hand still lags behind significantly and despite recent increases in infrastructure investments faces huge challenges in all aspects of physical infrastructure. This is expected to significantly limit the efficiency and efficacy of entrepreneurship in India in the near and intermediate future. *Again, this is an area where the United States continues to have a significant advantage. However, China is making huge investments in this area and, given the age of the US infrastructure, should be a concern for the United States. An opportunity for the United States is to invest in upgrading its infrastructure. This is also an area that presents big challenges to India.*

CAPITAL AVAILABILITY

The United States has very strong equity and debt markets, while the domestic debt market and stock markets are not so vibrant in China. In the case of India, the domestic debt market is weak as compared with its stock market or private credit. We explored the breadth and depth of financing available for entrepreneurial ventures across the three countries. In the United States, financial support is available from the US government through the Small Business Administration. More importantly, venture capital (VC) and angel investor communities are very well developed in the United States, and VCs have played a key role in the genesis of what are now major US and global corporations.

Compared with the United States, China has very little policy or government support for sponsoring entrepreneurship. Unlike in the United States, governmental funds in China are directly invested in the small businesses. But these funds have not been successful in stimulating other private funds to join in to help new businesses. In China, the VC industry began to develop in the 1980s. Although VC funds have grown in China in recent years, most of the sources of these funds are either the government or large corporations. Major stock exchanges were established in China in the 1990s, and an exchange was set up for small and medium enterprises very recently and has been growing rapidly. Although small and medium enterprises find it easier to obtain credit in the United States as compared with their counterparts in India and China, India fares better than China on this count. In spite of that, access to finance is one of the biggest limiting factors in achieving significantly higher levels of entrepreneurial growth in India. The role of banks, VCs, and angel investors continues to be highly underexploited for the advancement of entrepreneurial activities in India. *This is an area where the United States continues to have an advantage, although we are now starting to see increased activities in financing early-stage companies in both China and India.*

INTRAPRENEURSHIP

There are a lot of similarities between start-up entrepreneurship and corporate entrepreneurship, or intrapreneurship, and there are also some significant differences. While start-up entrepreneurship has played a huge role in the economic development of the United States through its early history, especially after the Civil War, corporate entrepreneurship was the dominant mechanism for technology-based innovation until about the 1970s. During this period, most significant innovations came through the efforts of major US corporations and their corporate labs. However, since about the 1970s, the intensity of corporate innovation has waxed and waned with the ups and downs of the US economy. This torch for innovation has been carried, to a large extent, in the United States by start-up ventures, very many of which have grown into giant corporations in their own rights and some of them have succeeded in maintaining their innovation and intrapreneurial culture. However, there is still a significant need for established corporations to show a steady commitment to pursue intrapreneurial activities with greater intensity.

In China and India by contrast, corporate entrepreneurship is quite nascent. In China, especially, the situation is fairly unique since a vast majority of large enterprises are state-owned, which have not felt any compelling need for corporate entrepreneurship in the past. That is beginning to change and intrapreneurship in state-owned enterprises is in the very early stages. In private enterprises, however, a strong movement is under way to promote intrapreneurship using various routes to accomplish those objectives. Similarly, in India, systems and procedures have not been in place to promote entrepreneurship within corporations. In recent years, however, there are a few examples of organizations that have overcome challenges of the past and have promoted entrepreneurial cultures. The most compelling examples of these are software subsidiaries of multinationals, which have been able to encourage entrepreneurial cultures within their subsidiaries in India. *The United States has a strong history of corporate innovation and entrepreneurship, although it has ebbed and flowed in recent times with the ups and downs in the US economy, and has a decided advantage over China and India.*

IMPACT ON THE ECONOMY

After having discussed innovation and entrepreneurship at great length and after having considered all of the above factors that contribute to and are conducive to innovation and entrepreneurship, we looked at the impact of innovation and entrepreneurship on the economy and, more specifically, on economic growth.

We provided a review of economic growth theory. We traced the evolution of growth theory from the early years and through the work of Robert Solow. We reviewed how technology and innovation have been addressed in increasingly more complex models that have attempted to "endogenize" the impact of technological change and innovation, as they relate to the long-run "steady state" of the economy and associated economic growth.

We also provided an overview of a general macroeconomic framework that reviews approaches that have been taken to bring together the two major schools of thought—the Keynesian and the classical—into a common economic framework. This approach shows how the near-term and long-term dynamics of the economy relate to each other, with the latter being described by the models discussed previously. All of these models are described by equilibrium economic models and most generally by dynamic stochastic general equilibrium models.

We then proposed that processes such as innovation and entrepreneurship are nonlinear and nonequilibrium processes, in analogy with processes in the physical sciences. We referred to approaches and models that have been used to mathematically describe such processes in physical and now also in nonphysical systems. The qualitative factors that we have discussed in previous chapters are "micro" level of the larger system, the economy. These subsystems interact among themselves cooperatively to create "mesoscopic" effects at the firm level and cumulatively across the economy to have a "macro" level effect. In lieu of a truly nonequilibrium model, we treat the effects of innovation and entrepreneurship as jump diffusions, which augment the traditional equilibrium models. The net cumulative effect of these jumps is economic growth. The intensity level or the activity level of this jump diffusion is determined by the net effect of all the qualitative parameters discussed in previous chapters. *The intent of future work would be to build on this approach to treating the impact of innovation and entrepreneurship on economic growth.*

We also reviewed empirical data that are available to assess the degree of entrepreneurship. We reviewed these *entrepreneurship indices*, work supported notably by the World Bank and the OECD, as well as other *relevant macroeconomic data*. These data, while they provide snapshots in time, are difficult to come by in a time series format. *The ultimate goal, which we will defer to future work, is, of course, to be able to use a model such as the one we proposed here and relate that to a time series of entrepreneurship data and key macroeconomic factors.*

Looking at the previous few pages, it is clear from our study of the factors that affect innovation and entrepreneurship, and hence their contribution to long-term economic growth, that in most of these areas the United States continues to have an advantage. While China and India have had glorious histories of innovation and entrepreneurship in the distant past, and have shown very encouraging signs in recent years, they both still have huge challenges to overcome. We reviewed each of the key areas and have compared the United States, China, and India in these areas with facts and figures. It is apparent from these comparisons that both face significant hurdles. While each may have some areas where it fares better than the other, on the whole, it appears that as the result of a strong and coordinated government effort since the late 1970s, China may be better positioned than India. Most long-term economic projections seem to indicate that despite serious questions regarding the long-term viability of state-sponsored capitalism, China is very well positioned for long-term growth with the potential to surpass the United States. India on the other hand, while more democratic in its traditions and more entrepreneurial in recent years, is burdened by its own heritage of bureaucracy and corruption. Given our detailed comparisons of innovation and entrepreneurship in these three countries, it appears that neither one of them poses a near-term threat in these areas to the United States. In that regard, our analysis would suggest that from the standpoint of the level of innovation and entrepreneurship, we would agree with Joffe (2014) that the notion of a rapidly declining America is probably overblown.

That said, the United States does have some serious new challenges that it did not have until roughly the last 20–30 years. Advances in telecommunications technologies as well as the advent of the Internet have proved to be the great equalizer, enabling instant global access to information sharing, as well as new Internet-based business models. See, for example, the work by Mary Meeker and Liang Wu of KPCB (Meeker and Wu, 2013; Figs. 22.1–22.4). Furthermore, as discussed earlier, some of the other challenges the United States faces are in the areas of strong cultural shifts that no longer emphasize the importance of education and its contribution to innovation and entrepreneurship; declining quality of education, especially STEM education in high schools; declining performance of high school students due to a widening income gap; quality challenges and financial burden associated with college education; an economy that has transitioned to primarily a service economy rather than a manufacturing economy; the dysfunction in Washington and the lack of political will to have a comprehensive US policy that coordinates science, technology, and innovation as it did in the past; and a lack of commitment to upgrade the aging US physical infrastructure, to name a few of the challenges that pertain to the spirit of innovation and entrepreneurship and the economic prosperity that flows from it. In this regard, we agree with

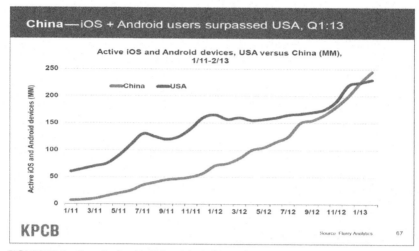

FIGURE 22.1 Growth of active iOS and Android usage in China and the United States (Meeker and Wu, 2013).

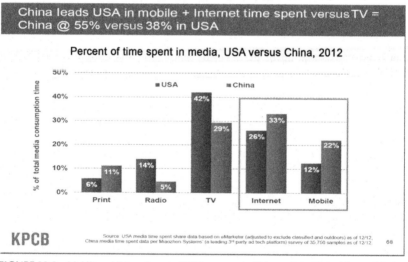

FIGURE 22.2 Mobile and Internet versus TV time spent in China and the United States (Meeker and Wu, 2013).

the concerns raised by Atkinson and Ezell (2012), Friedman and Mandelbaum (2011), and Currall et al. (2014) and that with timely intervention, the history of innovation and entrepreneurship and ensuing economic growth in the United States can be sustained over the long haul in relation to the rising powers in the East.

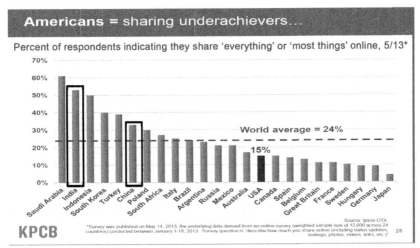

FIGURE 22.3 Online information sharing in major global markets (Meeker and Wu, 2013).

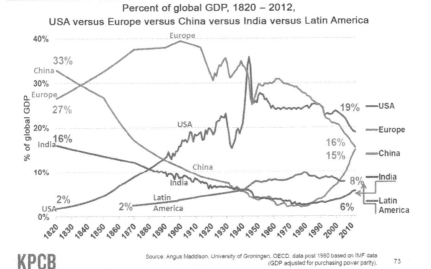

FIGURE 22.4 Impressive GDP gains of China since the 1980s (Meeker and Wu, 2013).

REFERENCES

Atkinson, R.D., Ezell, S.J., 2012. Innovation Economics—The Race for Global Advantage. Yale University Press.

Bardhan, P., 2010. Awakening Giants, Feet of Clay—Assessing the Economic Rise of China and India. Princeton University Press.

Currall, S.C., Frauenheim, E., Perry, S.J., Hunter, E.M., 2014. Organized Innovation—A Blueprint for Renewing America's Prosperity. Oxford University Press, New York.

Eichengreen, B., Gupta, P., Kumar, R., 2010. Emerging Giants—China and India in the World Economy. Oxford University Press.

Friedman, T., Mandelbaum, M., 2011. That Used to be US—How America Fell Behind in the World It Invented and How We Can Come Back. Farrar, Straus and Giroux.

Gupta, A.K., Wang, H., 2009. Getting India and China Right—Strategies for Leveraging The World's Fastest-Growing Economies for Global Advantage. Jossey-Bass/Wiley.

Joffe, J., 2014. The Myth of America's Decline—Politics, Economics, and a Half Century of False Prophecies. Liveright Publishing.

Khanna, T., 2011. Billions of Entrepreneurs—How China and India are Reshaping their Futures and Yours. Harvard Review Press.

Li, P.P., 2013. Disruptive Innovation in Chinese and Indian Businesses—The Strategic Implications for Local Entrepreneurs and Global Incumbents. Routledge/Taylor and Francis.

McKinsey & Company, 2013. Reimagining India—Unlocking the Potential of Asia's Next Superpower. Simon & Schuster.

Meeker, M., Wu, L., 2013. Internet trends. In: D11 Conference, May 29. Kleiner, Perkins, Caulfield and Byers (KPCB).

Rajan, R., 2006. From paternalistic to enabling. Finance Dev. 43 (3), 54–56.

Sharma, S.D., 2009. China and India in the Age of Globalization. Cambridge University Press.

Appendix 1

United States

Year	GDP in Current $ (World Bank)	GDP in Chained 2005 $ (World Bank)	PPP Converted GDP Per Capita (Chain Series), at 2005 Constant Prices (PennWorld)	Capital (PennWorld) 2005 $	Human Capital (www.Barroloe.com) Weighted Average of Years of Education	Labor (World Bank) at in Labor Force	R&D in Current $ (World Bank)
1950			13,069.2				
1951			14,173.04				
1952			14,648.24				
1953			15,028.82				
1954			14,438.89				
1955			15,161.82				
1956			15,163.51				
1957			15,128.66				
1958			14,741.1				
1959			15,307.41				
1960	5.20531E+11	2.79481E+12	15,397.75	3,297,586.46			
1961	5.39051E+11	2.85909E+12	15,487.26	3,352,100.395			
1962	5.79748E+11	3.0335E+12	16,221.28	3,397,376.677			
1963	6.1167E+11	3.16697E+12	16,706.08	3,767,349.283			

1964	6.56912E+11	3.35066E+12	17,412.19	3,547,488.206	10.17367044
1965	7.12082E+11	3.5651E+12	18,326.81	3,642,138.189	10.26472468
1966	7.80761E+11	3.79683E+12	19,278.48	3,769,803.339	10.35758982
1967	8.25056E+11	3.89175E+12	19,542.44	3,915,882.587	10.45353029
1968	9.01456E+11	4.07855E+12	20,334.34	4,033,084.401	10.56778499
1969	9.73385E+11	4.20499E+12	20,763.44	4,159,354.234	10.66138283
1970	1.0759E+12	4.33987E+12	20,435.85	4,296,408.233	10.76486598
1971	1.1678E+12	4.4827E+12	20,848.45	4,394,207.529	10.86225334
1972	1.2824E+12	4.71801E+12	21,732.33	4,513,124.135	11.02561345
1973	1.4285E+12	4.98423E+12	22,744.74	4,661,770.656	11.14118512
1974	1.5488E+12	4.95847E+12	22,357.68	4,839,006.243	11.26022347
1975	1.6889E+12	4.94863E+12	22,071.94	4,974,132.519	11.37915002
1976	1.8776E+12	5.21522E+12	23,112.33	5,035,236.47	11.52867528
1977	2.086E+12	5.45559E+12	23,987.66	5,147,526.359	11.62696699
1978	2.3566E+12	5.75897E+12	25,039.28	5,299,237.849	11.70552923	102,233.25
1979	2.6321E+12	5.94185E+12	25,473.57	5,490,832.926	11.84099924	104,960.5833
1980	2.8625E+12	5.92732E+12	24,951.58	5,681,298.515	11.92706792	106,974
1981	3.2109E+12	6.08112E+12	25,328.76	5,806,516.118	11.98630539	108,675.9167

Continued

United States

Year	GDP in Current $ (World Bank)	GDP in Chained 2005 $ (World Bank)	PPP Converted GDP Per Capita (Chain Series), at 2005 Constant Prices (PennWorld)	Capital (PennWorld) 2005 $	Human Capital (www.Barroloe.com) Weighted Average of Years of Education	Labor (World Bank) at in Labor Force	R&D in Current $ (World Bank)
1982	3.345E+12	5.96494E+12	24,673.91	5,954,062.272	12.10104334	110,244.0833	
1983	3.6381E+12	6.24128E+12	25,660.12	6,023,430.439	12.21788871	111,515.4167	
1984	4.0407E+12	6.69433E+12	27,373.71	6,121,084.16	12.30237794	113,531.8333	
1985	4.3467E+12	6.97812E+12	28,255.04	6,328,940.757	12.36038572	115,467.4167	
1986	4.5901E+12	7.22319E+12	28,944.4	6,523,911.825	12.41122464	117,845.5833	
1987	4.8702E+12	7.47322E+12	29,574.83	6,704,997.348	12.49199767	119,852.8333	
1988	5.2526E+12	7.78736E+12	30,454.07	6,884,434.413	12.5505655	121,670.6667	
1989	5.6577E+12	8.07401E+12	31,225.4	7,057,304.655	12.63083585	123,850.6667	
1990	5.9796E+12	8.22892E+12	31,388.79	7,242,761.676	12.68330373	125,856.6667	
1991	6.174E+12	8.22294E+12	30,794.4	7,398,305.227	12.74343705	126,352.4167	
1992	6.5393E+12	8.51528E+12	31,464.96	7,499,159.85	12.87851231	128,099.0833	
1993	6.8787E+12	8.74903E+12	32,045.52	7,625,333.676	12.95731333	129,185.3333	
1994	7.3087E+12	9.10218E+12	33,090.7	7,778,601.267	13.04198782	131,046.6667	

Year							
1995	7.664E+12	9.34964E+12	33,560.13	7,985,942.75	13.13063423	132,315.1667	2.067E+11
1996	8.1002E+12	8.70454E+12	34,516.18	8,195,775.654	13.17634251	133,951.25	2218E+11
1997	8.6085E+12	1.014E+13	35,780.47	8,441,985.043	13.21525844	136,301	2.360E+11
1998	9.0891E+12	1.05912E+13	37,026.11	8,750,184.242	13.27891947	137,679.8333	2.552E+11
1999	9.6657E+12	1.11045E+13	38,454.15	9,104,916.381	13.31261151	139,379.9167	2.552E+11
2000	1.02897E+13	1.15588E+13	39,668.69	9,504,208.947	13.41119101	142,585.75	2.78E+11
2001	1.06253E+13	1.16684E+13	39,526.88	9,928,847.155	13.45746692	143,768.9167	2.889E+11
2002	1.09802E+13	1.18757E+13	39,776.12	10,263,183.81	13.47857166	144,856.0833	2.873E+11
2003	1.15122E+13	1.26708E+13	40,437.44	10,563,834.59	13.52739992	146,499.5	3.008E+11
2004	1.2277E+13	1.26708E+13	41,540.43	10,869,770.62	13.58486911	147,379.5833	3.125E+11
2005	1.30954E+13	1.30954E+13	42,482.39	11,227,016.83	13.58035719	149,289.1667	3.397E+13
2006	1.38579E+13	1.34446E+13	43,215.47	11,598,462.61	13.6202784	151,408.8333	3.677E+11
2007	1.44803E+13	1.36852E+13	43,511.59	11,965,223.27	13.67660742	153,123.0833	3.942E+11
2008	1.47203E+13	1.36455E+13	42,723.8	12,271,137.58	13.76483024	154,321.5833	3.942E+11
2009	1.44179E+13	1.32631E+13	40,390.71	12,464,111.98	13.77281943	154,188.5	4.206E+11
2010	1.49583E+13	1.35956E+13	41,365	124,473,701.95	13.81615382	153,885.6667	4.202E+11
2011	1.55338E+13	1.38468E+13			13.86985408	153,615.25	4.302E+11
2012	1.62446E+13	1.42316E+13			13.90559147	154,961.5	
2013					13.97722077	155,378.8333	
2014						155,460	

China

Year	GDP in Current $ (World Bank)	GDP in Chained 2005 $ (World Bank)	PPP Converted GDP Per Capita (Chain Series), at 2005 Constant Prices (PennWorld)	Capital (PennWorld) 2005 $	Human Capital (www.Barroloe.com) Weighted Average of Years of Education	Labor (World Bank) at in Labor Force	R&D in Current $ (World Bank)
1950					0.4147.26		
1951							
1952			217.61				
1953			233.22				
1954			236.73				
1955			242.57		0.577065		
1956			264.47				
1957			272.26				
1958			313.61				
1959			337.35				
1960	61,377,930,682	83,178,386,964	330.79	105,539	0.848431		
1961	50,100,934,946	60,635,478,879	252.53	110,052			
1962	46,464,003,927	56,933,477,540	238.36	106,080			

1963	50,280,424,169	62,821,544,924	257.48	100,042	
1964	58,613,239,133	72,770,566,465	286.58	96,503	
1965	69,709,152,023	84,678,027,169	318.89	95,152	1.2114617
1966	75,879,433,528	93,738,576,076	341.49	96,179	
1967	72,057,026,116	88,395,477,239	311.02	99,090	
1968	69,993,499,400	84,771,262,673	295.12	98,344	
1969	78,718,820,946	99,097,606,064	318.6	97,428	
1970	91,506,213,646	1.18329E+11	360.63	97,546	1.779749
1971	98,562,021,764	1.26605E+11	378.76	102,278	
1972	1.1216E+11	1.31416E+11	374.92	107,458	
1973	1.3677E+11	1.41798E+11	404.05	111,102	
1974	1.42255E+11	1.45059E+11	405.44	116,089	
1975	1.61162E+11	1.5768E+11	428.74	120,758	2.291892
1976	1.51628E+11	1.55157E+11	421.75	126,604	
1977	1.72349E+11	1.66949E+11	441.42	130,358	
1978	1.48179E+11	1.86482E+11	499.41	135,050	
1979	1.76635E+11	2.00654E+11	528.93	143,439	
1980	1.894E+11	2.16305E+11	562.88	151,368	3.097788
1981	1.94111E+11	2.27553E+11	580.93	159,484	

Continued

China

Year	GDP in Current $ (World Bank)	GDP in Chained 2005 $ (World Bank)	PPP Converted GDP Per Capita (Chain Series) at 2005 Constant Prices (PennWorld)	Capital (PennWorld) 2005 $	Human Capital (www.Barroloe.com) Weighted Average of Years of Education	Labor (World Bank) at in Labor Force	R&D in Current $ (World Bank)
1982	2.03183E+11	2.4826E+11	623.16	166,354			
1983	2.28456E+11	2.75321E+11	681.2	173,693			
1984	2.57432E+11	3.17169E+11	845.22	182,989			
1985	3.06667E+11	3.59987E+11	959.67	188,880	3.565428		
1986	2.97832E+11	3.91666E+11	1017.24	201,527			
1987	2.70372E+11	4.37099E+11	1083.37	213,997			
1988	3.09523E+11	4.86492E+11	1138.26	226,918			
1989	3.43974E+11	5.06438E+11	1102.03	242,131			
1990	3.56937E+11	5.25683E+11	1154.3	255,971	3.863948	633,236,930	
1991	3.79469E+11	5.74045E+11	1244.18	267,900		642,323,210	
1992	4.22661E+11	6.5556E+11	1407.62	280,451		651,196,155	
1993	4.40501E+11	7.47338E+11	1590.08	296,872		659,797,391	
1994	5.59225E+11	8.45239E+11	1774.01	325,478		668,088,191	
1995	7.28007E+11	9.3737E+11	1931.26	358,994	4.729101	677,071,846	

Year							
1996	8.56085E+11	1.03111E+12	2102.44	398,375		685,951,508	4.865E+09
1997	9.52653E+11	1.127E+12	2276.14	439,208		695,649,736	6.142E+09
1998	1.01946E+12	1.21491E+12	2440.14	478,594		70,515,909	6.670E+09
1999	1.08328E+12	1.30724E+12	2616.37	517,872		714,378,563	8.201E+09
2000	1.19847E+12	1.41705E+12	2822.38	556,716	5.55495	724,325,746	1.082E+10
2001	1.32481E+12	1.53466E+12	3042.54	595,763		731,359,727	1.259E+10
2002	1.45383E+12	1.67432E+12	3293.61	641,155		738,923,141	1.556E+10
2003	1.64096E+12	1.84175E+12	3589.88	693,894		746,320,096	1.860E+10
2004	1.93164E+12	1.84175E+12	3915.71	760,168		752,711,357	2.376E+10
2005	2.2569E+12	2.2569E+12	4335.12	837,569	6.115157	758,612,920	2.990E+10
2006	2.71295E+12	2.54353E+12	4855.38	922,578		763,693,185	3.766E+10
2007	3.49406E+12	290471E+12	5511.87	1,021,088		768,074,459	4.877E+10
2008	4.52183E+12	3.18356E+12	6014.14	1,136,754		770,992,463	6.646E+10
2009	4.99126E+12	3.47645E+12	6519.51	1,263,644		773,686,144	8.495E+10
2010	5.93053E+12	3.838E+12	7129.56	1,426,550	6.701211	774,172,295	1.043E+11
2011	7.32194E+12	4.19494E+12	7129.56	1,426,550	6.701211	774,172,295	1.043E+11
2012	8.2271E+12	4.52214E+12				787,632,272	
2013							
2014							

India

Year	GDP in Current $ (World Bank)	GDP in Chained 2005 $ (World Bank)	PPP Converted GDP Per Capita (Chain Series), a= 2005 Constant Prices (PennWorld)	Capital (PennWorld) 2005 $	Human Capital (www.Barroloe.com) Weighted Average of Years of Education	Labor (World Bank) at in Labor Force	R&D in Current $ (World Bank)
1950			592.32		0.221008		
1951			598.32				
1952			612.48				
1953			635.51				
1954			648.26				
1955			650.89		0.242064		
1956			661.32				
1957			651.32				
1958			682.23				
1959			681.28				
1960	37,679,274,491	1.0266E+11	720.36	117,278	0.276808		
1961	39,920,452,403	1.06482E+11	730.29	119,596			
1962	42,900,864,970	1.09603E+11	743.78	121,350			

1963	49,271,095,508	1.16173E+11	779.86	124,054	
1964	57,470,781,033	1.24831E+11	819.32	127,395	
1965	60,599,264,112	1.21541E+11	786.92	131,595	0.321442
1966	46,669,801,600	1.21473E+11	767.55	135,552	
1967	51,014,155,360	1.3098E+11	807.37	139,103	
1968	54,016,411,987	1.35417E+11	827.28	141,972	
1969	59,472,993,627	1.44273E+11	896.9	143,540	
1970	63,517,182,000	1.51714E+11	892.7	145,958	0.456125
1971	68,532,271,313	1.54206E+11	906.93	148,953	
1972	72,716,595,884	1.53353E+11	884.17	152,806	
1973	87,014,945,186	1.58407E+11	898.79	154,889	
1974	1.01271E+11	1.60285E+11	886.87	158,520	
1975	1.002E+11	1.74951E+11	928.69	161,751	0.558602
1976	1.4518E+11	1.7786E+11	952.66	165,294	
1977	1.23618E+11	1.90763E+11	979.84	169,099	
1978	1.39709E+11	2.01661E+11	1039.07	172,860	
1979	1.55674E+11	1.91098E+11	997.46	178,520	
1980	1.89594E+11	2.0397E+11	1028.48	182,552	0.673904
1981	1.96883E+11	2.1622E+11	1075.98	185,190	

Continued

India

Year	GDP in Current $ (World Bank)	GDP in Chained 2005 $ (World Bank)	PPP Converted GDP Per Capita (Chain Series), a 2005 Constant Prices (PennWorld)	Capital (PennWorld) 2005 $	Human Capital (www.Barroloe.com) Weighted Average of Years of Education	Labor (World Bank) at in Labor Force	R&D in Current $ (World Bank)
1982	2.04234E+11	2.23736E+11	1085.92	190,936			
1983	2.2209E+11	2.40043E+11	1104.99	195,112			
1984	2.15878E+11	2.49215E+11	1142.67	198,248			
1985	2.36589E+11	2.62309E+11	1193.78	201,020	1.021347		
1986	2.53352E+11	2.74839E+11	1219	207,030			
1987	2.83927E+11	2.85737E+11	1260.43	212,205			
1988	3.01791E+11	3.13247E+11	1339.79	217,382			
1989	3.01234E+11	3.31877E+11	1375.28	226,101			
1990	3.26608E+11	3.50241E+11	1430.57	234,096	1.416914	330,720,108	
1991	2.74842E+11	3.53943E+11	1389.65	244,271		338,668,430	
1992	2.93262E+11	3.73347E+11	1425.8	249,524		346,802,576	
1993	2.84194E+11	3.91084E+11	1432.86	257,123		355,116,385	
1994	3.33014E+11	4.17162E+11	1496.13	262,137		363,000,334	

1995	3.666E+11	4.48722E+11	1611.27	271,774	1.715463	369,789,237	
1996	3.99787E+11	4.82598E+11	1638.49	287,129		377,265,860	2.511E+09
1997	4.2316E+11	5.2142E+11	1679.76	296,121		384,187,272	2.856E+09
1998	4.28741E+11	5.33197E+11	1746.7	307,500		391,155,410	2.965E+09
1999	4.66867E+11	5.80362E+11	1910.029	318,619		398,160,552	3.341E+09
2000	4.76609E+11	6.2654E+11	1921.9	335,370	2.072165	405,190,192	3.560E+09
2001	4.93954E+11	6.31726E+11	1984.2	347,700		417,144,863	3.584E+09
2002	5.23969E+11	6.55756E+11	2045.64	359,682		428,601,673	3.745E+09
2003	6.18356E+11	7.07301E+11	2145.76	374,360		440,212,535	4.377E+09
2004	7.21586E+11	7.633E+11	2317.34	393,496		451,934,600	5.368E+09
2005	8.34215E+11	8.34215E+11	2491.53	422,249	2.551313	494,498,005	6.500E+09
2006	9.49177E+11	9.11496E+11	2675.39	457,722		465,456,461	7.280E+09
2007	1.2387E+12	1.00084E+12	2921.54	499,972		466,033,315	9.383E+09
2008	1.2241E+12	1.03978E+12	2949.57	551,327		466,233,702	
2009	1.36537E+12	1.12795E+12	3211.61	593,764		466,896,011	
2010	1.710191E+12	1.24691E+12	3477.31	643,610	3.006246	466,390,538	
2011	1.87284E+12	1.32584E+12				475,806,212	
2012	1.84171E+12	1.36876E+12				484,343,281	
2013							
2014							

Appendix 2

Innovation Data

DATA FROM GLOBAL INNOVATION INDICES FOR VARIOUS SUBINDICES

The tables below provide rankings of China, India and the United States among the total group of 142 countries in the data.

	2009–2010			2011			2012			2013		
	China	India	United States	China	India	United States	China	India	United States	China	India	United States
Institutions	92	73	18	98	54	15	121	125	17	113	102	17
Political environment	58	82	22	108	56	27	133	109	29	126	108	25
Regulatory environment	64	66	21	76	71	8	112	78	13	116	77	13
Business environment	124	74	13	95	111	35	99	139	13	98	124	15

	2011			2012			2013		
	China	India	United States	China	India	United States	China	India	United States
Human capital and research	56	104	13	84	131	22	36	105	6
Education	51	115	36	67	133	31	20	127	27
Tertiary education	102	119	46	125	135	54	120	133	52
Research and development	32	35=	5	39	55	12	24	30	1

	2011			2012			2013		
	China	India	United States	China	India	United States	China	India	United States
Market sophistication	26	45	4	35	46	2	35	49	2
Credit	36	67	4	62	70	2	55	76	4
Investment	8	15	3	16	17	2	21	24	2
Trade and competition	67	88	83	94	118	69	38	106	10

	2011			2012			2013		
	China	India	United States	China	India	United States	China	India	United States
Infrastructure	33	63	14	39	78	14	44	89	17
ICT	59	94	9	73	94	5	75	96	6
General infrastructure	2	11	63	10	44	12	13	46	12
Ecological sustainability	92	72	18	37	87	73	38	102	74

	2011			2012			2013		
	China	India	United States	China	India	United States	China	India	United States
Business sophistication	29	84	15	28	75	9	33	94	2
Knowledge workers	30	104	12	27	74	6	28	95	5
Innovation linkages	46	52	22	73	59	8	61	51	3
Knowledge absorption	19	65	47	20	81	46	24	122	16

	2011			2012			2013		
	China	India	United States	China	India	United States	China	India	United States
Knowledge and technology output	9	60	5	5	47	11	2	37	7
Knowledge creation	12	62	9	4	54	9	3	53	7
Knowledge impact	9	85	11	6	67	31	2	62	11
Knowledge diffusion	21	33	12	23	33	13	21	22	15

	2011			2012			2013		
	China	India	United States	China	India	United States	China	India	United States
Creative outputs	35	38	24	56	34	33	96	65	19
Intangible assets	30	38	51	38	10	84	72	44	86
Creative goods and services	45	39	18	33	42	27	69	53	12
Online creativity				120	109	20	136	105	1

The graphs that follow provide the actual scores for China, India and the United States for the Global Innovation Index.

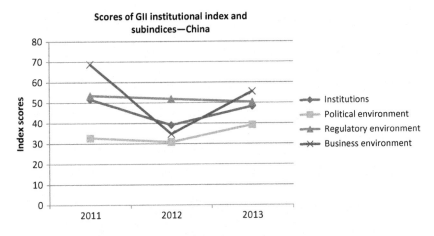

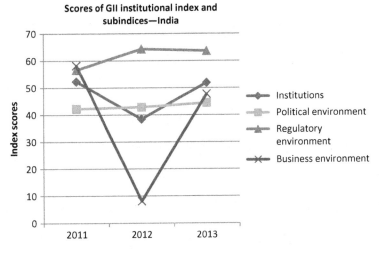

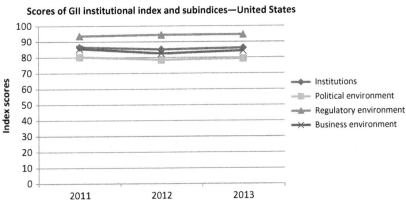

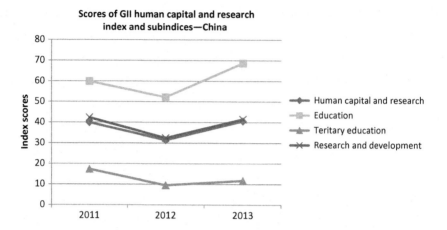

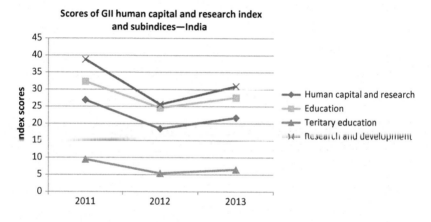

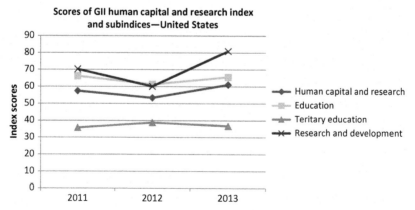

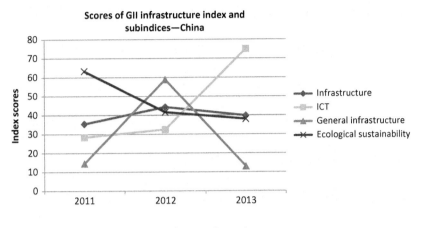

Scores of GII infrastructure index and subindices—China

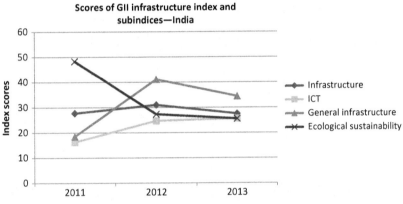

Scores of GII infrastructure index and subindices—India

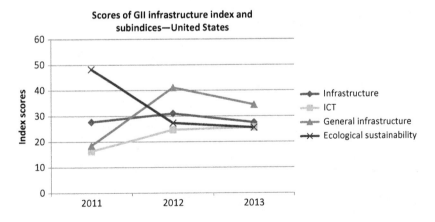

Scores of GII infrastructure index and subindices—United States

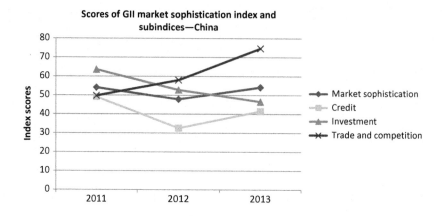

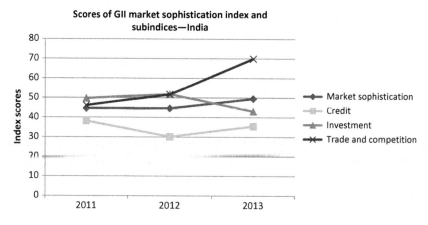

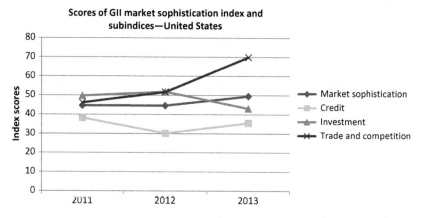

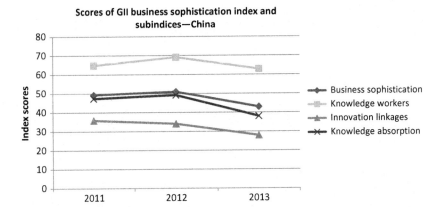

Scores of GII business sophistication index and subindices—China

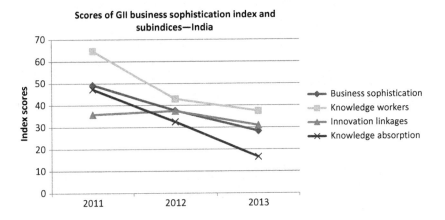

Scores of GII business sophistication index and subindices—India

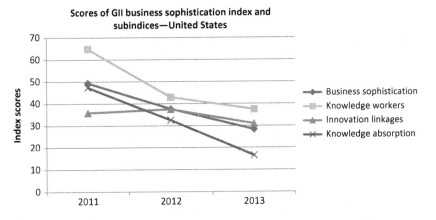

Scores of GII business sophistication index and subindices—United States

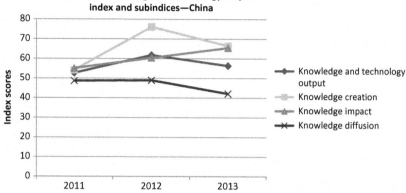

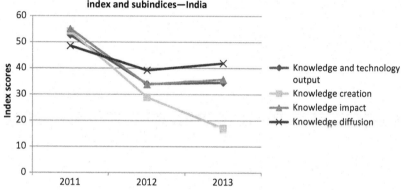

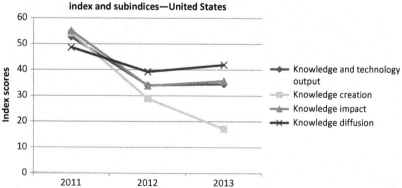

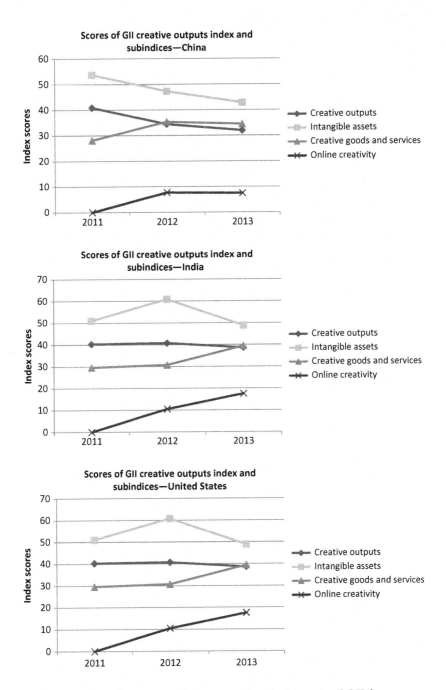

Constructed from data sourced from several annual reports of GII from www. globalinnovationindex.org.

Index

Note: Page numbers followed by *"b"* indicate boxes, *"t"* indicate tables, *"f"* indicate figures and *"np"* indicate footnotes.

Working-age population changes, in China,
102–104, 103*t*, 104*f*
World Intellectual Property Organization
(WIPO), 70
WTO's trading system, 73–74

Y

Yangtze River Delta, industry clusters, 150–153
Youth Employment and Demonstration Projects
Act, 232–233

Printed in the United States
By Bookmasters